SPURGEON'S TEACHING ON THE BL(

By Charles H. Spurgeon

ISBN: 9781521444337

June 2017

MAIN CONTENTS

THE BLOOD-SHEDDING

"Without shedding of blood is no remission."
Hebrews 9:22

I WILL show you three fools. One is yonder soldier, who has been wounded on the field of battle, grievously wounded, well near unto death. The surgeon is by his side and the soldier asks him a question. Listen and judge of his folly. What question does he ask? Does he raise his eyes with eager anxiety and inquire if the wound is mortal, if the practitioner's skill can suggest the means of healing, or if the remedies are within reach and the medicine at hand? No, nothing of the sort. Strange to tell, he asks, "Can you inform me with what sword I was wounded and by what Russian I have been thus grievously mauled? I want," he adds, "to learn every minute particular respecting the origin of my wound." The man is delirious or his head is affected. Surely such questions at such a time are proof enough that he is bereft of his senses.

There is another fool. The storm is raging, the ship is flying impetuously before the gale, the dark scud moves swiftly over head, the masts are creaking, the sails are rent to rags and still the gathering tempest grows more fierce. Where is the captain? Is he busily engaged on the deck? Is he manfully facing the danger and skillfully suggesting means to avert it? No, Sir, he has retired to his cabin and there with studious thoughts and crazy fancies he is speculating on the place where this storm took its rise. "It is mysterious, this wind," he says, "no one yet has been able to discover it." And so the lives of the passengers and his own in grievous danger, he is careful only to solve his curious questions. The man is mad, Sir. Take the rudder from his hand. He is clean gone mad! If he should ever run on shore, shut him up as a hopeless lunatic.

The third fool I shall doubtless find among yourselves. You are sick and wounded with sin, you are in the storm and hurricane of Almighty vengeance and yet the question which you would ask of me this morning would be, "Sir, what is the origin of evil?" You are mad, Sir, spiritually

4

mad. That is not the question you would ask if you were in a sane and healthy state of mind. Your question should be–"How can I get rid of the evil?" Not, "How did it come into the world?" but, "How am I to escape from it?" Not, "How is it that hail descends from Heaven upon Sodom?" but, "How may I, like Lot, escape out of the city to Zoar." Not, "How is it that I am sick?" but, "Are there medicines that will heal me? Is there a physician to be found that can restore my soul to health?"

Ah, you trifle with subtleties while you neglect certainties! More questions have been asked concerning the origin of evil than upon anything else. Men have puzzled their heads and twisted their brains into knots in order to understand what men can never know–how evil came into this world and how its entrance is consistent with Divine goodness. The broad fact is this–there is evil. And your question should be, "How can I escape from the wrath to come, which is engendered of this evil?" In answering that question this verse stands right in the middle of the way (like the angel with the sword, who once stopped Balaam on the road to Barak)–"Without shedding of blood is no remission."

Your real want is to know how you can be saved. If you are aware that your sin must be pardoned or punished, your question will be, "How can it be pardoned?" and then point blank in the very teeth of your enquiry, there stands out this fact–"Without shedding of blood there is no remission." Mark you, this is not merely a Jewish maxim. It is a worldwide and eternal Truth. It pertains not to the Hebrews only but to the Gentiles likewise. Never in any time, never in any place, never in any person can there be remission apart from shedding of blood. This great fact, I say, is stamped on nature. It is an essential Law of God's moral government. It is one of the fundamental principles which can neither be shaken nor denied. Never can there be any exception to it. It stands the same in every place throughout all ages–"Without shedding of blood there is no remission."

It was so with the Jews. They had no remission without the shedding of blood. Some things under the Jewish Law might be cleansed by water or by fire but in no case where absolute sin was concerned was there ever purification without blood—teaching this doctrine, that blood and blood alone, must be applied for the remission of sin. Indeed the very heathen seems to have an inkling of this fact. Do not I see their knives gory with the blood of victims? Have I not heard horrid tales of human immolations, of holocausts, of sacrifices? And what mean these but that there lies deep in the human breast, deep as the very existence of man, this Truth—"that without shedding of blood there is no remission."

And I assert once more, that even in the hearts and consciences of my hearers there is something which will never let them believe in remission apart from a shedding of blood. This is the grand Truth of Christianity and it is a Truth which I will endeavor now to fix upon your memory. And may God by His grace bless it to your souls. "Without shedding of blood is no remission."

First, let me show you the blood-shedding, before I begin to dwell upon the text. Is there not a special blood shedding meant? Yes, there was a shedding of most precious blood, to which I must refer you. I shall not tell you now of massacres and murders, nor of rivers of blood of goats and rams. There was a blood-shedding once, which did out vie all other shedding of blood by far. It was a Man—a God—that shed His blood at that memorable season. Come and see it. Here is a garden dark and gloomy. The ground is crisp with the cold frost of midnight. Between those gloomy olive trees I see a Man, I hear Him groan out His life in prayer.

Hearken, angels, hearken men and wonder. It is the Savior groaning out His soul! Come and see Him. Behold His brow! O Heavens! Drops of blood are streaming down His face and from His body. Every pore is open and it sweats. But not the sweat of men that toil for bread. It is the sweat of One that toils for Heaven—He "sweats great drops of blood"! That is the blood-shedding, without which there is no remission. Follow that Man further. They have dragged Him with sacrilegious hands from the place of His prayer and His agony and they have taken Him to the hall of Pilate. They seat Him in a chair and mock Him. A robe of purple is put on His shoulders in mockery.

And mark His brow—they have put about it a crown of thorns and the crimson drops of gore are rushing down His cheeks! Angels! The drops of blood are running down His cheeks! But turn aside that purple robe for a moment. His back is bleeding. Tell me demons did this. They lift up the thongs, still dripping clots of gore. They scourge and tear His flesh and make a river of blood to run down His shoulders! That is the shedding of blood without which there is no remission. Not yet have I done—they hurry Him through the streets. They fling Him on the ground. They nail His hands and feet to the transverse wood. They hoist it in the air. They dash it into its socket. It is fixed and there He hangs—the Christ of God.

Blood from His head. Blood from His hands. Blood from His feet! In agony unknown He bleeds away His life. In terrible throes He exhausts His soul. "Eloi, Eloi, lame Sabacthani." And then look! They pierce His side and forthwith runs out blood and water. This is the shedding of blood, Sinners and Saints. This is the awful shedding of blood, the terrible pouring out of blood without which for you and for the whole human race, there is no remission.

I have to you, I hope, brought my text fairly out—without this shedding of blood there is no remission. Now I shall come to dwell upon it more particularly.

Why is it that this story does not make men weep? I told it ill, you say. Yes, so I did. I will take all the blame. But, Sirs, if it were told as ill as men could speak, were our hearts what they should be, we should bleed away our lives in sorrow. Oh, it was a horrid murder that! It was not an act of regicide. It was not the deed of a fratricide, or of a parricide. It was—what shall I say? I must make a word—a deicide. The killing of a God—the slaying of Him who became incarnate for our sins. Oh, if our hearts were but soft as iron, we must weep! If they were but tender as the marble of the mountains, we should shed great drops of grief. But they are harder than the nether millstone. We forget the griefs of Him that died this ignominious death. We pity not His sorrows, nor do we account the interest we have in Him as though He suffered and accomplished all for us.

Nevertheless, here stands the principle—"Without shedding of blood is no remission." Now, I take it, there are two things here. First, there is a negative expressed—"No remission without shedding of blood." And then there is a positive implied, indeed, with shedding of blood there is remission.

First, I say, here is A NEGATIVE EXPRESSION—there is no remission without blood—without the blood of Jesus Christ. This is of Divine Authority. When I utter this sentence I have Divinity to plead. It is not a thing which you may doubt, or which you may believe. It must be believed and received, otherwise you have denied the Scriptures and turned aside from God. Some truths I utter, perhaps, have little better basis than my own reasoning and inference, which are of little value enough. But this I utter, not with quotations from God's Word to back up my assertion but from the lips of God Himself. Here it stands in great letters,
"There is no remission."

So Divine is its Authority perhaps you will kick at it—but remember, your rebellion is not against me but against God. If any of you reject this Truth, I shall not argue with you. God forbid I should turn aside from proclaiming His Gospel to dispute with men. I have God's irrevocable statute to plead now—here it stands—"Without shedding of blood there is no remission." You may believe or disbelieve many things the preacher utters. But this you disbelieve at the peril of your souls. It is God's utterance—will you tell God to His face you do not believe it? That were impious. The negative is Divine in its Authority—bow yourselves to it. And accept its solemn warning.

But some men will say that God's way of saving men, by shedding of blood, is a cruel way, an unjust way, an unkind way. And all kinds of things they will say of it. Sirs, I have nothing to do with your opinion of the matter. It is so. If you have any faults to find with your Maker, fight your battles out with Him at last. But take heed before you throw the gauntlet down. It will go ill with a worm when he fights with his Maker and it will go ill with you when you contend with Him. The doctrine of atonement when rightly understood and faithfully received, is delightful, for it exhibits boundless love, immeasurable goodness and infinite Truth. But to unbelievers it will always be a hated doctrine. So it must be, Sirs. You hate your own mercies. You despise your own salvation. I tarry not to dispute with you—I affirm it in God's name—"Without shedding of blood there is no remission."

And note how decisive this is in its character—"Without shedding of blood there is no remission." "But, Sir, can't I get my sins forgiven by my repentance? If I weep and plead and pray, will not God forgive me for the sake of my tears?" "No remission," says the text, "without shedding of blood." "But, Sir, if I never sin again and if I serve God more zealously than other men, will He not forgive me for the sake of my obedience?" "No remission," says the text, "without shedding of blood." "But, Sir, may I not trust that God is merciful and will forgive me without the shedding of blood?" "No," says the text, "without shedding of blood there is no remission." None whatever.

It cuts off every other hope. Bring your hopes here and if they are not based in blood and stamped with blood, they are as useless as castles in the air and dreams of the night. "There is no remission," says the text, in positive and plain words. And yet men will be trying to get remission in fifty other ways, until their special pleading becomes as irksome to us as it is useless for them. Sirs, do what you like, say what you please but you are as far off remission when you have done your best, as you were when you began. Unless you put confidence in the shedding of our Savior's blood and in the blood-shedding alone, there is no remission.

And note again how universal it is in its character. "What? I may not get remission without blood-shedding?" says the king and he comes with the crown on his head. "May not I in all my robes, with this rich ransom, get pardon without the blood-shedding?" "None," is the reply. "None." Then comes the wise man, with a number of letters after his name—"Can I not get remission by these grand titles of my learning?" "None, none." Then comes the benevolent man–"I have dispersed my money to the poor and given my bounty to feed them. Shall not I get remission? "None." says the text, "Without shedding of blood there is no remission." How this puts everyone level! My Lord, you are no bigger than your coachman. Sir, Squire, you are no better off than John that plows the ground. Minister, your office does not serve you with any exemption–your poorest hearer stands on the very same footing. "Without shedding of blood there is no remission."

No hope for the best, any more than for the worst, without this shedding of blood . Oh, I love the Gospel, for this reason among others, because it is such a leveling Gospel! Some persons do not like a leveling Gospel. Nor would I, in some senses of the word. Let men have their rank and their titles and their riches if they will. But I do like and I am sure all good men like, to see rich and poor meet together and feel that they are on a level. The Gospel makes them so. It says, "Put up your money-bags, they will not procure you remission. Roll up your diploma, that will not get you remission. Forget your farm and your park, they will not get you remission. Cover up that escutcheon, that coat of arms will not get you remission.

Come, you ragged beggars, filthy off-scouring of the world, penniless. Come here, here is remission as much for you, ill-bred and ill-mannered though you are, as for the noble, the honorable, the titled and the wealthy. All stand on a level here. The text is universal–"Without shedding of blood there is no remission."

Mark too, how perpetual my text is. Paul said, "there is no remission!" I must repeat this testimony, too. When thousands of years have rolled away some minister may stand on this spot and say the same. This will never alter at all. It will always be so, in the next world as well as this–no remission without shedding of blood. "Oh! yes there is," says one, "the priest takes the shilling and he gets the soul out of purgatory." That is a mere presence. It never was in. But without shedding of blood there is no real remission. There may be tales and fancies but there is no true remission without the blood of propitiation.

Never, though you strained yourselves in prayer. Never, though you wept yourselves away in tears. Never, though you groaned and cried till your heart-strings break. Never in this world, nor in that which is to come, can the forgiveness of sins be procured on any other ground than redemption by the blood of Christ. And never can the conscience be cleansed but by faith in that sacrifice. The fact is, Beloved, there is no use for you to satisfy your hearts with anything less than what satisfied God the Father. Without the shedding of blood nothing would appease His justice. And without the application of that same blood nothing can purge your consciences.

II. But as there is no remission without blood-shedding, IT IS IMPLIED THAT THERE IS REMISSION WITH IT. Mark it well, this remission is a present fact. The blood having been already shed, the remission is already obtained. I took you to the garden of Gethsemane and the mount of Calvary to see the blood-shedding. I might now conduct you to another garden and another mount to show you the grand proof of the remission. Another garden, did I say? Yes, it is a garden filled with many pleasing and even triumphant reminiscences. Aside from the haunts of this busy world, in it was a new sepulcher, hewn out of a rock where Joseph of Arimathea thought his own poor body should presently be laid. But there they laid Jesus after His crucifixion.

He had stood Surety for His people and the Law had demanded His blood–death had held Him with strong grasp. And that tomb was, as it were, the dungeon of His captivity, when, as the Good Shepherd, He laid down His life for the sheep. Why, then, do I see in that garden, an open, untenanted grave? I will tell you. The debts are paid, the sins are cancelled, the remission is obtained. That great Shepherd of the sheep has been brought again from the dead by the blood of the Everlasting Covenant and in Him also we have obtained redemption through His blood. There, Beloved, is the first proof.

Do you ask for further evidence? I will take you to Mount Olives. You shall behold Jesus there with His hands raised like the High Priest of old to bless His people and while He is blessing them, He ascends, the clouds receiving Him out of their sight. But why, you ask, oh why has He thus ascended and where is He gone? Behold He enters, not into the holy place made with hands but He enters into Heaven itself with His own blood, there to appear in the presence of God for us. Now, therefore, we have boldness to draw near by the blood of Christ. The remission is obtained, here is the second proof. Oh Believer, what springs of comfort are there here for you.

And now let me commend this remission by the shedding of blood to those who have not yet believed. Mr. Innis, a great Scotch minister, once visited an infidel who was dying. When he came to him the first time, he said, "Mr. Innis, I am relying on the mercy of God. God is merciful and He will never damn a man forever." When he got worse and was nearer death, Mr. Innis went to him again and he said, "Oh, Mr. Innis, my hope is gone. For I have been thinking if God is merciful, God is Just, too. And what if, instead of being merciful to me, He should be just to me? What would then become of me? I must give up my hope in the mere mercy of God. Tell me how to be saved!"

Mr. Innis told him that Christ had died in the place of all Believers—that God could be Just and yet the justifier through the death of Christ. "Ah," he said, "Mr. Innis, there is something solid in that. I can rest on that. I cannot rest on anything else." And it is a remarkable fact that none of us ever met with a man who thought he had his sins forgiven unless it was through the blood of Christ. Meet a Muslim. He never had his sins forgiven. He does not say so. Meet an Infidel. He never knows that his sins are forgiven. Meet a Legalist. He says, "I hope they will be forgiven." But he does not pretend they are. No one ever gets even a fancied hope apart from this—that Christ and Christ alone must save by the shedding of His blood.

Let me tell a story to show how Christ saves souls. Mr. Whitfield had a brother who had been like he, an earnest Christian, but he had backslidden. He went far from the ways of godliness. And one afternoon, after he had been recovered from his backsliding, he was sitting in a room in a chapel house. He had heard his brother preaching the day before and his poor conscience had been cut to the very quick. Said Whitfield's brother, when he was at tea, "I am a lost man" and he groaned and cried and could neither eat nor drink. Said Lady Huntingdon, who sat opposite, "What did you say, Mr. Whitfield?" "Madam," said he, "I said, I am a lost man." "I'm glad of it," said she, "I'm glad of it."

"Your Ladyship, how can you say so? It is cruel to say you are glad that I am a lost man." "I repeat it, Sir," said she, "I am heartily glad of it." He looked at her, more and more astonished at her barbarity. "I am glad of it," said she, "because it is written, 'The Son of Man came to seek and to save that which was lost.'" With the tears rolling down his cheeks, he said, "What a precious Scripture. And how is it that it comes with such force to me? Oh, Madam," said he, "Madam, I bless God for that. Then He will save me. I trust my soul in His hands. He has forgiven me." Shortly thereafter he went outside the house, felt ill, fell upon the ground and died.

I may have a lost man here this morning. As I cannot say much, I will leave you good people. You do not need anything. Have I got a lost man here, Lost Man! Lost Woman! Where are you? Do you feel yourself to be lost? I am so glad of it. For there is remission by the blood-shedding. O Sinner, are there tears in your eyes? Look through them. Do you see that Man in the garden? That Man sweats drops of blood for you. Do you see that Man on the Cross? That Man was nailed there for you. Oh, if I could be nailed on a cross this morning for you all, I know what you would do—you would fall down and kiss my feet and weep that I should have to die for you! But Sinner, lost Sinner, Jesus died for you—for YOU. And if He died for you, you cannot be lost. Christ died in vain for no one.

Are you, then, a sinner? Are you convicted of sin because you believe not in Christ? I have authority to preach to you. Believe in His name and you cannot be lost. Do you say you are no sinner? Then I do not know that Christ died for you. Do you say that you have no sins to repent of? Then I have no Christ to preach to you. He did not come to save the righteous. He came to save the wicked. Are you wicked? Do you feel it? Are you lost? Do you know? Are you sinful? Will you confess it? Sinner, if Jesus were here this morning, He would put out His bleeding hands and say, "Sinner, I died for you, will you believe Me?" He is not here in Person—He has sent His servant to tell you. Won't you believe Him?

"Oh!" but you say, "I am such a sinner." "Ah," He says, "that is just why I died for you, because you are a sinner." "But," you say, "I do not deserve it." "Ah," says He, "that is just why I did it." Say you, "I have hated You." "But," says He, "I have always loved you." "But, Lord, I have spat on Your minister and scorned Your Word." "It is all forgiven," says He, "all washed away by the blood which did run from My side. Only believe Me. That is all I ask. And that I will give you. I will help you to believe." "Ah," says one, "but I do not want a Savior." Sir, I have nothing to say to you except this—"The wrath to come! The wrath to come!" But there is one who says, "Sir, you do not mean what you say! Do you mean to preach to the most wicked men or women in the place?"

I mean what I say. There she is! She is a harlot, she has led many into sin and many into Hell. There she is. Her own friends have turned her out of doors. Her father called her a good-for nothing whore and said she should never come to the house again. Woman! Do you repent? Do you feel yourself to be guilty? Christ died to save you and you shall be saved! There he is. I can see him. He was drunk. He has been drunk very often. Not many nights ago I heard his voice in the street, as he went home at a late hour on Saturday night, disturbing everybody. And he beat his wife, too. He has broken the Sabbath. And as to swearing, if oaths be like soot, his throat must want sweeping bad enough, for he has cursed God often. Do you feel yourself to be guilty, my Hearer? Do you hate your sins and are you willing to forsake them? Then I bless God for you. Christ died for you. Believe!

I had a letter a few days ago from a young man who heard that during this week I was going to a certain town. Said he, "Sir, when you come,

14

do preach a sermon that will fit me, for do you know, Sir, I have heard it said that we must all think ourselves to be the most wicked people in the world, or else we cannot be saved. I try to think so but I cannot, because I have not been the most wicked. I want to think so but I cannot. I want to be saved but I do not know how to repent enough." Now, if I have the pleasure of seeing him, I shall tell him, God does not require a man to think himself the most wicked in the world, because that would sometimes be to think a falsehood. There are some men who are not so wicked as others are.

What God requires is this—that a man should say, "I know more of myself than I do of other people. I know little about them and from what I see of myself, not of my actions but of my heart, I do think there can be few worse than I am. They may be more guilty openly but then I have had more light, more privileges, more opportunities, more warnings and therefore I am still guiltier." I do not want you to bring your brother with you and say, "I am more wicked than he is." I want you to come yourself and say, "Father, I have sinned." You have nothing to do with your brother William, whether he has sinned more or less. Your cry should be, "Father, I have sinned." You have nothing to do with your cousin Jane, whether or not she has rebelled more than you. Your business is to cry, "Lord, nave mercy upon me, a sinner!" That is all. Do you feel yourselves lost? Again, I say, –

"Come and welcome, Sinner, come!"

To conclude. There is not a sinner in this place, who knows himself to be lost and ruined, who may not have all his sins forgiven and "rejoice in the hope of the glory of God." You may, though black as Hell, be white as Heaven this very instant. I know 'tis only by a desperate struggle that faith takes hold of the promise but the very moment a sinner believes, that conflict is past. It is his first victory and a blessed one. Let this verse be the language of your heart—adopt it and make it your own—

"A guilty, weak and helpless worm
In Christ's kind arms I fall;

He is my strength and righteousness.
My Jesus and my All."

THE VOICE OF THE BLOOD OF CHRIST

"The blood of sprinkling, that speaks better things than that of Abel."
Hebrews 12:24

OF all substances blood is the most mysterious and in some senses the most sacred. Scripture teaches us–and after all there is very much philosophy in Scripture–that "the blood is the life thereof"–that the life lies in the blood. Blood, therefore, is the mysterious link between matter and spirit. How it is that the soul should in any degree have an alliance with matter through blood we cannot understand. But certain it is that this is the mysterious link which unites these apparently dissimilar things together so that the soul can inhabit the body and the life can rest in the blood. God has attached awful sacredness to the shedding of blood.

Under the Jewish dispensation, even the blood of animals was considered sacred. Blood might never be eaten by the Jews. It was too sacred a thing to become the food of man. The Jew was scarcely allowed to kill his own food–certainly he must not kill it except he poured out the blood as a sacred offering to Almighty God. Blood was accepted by God as the symbol of the atonement. "Without shedding of blood there is no remission of sin," because, I take it, blood has such an affinity with life, that inasmuch as God would accept nothing but blood, He signified that there must be a life offered to Him and that His great and glorious Son must surrender His life as a sacrifice for His sheep.

Now we have in our text "blood" mentioned–two-fold blood. We have the blood of murdered Abel and the blood of murdered Jesus. We have also two things in the text–A comparison between the blood of sprinkling and the blood of Abel. And then a certain condition mentioned. Rather, if we read the whole verse in order to get its meaning we find that the righteous are spoken of as coming to the blood of sprinkling, that speaks better things than the blood of Abel–so that the condition which will constitute the second part of our discourse is coming to that blood of sprinkling for our salvation and glory.

Without further preface I shall at once introduce to you the CONTRAST AND COMPARISON IMPLIED IN THE TEXT. "The blood of sprinkling, that speaks better things than that of Abel." I confess I was very much astonished when looking at Dr. Gill and Albert Barnes and several of the more eminent commentators, while studying this passage, to find that they attach a meaning to this verse which had never occurred to me before. They say that the meaning of the verse is not that the blood of Christ is superior to the blood of murdered Abel, although that is certainly a Truth of God, but that the sacrifice of the blood of Christ is better and speaks better things than the sacrifice which Abel offered. Now, although I do not think this is the meaning of the text and I have my reasons for believing that the blood here contrasted with that of the Savior is the blood of the murdered man Abel, yet on looking to the original there is so much to be said on both sides of the question that I think it fair in explaining the passage to give you both meanings. They are not conflicting interpretations. There is indeed a shade of difference but still they amount to the same idea.

First, then, we may understand here a comparison between the offerings Abel presented and the offerings Jesus Christ presented when He gave His blood to be a ransom for the flock.

Let me describe Abel's offering. I have no doubt Adam had from the very first of his expulsion from the garden of Eden offered a sacrifice to God. We have some dim hint that this sacrifice was of a beast, for we find that the Lord God made Adam and Eve skins of beasts to be their clothing and it is probable that those skins were procured by the slaughter of victims offered in sacrifice. However, that is but a dim hint–the first absolute record that we have of an obligatory sacrifice is the record of the sacrifice offered by Abel. Now, it appears that very early there was a distinction among men. Cain was the representative of the seed of the serpent and Abel was the representative of the seed of the woman.

Abel was God's elect and Cain was one of those who rejected the Most High. However, both Cain and Abel united together in the outward service of God. They both of them brought on certain high days a sacrifice. Cain took a different view of the matter of sacrifice from that which presented itself to the mind of Abel. Cain was proud and haughty—he said, "I am ready to confess that the mercies which we receive from the soil are the gift of God, but I am not ready to acknowledge that I am a guilty sinner, deserving God's wrath, therefore," said he, "I will bring nothing but the fruit of the ground."

"Ah but," said Abel, "I feel that while I ought to be grateful for temporal mercies, at the same time I have sins to confess, I have iniquities to be pardoned and I know that without shedding of blood there is no remission of sin. Therefore," said he, "O Cain, I will not be content to bring an offering of the ground, of the ears of corn, or of first ripe fruits. I will bring of the firstlings of my flock and I will shed blood upon the altar, because my faith is that there is to come a great Victim who is actually to make atonement for the sins of men and by the slaughter of this lamb, I express my solemn faith in Him."

Not so Cain. He cared nothing for Christ. He was not willing to confess his sin. He had no objection to present a thank-offering, but a sin-offering he would not bring. He did not mind bringing to God that which he thought might be acceptable as a return for favors received, but he would not bring to God an acknowledgment of his guilt, or a confession of his inability to make atonement for it, except by the blood of a Substitute. Cain, moreover, when he came to the altar, came entirely without faith. He piled the unhewn stones as Abel did. He laid his sheaves of corn upon the altar and there he waited. It was to him a matter of comparative indifference whether God accepted him or not.

He believed there was a God, doubtless, but he had no faith in the promises of that God. God had said that the seed of the woman should bruise the serpent's head—that was the Gospel as revealed to our first parents. But Cain had no belief in that Gospel—whether it were true or not, he cared not—it was sufficient for him that he acquired enough for his own sustenance from the soil. He had no faith. But holy Abel stood by the side of the altar and while Cain, the infidel, perhaps laughed and jeered at his sacrifice, he boldly presented there the bleeding lamb as a testimony to all men, both of that time and all future times, that he believed in the seed of the woman—that he looked for Him to come who should destroy the serpent and restore the ruins of the Fall.

Do you see holy Abel, standing there, ministering as a priest at God's altar? Do you see the flush of joy which comes over his face when he sees the heavens opened and the living fire of God descend upon the victims? Do you note with what a grateful expression of confident faith he lifts to Heaven his eyes which had been before filled with tears and cries, "I thank You, O Father, Lord of Heaven and earth, that You have accepted my sacrifice, inasmuch as I presented it through faith in the blood of Your Son, my Savior, who is to come"?

Abel's sacrifice, being the first on record and being offered in the teeth of opposition, has very much in it which puts it ahead of many other of the sacrifices of the Jews. Abel is to be greatly honored for his confidence and faith in the coming Messiah. But compare for a moment the sacrifice of Christ with the sacrifice of Abel and the sacrifice of Abel shrinks into insignificance. What did Abel bring? He brought a sacrifice which showed the necessity of blood-shedding—but Christ brought the blood-shedding itself. Abel taught the world by his sacrifice that he looked for a victim, but Christ was the actual Victim. Abel brought but the type and the figure, the Lamb which was but a picture of the Lamb of God which takes away the sins of the world. But Christ was that Lamb. He was the Substance of the shadow, the Reality of the type.

Abel's sacrifice had no merit in it apart from the faith in the Messiah with which he presented it. But Christ's sacrifice had merit of itself. It was in itself meritorious. What was the blood of Abel's lamb? It was nothing but the blood of a common lamb that might have been shed anywhere. Except for the faith in Christ the blood of the lamb was but as water, a contemptible thing. But the blood of Christ was a sacrifice indeed, richer far than all the blood of beasts that ever were offered upon the altar of Abel, or the altar of all the Jewish high priests. We may say of all the sacrifices that were ever offered, however costly they might be and however acceptable to God, though they were rivers of oil and tens of thousands of fat beasts—they were less than nothing and contemptible in comparison with the one sacrifice which our High Priest has offered once and for all whereby He has eternally perfected them that are sanctified.

We have thus found it very easy to set forth the difference between the blood of Christ's sprinkling and the blood which Abel sprinkled. But now I take it that there is a deeper meaning than this, despite what some commentators have said. I believe that the allusion here is to the blood of murdered Abel. Cain smote Abel and doubtless his hands and the altar were stained with the blood of him who had acted as a priest. "Now," says our Apostle, "that blood of Abel spoke." We have evidence that it did, for God said to Cain, "The voice of your brother's blood cries unto Me from the ground," and the Apostle's comment upon that in another place is—"By faith Abel offered unto God a more excellent sacrifice than Cain, by which he obtained witness that he was righteous, God testifying of his gifts and by it he being dead yet speaks," speaks through his blood, his blood crying unto God from the ground. Now, Christ's blood speaks, too. What is the difference between the two voices?—for we are told in the text that it "speaks better things than that of Abel."

Abel's blood spoke in a threefold manner. It spoke in Heaven. It spoke to the sons of men. It spoke to the conscience of Cain. The blood of Christ speaks in a like threefold manner and it speaks better things.

First, the blood of Abel spoke in Heaven. Abel was a holy man and all that Cain could bring against him was, "his own works were evil and his brother's were righteous." You see the brothers going to the sacrifice together. You mark the black scowl upon the brow of Cain, when Abel's sacrifice is accepted while his remains untouched by the sacred fire. You note how they begin to talk together—how quietly Abel argues the question and how ferociously Cain denounces him. You note again how God speaks to Cain and warns him of the evil which he knew was in his heart. And you see Cain, as he goes from the presence chamber of the

Most High, warned and forewarned—with the dreadful thought in his heart that he will imbrue his hands in his brother's blood.

He meets his brother. He talks friendly with him—he gives him, as it were, the kiss of Judas. He entices him into the field where he is alone. He takes him unaware. He smites him and smites him yet again, till there lies the murdered bleeding corpse of his brother. O earth! Earth! Earth! Cover not his blood. This is the first murder you have ever seen! The first blood of man that ever stained your soil. Hark, there is a cry heard in Heaven, the angels are astonished. They rise up from their golden seats and they enquire, "What is that cry?"

God looks upon them and He says, "It is the cry of blood, a man has been slain by his fellow. A brother by him who came from the bowels of the self-same mother has been murdered in cold blood, through malice. One of my saints has been murdered and here he comes. And Abel enters into Heaven blood-red, the first of God's elect who had entered Paradise and the first of God's children who had worn the blood-red crown of martyrdom. And then the cry was heard, loud and clear and strong. And thus it spoke—"Revenge! Revenge! Revenge!" And God Himself, rising from His throne, summoned the culprit to His presence, questioned Him, condemned Him out of his own mouth and made him henceforth a fugitive and a vagabond to wander over the surface of the earth, which was to be sterile henceforth to his plow.

And now, Beloved, just contrast with this the blood of Christ. That is Jesus Christ, the Incarnate Son of God. He hangs upon a tree. He is murdered—murdered by His own Brethren. "He came unto His own and His own received Him not, but His own led him out to death." He bleeds. He dies. And then is heard a cry in Heaven. The astonished angels again start from their seats and they say, "What is this? What is this cry that we hear?" And the Mighty Maker answers yet again, "It is the cry of blood. It is the cry of the blood of My only-begotten and well-beloved Son!" And God, rising up from His throne, looks down from Heaven and listens to the cry. And what is the cry? It is not revenge. But the voice cries, "Mercy! Mercy! Mercy!" Did you hear it? It said, "Father, forgive them, for they know not what they do."

Herein, the blood of Christ "speaks better things than that of Abel," for Abel's blood said, "Revenge!" and made the sword of God start from its scabbard. But Christ's blood cried "Mercy!" and sent the sword back again and bade it sleep forever–

"Blood has a voice to pierce the skies,
'Revenge!' the blood of Abel cries;
But the rich blood of Jesus slain,
Speaks peace as loud from every vein."

You will note, too, that Abel's blood cried for revenge upon one man only–upon Cain. It required the death of but one man to satisfy it, namely, the death of the murderer. "Blood for blood!" The murderer must die the death. But what says Christ's blood in Heaven? Does it speak for only one? Ah, no, Beloved. "The free gift has come upon many." Christ's blood cries mercy! Mercy! Mercy! Not on one, but upon a multitude whom no man can number–ten thousand times ten thousand.

Again–Abel's blood cried to Heaven for revenge, for one transgression of Cain. What Cain had done, worthless and vile before, the blood of Abel did not demand any revenge. It was for the one sin that blood clamored at the Throne of you hear that cry, that all-prevailing cry, as now it comes up from Calvary's summit–"Father, forgive them!" Not one, but many. "Father, forgive them." And not only forgive them this offense, but forgive them all their sins and blot out all their iniquities. Ah, Beloved, we might have thought that the blood of Christ would have demanded vengeance at the hands of God.

Surely, if Abel is revenged seven fold, then must Christ be revenged seventy times seven. If the earth would not swallow up the blood of Abel till it had had its fill, surely we might have thought that the earth never would have covered the corpse of Christ until God had struck the world with fire and sword and banished all men to destruction. But, O precious blood! You say not one word of vengeance! All that this blood cries is peace! Pardon! Forgiveness! Mercy! Acceptance! Truly it "speaks better things than that of Abel."

Again—Abel's blood had a second voice. It spoke to the whole world. "He being dead yet speaks"—not only in Heaven, but on earth. God's Prophets are a speaking people. They speak by their acts and by their words as long as they live and when they are buried they speak by their example which they have left behind. Abel speaks by his blood to us. And what does it say? When Abel offered up his victim upon the altar he said to us, "I believe in a sacrifice that is to be offered for the sins of men," but when Abel's own blood was sprinkled on the altar he seemed to say, "Here is the ratification of my faith. I seal my testimony with my own blood. You have now the evidence of my sincerity, for I was prepared to die for the defense of this Truth of God which I now witness unto you."

It was a great thing for Abel thus to ratify his testimony with his blood. We should not have believed the martyrs half so easily if they had not been ready to die for their profession. The Gospel in ancient times would never have spread at such a marvelous rate if it had not been that all the preachers of the Gospel were ready at any time to attest their message with their own blood. But Christ's blood "speaks better things than that of Abel." Abel's blood ratified his testimony and Christ's blood has ratified His testimony, too. But Christ's testimony is better than that of Abel. For what is the testimony of Christ? The Covenant of Grace—that Everlasting Covenant.

He came into this world to tell us that God had from the beginning chosen His people—that He had ordained them to eternal life and that He had made a Covenant with His son Jesus Christ that if He would pay the price they should go free—if He would suffer in their stead they should be delivered. And Christ cried before, "He bowed His head and gave up the ghost," "It is finished." The Covenant purpose is finished. That purpose was "to finish the transgression and to make an end of sins and to make reconciliation for iniquity and to bring in everlasting righteousness." Such was the testimony of our Lord Jesus Christ, as His own blood gushed from His heart to be the die stamp and seal that the Covenant was ratified. When I see Abel die I know that his testimony was true. But when I see Christ die I know that the Covenant is true–

"This Covenant, O Believer, stands
Your rising fears to quell;
'Tis signed and sealed and ratified,
In all things ordered well."

When He bowed His head and gave up the ghost, He did as much say, "All things are made sure unto the seed by My giving Myself as Victim." Come, Saint, and see the Covenant all blood-stained and know that it is sure. He is "the faithful and true Witness, the Prince of the kings of the earth." First of martyrs, my Lord Jesus, You had a better testimony to witness than they all, for You have witnessed to the Everlasting Covenant. You have witnessed that You are the Shepherd and Bishop of souls. You have witnessed to the putting away of sin by the sacrifice of Yourself. Again–I say, come, you people of God and read over the golden roll. It begins in election–it ends in everlasting life and all this the blood of Christ cries in your ears. All this is true. For Christ's blood proves it to be true and to be sure to all the seed. It "speaks better things than that of Abel."

Now we come to the third voice, for the blood of Abel had a three-fold sound. It spoke in the conscience of Cain. Hardened though he was and like a very devil in his sin, yet he was not so deaf in his conscience that he could not hear the voice of blood. The first thing that Abel's blood said to Cain was this–"Ah, guilty wretch, to spill your brother's blood!"–as he saw it trickling from the wound and flowing down in streams. He looked at it and as the sun shone on it and the red glare came into his eye, it seemed to say, "Ah, cursed wretch, for the son of your own mother you have slain. Your wrath was vile enough, when your countenance fell, but to rise up against your brother and take away his life, Oh,

It seemed to say to him, "What had he done that you should take his life? Wherein had he offended you? Was not his conduct blameless and his conversation pure? If you had smitten a villain or a thief, men might not have blamed you. But this blood is pure, clean, perfect blood. How could you kill such a man as this?" And Cain put his hand across his brow and felt there was a sense of guilt there that he had never felt before. And then the blood said to him again, "Why, where will you go? You shall be a vagabond as long as you live." A cold chill ran through him and he said, "Whoever finds me will kill me." And though God promised him he should live, no doubt he was always afraid. If he saw a company of men together, he would hide himself in a thicket, or if in his solitary wanderings he saw a man at a distance, he started back and sought to bury his head, so that none should observe him. In the stillness of the night he started up in his dreams.

It was but his wife that slept by his side. But he thought he felt someone's hands gripping his throat and about to take away his life. Then he would sit up in his bed and took around at the grim shadows, thinking some fiend was hunting him and seeking after him. Then, as he rose to go about his business, he trembled. He trembled to be alone, he trembled to be in company. When he was alone he seemed not to be alone. The ghost of his brother seemed staring him in his face. And when he was in company he dreaded the voice of men, for he seemed to think everyone cursed him and he thought everyone knew the crime he had committed and no doubt they did and every man shunned him.

No man would take his hand, for it was red with blood and his very child upon his knee was afraid to look up into his father's face, for there was the mark which God had set upon him. His very wife could scarcely speak to him–for she was afraid that from the lips of him who had been cursed of God some curse might fall on her. The very earth cursed him. He no sooner put his foot upon the ground where had been a garden before it suddenly turned into a desert and the fair rich soil became hardened into an arid rock. Guilt, like a grim chamberlain with fingers bloody red, did draw the curtain of his bed each night. His crime refused him sleep. It spoke in his heart and the walls of his memory reverberated the dying cry of his murdered brother.

And no doubt that blood spoke one more thing to Cain. It said, "Cain, although you may now be spared there is no hope for you. You are a man accursed on earth and accursed forever. God has condemned you here and He will damn you hereafter." And so wherever Cain went, he never found hope. Though he searched for it in the mountaintop, yet he found it not there. Hope that was left to all men, was denied to him–a hopeless, houseless, helpless vagabond–he wandered up and down the surface of the earth. Oh, Abel's brood had a terrible voice indeed.

But now see the sweet change as you listen to the blood of Christ. It "speaks better things than that of Abel." Friend, have you ever heard the blood of Christ in your conscience? I have and I thank God I ever heard that sweet soft voice–

"Once a sinner near despair;
Sought the mercy seat by prayer."

He prayed–he thought he was praying in vain. The tears gushed from his eyes; his heart was heavy within him. He sought, but he found no mercy. Again, again and yet again, he besieged the Throne of heavenly Grace and knocked at Mercy's door. Oh, who can tell the millstone that lay upon his beating heart and the iron that did eat into his soul? He was a prisoner in sore bondage–deep, as he thought–in the bondage of despair was he chained, to perish forever. That prisoner one day heard a voice, which said to him, "Away, away to Calvary!" Yet he trembled at the voice, for he said, "Why should I go there, for there my blackest sin was committed. There I murdered the Savior by my transgressions? Why should I go to see the murdered corpse of Him who became my brother born for adversity?"

But mercy beckoned and she said, "Come, come away, Sinner!" And the sinner followed. The chains were on his legs and on his hands and he could scarcely creep along. Still the black vulture Destruction seemed hovering in the air. But he crept as best he could, till he came to the foot of the hill of Calvary. On the summit he saw a Cross—blood was distilling from the hands and from the feet and from the side and Mercy touched his ears and said, "Listen!" And he heard that blood speak. And as it spoke the first thing it said was, "Love!" And the second thing it said was, "Mercy!" The third thing it said was, "Pardon." The next thing it said was, "Acceptance." The next thing it said was, "Adoption." The next thing it said was, "Security." And the last thing it whispered was, "Heaven."

And as the sinner heard that voice, he said within himself, "And does that blood speak to me?" And the Spirit said, "To you—to you it speaks." And he listened and oh, what music did it seem to his poor troubled heart, for in a moment all his doubts were gone. He had no sense of guilt. He knew that he was vile but he saw that his vileness was all washed away. He knew that he was guilty, but he saw his guilt all atoned for through the precious blood that was flowing there. He had been full of dread before. He dreaded life, he dreaded death. But now he had no dread at all. A joyous confidence took possession of his heart. He looked to Christ and he said, "I know that my Redeemer lives." He clasped the Savior in his arms and he began to sing—"Oh, confident am I. For this blest blood was shed for me." And then despair fled and destruction was driven clean away and instead thereof came the bright white-winged angel of Assurance and she dwelt in his bosom, saying evermore to him, "You are accepted in the Beloved. You are chosen of God and precious. You are His child now and you shall be His favorite throughout eternity." "The blood of Christ speaks better things than that of Abel."

And now I must have you notice that the blood of Christ bears a comparison with the blood of Abel in one or two respects, but it excels in them all.

The blood of Abel cried "Justice!" It was but right that the blood should be revenged. Abel had no private resentment against Cain. Doubtless could Abel have done so, he would have forgiven his brother. But the blood spoke justly and only asked its due when it shouted, "Vengeance! Vengeance! Vengeance!" And Christ's blood speaks justly, when it says,

28

"Mercy!" Christ has as much right to demand mercy upon sinners as Abel's blood had to cry vengeance against Cain. When Christ saves a sinner, He does not save him on the sly, or against Law or justice, but He saves him justly. Christ has a right to save whom He will save, to have mercy on whom He will have mercy, for He can do it justly, He can be just and yet be the Justifier of the ungodly.

Again—Abel's blood cried effectively. It did not cry in vain. It said, "Revenge," and revenge it had. And Christ's blood, blessed be His name, never cries in vain. It says, "Pardon," and pardon every Believer shall have. It says, "Acceptance," and every penitent is accepted in the Beloved. If that blood cries for me, I know it cannot cry in vain. That allprevailing blood of Christ shall never miss its due. It must, it shall, be heard. Shall Abel's blood startle Heaven and shall not the blood of Christ reach the ears of the Lord God of Sabaoth?

And again—Abel's blood cries continually—there is the mercy seat and there is the Cross and the blood is dropping on the mercy seat. I have sinned a sin. Christ says, "Father, forgive him." There is one drop. I sin again—Christ intercedes again. There is another drop. In fact, it is the drop that intercedes, Christ need not speak with His mouth. The drops of blood as they fall upon the mercy seat, each seems to say, "Forgive him! Forgive him! Forgive him!"

Dear Friend, when you hear the voice of conscience, stop and try to hear the voice of the blood, too. Oh, what a precious thing it is to hear the voice of the blood of Christ. You who do not know what that means, do not know the very essence and joy of life. But you who understand that can say, "The dropping of the blood is like the music of Heaven upon earth." Poor Sinner! I would ask you to come and listen to that voice that distils upon your ears and your heart today. You are full of sin. The Savior bids you lift your eyes to Him. See, there, His blood is flowing from His head, His hands, His feet and every drop that falls, still cries, "Father, O forgive them! Father, O forgive them." And each drop seems to cry also as it falls, "It is finished—I have made an end of sin, I have brought in everlasting righteousness." Oh, sweet, sweet language of the dropping of the blood of Christ." It "speaks better things than that of Abel."

II. Having thus, I trust, sufficiently enlarged upon this subject, I shall now close by addressing you with a few earnest words concerning the second point.—The CONDITION INTO WHICH EVERY CHRISTIAN IS BROUGHT. He is said to "come to the blood of sprinkling." I shall make this a very brief matter, but a very solemn and pointed one. My Hearers, have you come to the blood of Christ? I do not ask you whether you have come to a knowledge of doctrine, or of an observance of ceremonies, or of a certain form of experience. But I ask you if you have come to the blood of Christ. If you have, I know how you came. You must come to the blood of Christ with no merits of your own. Guilty, lost and helpless, you must come to that blood and to that blood, alone, for your hopes. You come to the Cross of Christ and to that blood, too, I know, with a trembling and an aching heart.

Some of you remember how you first came—cast down and full of despair. But that blood recovered you. And this one thing I know—if you have come to that blood once, you will come to it every day. Your life will be just this—"Looking unto Jesus." And your whole conduct will be epitomized in this—"To whom coming as unto a living stone." Not to whom I have come, but to whom I am always coming. If you have ever come to the blood of Christ you will feel your need of coming to it every day. He that does not desire to wash in that fountain every day has never washed in it at all. I feel it every day to be my joy and my privilege that there is still a fountain opened. I trust I came to Christ years ago but ah, I could not trust to that unless I could come again today. Past experiences are doubtful things to a Christian. It is present coming to Christ that must give us joy and comfort. Did you not, some of you, sing twenty years ago that hymn—

"My faith does lay her hand
On that dear head of Yours
While like a penitent I stand,
And there confess my sin"?

Why, Beloved you can sing it as well today as you did then. I was reading the other day some book in which the author states that we are not to come to Christ as sinners as long as we live. He says we are to grow into saints. Ah, he did not know much, I am sure. For saints are sinners, still, and they have always to come to Christ as sinners. If ever I go to the Throne of God as a saint, I get repulsed. But when I go just as a poor, humble, seeking sinner–relying upon nothing but Your blood, O Jesus–I never can be turned away, I am sure. To whom coming as unto "blood that speaks better things than that of Abel." Let this be our experience every day.

But there are some here who confess that they never did come. I cannot exhort you, then, to come every day but I exhort you to come now for the first time. But you say, "May I come?" Yes, if you are wishing to come you may come. If you feel that you have need to come you may come–

"All the fitness He requires,
Is to feel your need of Him."

And even–

"This He gives you,
'Tis His Spirit's rising beam."

But you say, "I must bring some merits." Hark to the blood that speaks! It says, "Sinner, I am full of merit–why bring your merits here?" "Ah, but," you say "I have too much sin." Hark to the blood–as it falls, it cries, "Of many offenses unto justification of life." "Ah, but," you say, "I know I am too guilty." Hark to the blood! "Though your sins are as scarlet I will make them as wool; though they are red like crimson they shall be whiter than snow." "No," says one, "but I have such a poor desire, I have such a little faith." Hark to the blood! "The bruised reed I will not break and smoking flax I will not quench."

31

"No, but," you say, "I know He will cast me out, if I do come." Hark to the blood! "All that the Father gives Me shall come to Me and him that comes to Me I will in no wise cast out." "No, but," you say, "I know I have so many sins that I cannot be forgiven." Now, hear the blood once more and I have done. "The blood of Jesus Christ, His Son, cleans us from all sin." That is the blood's testimony and its testimony to you. "There are three that bear witness on earth, the Spirit and the water and the blood." And behold the blood's witness is–"The blood of Jesus Christ, His Son, cleans us from all sin." Come, poor Sinner, cast yourself simply on that Truth of God. Away with your good works and all your trust! Lie simply flat on that sweet word of Christ. Trust His blood. And if you can put your trust alone in Jesus, in His sprinkled blood, it shall speak in your conscience better things than that of Abel.

I am afraid there are many that do not know what we mean by believing. Good Dr. Chalmers, once visiting a poor old woman, told her to believe in Christ and she said, "But that is just the thing I do not know what you mean by." So Dr. Chalmers said, "Trust Christ." Now, that is just the meaning of believing. Trust Him with your soul. Trust Him with your sins. Trust Him with the future. Trust Him with the past. Trust Him with everything. Say–

"A guilty, weak and worthless worm,
On Christ's kind arms I fall
Be You my strength and righteousness,
My Jesus and my all."

THE BLOOD

"When I see the blood, I will pass over you."
Exodus 12:13

GOD'S people are always safe. "All the saints are in His hand." And the hand of God is a place of safety, as well as a place of honor. Nothing can hurt the man who has made his refuge God. "You have given commandment to save me," said David. And every believing child of God may say the same. Plague, famine, war, tempest–all these have received commandment of God to save His people. Though the earth should rock beneath the feet of man, yet the Christian may stand fast and though the heavens should be rolled up and the firmament should pass away like a scroll that is burned by fervent heat, yet need not a Christian fear. God's people shall be saved–if they cannot be saved under the heavens, they shall be saved in the heavens. If there is no safety for them in the time of trouble upon this solid earth, they shall be "caught up together with the Lord in the air and so shall they be ever with the Lord," and ever safe.

Now, at the time of which this Book of Exodus speaks, Egypt was exposed to a terrible peril. Jehovah Himself was about to march through the streets of all the cities of Egypt. It was not merely a destroying angel, but Jehovah Himself. For thus it is written, "I will pass through the land of Egypt this night and will smite all the first-born in the land of Egypt, both man and beast." No one less than I AM, the great God, had vowed to "cut Rahab" with the sword of vengeance. Tremble, you inhabitants of the earth, for God has come down among you, provoked, incensed and at last awakened from His seeming sleep of patience. He has girded on His terrible sword and He has come to smite you. Quake for fear, all you that have sin within you, for when God walks through the streets, sword in hand, will He not smite you all?

But hark! The voice of Covenant mercy speaks. God's children are safe, even though an angry God is in the streets. As they are safe from the rod of the wicked, so are they safe from the sword of justice–always and ever safe. For there was not a hair of the head of an Israelite that was so much as touched—Jehovah kept them safe beneath His wings. While He did rend His enemies like a lion, yet did He protect His children, every one of them. But, Beloved, while this is always true, that God's people are safe, there is another fact that is equally true, namely, that God's people are only safe through the blood. The reason why God spares His people in the time of calamity is because He sees the mark of blood on their brow.

What is the basis of that great Truth of God, that all things work together for good to them that love God? What is the cause that all things so produce good to them but this—that they are bought with the precious blood of Christ? Therefore it is that nothing can hurt them, because the blood is upon them and every evil thing must pass them by. It was so that night in Egypt. God Himself was abroad with His sword. But He spared them, because He saw the mark of blood on the lintel and on the two side-posts. And so it is with us. In the day when God in His fierce anger shall come forth from His dwelling place, to frighten the earth with terrors and to condemn the wicked, we shall be secure. If covered with the Savior's righteousness and sprinkled with His blood, we are found in Him.

Do I hear someone say that I am now coming to an old subject? This thought struck me when I was preparing for preaching, that I should have to tell you an old story over again. And just as I was thinking of that, happening to turn over a book, I met with an anecdote of Judson the missionary to Burma. He had passed through unheard-of hardships and had performed dangerous exploits for his Master. He returned, after thirty years' absence, to America. Announced to address an assembly in a provincial town and a vast concourse having gathered from great distances to hear him, he rose at the close of the usual service and, as all eyes were fixed and every ear attentive, he spoke for about fifteen minutes, with much pathos, of the precious Savior, of what He had done for us and of what we owed to Him. And he sat down, visibly affected.

"The people are very much disappointed," said a friend to him on their way home–"they wonder you did not talk of something else." "Why what did they want?" he replied, "I presented, to the best of my ability, the most interesting subject in the world." "But they wanted something different–a story." "Well, I am sure I gave them a story–the most thrilling one that can be conceived of." "But they had heard it before. They wanted something new of a man who had just come from the antipodes." "Then I am glad they have it to say, that a man coming from the antipodes had nothing better to tell than the wondrous story of the dying love of Jesus. My business is to preach the Gospel of Christ. And when I can speak at all, I dare not trifle with my commission. When I looked upon those people today and remembering where I should next meet them, how could I stand up and furnish food to vain curiosity–tickle their fancy with amusing stories, however decently strung together on a thread of religion? That is not what Christ meant by preaching the Gospel. And then how could I hereafter meet the fearful charge, 'I gave you one opportunity to tell them of ME. You spent it in describing your own adventures!' "

So I thought, Well, if Judson told the old story after he had been thirty years away and could not find anything better, I will just go back to this old subject, which is always new and always fresh to us–the precious blood of Christ, by which we are saved. First, then, the blood. Secondly, its efficacy. Thirdly, the one condition appended to it–"When I see the blood." And fourthly, the practical lesson.

First, then, THE BLOOD ITSELF. In the case of the Israelites it was the blood of the Paschal Lamb. In our case, Beloved, it is the blood of the Lamb of God, which takes away the sins of the world.
The blood of which I have solemnly to speak this morning, is, first of all, the blood of a Divinely appointed Victim. Jesus Christ did not come into this world unappointed. He was sent here by His Father. This, indeed, is one of the underlying groundworks of the Christian's hope. We can rely upon Jesus Christ's acceptance by His Father because His father ordained Him to be our Savior from before the foundation of the world. Sinner, when I preach to you the blood of Christ this morning, I am

preaching something that is well-pleasing to God. For God Himself did choose Christ to be the Redeemer. He Himself set Him apart from before the foundation of the world and He Himself, even Jehovah the Father, did lay upon Him the iniquity of us all. The sacrifice of Christ is not brought to you without warrant. It is not something which Christ did surreptitiously and in secret. It was written in the great decree from all eternity, that He was the Lamb slain from before the foundation of the world. As He Himself said, "Lo, I come. In the volume of the book it is written of Me, I delight to do Your will O God." It is God's will that the blood of Jesus should be shed. Jesus is God's chosen Savior for men. And here, when addressing the ungodly, here, I say, is one potent argument with them. Sinner! You may trust in Christ, that He is able to save you from the wrath of God, for God Himself has appointed Him to save.

Christ Jesus, too, like the lamb, was not only a Divinely appointed Victim, but he was spotless. Had there been one sin in Christ, He had not been capable of being our Savior. But He was without spot or blemish—without original sin, without any practical transgression. In Him was no sin, though He was "tempted in all points like as we are." Here, again, is the reason why the blood is able to save, because it is the blood of an innocent Victim, a Victim only because His death lay in us and not in Himself. When the poor innocent lamb was put to death, by the head of the household of Egypt, I can imagine that thoughts like these ran through his mind. "Ah," he would say, as he struck the knife into the lamb, "This poor creature dies, not for any guilt that it has ever had, but to show me that I am guilty and that I deserved to die like this." Turn, then, your eye to the Cross and see Jesus bleeding there and dying for you. Remember—

"For sins not His own, He died to atone."

Sin had no foothold in Him, never troubled Him. The prince of this world came and looked, but he said, "I have nothing in Christ. There is no room for me to plant my foot—no piece of corrupt ground, which I may call my own." O Sinner, the blood of Jesus is able to save you because

He was perfectly innocent Himself and, "He died, the Just for the unjust, to bring us to God."

But some will say, "Why has the blood of Christ such power to save?" My reply is not only because God appointed that blood and because it was the blood of an innocent and spotless being, but because Christ Himself was God. If Christ were a mere man, my Hearers, you could not be exhorted to trust Him. Were He ever so spotless and holy, there would be no efficacy in His blood to save. But Christ was "very God of very God." The blood that Jesus shed was God-like blood. It was the blood of man, for He was Man like ourselves. But the Divinity was so allied with the manhood, that the blood derived efficacy from it.

Can you imagine what must be the value of the blood of God's own dear Son? No, you cannot put an estimate upon it that should so much as reach to a millionth part of its preciousness. I know you esteem that blood as beyond all price if you have been washed in it. But I know also that you do not esteem it enough. It was the wonder of angels that God should condescend to die. It will be the wonder of all wonders, the unceasing wonder of eternity, that God should become Man to die. Oh, when we think that Christ was Creator of the world and that on His all-sustaining shoulders did hang the universe, we cannot wonder that His death is mighty to redeem and that His blood should cleanse from sin.

Come here, Saints and Sinners. Gather in and crowd around the Cross and see this Man, overcome with weakness, fainting, groaning, bleeding and dying. This Man is also "God over all, blessed forever," Is there not power to save? Is there not efficacy in blood like that? Can you imagine any stretch of sin which shall prove greater than the power of Divinity— any height of iniquity that shall overtop the topless steeps of the Divine? Can I conceive a depth of sin that shall be deeper than the Infinite? A breadth of iniquity that shall be broader than the Godhead? Because He is Divine, He is "able to save to the uttermost, them that come unto God by Him." Divinity appointed, spotless and Divine—His blood is the blood whereby you may escape the anger and the wrath of God.

Once more–the blood of which we speak today is blood once shed for many for the remission of sin. The paschal lamb was killed every year, but now Christ has appeared to take away sin by the offering up of Himself and there is now no more mention of sin, for Christ once and for all has put away sin by the offering of Himself. The Jew sacrificed the lamb every morning and every evening, for there was a continual mention of sin. The blood of the lamb could not take it away. The lamb availed for today, but there was the sin of tomorrow–what was to be done with that? Why, a fresh victim must bleed.

But oh, my Hearer, our greatest joy is that the blood of Jesus has been once shed and He has said, "It is finished." There is no more need of the blood of bulls or of goats, or of any other sacrifice. That one sacrifice has "perfected forever them that are sanctified." Trembling Sinner! Come to the Cross again. Your sins are heavy and many but the atonement for them is completed by the death of Christ. Look, then, to Jesus and remember that Christ needs nothing to supplement His blood! The road between God and man is finished and open–the robe to cover your nakedness is complete–without a rag of yours. The bath in which you are to be washed is full, full to the brim and needs nothing to be added thereunto. "It is finished!" Let that ring in your ears. There is nothing now that can hinder your being saved, if God has made you willing now to believe in Jesus Christ. He is a complete Savior, full of Grace for an empty sinner.

And yet I must add one more thought and then leave this point. The blood of Jesus Christ is blood that has been accepted. Christ died–He was buried. But neither Heaven nor earth could tell whether God had accepted the ransom. There was wanted God's seal upon the great Magna Charta of man's salvation and that seal was put, my Hearer, in that hour when God summoned the angel and bade Him descend from Heaven and roll away the stone. Christ was put in vile confinement in the prison of the grave, as a hostage for His people. Until God had signed the warrant for acquittal of all His people, Christ must abide in the bonds of death. He did not attempt to break out of His prison. He did not come out illegally, by wrenching down the bars of His dungeon, He waited–He wrapped up the napkin, folding it by itself—He laid the grave clothes in a separate place.

He waited, waited patiently. And at last down from the skies, like the flash of a meteor, the angel descended, touched the stone and rolled it away. And when Christ came out, rising from the dead in the glory of His Father's power, then was the seal put upon the great charts of our redemption. The blood was accepted and sin was forgiven. And now, Soul, it is not possible for God to reject you, if you come this day to Him, pleading the blood of Christ. God cannot—and here we speak with reverence, too—the everlasting God cannot reject a sinner who pleads the blood of Christ—for if He did, it were to deny Himself. And to contradict all His former acts. He has accepted blood and He will accept it. He never can revoke that Divine acceptance of the resurrection. And if you go to God, my Hearer, pleading simply and only the blood of Him that hung upon the tree, God must un-God Himself before He can reject you, or reject that blood.

And yet I fear that I have not been able to make you think of the blood of Christ. I beseech you, then, just for a moment, try to picture to yourself Christ on the Cross. Let your imagination figure the motley crew assembled round about that little hill of Calvary. Lift now your eyes and see the three crosses put upon that rising knoll. See in the center the thorn-crowned brow of Christ. Do you see the hands that have always been full of blessing, nailed fast to the accursed wood? Look at His dear face, more marred than that of any other man? Do you see it now, as His head bows upon His bosom in the extreme agonies of death? He was a real Man, remember. It was a real Cross. Do not think of these things as figments and fancies and romances There was such a Being and He died as I describe it. Let your imagination picture Him and then sit still a moment and think over this thought—"The blood of that man, whom now I behold dying in agony, must be my redemption. And if I would be saved, I must put my only trust in what He suffered for me, when He Himself did 'bear our sins in His own body on the tree.' " If God the Holy Spirit should help you, you will then be in a right state to proceed to the second point.

II. THE EFFICACY OF THIS BLOOD. "When I see the blood I will pass over you."

The blood of Christ has such a Divine power to save that nothing but it can ever save the soul. If some foolish Israelite had despised the command of God and had said, "I will sprinkle something else upon the doorposts," or, "I will adorn the lintel with jewels of gold and silver," he would have perished. Nothing could save his household but the sprinkled blood. And now let us all remember, that "other foundation can no man lay than that which is laid, Jesus Christ," for "there is none other name given among men whereby we must be saved." My works, my prayers, my tears, cannot save me. The blood, the blood alone, has power to redeem. Sacraments, however well they may be attended to, cannot save me. Nothing but Your blood, O Jesus, can redeem me from the guilt of sin.

Though I should give rivers of oil and ten thousand of the fat of fed beasts. Yes, though I should give my first-born for my transgression, the fruit of my body for the sin of my soul—all would be useless. Nothing but the blood of Jesus has in it the slightest saving power. Oh, you that are trusting in your infant Baptism, your Confirmation and your Lord's Supper, you are trusting in a lie! Nothing but the blood of Jesus can save. I care not how right the ordinance, how true the form, how Scriptural the practice, it is all a vanity to you if you rely in it. God forbid I should say a word against ordinances, or against holy things, but keep them in their places. If you make them the basis of your soul's salvation, they are lighter than a shadow and when you need them most you shall find them fail you.

There is not, I repeat it again, the slightest atom of saving power anywhere but in the blood of Jesus. That blood has the only power to save and anything else that you rely upon shall be a refuge of lies. This is the rock and this is the work that is perfect. But all other things are day dreams. They must be swept away in the day when God shall come to try our work of what sort it is. THE BLOOD stands out in solitary majesty, the only rock of our salvation.

This blood is not simply the only thing that can save, but it must save alone. Put anything with the blood of Christ and you are lost. Trust to anything else with this and you perish. "It is true," says one, "that the Sacrament cannot save me, but I will trust in that, and in Christ, too." You are a lost man, then. So jealous is Christ of His honor, that anything you put with Him, however good it is, becomes, from the fact of your putting it with Him, an accursed thing. And what is it that you would put with Christ? Your good works? What? Will you yoke a reptile with an angel–yoke yourself to the chariot of salvation with Christ? What are your good works? Your righteousnesses are "as filthy rags." And shall filthy rags be joined to the spotless celestial righteousness of Christ? It must not and it shall not be.

Rely on Jesus only and you cannot perish. But rely on anything with Him and you are as surely damned as if you should rely upon your sins. Jesus only–Jesus only–Jesus only! This is the Rock of our salvation. And here let me stop and combat a few forms and shapes which our self-righteousness always takes. "Oh," says one, "I could trust in Christ if I felt my sins more." Sir, that is a damning error. Is your repentance, your sense of sin, to be a part-Savior? Sinner! The blood is to save you, not your tears–Christ's death, not your repentance! You are bid this day to trust in Christ. Not in your feelings, not in your pangs on account of sin. Many a man has been brought into great soul distress, because he has looked more at his repentance than at the obedience of Christ–

"Could your tears forever flow,
Could your zeal no respite know–
All for sin could not atone,
Christ must save and Christ alone."

"No, says another, "but I feel that I do not value the blood of Christ as I ought and therefore I am afraid to believe." My Friend, that is another insidious form of the same error. God does not say, "When I see your estimate of the blood of Christ, I will pass over you. No, but when I see the blood." It is not your estimate of that blood, it is the blood that saves you. As I said before, that magnificent, solitary blood, must be alone. "No," says another, "but if I had more faith then I should have hope." That, too, is a very deadly shape of the same evil. You are not to be saved by the efficacy of your faith, to look to your believing as salvation. No man will go to Heaven if he trusts to his own faith. You may as well trust to your own good works as trust to your faith. Your faith must deal with Christ not with itself.

The world hangs on nothing–but faith cannot hang upon itself–it must hang on Christ. Sometimes, when my faith is vigorous, I catch myself doing this. There is joy flowing into my heart and after awhile I begin to find that my joy suddenly departs. I ask the causes and I find that the joy came because I was thinking of Christ. But when I begin to think about my joy, then my joy fled. You must not think of your faith but of Christ. Faith comes from meditation upon Christ. Turn, then, your eye, not upon faith but upon Jesus. It is not your hold of Christ that saves you, it is His hold of you. It is not the efficacy of your believing in Him. It is the efficacy of His blood applied to you through the Spirit.

I do not know how sufficiently to follow Satan in all his windings into the human heart but this. I know he is always trying to keep back this great Truth of God–the blood, and the blood alone, has power to save. "Oh," says another, "if I had such-and-such an experience then I could trust." Friend, it is not your experience, it is the BLOOD. God did not say, "When I see your experience," but, "When I see the blood of Christ." "No," says one, "but if I had such-and-such graces, I could hope." No, but He did not say, "When I see your graces," but, "When I see the blood." Get grace, get as much as you can of faith and love and hope, but oh, do not put them where Christ's blood ought to be. The only pillar of your hope must be the Cross and anything else that you put to buttress up the Cross of Christ is obnoxious to God and ceases to have any virtue in it, because it is an anti-Christ. The blood of Christ, then, ALONE, saves. But anything with it and it does not save.

Yet again we may say of the blood of Christ, it is all-sufficient. There is no case which the blood of Christ cannot meet. There is no sin which it cannot wash away. There is no multiplicity of sin which it cannot cleanse, no aggravation of guilt which it cannot remove. You may be double-dyed like scarlet. You may have lain in the lye of your sins these seventy years, but the blood of Christ can take out the stain. You may have blasphemed Him almost as many times as you have breathed, you may have rejected Him as often as you have heard His name. You may have broken His Sabbath, you may have denied His existence, you may have doubted His Godhead, you may have persecuted His servants, you may have trampled on His blood, but all this the blood can wash away. You may have committed whoredom without number—no, murder itself may have defiled your hands—but this fountain filled with blood can wash all the stains away.

The blood of Jesus Christ cleans us from all sin. There is no sort of a man, there is no abortion of mankind, no demon in human shape that this blood cannot wash. Hell may have sought to make a paragon of iniquity, it may have strived to put sin and sin and sin together, till it has made a monster in the shape of man, a monster abhorred of mankind— but the blood of Christ can transform that monster. Magdalene's seven devils it can cast out. It can ease the deep-seated leprosy, it can cure the wound of the maimed, yes, the lost limb it can restore. There is no spiritual disease which the great Physician cannot heal. This is the great panacea, the medicine for all diseases. No case can exceed its virtue, be it ever so black or vile. All-sufficient, all-sufficient blood.

But go further. The blood of Christ saves surely. Many people say, "Well, I hope I shall be saved through the blood of Christ." And perhaps, says one here, who is believing in Christ, "Well, I hope it will save." My dear Friend, that is a slur upon the honor of God. If any man gives you a promise and you say, "Well, I hope he will fulfill it"—is it not implied that you have at least some small doubt as to whether he will or not? Now, I do not hope that the blood of Christ will wash away my sin. I know it is washed away by His blood and that is true faith which does not hope about Christ's blood, but says, "I know it is so. That blood does cleanse.

The moment it was applied to my conscience it did cleanse and it does cleanse still."

The Israelite, if he were true to his faith, did not go inside and say, "I hope the destroying angel will pass by me." But he said, "I know he will. I know God cannot smite me. I know He will not. There is the mark of blood there, I am secure beyond a doubt, there is not the shadow of a risk of my perishing. I am, I must be saved." And so I preach a sure Gospel this morning–"Whosoever believes on the Lord Jesus Christ shall not perish but have everlasting life." "I give unto My sheep eternal life," said He, "and they shall not perish, neither shall any pluck them out of My hand." O, Sinner, I have not the shadow of a doubt as to whether Christ will save you if you trust in His blood. O no, I know He will. I am certain His blood can save. And I beg you, in Christ's name, believe the same. Believe that that blood is sure to cleanse, not only that it may cleanse, but that it must cleanse, "whereby we must be saved," says the Scripture. If we have that blood upon us we must be saved, or else we are to suppose a God unfaithful and a God unkind. In fact, a God transformed from everything that is God-like into everything that is base.

And yet again–he that has this blood sprinkled upon him is saved completely. Not the hair of the head of an Israelite was disturbed by the destroying angel. They were completely saved–so he that believes in the blood is saved from all things. I like the old translation of the chapter in the Romans. There was a martyr once summoned before Bonner. And after he had expressed his faith in Christ, Bonner said, "You are a heretic and will be damned." "No" said he, quoting the old version, "There is therefore now no damnation to them that believe in Christ Jesus." And that brings a sweet thought before us. There is no damnation to the man who has the blood of Christ upon him–he cannot be condemned of God. It is impossible. There is no such a thing, there can be no such thing. There is no damnation. He cannot be damned. For there is no damnation to him that is in Christ Jesus. Let the blood be applied to the lintel and to the doorpost–there is no destruction.

There is a destroying angel for Egypt, but there is none for Israel. There is a Hell for the wicked, but none for the righteous. And if there is none, they cannot be put there. If there is no damnation they cannot suffer it. Christ saves completely—every sin is washed, every blessing ensured—perfection is provided and glory everlasting is the sure result. I think then, I have dwelt sufficiently long upon the efficacy of His blood. But no tongue of seraph can ever speak its worth. I must go home to my chamber and weep because I am powerless to tell this story and yet I have labored to tell it simply, so that all can understand. And I pray, therefore, that God the Spirit may lead some of you to put your trust simply, wholly and entirely, on the blood of Jesus Christ.

III. This brings us to the third point, upon which I must be very brief and the third point is—THE ONE CONDITION. "What?" says one, "Do you preach a conditional salvation?" Yes I do, there is the one condition—"Where I see the blood I will pass over you." What a blessed condition! God does not say, when you see the blood but when I see it. Your eye of faith may be so dim that you cannot see the blood of Christ. Yes, but God's eyes are not dim—He can see it—yes, He must see it. For Christ in Heaven is always presenting His blood before His Father's face. The Israelite could not see the blood—he was inside the house. He could not see what was on the lintel and the doorpost—but God could see it. And this is the only condition of the sinner's salvation—God's seeing the blood. Not your seeing it.

O how safe, then, is everyone that trusts in the Lord Jesus Christ. It is not his faith that is the condition of his assurance. It is the simple fact that Calvary is set perpetually before the eyes of God in a risen and ascended Savior. "When I see the blood, I will pass over you." Fall on your knees, then, in prayer, you doubting souls and let this be your plea—"Lord, have mercy upon me for the blood's sake. I cannot see it as I could desire, but Lord, You see it and You have said, 'When I see it, I will pass over you.' Lord, you see it this day, pass over my sin and forgive me for its dear sake alone."

IV. And now, lastly, WHAT IS THE LESSON? The lesson of the text is this to the Christian. Christian, take care that you do always remember that nothing but the blood of Christ can save you. I preach to myself today what I preach to you. I often find myself like this—I have been praying that the Holy Spirit might rest in my heart and cleanse out an evil passion and presently I find myself full of doubts and fears and when I ask the reason, I find it is this—I have been looking to the Spirit's work until I put the Spirit's work where Christ's work ought to be. Now, it is a sin to put your own works where Christ's should be, but it is just as much a sin to put the Holy Spirit's work there. You must never make the Spirit of God an anti-Christ and you virtually do that when you put the Spirit's work as the groundwork of your faith.

Do you not often hear Christian men say, "I cannot believe in Christ today as I could yesterday, for yesterday I felt such sweet and blessed enjoyments." Now, what is that but putting your frames and feelings where Christ ought to be? Remember, Christ's blood is able to save you in a good frame or in a bad frame. Christ's blood must be your trust, as much when you are full of joy as when you are full of doubt. And here it is that your happiness will be in danger, by beginning to put your good frames and good feelings in the place of the blood of Christ. O, Brethren, if we could always live with a single eye fixed on the Cross, we should always be happy. But when we get a little peace and a little joy, we begin to prize the joy and peace so much, that we forget the source from where they come. As Mr. Brooks says, "A husband that loves his wife will, perhaps, often give her jewels and rings—but suppose she should sit down and begin to think of her jewels and rings so much that she should forget her husband? It would be a kind husband's business to take them away from her so that she might fix her affections entirely on him."

And it is so with us. Jesus gives us jewels of faith and love and we get trusting to them and He takes them away in order that we may come again as guilty, helpless sinners and put our trust in Christ. To quote a verse I often repeat—I believe the spirit of a Christian should be, from his first hour to his last, the spirit of these two lines—

"Nothing in my hand I bring,
Simply to Your Cross I cling."

That is the lesson to the saint.

But another minute, there is a lesson here to the sinner. Poor, trembling, guilty self-condemned Sinner, I have a word from the Lord for you. "The blood of Jesus Christ cleans us," that is, you and me, "cleans us from all sin." That "us" includes you, if now you are feeling your need of a Savior. Now that blood is able to save you and you are bid simply to trust that blood and you shall be saved. But I hear you say, "Sir," you said, "If I feel my need. Now I feel that I do not feel, I only wish I did feel my need enough." Well do not bring your feelings then, but trust only in the blood. If you can rely simply on the blood of Christ, whatever your feelings may be, or may not be, that blood is able to save.

But you are saying, "How am I to be saved? What must I do?" Well there is nothing that you can do. You must leave off doing altogether, in order to be saved. There must be a denial of all your doings. You must get Christ first and then you may do as much as you like. But you must not trust in your doings. Your business is now to lift up your heart in prayer like this—"Lord, You have shown me something of myself, show me something of my Savior." See the Savior hanging on the Cross, turn your eye to Him and say, "Lord, I trust You, I have nothing else to trust to, but I rely on You. Sink or swim, my Savior, I trust You."

And as surely, Sinner, as you can put your trust in Christ, you are as safe as an Apostle or Prophet. Not death nor Hell can slay that man whose firm reliance is at the foot of the Cross. "Believe on the Lord Jesus Christ and you shall be saved." "He that believes and is baptized shall be saved. He that believes not shall be damned." He that believes shall be saved, be his sins ever so many. He that believes not shall be damned, be his sins ever so few and be his virtues ever so many. Trust in Jesus NOW! Sinner, trust in Jesus ONLY.

"Not all the blood of beasts

On Jewish altars slain
Could give the guilty conscience peace,
Or wash away the stain.
But Christ, the heavenly Lamb,
Takes all our sins away–
A sacrifice of nobler name
And richer blood than they."

THE BLOOD OF THE EVERLASTING COVENANT

"The blood of the Everlasting Covenant."
Hebrews 13:20

ALL God's dealings with men have had a covenant character. It has so pleased Him to arrange it, that He will not deal with us except through a covenant, nor can we deal with Him except in the same manner. Adam in the garden was under a covenant with God and God was in covenant with him. That covenant Adam speedily broke. There is a covenant still existing in all its terrible power–terrible I say, because it has been broken on man's part and therefore God will most surely fulfill its solemn threats and sanctions. That is the Covenant of Works. By this He dealt with Moses and in this does He deal with the whole race of men as represented in the first Adam.

Afterwards when God would deal with Noah, it was by a covenant, And when in succeeding ages He dealt with Abraham, He was still pleased to bind himself to him by a covenant. That covenant He preserved and kept and it was renewed continually to many of his seed. God dealt not even with David, the man after His own heart, except with a covenant. He made a covenant with His anointed. And, Beloved, He deals with you and me this day still by covenant. When He shall come in all His terrors to condemn, He shall smite by covenant–namely, by the sword of the covenant of Sinai–and if He comes in the splendors of His grace to save, He still comes to us by covenant–namely, the Covenant of Zion. The covenant which He has made with the Lord Jesus Christ, the Head and representative of His people.

And mark, whenever we come into close and intimate dealings with God, it is sure to be, on our part, also by covenant. We make with God, after conversion, a covenant of gratitude. We come to Him sensible of what He has done for us and we devote ourselves to Him. We set our seal to that covenant when in Baptism we are united with His Church. And day by day, so often as we come around the table of the breaking of the bread, we renew the vow of our covenant and thus we have personal

49

communion with God. I cannot pray to Him except through the Covenant of Grace. And I know that I am not His child unless I am His, first, through the covenant whereby Christ purchased me and secondly, through the covenant by which I have given up myself and dedicated all that I am and all that I have to Him.

It is important, then, since the covenant is the only ladder which reaches from earth to Heaven–since it is the only way in which God has communion with us and by which we can deal with Him, that we should know how to discriminate between covenant and covenant. We should not be in any darkness or error with regard to what is the Covenant of Grace and what is not. It shall be our endeavor, this morning, to make as simple and as plain as possible, the matter of the covenant spoken of in our text and I shall thus speak–first upon the Covenant of Grace. Secondly, its everlasting character. And thirdly, the relationship which the blood bears to it. "The blood of the Everlasting Covenant."

First of all, then, I have to speak this morning of THE COVENANT mentioned in the text. And I observe that we can readily discover at first sight what the covenant is not. We see at once that this is not the Covenant of Works, for the simple reason that this is the Everlasting Covenant. Now the Covenant of Works was not everlasting in any sense whatever. It was not eternal. It was first made in the garden of Eden. It had a beginning, it has been broken. It will be violated continually and will soon be wound up and pass away–therefore, it is not everlasting in any sense. The Covenant of Works cannot bear an everlasting title. But as the one in my text is the Everlasting Covenant, therefore it is not a Covenant of Works. God made a covenant first of all with the human race, which ran in this wise–"If you, O man, will be obedient, you shall live and be happy, but if you will be disobedient, you shall perish. In the day that you disobey Me you shall die. That covenant was made with all of us in the person of our representative, the first Adam.

If Adam had kept that covenant, we believe we should everyone of us have been preserved. But inasmuch as he broke the covenant, you and I–all of us–fell down and were considered henceforth as the heirs of wrath, as inheritors of sin as prone to every evil and subject to every misery. That covenant has passed away with regard to God's people. It has been put away through the new and better covenant which has utterly and entirely eclipsed it by its gracious glory.

Again—I may remark that the covenant here meant is not the covenant of gratitude which is made between the loving child of God and his Savior. Such a covenant is very right and proper. I trust all of us who know the Savior have said in our very hearts—

"'Tis done! The great transaction's done;
I am my Lord's and He is mine."

We have given up everything to Him. But that covenant is not the one in the text, for the simple reason that the covenant in our text is an everlasting one. Now ours was only written out some few years ago. It would have been despised by us in the earlier parts of our life and cannot at the very utmost be so old as ourselves.

Having thus readily shown what this covenant is not, let us now observe what this covenant is. And here it will be necessary for me to subdivide this head again and to speak of it thus—to understand a covenant, you must know who are the contracting parties. Secondly, what are the stipulations of the contract. Thirdly, what are the objects of it. And then, if you would go still deeper, you must understand something of the motives which lead the contracting parties to form the covenant between themselves.

Now, in this Covenant of Grace, or the Everlasting Covenant, we must first of all observe the high contracting parties between whom it was made. The Covenant of Grace was made before the foundation of the world between God the Father and God the Son. Or to put it in a yet more Scriptural light, it was made mutually between the three Divine Persons of the adorable Trinity. This covenant was not made mutually between God and man. Man did not at that time exist. But Christ stood in the covenant as man's representative. In that sense we will allow that it was a covenant between God and man, but not a covenant between God and any man personally and individually.

It was a covenant between God with Christ and through Christ indirectly with all the blood-bought seed who were loved of Christ from before the foundation of the world. It is a noble and glorious thought, the very poetry of that old Calvinistic doctrine which we teach, that long before the day-star knew its place, before God had spoken existence out of nothing, before angel's wing had stirred the unnavigated ether, before a solitary song had distributed the solemnity of the silence in which God reigned supreme, He had entered into solemn council with Himself, with His Son and with His Spirit and had in that council decreed, determined, proposed and predestinated the salvation of His people.

He had, moreover, in the Everlasting Covenant, arranged the ways and means and fixed and settled everything which should work together for the effecting of the purpose and the decree. My soul flies back now, winged by imagination and by faith and looks into that mysterious council chamber and by faith I behold the Father pledging Himself to the Son and the Son pledging Himself to the Father, while the Spirit gives His pledge to both and thus that Divine compact, long to be hidden in darkness, is completed and settled–the Covenant which in these latter days has been read in the light of Heaven and has become the joy and hope and boast of all the saints.

And now, what were the stipulations of this Covenant? They were somewhat in the wise. God has foreseen that man after creation would break the Covenant of Works. That however mild and gentle the tenure upon which Adam had possession of Paradise, yet that tenure would be too severe for him and he would be sure to kick against it and ruin himself. God had also foreseen that His elect ones, whom He had chosen out of the rest of mankind would fall by the sin of Adam, since they, as well as the rest of mankind, were represented in Adam. The Everlasting Covenant, therefore, had for its end the restoration of the chosen people.

And now we may readily understands what were the stipulations. On the Father's part, thus runs the Covenant—I cannot tell you it in the glorious celestial tongue in which it was written—I am glad to bring it down to the speech which suits the ear of flesh and to the heart of the mortal. Thus, I say, runs the Covenant, in words like these—"I, the Most High Jehovah, do hereby give unto My only begotten and well-beloved Son, a people, countless beyond the number of stars, who shall be by Him washed from sin, by Him preserved and kept and led and by Him, at last, presented before My Throne, without spot, or wrinkle, or any such thing. I covenant by oath and swear by Myself, because I can swear by no greater, that these whom I now give to Christ shall be forever the objects of My eternal love.

"Them I will forgive through the merit of His blood. To these will I give a perfect righteousness. These will I adopt and make my sons and daughters and these shall reign with Me through Christ eternally." Thus runs that glorious side of the Everlasting Covenant. The Holy Spirit, also, as one of the high contracting parties on this side of the Covenant, gave His declaration, "I hereby covenant," said He, "that all whom the Father gives to the Son, I will in due time quicken. I will show them their need of redemption. I will cut off from them all groundless hope and destroy their refuges of lies. I will bring them to the blood of sprinkling. I will give them faith whereby this blood shall be applied to them. I will work in them every grace. I will keep their faith alive. I will cleanse them and drive out all depravity from them and they shall be presented at last spotless and faultless." This was the one side of the Everlasting Covenant, which is at this very day being fulfilled and scrupulously kept.

As for the other side of the covenant, that was the part of it, engaged and covenanted by Christ. He thus declared and covenanted with His Father—"My Father, on My part I covenant that in the fullness of time I will become man. I will take upon Myself the form and nature of the fallen race. I will live in their wretched world and for My people I will keep the Law perfectly. I will work out a spotless righteousness which shall be acceptable to the demands of Your just and holy Law. In due time I will bear the sins of all My people. You shall exact their debts on Me. The chastisement of their peace I will endure and by My stripes they shall be healed. My Father, I covenant and promise that I will be obedient unto death, even the death of the Cross. I will magnify Your Law and make it honorable. I will suffer all they ought to have suffered. I will endure the curse of Your Law and all the vials of Your wrath shall be emptied and spent upon My head. I will then rise again. I will ascend into Heaven. I will intercede for them at Your right hand. And I will make Myself responsible for every one of them, that not one of those whom You have given Me shall ever be lost, but I will bring all My sheep of whom, by My blood, You have constituted Me the Shepherd—I will bring every one safe to You at last."

Thus ran the Covenant of Grace. And now, I think, you have a clear idea of what it was and how it stands—the Covenant between God and Christ, between God the Father and God the Spirit and God the Son as the Covenant Head and representative of all God's elect. I have told you, as briefly as I could, what were the stipulations of it. You will please to remark, my dear Friends, that the Covenant is, on one side, perfectly fulfilled. God the Son has paid the debts of all the elect. He has, for us men and for our redemption, suffered the whole of Divine wrath. Nothing remains now on this side of the question except that He shall continue to intercede, that He may safely bring all His redeemed to glory.

On the side of the Father this part of the Covenant has been fulfilled to countless myriads. God the Father and God the Spirit have not been behind-hand in their Divine contract. And mark you, this side shall be as fully and as completely finished and carried out as the other. Christ can say of what He promised to do. "It is finished!" and the like shall be said by all the glorious covenanters. All for whom Christ died shall be pardoned, all justified, all adopted. The Spirit shall quicken them all, shall give them all faith, shall bring them all to Heaven and they shall, every one of them, without obstruction or hindrance, stand accepted in the Beloved, in the day when the people shall be numbered and Jesus shall be glorified.

And now having seen who were the high contracting parties and what were the terms of the covenant made between them, let us see what were the objects of this covenant. Was this covenant made for every man of the race of Adam? Assuredly not. We discover the secret by the visible. That which is in the covenant is to be seen in due time by the eye and to be heard with the ear. I see multitudes of men perishing, continuing wantonly in their wicked ways, rejecting the offer of Christ which is presented to them in the Gospel day after day, treading under foot the blood of the Son of Man, defying the Spirit who strives with them. I see these men going on from bad to worse and at last perishing in their sins. I have not the folly to believe that they have any part in the Everlasting Covenant. Those who die impenitent, the multitudes who reject the Savior, are clearly proved to have no part and no lot in the sacred Covenant of Divine Grace. For if they were interested in that, there would be certain marks and evidences which would show us this.

We should find that in due time in this life they would be brought to repentance, would be washed in the Savior's blood and would be saved. The covenant–to come at once straight to the matter, however offensive the doctrine may be–the covenant has relationship to the elect and none besides. Does this offend you? Be you offended ever more. What said Christ? "I pray for them: I pray not for the world, but for them which You have given Me: for they are Yours." If Christ prays for none but for the chosen, why should you be angry that you are also taught from the Word of God that in the Covenant there was provision made for the same persons–that they might receive eternal life? As many as shall believe, as many as shall trust in Christ, as many as shall persevere unto the end, as many as shall enter into the eternal rest, so many and no more are interested in the Covenant of Divine Grace.

Furthermore, we have to consider what were the motives of this Covenant. Why was the Covenant made at all? There was no compulsion or constraint on God. As yet there were no creatures. Even could the creature have an influence on the Creator, there was none existing in the period when the Covenant was made. We can look nowhere for God's motive in the Covenant except it is in Himself, for of

God it could be said literally in that day, "I AM, and there are none beside Me." Why then did He make the Everlasting Covenant? I answer, absolute Sovereignty dictated it. But why were certain men the objects of it and why not others? I answer, Sovereign Grace guided the pen. It was not the merit of man, it was nothing which God foresaw in us that made Him choose many and leave others to go on in their sins. It was nothing in them, it was sovereignty and grace combined that made the Divine choice. If you, my Brothers and Sisters, have a good hope that you are interested in the Covenant of Grace, you must sing that song–

"What was there in me to merit esteem,
Or give the Creator delight?
'Twas even so Father I ever sing,
For so it seemed good in Your sight."

"He will have mercy on whom He will have mercy," "for it is not of him that wills, nor of him that runs, but of God that shows mercy." His sovereignty elected and His Grace distinguished and immutability decreed. No motive dictated the election of the individuals, except a motive in Himself of love and of Divine Sovereignty. Doubtless the grand intention of God in making the Covenant at all was His own glory–any motive inferior to that would be beneath His dignity. God must find His motives in Himself–He has not to look to moths and worms for motives for His deeds. He is the "I AM."–

"He sits on no precarious throne,
Nor borrows leave to be."

He does as He wills in the armies of Heaven. Who can stay His hand and say unto Him, "What are You doing?" Shall the clay ask the potter for the motive for his making it into a vessel? Shall the thing formed before its creation dictate to its Creator? No, let God be God and let man shrink into his native nothingness and if God exalts him, let him not boast as though God found a reason for the deed in man. He finds His motives in Himself. He is self-contained and finds nothing beyond nor need anything from any but Himself. Thus have I, as fully as time

56

permits this morning, discussed the first point concerning the Everlasting Covenant. May the Holy Spirit lead us into this sublime Truth of God.

II. But now, in the second place, we come to notice ITS EVERLASTING CHARACTER. It is called the Everlasting Covenant. And here you observe at once its antiquity. The Everlasting Covenant is the oldest of all things. It is sometimes a subject of great joy to me to think that the Covenant of Grace is older than the Covenant of Works. The Covenant of Works had a beginning, but the Covenant of Grace had not. And blessed be God, the Covenant of Works has its end, but the Covenant of Grace shall stand fast when Heaven and earth shall pass away. The antiquity of the Covenant of Grace demands our grateful attention. It is a Truth of God which tends to elevate the mind. I know of no doctrine more grand than this. It is the very soul and essence of all poetry and in sitting down and meditating upon it, I do confess my spirit has sometimes been ravished with delight.

Can you conceive the idea that before all things God thought of you? That when as yet He had not made His mountains, He had thought of you, poor puny worm? Before the magnificent constellations began to shine and before the great center of the world had been fixed and all the mighty planets and many worlds had been made to revolve around it, then had God fixed the center of His covenant and ordained the number of those lesser stars which should revolve round that blessed center and derive light from there. Why, when one is taken up with some grand conceptions of the boundless universe, when with the astronomers we fly through space, when we find it without end and the starry hosts without number, does it not seem marvelous that God should give poor insignificant man the preference beyond even the whole universe besides?

Oh this cannot make us proud, because it is a Divine Truth, but it must make us feel happy. Oh Believer, you think yourself nothing, but God does not think so of you. Men despise you but God remembered you before He made anything. The Covenant of Love which He made with His Son on your behalf is older than the hoary ages. If you fly back when as yet time had not begun, before those massive rocks that bear the marks of gray old age upon them, had begun to be deposited—He had loved and chosen you and made a Covenant on your behalf. Remember well these ancient things of the

Then, again, it is the Everlasting Covenant from its sureness. Nothing is everlasting which is not secure. Man may erect his structures and think they may last forever, but the Tower of Babel has crumbled and the very Pyramids bear signs of ruin. Nothing which man has made is everlasting, because he cannot ensure it against decay. But as for the Covenant of Grace, well did David say of it, "It is ordered in all things and sure." It is—

"Signed and sealed and ratified,
In all things ordered well."

There is not an "if" or a "but" in the whole of it from beginning to end. Free will hates God's "shalls" and "wills," and likes man's "ifs" and "buts," but there are no "ifs" and "buts" in the Covenant of Grace. Thus the tenure runs—"I will" and "they shall." Jehovah swears it and the Son fulfills it. It is—it must be true. It must be sure, for "I AM" determines it.

"Has He said and shall He not do it? Or has He spoken and shall He not make it good?" It is a sure Covenant. I have sometimes said if any man were about to build a bridge or a house if he would leave me just one single stone or one timber to put where I liked, I would undertake that his house would fall down. Let me, if there is anyone about to construct a bridge, have just simply the placing of one stone—I will select which stone it shall be and I will defy him to build a bridge that shall stand. I should simply select the keystone and then he might erect whatever he pleased and it should soon fall.

Now, the Arminian's covenant is one that cannot stand because there are one or two bricks in it (and that is putting it in the slightest form—I might have said, "because every stone in it," and that would be nearer the mark) that are dependent on the will of man. It is left to the will of the creature whether he will be saved or not. If he wills not, there is no constraining influence that can master and overcome his will. There is no promise that any influence shall be strong enough to overcome him, according to the Arminian. So the question is left to man—and God, the mighty Builder, though He puts stone on stone massive as the universe— yet may be defeated by this creature. Away with such blasphemy!

The whole structure, from beginning to end, is in the hand of God. The very terms and conditions of that Covenant are become its seals and guarantees, seeing that Jesus has fulfilled them all. Its full accomplishment in every jot and title is sure and must be fulfilled by Christ Jesus, whether man will or man will not. It is not the creature's covenant, it is the Creator's. It is not man's covenant, it is the Almighty's Covenant and He will carry it out and perform it, the will of man notwithstanding. For this is the very glory of Grace—that man hates to be saved—that he is enmity to Him, yet God will have him redeemed—that God's consensus is, "You shall," and man's intention is "I will not," and God's "shall" conquers man's "I will not." Almighty Grace rides victoriously over the neck of free will and leads it captive in glorious captivity to the all-conquering power of irresistible grace and love. It is a sure Covenant and therefore deserves the title of Everlasting.

Furthermore, it is not only sure, but it is immutable. If it were not immutable, it could not be everlasting. That which changes passes away. We may be quite sure that anything that has the word "change" in it, will sooner or later die and be put away as a thing of nothing. But in the Everlasting Covenant, everything is immutable. Whatever God has established must come to pass and not word, or line, or letter, can be altered. Whatever the Spirit vows shall be done and whatever God the Son promised has been fulfilled and shall be consummated at the day of His appearing. Oh, if we could believe that the sacred lines could be erased—that the Covenant could be blotted and blurred, why then, my dear Friends, we might lie down in despair. I have heard it said by some preachers that when the Christian is holy, he is in the Covenant. That when he sins, he is crossed out again—that when he repents, he is put in again and if he fails he is scratched out once more.

And so he goes in and out of the door, as he would in and out of his own house. He goes in at one door and out of another. He is sometimes the child of God and sometimes the child of the devil—sometimes an heir of Heaven and now and then an heir of Hell. And I know one man who went so far as to say that although a man might have persevered through grace for sixty years, yet should he fall away the last year of his life—if he should sin and die so, he would perish everlastingly and all his faith and all the love which God had manifested to him in the day's gone by would go for nothing!

I am very happy to say that such a notion of God is just the very notion I have of the devil. I could not believe in such a god and could not bow down before him. A god that loves today and hates tomorrow. A god that gives a promise and yet foreknows, after all, that man shall not see the promise fulfilled. A god that forgives and punishes—that justifies and afterwards executes—is a god that I cannot endure. He is not the God of the Scriptures, I am certain. The God of Scripture is immutable, just, holy and true and having loved His own, He will love them to the end. And if He has given a promise to any man, the promise shall be kept and that man, once in grace, is in grace forever and shall without fall byand-by enter into glory.

And then to finish up this point. The Covenant is everlasting because it will never run itself out. It will be fulfilled but it will stand firm. When Christ has completed all and brought every Believer to Heaven. When the Father has seen all His people gathered in—the Covenant—it is true, will come to a consummation, but not to a conclusion, for thus the Covenant runs—the heirs of grace shall be blessed forever and as long as "forever" lasts, this Everlasting Covenant will demand the happiness, the security, the glorification, of every object of it.

III. Having thus noticed the everlasting character of the Covenant, I conclude by the sweetest and most precious portion of the doctrine—the relation which the blood bears to it—THE BLOOD OF THE EVERLASTING COVENANT. The blood of Christ stands in a fourfold relationship to the Covenant. With regard to Christ, His precious blood shed in Gethsemane, in Gabbatha, and Golgotha, is the fulfillment of the Covenant. By this blood sin is canceled. By Jesus' agonies justice is satisfied–by His death the Law is honored. And by that precious blood in all its mediatorial efficacy and in all its cleansing power, Christ fulfills all that He stipulated to do on the behalf of His people towards God.

Oh, Believer, look to the blood of Christ and remember that there is Christ's part of the Covenant carried out. And now, there remains nothing to be fulfilled but God's part, there is nothing for you to do–Jesus has done it all. There is nothing for free will to supply–Christ has done everything that God can demand. The blood is the fulfillment of the debtor's side of the Covenant and now God becomes bound by His own solemn oath to show grace and mercy to all whom Christ has redeemed by His blood. With regard to the blood in another respect, it is to God the Father the bond of the Covenant. When I see Christ dying on the Cross, I see the everlasting God from that time, if I may use the term, of Him who ever must be free, bound by His own oath and covenant to carry out every stipulation.

Does the Covenant say, "A new heart will I give you and a right spirit will I put within you"? It must be done, for Jesus died and Jesus' death is the seal of the Covenant. Does it say, "I will sprinkle pure water upon them and they shall be clean; from all their iniquities will I cleanse them"? Then it must be done, for Christ has fulfilled His part. And, therefore, now we can present the Covenant no more as a thing of doubt–but as our claim on God through Christ and coming humbly on our knees, pleading that Covenant, our heavenly Father will not deny the promises contained therein, but will make every one of them yes and amen to us through the blood of Jesus Christ.

Then, again, the blood of the Covenant has relation to us as the objects of the Covenant and that is its third light. It is not only a fulfillment as regards Christ and a bond as regards His Father, but it is an evidence as regards ourselves. And here, dear Brothers and Sisters, let me speak affectionately to you. Are you relying wholly upon the blood? Has His blood—the precious blood of Christ—been laid to your conscience? Have you seen your sins pardoned through His blood? Have you received forgiveness of sins through the blood of Jesus? Are you glorying in His sacrifice and is His Cross your only hope and refuge?

Then you are in the Everlasting Covenant. Some men want to know whether they are elect. We cannot tell them unless they will tell us this. Do you believe? Is your faith fixed on the precious blood? Then you are in the Covenant. And oh, poor Sinner, if you have nothing to recommend you. If you are standing back and saying, "I dare not come! I am afraid! I am not in the Covenant!" still, Christ bids you come. "Come unto Me," He says. "If you cannot come to the Covenant Father, come to the Covenant Surety. Come unto Me and I will give you rest." And when you have come to Him and His blood has been applied to you, doubt not—the red roll of election contains your name! Can you read your name in the bloody characters of a Savior's atonement? Then shall you read it one day in the golden letters of the Father's election. He that believes is elected!

The blood is the symbol, the token, the earnest, the surety, the seal of the Covenant of Grace to you. It must ever be the telescope through which you can look to see the things that are afar off. You cannot see election with the naked eye, but through the blood of Christ you can see it clear enough. Trust in the blood, poor Sinner and then the blood of the Everlasting Covenant is a proof that you are an heir of Heaven.

Lastly, the blood stands in a relationship to all three, and here I may add that the blood is the glory of all. To the Son it is the fulfillment, to the Father the bond, to the sinner the evidence and to all—to Father, Son and sinner—it is the common glory and the common boast. In this the Father is well pleased. In this the Son also, with joy, looks down and sees the purchase of His agonies. And in this must the sinner ever find his comfort and his everlasting song—"Jesus, Your blood and righteousness are my glory, my song, forever and ever!"

And now, my dear Hearers, I have one question to ask and I have done. Have you the hope that you are in the Covenant? Have you put your trust in the blood? Remember—though you imagine, perhaps, from what I have been saying, that the Gospel is restricted—the Gospel is freely preached to all. The decree is limited, but the good news is as wide as the world. The Gospel, the good news, is as wide as the universe. I tell it to every creature under Heaven, because I am told to do so. The secret of God, which is to deal with the application—that is restricted to God's chosen ones, but not the message—for that is to be proclaimed to all nations.

Now you have heard the Gospel many and many a time in your life. It runs thus—"This is a faithful saying and worthy of all acceptation, that Christ Jesus came into the world to save sinners." Do you believe that? And this is your hope—something like this—"I am a sinner. I trust Christ has died for me. I put my trust in the merit of His blood and sink or swim, I have no other hope but this—

"Nothing in my hand I bring,
Simply to Your Cross I cling."

You have heard it. Have you received it in your heart and laid hold on it? Then you are one of those in the Covenant! And why should election frighten you? If you have chosen Christ, depend upon it, He has chosen you. If your tearful eyes are looking to Him, then His omniscient eyes have long looked on you. If your heart loves Him, His heart loves you more than ever you can love, and if now you are saying, "My Father, You shall be the guide of my youth," I will tell you a secret—He has been your Guide and has brought you to be what you now are—a humble seeker—and He will be your guide and bring you safe at last.

But are you a proud, boastful, free willer, saying, "I will repent and believe whenever I choose. I have as good a right to be saved as anybody, for I do my duty as well as others and I shall doubtless get my reward"? If you are claiming an universal atonement which is to be received at the option of man's will, go and claim it and you will be disappointed in your claim. You will find God will not deal with you on that ground at all, but will say, "Get away from Me, I never knew you. He that comes not to Me through My Son comes not at all." I believe the man who is not willing to submit to the electing love and Sovereign Grace of God has great reason to question whether he is a Christian at all–for the spirit that kicks against that is the spirit of the devil and the spirit of the unhumbled, unrenewed heart.

May God take away the enmity out of your heart to His own precious Truth and reconcile you to Himself through THE BLOOD of His Son, which is the bond and seal of the Everlasting Covenant.

AM I CLEAR OF HIS BLOOD?

"The voice of your brother's blood cries out to Me from the ground."
Genesis 4:10

CAIN was of the Wicked One and slew his brother. "The way of Cain" is not hard to describe. He is too proud to offer atonement for his sin. He prefers his own way of sacrifice. He presents a bloodless oblation. He hates the obedience of faith. He smites the faithful Abel. Beware of the way of Cain, O proud self-righteous ones, lest you run therein, for the steps are few from self-righteous pride to hatred of true Believers and murder is not far thereafter. There is the seed of every infamy in the proud spirit of self-justification, and it is a great mercy that it does not more often show itself in all its terrific ripeness.

Look, bold boasters of your own merits, at the mangled body of the first martyr, for this is the full-blown development of your rebellious self-conceit. From all pride and vainglory, from all self-righteousness and hatred of the Cross of Christ, good Lord deliver us.

This is not, however, the drift of my discourse this morning. I have rather to indicate the method in which we also may be guilty of this sin of blood-guiltiness concerning our brother.

Dear Friends, I feel assured that the text of this morning, terrible as it must have been in the ears of Cain, ought to ring in your ears, and mine. And it may be that while that cry is heard again, though at the distance of many thousand years, it may awaken some here present to a sense of guilt, and to a desire for amendment. And thus the blood of Abel may speak good, though terrible things to them, and prepare their ears to listen to the voice of that other blood, "which speaks better things than that of Abel."

First, we shall this morning enquire for the criminals whose brother's blood cries from the ground. Next, we will endeavor to show the hateful character of the crime. Then, thirdly, we will select the judgment. And fourthly, we will exhort the guilty ones to turn from their ways and to hear the voice of mercy.

First, then, we are to MAKE A SEARCHING ENQUIRY FOR THE CRIMINALS.
I do not intend to say much, this morning, about the act of actually slaying one's brother. The question of the rightness of war is a moot point even among moral men. Among those who read their Bibles, the allowance of defensive war may, perhaps, still be a question. But any other sort of war must certainly be condemned by the man who is a disciple of the Lord Jesus Christ. We shall say nothing, however, or but very little, concerning the criminality of those ambitious and unscrupulous persons who hurry nations into war without cause.

Lust of dominion and a false pride are setting the United States on a blaze. I know at this time a tragic incident connected with the present war in America. Four brothers left one of our villages in Oxfordshire, two of whom, if now alive, are in one army and two of them in the other. And, I doubt not, as desperately as any of their comrades, they are thirsting for each other's blood. What horrors cluster around the iniquity of civil war. On yonder soil it is the blood of brothers that cries from the ground. Men are fighting, one against the other, in this lamentable conflict for no justifiable cause. The one cause which justified the war, as we thought—the snapping of the fetters of the slave—is gone. Emancipation is not proclaimed, the slave is forgotten.

What might have been a struggle for the rights of man is now a shameful and abominable slaughter of brothers by brothers. And a cry is going up to Heaven from those blood-red fields which God will hear, and will yet avenge on both sides. Oh that they would sheathe their swords and end it once and for all! What matters it if there are two nations or one? Better two in peace, than one divided with intestine strife! How much better to have even twenty nations of living men, than one nation of mangled corpses! What difference is it to the survivors if they have all the honor and dignity of conquerors, when they are stained up to their elbows in the blood of their fellow men?

Thus says the Lord, the God of Israel, "Consider your ways." Arise, you that draw your sword against your fellows and weep like the weeping of Ramah of old, and make your cities like Bochim, because of your iniquities! Go back to your homes in peace, beat your swords into plowshares, and your spears into pruning hooks, for Jehovah will have none of them. He casts out your armies like dung upon the field because every man of you smites his kinsman and his fellow!

That, however, is not my subject this morning. May God grant that whatever may come of this terrible struggle, His name may be glorified. At present I see nothing but a carnival of madmen–Hell let loose. And I fear that an evil demon has deceived both nations, and made them like ravening wolves and roaring lions.

I have to deal with you, however and not with those across the ocean. Let us come, therefore, to the point. There are many persons whose brother's blood cries to God from the ground. There is the seducer. He spoke with honeyed words and talked of love, but the poison of asps was under his tongue, for lust was in his heart. He came to a fair temple as a worshipper, but he committed infamous sacrilege and left that to be the haunt of demons which once was the palace of purity. Such men are received into society. They are looked upon as gentlemen, while the fallen woman, the harlot sister–she has to hide herself beneath the shadow of night.

None will make excuse for her sin. But the man, the criminal–he is called a respectable and reputable man–he may fill places of trust and posts of honor. And there are none who point the finger of scorn at him. Sir, the voice of that poor fallen sister's blood cries to Heaven against you! And in the day of judgment, her damnation shall be on your garments. All the infamy into which you have plunged her shall lie at your door. And among the dreadful sights of Hell, two eyes shall glare at you through the murky darkness like the eyes of serpents, burning their way into your inmost soul.

"You did deceive and decoy me to the pit," she says, "your arms dragged me down to Hell and here I lie to curse you forever and ever as the author of my eternal ruin." I know I address some such this morning. It were not possible that all men here were pure and spotless. Hear while yet there is time for your repentance, for the voice of her blood cries unto God from the ground for vengeance.

Then there are men who educate youth in sin. Satan's captains and marshals–strong men with corrupt hearts–who are never better pleased than when they see the buds of evil swelling and ripening into crime. We have known some such–men of an evil eye, who not only loved sin, themselves, but delighted in it in others. They pat the boy on his back when he utters his first oath. They reward him when he commits his first theft. Satan has his Sunday school teachers. Hell has its missionaries who compass sea and land to make one proselyte, and make him tenfold more a child of Hell than they are themselves. Most of our villages are cursed with one such wretch–and is there a street in London which is not the haunt of one such fiend, or more?

Oh, do I speak to any here who have applauded and praised young persons when they have commenced walking in the paths of infamy? Wretch! Have you sought to entangle them in your net? Have you, like the spider, thrown first one film about them, and then another, till you have them safely in your coils to drag them down to the den of Beelzebub? Then the voice of your brother's blood cries from the ground, and at the judgment will be a witness which you shall not be able to confute–the witness of the blood of souls ruined by your foul and evil training. Beware you who hunt for the precious life!

Yes, and I know some base men who, if they see young converts, will take a pride in putting stumbling blocks in their way. They no sooner discover that there is some little working of conscience, than they laugh, they sneer, they point the finger. How often have I seen this in the husband who seeks to prevent the wife's attendance at the House of God and in the young man who jeers at his companion because he felt something of the power of religion! Is not this too frequent in our great establishments in London–where one young man kneels to pray and many are found to laugh at him and hurl some foul term at his head? Not content to perish, themselves, like dogs pursuing a rabbit, so will the wicked haunt the godly.

Oh, you who are the enlisting sergeants for the Black Prince of Darkness, you who seem never as happy as when you set your traps for souls to lure them to destruction–solemnly do I warn you. Oh, take the warning, lest God's avenging angel, without earnest, should soon overtake you with the dividing sword which shall smite you even to the neck, and make you feel how terrible a thing it is to have tried to ruin the servants of the living God.

Then there is the infidel, the man who is not content to keep his sin in his own breast but must publish his infamy. He ascends the platform and blasphemes the Almighty to His face! He defies the Eternal. He takes Scripture to make it the subject of unhallowed jest. He makes religion a theme for comedy. Take heed, Sir, there will be a tragedy by-and-by, in which you shall be the chief sufferer! What shall I say of those men who are more diligent by far than half of God's ministers are? Whose names we see plastered on every wall? They go from town to town, especially where in greatest numbers artisans are dwelling, and never seem content unless they are preaching against everything that is pure and lovely and of good report.

They utter things which would make your cheeks blush if you heard them, and at the very reading of which, the marrow of your bones might melt–dreadful things against the Most High–such as David heard when he said, "Horror has taken hold of me because of the wicked that keep not Your Law." Oh, Sirs! Should I address such persons here, the voice of your brother's blood cries to Jehovah this day. The young men you have deluded, the working men you have led astray, the sinners whose lullaby you have sung, the souls that you have poisoned with your foul draughts, the multitudes–the multitudes that you have deceived–all these shall stand up at the last, an exceedingly great army, and pointing their fingers at you, shall demand your swift destruction because you decoyed them to their doom.

And what shall I say of the unfaithful preacher? The slumbering watchman of souls, the man who swore at God's altar that he was called of the Holy Spirit to preach the Word of God? The man upon whose lips men's ears waited with attention while he stood like a priest at God's altar to teach Israel God's Law? The man who performed his duties half-a-sleep, in a dull and careless manner until men slept, too, and thought religion but a dream? What shall I say of the minister of unholy life, whose corrupt practice out of the pulpit has made the most telling things in the pulpit to be of no avail, has blunted the edge of the sword of the Spirit and turned the back of God's army in the day of battle?

Yes, what shall I say of the man who has amused his audience with pretty things when he ought to have roused their consciences, who has been rounding periods when he ought to have announced the judgment of God? Who has been preaching a dead morality when he ought to have lifted Christ on high as Moses lifted the serpent in the wilderness? What shall I say, Brothers and Sisters, of those who have dwindled away their congregations, who have sown strife and schism in Churches of Christ once happy, peaceful and prosperous? What shall I say of the men who, out of the pulpit, have made a jest of the most solemn things, whose life has been so devoid of holy passion and devout enthusiasm that men have thought the Truth of God to be fiction, religion a stage play, prayer a nullity, the Spirit of God a phantom, and eternity a joke?

Among all who will need eternal compassion, surely the unfaithful, unholy, unearnest minister of Christ will be the most pitiable! What did I say? No, rather the most contemptible, the most despicable, the most accursed! Surely, every thunderbolt shall make his brow its target and every arrow of God shall seek his conscience as its mark.

If I must perish, let me suffer any way but as a minister who has desecrated the pulpit by a slumbering style of ministry, by a want of passion for souls. God knows how oftentimes this body trembles with horror at the thought the blood of souls should be required at my hands. And I cannot, and I hope I never may–I cannot understand that lifeless performance of duty, that cold and careless going through of services which, alas, is too common. How shall such men answer for it at the bar of God–the smooth things, the polite and honeyed words, the daubing of men with the untempered mortar of peace, peace, when they should have dealt with them honestly as in God's name?

Oh, Sirs, if we ever play the Boanerges, we shall hear God's thunder in our ears and that forever and ever and, cursed of men, and cursed of the Most High shall we be without end. In Tophet we shall have this wail peculiar to ourselves, "We preached what we did not feel. We testified of what we did not know. Men received not our witness, for we were hypocrites, and deceivers, and now we go down, richly deserving it, to the very lowest depths of perdition."

But, my Hearers, think not when I thus speak of the ministry, that I am about to permit you to escape. The voice of your brother's blood cries to God from the ground, even though you are no infidel lecturer, though you have never been debauched, though you have taught no heresy, though you have spread no schism. If your life is unholy, your brother's blood is on your garments. "Oh," says one, "if I sin, I sin to myself." Impossible! As well might the gasses say "I am deadly to myself alone." As well might the cholera say "my deadly breath is for myself only." Your example spreads. You, like the leper, leave uncleanliness on everything you touch. The very atmosphere which surrounds you breeds contagion.

What others see you do, they learn to do. Some may rival you and exceed you, but if you taught them their letters, and they learn to read in Hell's book better than you, all that they learn afterwards will come to your door, because the elements of sin they learned from your practice. I am afraid many people never look at their transgressions in this light. Why, you cannot help being leaders and teachers. If in your own house you are a drunkard, your boys will be drunkards, too! I have heard of a man who flogged his boy for swearing, swearing at him all the time he did it. We know instances of men who feel as if they would sooner bury their children than see them grow up such as they are themselves—but yet how can it be helped?

Your practice must, and will, influence your children. No, not your children only, but all with whom you come into connection in the mercantile world. Do not think, Sir, if you are a great employer, that your men can know what your life is without being affected by that knowledge? There may be some among them who have an inward principle which will not yield to temptation, but I know of hardly anything more dangerous than for a number of operatives to come constantly into contact with one whom they look up to as a master—who is also a master of the arts of sin and a doctor of damnation to their souls. Oh, take care, if not for yourselves, yet for others, or else, as sure as you live, the voice of your brother's blood will cry unto God from the ground.

To come yet closer home to this present audience. How much of the blood of man will die at the door of careless professors. You that make a profession of being Christians, and yet live in sin, you are the murderers of souls by the thousands. And you, too, who are moral enough in your conversation, and regular in your attendance on the outward forms of religion—you who never weep over sinners, you who never pray for them, you who never speak to them—you who leave all that to your minister, and think you have nothing to do with it—the voice of your brother's blood cries from the ground to Heaven.

There died a man in your court the other day. You spoke not to him about his soul—his blood cries to Heaven against you! You live in a villa in the country. There was a neighbor of yours—you were on speaking terms with him but you talked not to him about his soul—he is dead. He is gone—his blood cries to God against you! You have relations, relations to whom you could speak with familiarity. You have talked to them of business. You have befriended them, perhaps, in their needs, but you have never said a word to them about escaping from Hell and fleeing to Heaven. When you shall hear the mournful news that they have departed this life—will not their blood cry against you from the ground where they are buried?

You work, young man, in an establishment where you are somewhat respected, and, without intrusiveness you might often say a good word for your Master, but you do not. The blood of your fellows shall cry against you if they perish! Do not think the minister is the only man who is responsible for souls? God has made you all watchmen. All of you, in your spheres, are to be watchers for the souls of men. And, "If the watchman warns them not," says the Lord, "they shall perish but their blood will I require at the watchman's hands."

I know you do not think of this, and I am sorrowfully conscious that I do not feel it myself so much as I ought to do. Ah, the servants of Satan shame me! They shame me, they shame me! There comes at night a message to some of you who are the servants of Satan—"The master is come, and he calls for you." You leave your wife and your children without a tear. You go to your master's house and there are cups, foul cups, passing round, and you will drink, and drink, and drink, and drink on—never denying your master, confessing him with many an oath— saying to your comrades many things which injure your poor souls, and yet you do it so bravely, oh, so bravely!

You hardly know how you get home at night, but when the morning comes and you awake, there is the redness of the eyes, the headache, and the sickness. But the next night when your master wants you, you go again. And so you will do year after year, even though delirium tears you like a whirlwind. But here am I, a servant of God, and when my Master calls for me, and bids me go and confess Him, I am tempted to be still. And when He tells me to speak to yonder man, I would wickedly avoid the task. And whereas you confess your master and imprecate a curse upon your heads, how often do some of us confess our Master as timidly as if we feared a curse, when instead it is by confession that the curse is turned away!

Oh, it is enough to make us Christians ashamed to think how sinners will confess their god! Hear them at night as they reel home through the streets! They are not ashamed of their lord and master. Hear how they swear and defy Heaven! They are ashamed of nothing for their lord. And yet we, who have Heaven for our reward, and such a Christ to serve, and One so good and gracious to us–look at us–look at us! What poor lovers of our Savior are we! What poor lovers of the souls of men! I know this is not true of all of you, for there are some of you who love men's souls. I have delighted to see in many of you that deep earnestness which makes you yearn for the conversion of others. You will sometimes take your stand at the corner of the street, and though you cannot speak as you would, yet, the tears running down your cheeks prove your earnestness.

There are many women among you, too, who have spoken a good word for Christ in strange places, and have never been ashamed of Him. But oh, there are some of you, the members of this Church, over whom the angels of glory might weep, for what do you do for Christ? What do you give to Christ? You are content to go to Heaven, yourselves, but you let your neighbors perish for lack of knowledge, and neither the Mission will you help, nor anything else besides. The blood, the blood of dying London cries from the ground against you before God!

The perishing crowds of every street, and every court and every alley send up their wail to Heaven–"O, God! Your professing people have forgotten us." The daughter of Zion is become like the ostrich of the desert. The tongue of the sucking child cleaves to the roof of its mouth for want of moisture! O, God, will You not visit Your Church for this, and make these, Your people, that forget the souls of men, smart even to the quick?

I do not know whether I have seized hold of any of your consciences, but if I have, may God the Holy Spirit get such a grip of you that He may never let you rest till you say, "Great God, in Your name I will do something, that the next time I hear the bell toll I may be able to say, 'I did what I could for that man and if his soul has perished, his blood does not lie at my door, for I did tell him the way of salvation, I did exhort him to flee from the wrath to come.' " I am afraid none of us are altogether guiltless here. We must all take some degree of sin to our own consciences. I fear against everyone of us, to some extent, the voice of our brother's blood cries unto Heaven because of our sloth.

II. But to pass on. I was, in the second place, to HOLD UP THIS CRIME TO SCORN–the chief point being whose blood it is. It is the blood of our Brethren. "The voice of your brother's blood cries out to Me from the ground." All men are our Brethren. If any of them perish, and if we have not done our best for their conversion, their blood has a fearful and telling cry against us when it reaches to Heaven. But I shall rather dwell this morning upon certain special cases. Perhaps, young man, it is your natural brother's blood that cries against you. You have been converted to God, say, these three, four, ten, or twenty years. You have done nothing for your brother's conversion–never written him a letter begging him to think of his state. Never spoken a kind and gentle word to him about Christ.

No, you have been content to let him know you were a Christian, and were half afraid of that, but you have done nothing for him. Will not your brother, if he perishes, be well able to say, "My brother and I did hang at the same breast, and were rocked in the same cradle. We played together. We filled one home with glee–he professed to know the way of life but he never told me the way. He professed to have pardon for his sins, but he never told me how I might find it, too. He suffered me to go unpitied to my doom without a tear"? Will not the voice of such blood as that cry against us if we have been guilty?

It may be, however, it is the blood of your father or mother. Some of you young people have come to London and God has met with you in this House of Prayer. You still have ungodly parents in the country–have you quite forgotten them? What if your gray-headed sire should die! You know he never thinks of God. What if he should die before his son has talked to him! Oh, you have a strange power, you sons and daughters. If you will only pluck the old man by the sleeve and say, "Father, by the child's love I bear you, I would desire to see you saved!"

And do you fling this power away? Would you see your father and mother sold to slavery, and if it were in your power to redeem them, would you keep the sordid pelf? Or if you saw them sick, would you spare your feet and not run for a physician? Or if you saw them sinking in the stream, would you not leap in, at the peril of your own life, and rescue them? And will you let them perish, perish forever, without a struggle on your part? Will you see them go down to the depths without stretching out a helping hand? I cannot think thus of you, if God has truly touched your hearts!

But what shall I say to those who are not only careless of parents but are neglecting their own children? Mother, what if the voice of your child's blood should cry to God against you? You trained that child up without the fear of God. You sent your boy and girl to school on the Sunday, it is true, but that was only to get rid of them. What was your own example to them? Bad. What was the father's example? Vicious. When your boy grows up he becomes reckless. You cannot get him to come to a place of worship with you now. No, but if you had brought him when he was a child, it may be he would have been here now. And, inasmuch as you have tutored him for Satan, if that boy of yours goes down to the pit, his soul shall cry against you.

Up to Heaven shall it send its shriek–"Oh God! The mother that did bear me, and the man that did beget me were as cruel to me as if I were not their child, for they suffered me to come here without weeping for me, without praying for me, without taking me in their arms of loving supplication and pleading that I might be saved!"

Look at this again in the case of some of you against whom the indictment lies, that you have done injury to your servants. Oh, I know great cotton growers, builders and traders, that have many men in their employment and have much to answer for. Sirs, though it is your skill and your capital that brings in your wealth, have you no responsibility towards the men who day and night toil for you? You pay them their wages, but do you think your responsibility has ceased with that? Are they not the very bones and sinews of your establishment, and after taking everything into consideration, do you not owe far more to them than ever the best remuneration can pay?

And what if you have left their spiritual state uncared for? Have you said, "Oh, it is no business of mine what they do with their Sundays. I do not care what they do when they are out of the mill, or away from the workshop"? What? Sirs, do you think that as those hundreds of souls go before God they will lay no impeachment against you? Do you think they will not arraign you at God's bar? I tell you, and I think I speak in the Spirit of God when I say this, you shall find that the voices of your neglected workers, the voices of those whom you never sought to bless with spiritual instruction, shall cry against you from the ground!

Would that I had an audience, for the moment, consisting more largely of such persons! There are some here who can, I think, plead exemption, for they have done much to spread spiritual light among those who toil for them. But I do fear they are rather the exception than the rule, and that there are many who think no more of the men that work for them than of their horses–and some not as much. They take as much interest in the spirit of the beast that goes downwards as in the soul of man that goes upwards. Let it be so no more! Employers, contractors, you that have great influence, I do entreat you–shall I fall upon my knees to do it? I could not then do it more earnestly–see to it that your brothers' blood lie not on your garments throughout eternity!

Oh, there is one sinner who can look upon this in a solemn light! Who is it that has gone down to the pit? You, Man, yonder–who is it that died but a few days ago? The woman that loved you as she loved her own soul! The woman who idolized you–who thought you an angel. Shall I say it before God and to your face?–you ruined her! And what next, Sir? You cast her off as though she were but dirt, and threw her into the kennel with a broken heart. And being there, her god having cast her off–for you were her god–she fell into despair. And despair led to dreadful consequences and to direr ruin, still. She has gone, and you are glad of it–glad of it–for you will hear no more of her now, you say.

Sir, you shall hear of it. You shall hear of it. You shall hear of it! As long as you live her spirit shall haunt you, track you to the filthy joy which you have planned for a future day. And on your death bed she shall be there to twist her fingers in your hair, to tear your soul out of your body, and drag it down to the Hell appointed for such fiends as you—for you spilt her blood, the blood of her that trusted you—a fair, frail thing, worthy to be an angel's sister. And you pulled her down and made her a devil's tool! God save you! For if He does not, your damnation shall be seven-fold. Oh, you son of Belial, what shall be your doom when God deals with you as you deserve?

Are these hot words? Not half so hot as I would make them. I would send them hissing into your souls if I were able. Not so much to condemn you, as with the hope that though you cannot make good the mischief you have done, you may yet turn from the error of your ways to seek a Savior's blood and find pardon for this great iniquity! Oh, dear Friends, let us all take something of our text home. When we think of friends who are dead and gone, are there none over whose corpses we must say, "I did not do what I could for this man. I did not do what I could for this woman"?

I know when I go down to the village where I used to preach, and as I look upon the houses, I am apt to question myself—Was I as earnest with the people as I used to be? I can say I hope I never flinched from telling them all the Truth of God, though sometimes it had to be very rudely and roughly spoken. But yet God knows I do sometimes smite myself to think I did not weep over them more and did not entreat them more to be won to Christ.

And you, too, that sit in these pews so often—many of you are joyful converts to Christ—but numbers of you are still unsaved. What if any of you should be able to say at the last, "We trusted our minister. We hung upon his lips. We were never absent. We loved the Sunday, but oh, he did not tell us of our sin. He did not plead with us to be saved. He left us to ourselves—he was cold when his heart should have been hot. He was a man without tears and had a heart without sympathy for us!"

Oh, Sirs, God grant you may never be able to say that of me! God save you, for my soul longs for you. He is my witness how earnestly I long for you all to be in the heart of my Lord and Savior, Jesus Christ! Come unto Him! Come unto Him! I let not your blood cry out against me! Oh, believe in the Lord Jesus Christ and trust Him! Trust Him now, that you may be saved, and that at last I may be able to say, "Here am I and the children whom You have given me. You have kept them through Your power and they are preserved even to the end. Unto You be glory forever and ever!"

III. We are in the third place, and that only for a moment, TO EXPECT THE JUDGMENT. "The voice of your brother's blood cries out to Me from the ground." It does not cry to a deaf ear but to the ear of One who hears and feels the cry, and will certainly make bare His arm to smite the offender and to avenge the wrong. Seducer, Infidel, Tempter of the young, God hears the cry that goes up against you, and this is its burden—it comes from souls damned through your influence, and they say—"Lord give him his portion with the tormentors. Let him suffer, for we suffer. He slew us, avenge our death!" He will do it and the day shall come when swift destruction shall overtake you, and as with a rod of iron will He break you. As a potter's vessel so will He dash you in pieces, and who shall deliver you out of His hands?

The cry goes up to Heaven against barren, careless, cold-hearted professors, from many in London, untaught and untrained, who are on their beds today in the jaws of death. They cry out, I say, against you, careless Christians, and they say "Lord, take away their privileges from them! Lord, take them away from the Church which they disfigure and dishonor! Lord, take away these trees that bear no leaves for the healing of the nations! Sweep away this salt which has lost its savor! Lord, cast these candles that give no light into the fire! O Lord, take away, take away, once and for all, these cities that are not set on hills but are hidden from the sight of men."

What would you say if God should visit this Church, for instance, and take out of it all of you who are useless? How would the catalog be thinned! How would our lists show here and there the black mark of erasure! Unless you are doing something to win souls, the voice of your brother's blood cries to God from the ground—and it cries that your privileges may be taken away, and the candlestick moved out of its place. And it will be so, my Hearers, it will be so unless all of us arise to serve our Master. We are happy when God prospers us, but if we get many in our midst who do nothing for Christ, we shall have "Ichabod" written on these walls.

The walls that now ring with the song of the multitude shall hear only the wail of a desolate few. The pulpit that now thunders out God's own voice will become a dead, dreary, and voiceless platform. The time will come when your deacons and your elders shall be no more men of earnest hearts—and when you shall grope as the blind in the midnight and say—"Oh, that God would give us back once more such times as we used to have, which we frittered away through our carelessness, and lost through our lukewarmness."

Further, how awful must be the cry of this blood from the ground against a minister! I think I hear it, a cry from earth, from Heaven, from Hell—"Hurl him from his pulpit. Tear away his vestments! Snatch the book from his blood-stained hand! Smite upon the mouth the dog that will not bark. Let his corpse fall before men's eyes. Let him be made a hissing and a byword, because, being made a winner of souls, he dared to trifle, and being made a watchman of a besieged city, he dared to lie down and slumber. Tear him down! Tear him down! Tear him down," a hundred voices cry! Though he is a bishop or a great man in the Church. Though his eloquence is unrivalled. Though his power is matchless, pluck him down from his high places—miscreant that he is, to waste men's time—and ruin men's souls forever!"

And what shall the cry be against you who still continue by your ill-example to lead others into sin—open Sinners and Infidels? It would be an awful thing to pray for a man's damnation. But there are some people

I know of who while they live do so much mischief, that if they were dead, men would breathe more freely. I know a village where there lives a man who contaminates half the population. There is a sneer upon his face at which virtue blushes. There is a sneer at which even courage quails. He is a wretch so well taught, and so deeply instructed in the highest science of iniquity, that wherever he may go, he finds none a match for him—either in his reasoning or in the infamous conclusions which he draws. He is a deadly upas tree, dropping black poison upon all beneath his shadow.

I did think once I would half pray that the man might die and go to his doom, but one must not. And yet, were he gone, the saints might say, "It is well," and as over Babylon, when she is destroyed, and the smoke of her torment goes up forever, the saints will say "Hallelujah." So have I thought that over these against whom the blood of many young people cries to God from the ground, when they go, at last, to their doom, men might almost say, Hallelujah, for God has judged the great sinner who did make the people of the earth drunk with the wine of his fornication.

IV. I hope that these terrible things have prepared our minds to hear better THE VOICE OF EXHORTATION.

If there is the voice of blood crying against us today, and we affirm that none of us can altogether escape from it, what shall we do to be rid of the past? Can tears of repentance do it? No. Can promises of amendment make a blank page where there are so many blots and blurs? Ah, no! Nothing that we can do can put away our sin. But may not the future atone? May not future zeal wipe out past carelessness? May not the endeavor of our life that is yet to come make amends for the indolence or vice of the life that is past? No. The blood of our Brethren has been shed, and we cannot gather it up. The mischief we have done is not to be retrieved!

O God! Souls that are lost through us cannot be saved now. The gates of Hell are so shut that they can never be opened. We can make no restitution. The redemption of the soul is precious, and it ceases forever.

The sin is not to be washed away by repentance, nor retrieved by reformation. What then? Hopeless despair for you, and I, and everyone of us, were it not that there is another blood—the blood of One called Jesus—that cries from the ground, too, and the voice of that blood is, "Father, forgive them! Father, forgive them!" I hear a voice that says, "Vengeance, vengeance, vengeance," like the voice of Jonah in Nineveh, enough to make every man clothe himself in sackcloth.

But a sweeter, and a louder cry comes up—"Mercy, mercy, mercy." And the Father bows His head and says, "Whose blood is that?" And the voice replies, "It is the blood of Your only Begotten, shed on Calvary for sin. The Father lays His thunders by, sheathes His sword, stretches out His hands and cries to you, the sons of men, "Come unto Me and I will have mercy upon you. Turn, turn. I will pour out My Spirit upon you, and you shall live." "Repent and believe the Gospel." Hate the sin that is past, and trust in Jesus for the future. He is able to save to the uttermost all that come unto God by Him. For the blood of Jesus Christ, God's dear Son, cleans us from all sin.

Flee, Sinner, flee! The avenger of the blood that you have shed pursues you with hot haste, with feet that are winged—with a heart that is athirst for blood, he pursues you. Run, Man, run! The City of Refuge is before you. It is there, along the narrow way of faith. Fly, Man, fly, for unless you reach that city before he overtake you, he shall smite you and one blow shall be your everlasting ruin. For God's sake, do not loiter, Man! Those flowers on the left-hand side, care not for them. You will dye that field with your blood if you linger there!

That ale house on the right hand? Stay for none of these things. He comes! Listen! His footsteps on the hard highway! He comes, he comes, he comes now! Oh, that now you may pass the portals of the City of Refuge! Trust the Son of God, and sin is forgiven, and you have entered into everlasting life.

Good Lord, add Your blessing! We are powerless. We can say no more. For Christ's sake, "by His agony and bloody sweat, by His Cross and passion, by His precious death and burial," bless these souls. Amen.

THE PRECIOUS BLOOD OF CHRIST

"The precious blood of Christ."
1 Peter 1:19

IT is frequently my fear I should fall into the habit of preaching about the Gospel rather than directly preaching the Gospel. And then I labor to return to the first principle of our faith and often take a text upon which it would not be possible to say anything new, but which will compel me to recapitulate in your hearing those things which are vital, essential and fundamental to the life of our souls. With such a text as this before me, if I do not preach the Gospel I shall do violence both to the sacred Word and to my own conscience. Surely I may hope that while endeavoring to unfold my text and to proclaim the saving Word, the Holy Spirit will be present to take of the things of Christ and to show them unto us and make them saving to our souls.

Blood has from the beginning been regarded by God as a most precious thing. He has hedged about this fountain of vitality with the most solemn sanctions. The Lord thus commanded Noah and his descendants, "Flesh with the life thereof, which is the blood thereof, shall you not eat." Man had every moving thing that lives given him for meat, but they were by no means to eat the blood with the flesh. Things strangled were to be considered unfit for food, since God would not have man became too familiar with blood by eating or drinking it in any shape or form. Even the blood of bulls and goats thus had a sacredness put upon it by God's decrees.

As for the blood of man, you remember how God's threats ran, "And surely your blood of your lives will I require; at the hand of every beast will I require it and at the hand of man; at the hand of every man's brother will I require the life of man. Whoever sheds man's blood, by man shall his blood be shed: for in the image of God made He man." It is true that the first murderer had not his blood shed by man, but then the crime was new and the penalty had not then been settled and proclaimed. And therefore the case was clearly exceptional and one by itself. And, moreover, Cain's doom was probably far more terrible than if he had been slain upon the spot—he was permitted to fill up his measure of wickedness, to be a wanderer and a vagabond upon the face of the earth—and then to enter into the dreadful heritage of wrath, which his life of sin had doubtless greatly increased.

Under the theocratic dispensation, in which God was the King and governed Israel, murder was always punished in the most exemplary manner and there was never any toleration or excuse for it. Eye for eye, tooth for tooth, life for life was the stern inexorable law. It is expressly written, "You shall take no satisfaction for the life of a murderer which is guilty of death: but he shall surely be put to death." Even in cases where life was taken in chance medley or misadventure, the matter was not overlooked. The slayer fled at once to a City of Refuge, where, after having his case properly tried, he was allowed to reside. But there was no safety for him elsewhere until the death of the high priest.

The general law in all cases was, "So you shall not pollute the land wherein you are: for blood defiles the land: and the land cannot be cleansed of the blood that is shed there, but by the blood of him that shed it. Defile not, therefore, the land which you shall inhabit, wherein I dwell: for I, the Lord, dwell among the children of Israel." Strange is it that that very thing which defiles should turn out to be that which alone can cleanse! It is clear, then, that blood was ever precious in God's sight and He would have it so in ours.

He first forbids the blood of beasts as food of man, then avenges the blood of man shed in anger. And, furthermore, takes care that even accidents shall not pour it out unheeded. Nor is this all. We hear within us the echo of that law. We feel that God has truly made blood a sacred thing. Though some can, through use and habit, read the story of war with patience, if not with pleasure—though the sound of the trumpet and the drum and the tramp of soldiery will stir our heart and make us, for the moment, sympathize with the martial spirit—yet, if we could see war as it really is, if we could only walk but halfway across a battlefield or see but one wounded man, a cold shiver would shoot through the very marrow of our bones and we should have experimental proof that blood is, indeed, a sacred thing.

The other night, when I listened to one who professed to have come from battlefields of the American war, I felt a faintness and clammy sweat steal over me as he shocked and horrified us with the details of mutilated bodies and spoke of standing up to the tops of his boots in pools of human gore. The shudder which ran through us all was a sure confirmation of the sanctity with which God has forever guarded the symbol and nutriment of life. We cannot even contemplate the probability of the shedding of blood without fear and trembling.

And comforts which entail high risks in their production or procuring will lose all sweetness to men of humane dispositions. Who does not sympathize with David in his action with regard to the water procured by his three mighties! The three heroes broke through the hosts of the Philistines to bring David water from the well of Bethlehem. But as soon as he received that water, though very thirsty and much longing for it, yet he felt he could not touch it because these men had run such dreadful risks in breaking thrice through the Philistine hosts to bring it to him! He, therefore, took the water and poured it out before the Lord, as if it was not meet that men should run risk of life for any but God who gave life!

His words were very touching, "My God forbid it me, that I should do this thing! Shall I drink the blood of these men that have put their lives in jeopardy? For with the jeopardy or their lives they brought it." I wonder at the cruelty of the great crowds who delight to see men and women running such fearful risks of life in rope-dancing. How is it that they can feed their morbid curiosity on such dreadful food and greet the man who is foolish enough to run such hazards with acclamations because of his foolhardiness? How much more Christ-like the regret of David that he should have led any man to risk his life for his comfort! How much more laudable was his belief that nothing short of the highest benevolence to man, or the highest devotion to God can justify such jeopardy of life!

Further permit me to observe that the seal of the sanctity of blood is usually set upon the conscience even of the most depraved of men–not merely upon gentle souls and sanctified spirits–but even upon the most hardened. You will notice that men, bad as they are, shrink from the disgrace of taking blood money. Even those high priests who could sit down and gloat their eyes with the sufferings of the Savior would not receive the price of blood into the treasury. And even Judas, that son of perdition, who could contemplate without horror the treachery by which he betrayed his Master–yet when he had the thirty pieces of silver in his palm, found the money too hot to hold! He threw it down in the temple, for he could not bear or abide the sight of "the price of blood." This is another proof that even when virtue has become extinct and vice reigns, yet God has put the broad arrow of His own Sovereignty so manifestly upon the very thought of blood that even these worst of spirits are compelled to shrink from tampering with it.

Now, if in ordinary cases the shedding of life is thus precious, can you guess how fully God utters His heart's meaning when He says, "Precious in the sight of the Lord is the death of His saints"? If the death of a rebel is precious, what must be the death of a child? If He will not contemplate the shedding of the blood of His own enemies and of them that curse Him without proclaiming vengeance, what do you think He feels concerning His own elect, of whom He says, "Precious shall their blood be in His sight"? Will He not avenge them, though He bears long with them?

Shall the cup which the Harlot of Rome filled with the blood of the saints long remain unavenged? Shall not the martyrs from Piedmont and the Alps and from our Smithfield and from the hills of covenanting Scotland yet obtain from God the vengeance due for all that they suffered and all the blood which they poured forth in the defense of His cause? I have taken you up, you see, from the beast to man–from man to God's chosen men–the martyrs. I have another step to indicate to you–it is a far larger one–it is to the blood OF JESUS CHRIST.

Here powers of speech would fail to convey to you an idea of the preciousness! Behold here, a Person innocent–without taint within, or flaw without! A Person meritorious who magnified the Law and made it honorable–a Person who served both God and man even unto death. No, here you have a Divine Person–so Divine that in the Acts of the Apostles Paul calls His blood the "blood of God." Place innocence and merit and dignity and position and Godhead itself in the scale and then conceive what must be the inestimable value of the blood which Jesus Christ poured forth!

Angels must have seen that matchless blood-shedding with wonder and amazement, and even God Himself saw what never before was seen in creation or in Providence–He saw Himself more gloriously displayed than the whole universe beside. Let us come nearer to the text and try to show forth the preciousness of the blood of Christ. We shall confine ourselves to an enumeration of some of the many properties possessed by this precious blood.

I felt, as I was studying, that I should have so many divisions this morning that some of you would compare my sermon to the bones in Ezekiel's vision–they were very many and they were very dry–but I am in hopes that God's Holy Spirit may so descend upon the bones in my sermon–which would be but dry of themselves–that they being quickened and full of life you may admire the exceeding great army of God's thoughts of loving-kindness towards His people in the sacrifice of His own dear Son.

The precious blood of Christ is useful to God's people in a thousand ways–we intend to speak of twelve of them. After all, the real preciousness of a thing in the time of pinch and trial must depend upon its usefulness. A bag of pearls would be to us, this morning, far more precious than a bag of bread. But you have all heard the story of the man in the desert who stumbled, when near to death, upon a bag. He opened it, hoping that it might be the wallet of some passerby, and he found in it nothing but pearls! If they had been crusts of bread, how much more precious would they have been! I say, in the hour of necessity and peril, the use of a thing really constitutes the preciousness of it. This may not be according to political economy, but it is according to common sense.

The precious blood of Christ has a REDEEMING POWER. It redeems from the Law. We were all under the Law which says, "Do this and live." We were slaves to it–Christ has paid the ransom price and the Law is no longer our tyrant master. We are entirely free from it. The Law had a dreadful curse–it threatened that whoever should violate one of its precepts should die–"Christ has redeemed us from the curse of the Law, being made a curse for us."

By the fear of this curse the Law inflicted a continual dread on those who were under it. They knew they had disobeyed it and they were all their lifetime subject to bondage, fearful lest death and destruction should come upon them at any moment. But we are not under the Law, but under Grace, and consequently, "We have not received the spirit of bondage again to fear, but we have received the spirit of adoption whereby we cry, 'Abba, Father.' " We are not afraid of the Law now–its worst thunders cannot affect us for they are not hurled at us!

Its most tremendous lightning cannot touch us for we are sheltered beneath the Cross of Christ, where the thunder loses its terror and the lightning its fury. We read the Law of God with pleasure now! We look upon it as in the ark covered with the Mercy Seat and not thundering in tempests from Sinai's fiery brow. Happy is that man who knows his full redemption from the Law, its curse, its penalty, its present dread!

My Brethren, the life of a Jew, happy as it was compared with that of a heathen, was perfect drudgery compared to yours and mine! He was hedged in with a thousand commands and prohibitions. His forms and ceremonies were abundant and their details minutely arranged. He was always in danger of making himself unclean. If he sat upon a bed or upon a stool he might be defiled. If he drank out of an earthen pitcher, or even touched the wall of a house–a leprous man might have put his hand there before him and he would thus become defiled. A thousand sins of ignorance were like so many hidden pits in his way. He must be perpetually in fear lest he should be cut off from the people of God.

When he had done his best any one day, he knew he had not finished— no Jew could ever talk of a finished work. The bullock was offered, but he must bring another. The lamb was offered this morning, but another must be offered this evening, another tomorrow and another the next day. The Passover is celebrated with holy rites—it must be kept in the same manner next year. The high priest has gone within the veil once, but be must go there again. The thing is never finished—it is always beginning. He never comes any nearer to the end. "The Law could not make the comer thereunto perfect."

But see our position—we are redeemed from this! Our Law is fulfilled, for Christ is the end of the Law for righteousness! Our Passover is slain, for Jesus died! Our righteousness is finished, for we are complete in Him! Our victim is slain, our Priest has gone within the veil, the blood is sprinkled! We are clean and clean beyond any fear of defilement, "For He has perfected forever those that were set apart." Value this precious blood, my Beloved, because thus it has redeemed you from the thralldom and bondage which the Law imposed upon its votaries.

The value of the blood lies much in its ATONING EFFICACY. We are told in Leviticus, that, "it is the blood which makes an atonement for the soul." God never forgave sin apart from blood under the Law. This stood as a constant text—"Without shedding of blood there is no remission." Meal and honey, sweet spices and incense would not avail without shedding of blood. There was no remission promised to future diligence or deep repentance—without shedding of blood pardon never came. The blood, and the blood alone, put away sin and permitted a man to come to God's courts to worship—because it made him one with God.

The blood is the great at-one-ment. There is no hope of pardon for the sin of any man except through its punishment being fully endured. God must punish sin. It is not an arbitrary arrangement that sin shall be punished, but it is a part of the very constitution of moral government that sin must be punished. Never did God swerve from that and never will He. "He will by no means clear the guilty."

Christ, therefore, came and was punished in the place of all His people. Ten thousands times ten thousands are the souls for whom Jesus shed His blood. He, for the sins of all the elect, has made a complete Atonement. For every man born of Adam who has believed or shall believe on Him, or who is taken to Glory before being capable of believing, Christ has made a complete Atonement. And there is none other plan by which sinners can be made at one with God, except by Jesus' precious blood.

I may make sacrifices. I may mortify my body. I may be baptized. I may receive sacraments. I may pray until my knees grow hard with kneeling. I may read devout words until I know them by heart. I may celebrate masses. I may worship in one language or in fifty languages–but I can never be at one with God except by blood–and that blood, "the precious blood of Christ."

My dear Friends, many of you have felt the power of Christ's redeeming blood! You are not under the Law now, but under Grace–you have also felt the power of the atoning blood–you know that you are reconciled unto God by the death of His Son. You feel that He is no angry God to you, that He loves you with a love unchangeable. But this is not the case with you all. O that it were! I do pray that you may know, this very day, the atoning power of the blood of Jesus! Creature, would you not be at one with your Creator? Puny man, would you not have Almighty God to be your Friend? You can not be at one with God except through the at-one-ment. God has set forth Christ to be a Propitiation for our sins. Oh, take the Propitiation through faith in His blood and be at one with God!

Thirdly, the precious blood of Jesus Christ has A CLEANSING POWER. John tells us in his first Epistle, first chapter, seventh verse, "The blood of Jesus Christ His Son, cleanses us from all sin." Sin has a directly defiling effect upon the sinner, from which comes the need of cleansing. Suppose that God, the Holy One, were perfectly willing to be at one with an unholy sinner which is supposing a case that cannot be. Yet even should the pure eyes of the Most High wink at sin, still, as long as we are unclean we never could feel in our own hearts anything like joy and rest and peace.

Sin is a plague to the man who has it, as well as a hateful thing to the God who abhors it. I must be made clean. I must have my iniquities washed away or I never can be happy. The first mercy that is sung of in the one hundred and third Psalm is, "Who forgives all your iniquities." Now we know it is by the precious blood that sin is cleansed. Murder, adultery, theft–whatever the sin may be–there is power in the veins of Christ to take it away at once and forever! No matter how many, nor how deeply-seated our offenses may be, the blood cries, "Though your sins are as scarlet, they shall be as white as snow. Though they are red like crimson, they shall be as wool."

It is the song of Heaven–"We have washed our robes and made them white in the blood of the Lamb." This is the experience of earth, for none was ever cleansed except in this fountain opened for the house of David for sin and for uncleanness. You have heard this so often that perhaps if an angel told it to you, you would not take much interest in it–unless you have known experimentally the horror of uncleanness and the blessedness of being made clean. Beloved, it is a thought which ought to make our hearts leap within us, that through Jesus' blood there is not a spot left upon any Believer, not a wrinkle nor any such thing–

"Though in myself defiled I am,
And black as Kedar's tent, appear,
Yet when I put Your garment on,
Fair as the courts of Solomon."

You have no spiritual beauty, Beloved, apart from Christ. But, having Christ, He Himself says, "You are all fair, My Love, there is no spot in you." Oh, precious blood which makes the blackamoor white as snow and takes out the leopard's spots! Oh, precious blood removing the Hell-stains of abundant iniquity and permitting me to stand accepted in the

Beloved, notwithstanding all the many ways in which I have rebelled against my God!

A fourth property of the blood of Christ is ITS PRESERVING POWER. You will rightly comprehend this when went up from house to house as the first-born of all Egypt–from Pharaoh on the throne to the first-born of the woman behind the mill and the slave in the dungeon–all fell dead in a moment! The angel sped with noiseless wings through every street of Egypt's many cities.

But there were some houses which he could not enter–he sheathed his sword and breathed no malediction there. What was it which preserved the houses? The inhabitants were not better than others. Their habitations were not more elegantly built–there was nothing except the bloodstain on the lintel and on the two side posts–and it is written, "When I see the blood I will pass over you." There was nothing whatever which gained the Passover for Israel but the sprinkling of blood!

The father of the house had taken a lamb and killed it–had caught the blood in a basin. And while the lamb was roasted that it might be eaten by every inhabitant of the house, he took a bunch of hyssop, stirred the basin of blood and went outside with his children and began to strike the posts and to strike the door. And as soon as this was done they were all safe, all safe–no angel could touch them–the fiends of Hell themselves could not venture there.

Beloved, see, we are preserved in Christ Jesus! Did not God see the blood before you and I saw it and was not that the reason why He spared our forfeited lives when, like barren fig trees, we brought forth no fruit for Him? When we saw the blood, let us remember it was not our seeing it which really saved us–one sight of it gave us peace, but it was God's seeing it that saved us. "When I see the blood I will pass over you."

And today, if my eye of faith is dim and I see the precious blood so as to rejoice that I am washed but I can scarcely see it, yet God can see the blood and as long as the undimmed eyes of Jehovah look upon the atoning Sacrifice of the Lord Jesus, He cannot smite one soul that is covered with its scarlet mantle. Oh, how precious is this blood-red shield! My Soul, cower yourself down under it when the darts of Hell are flying! This is the chariot, the covering of purple–let the storm come and the deluge rise, let even the fiery hail descend beneath that crimson pavilion–my soul must rest secure, for what can touch me when I am covered with His precious blood?

The preserving power of that blood should make us feel how precious it is. Beloved, let me beg you to try and realize these points. You know I told you before I cannot say anything new upon the subject, neither can I embody these old thoughts in new words. I should only spoil them and be making a fool of myself by trying to make a display of myself and my own powers, instead of the precious blood. Let me ask you to get here, right under the shelter of the Cross. Sit down, now, beneath the shadow of the Cross and feel, "I am safe, I am safe, O you devils of Hell, or you angels of God–I could challenge you all and say, 'Who shall separate me from the love of God in Christ Jesus, or who shall lay anything to my charge, seeing that Christ has died for me?' "

When Heaven is on a blaze. When earth begins to shake. When the mountains rock. When God divides the righteous from the wicked, happy will they be who can find a shelter beneath the blood! But where will you be who have never trusted in its cleansing power? You will call to the rocks to hide you and to the mountains to cover you, but all in vain. God help you now, or even the blood will not help you then!

Fifthly, the blood of Christ is precious because of its PLEADING PREVALENCE. Paul says in the twelfth chapter of his Epistle to the Hebrews, at the twenty-fourth verse, "It speaks better things than that of Abel." Abel's blood pleaded and prevailed. Its cry was, "Vengeance!" and Cain was punished. Jesus' blood pleads and prevails. Its cry is "Father, forgive them!" and sinners are forgiven through it.

When I cannot pray as I would, how sweet to remember that the blood prays! There is no voice in my tongue, but there is always a voice in the blood. If I cannot, when I bow before my God, get farther than to say, "God be merciful to me, a sinner," yet my Advocate before the Throne is not dumb because I am and His plea has not lost its power because my faith in it may happen to be diminished. The blood is always alike prevalent with God. The wounds of Jesus are so many mouths to plead with God for sinners–what if I say they are so many chains with which love is lead captive and sovereign mercy bound to bless every favored child?

What if I say that the wounds of Jesus have become doors of Divine Grace through which Divine love comes forth to the vilest of the vile and doors through which our wants go up to God and plead with Him that He would be pleased to supply them? Next time you cannot pray. Next time you are crying and striving and groaning up in that upper room, praise the value of the precious blood which makes intercession before the eternal Throne of God!

Sixthly, the blood is precious where perhaps we little expect it to operate. It is precious, because of its MELTING INFLUENCE on the human heart. "They shall look upon Me whom they have pierced and they shall mourn for Him, as one that mourns for his only son and shall be in bitterness for Him, as one that is in bitterness for his first-born."

There is a great complaint among sinners, when they are a little awakened, that they feel their hearts so hard. The blood is a mighty melter. Alchemists of old sought after a universal solvent–the blood of Jesus is that. There is no nature so stubborn that a sight of the love of God in Christ Jesus cannot melt it, if Grace shall open the blind eye to see Christ. The stone in the human heart shall melt away when it is plunged into a bath of Divine blood. Cannot you say, dear Friends, that Toplady was right in his hymn–

"Law and terrors do but harden
All the while they work alone.

95

But a sense of blood-bought pardon,
Soon dissolves a heart of stone"?

Sinner, if God shall lead you to believe this morning in Christ to save you–if, then, you will trust your soul in His hands to have it saved–that hard heart of yours will melt at once! You would think differently of sin, my Friends, if you knew that Christ smarted for it. Oh, if you knew that out of those dear listless eyes there looked the loving heart of Jesus upon you, I know you would say, "I hate the sin that made Him mourn and fastened Him to the accursed tree." I do not think that preaching the Law generally softens men's hearts.

Hitting men with a hard hammer may often drive the particles of a hard heart more closely together and make the iron yet more hard. But oh, to preach Christ's love–His great love with which He loved us even when we were dead in sins and to tell to sinners that there is life in a look at the Crucified One–surely this will prove that Christ was exalted on high to give repentance and remission of sins! Come for repentance, if you cannot come repenting! Come for a broken heart, if you cannot come with a broken heart! Come to be melted, if you are not melted. Come to be wounded, if you are not wounded.

But then comes in a seventh property of the precious blood. The same blood that melts has A GRACIOUS POWER TO PACIFY. John Bunyan speaks of the Law as coming to sweep a chamber like a maid with a broom. And when she began to sweep there was a great dust which almost choked people and got into their eyes. But then came the Gospel with its drops of water and laid the dust and then the broom might be used far better.

Now it sometimes happens that the Law of God makes such a dust in the sinner's soul that nothing but the precious blood of Jesus Christ can make that dust lie still. The sinner is so disquieted that nothing can ever give him any relief except to know that Jesus died for him. When I felt the burden of my sin, I do confess all the preaching I ever heard never gave me one single atom of comfort. I was told to do this and to do that and when I had done it all, I had not advanced one inch farther.

I thought I must feel something, or pray a certain quantity. And when I had done that, the burden was quite as heavy. But the moment I saw that there was nothing whatever for me to do, that Jesus did it long, long ago–that all my sins were put on His back and that He suffered all I ought to have suffered–why then my heart had peace with God. Real peace by believing peace through the precious blood!

Two soldiers were on duty in the citadel of Gibraltar. One of them had obtained peace through the precious blood of Christ, the other was in very great distress of mind. It happened to be their turn to stand sentinel, both of them, the same night. And there are many long passages in the rock, which passages are adapted to convey sounds a very great distance. The soldier in distress of mind was ready to beat his breast for grief–he felt he had rebelled against God and could not find how he could be reconciled–when suddenly there came through the air what seemed to him to be a mysterious voice from Heaven saying these words, "The precious blood of Christ."

In a moment he saw it all–it was that which reconciled us to God–and he rejoiced with joy unspeakable and full of glory! Now did those words come directly from God? No. They did as far as the effect was concerned–they did come from the Holy Spirit. Who was it that had spoken those words? Curiously enough, the other sentinel at the far end of the passage was standing still and meditating when an officer came by and it was his duty, of course, to give the word for the night and with soldier-like promptness he did give it–but not accurately, for instead of giving the proper word, he was so taken up by his meditations that he said to the officer, "The precious blood of Christ."

He corrected himself in a moment. But he had said it and it had passed along the passage and reached the ear for which God meant it–and the man found peace and spent his life in the fear of God, being in after years the means of completing one of our excellent translations of the

Word of God into the Hindu language. Who can tell, dear Friends, how much peace you may give by only telling the story of our Savior! If I only had about a dozen words to speak and knew I must die, I would say, "This is a faithful saying and worthy of all acceptation, that Christ Jesus came into the world to save sinners." The doctrine of Substitution is the pith and marrow of the Gospel, and if you can hold that forth, you will prove the value of the precious blood by its peace-giving power.

We can only spare a minute now upon ITS SANCTIFYING INFLUENCE. The Apostle tells us in the ninth chapter and the fourteenth verse that Christ sanctified the people by His own blood. Certain it is that the same blood which justifies by taking away sin does, in its after-action, act upon the new nature and lead it onward to subdue sin and to follow out the commands of God. There is no motive for holiness so great as that which streams from the veins of Jesus. If you want to know why you should be obedient to God's will, my Brethren, go and look upon Him who sweat, as it were, great drops of blood and the love of Christ will constrain you, because you will thus judge, "That if one died for all, then were all dead: and that He died for all that we which live might not henceforth live unto ourselves, but unto Him that died for us and rose again."

In the ninth place, another blessed property of the blood of Jesus is ITS POWER TO GIVE ENTRANCE. We are told that the high priest never went within the veil without blood. And surely we can never get into God's heart, nor into the secret of the Lord which is with them that fear Him, nor into any familiar communion with our great Father and Friend, except by the sprinkling of the precious blood of Jesus.

"We have access with boldness into this grace wherein we stand," but we never dare go a step towards God except as we are sprinkled with this precious blood. I am persuaded some of us do not come near to God because we forget the blood. If you try to have fellowship with God in your graces, your experiences, your believing—you will fail. But if you try to come near to God as you stand in Christ Jesus—you will have courage to come. And on the other hand, God will run to meet you when

He sees you in the face of His Anointed. Oh, for power to get near to God! But there is no getting near to God except as we got near to the Cross. Praise the blood, then, for its power of giving you nearness to God.

Tenthly—a hint only. The blood is very precious, in the tenth place, for ITS CONFIRMING POWER. No covenant, we are told, was ever valid unless victims were slain and blood sprinkled. And it is the blood of Jesus which has ratified the New Covenant and made its promises sure to all the seed. Therefore it is called "the blood of the Everlasting Covenant." The Apostle changes the figure and he says that a testament is not of force except the testator is dead. The blood is a proof that the Testator died and now the Law holds good to every inheritor because Jesus Christ has signed it with His own gore.

Beloved, let us rejoice that the promises are yes, and amen, for no other reason than this—because Christ Jesus died and rose again. Had there been no bowing of the head upon the tree, no slumbering in the sepulcher, no rising from the tomb, then the promises had been uncertain, fickle things—not "immutable things wherein it is impossible for God to lie"—and consequently they could never have afforded strong consolation to those who have fled for refuge to Christ Jesus. See, then, the confirming nature of the blood of Jesus and count it very precious.

I am almost done. But there remains another. It is the eleventh one, and that is THE INVIGORATING POWER of the precious blood. If you want to know that, you must see it set forth as we often do when we cover the table with the white cloth and put the bread and wine on it. What do we mean by this ordinance? We mean by it that Christ suffered for us and that we, being already washed in His precious blood and so made clean, do come to the table to drink wine as an emblem of the way in which we live and feed upon His body and upon His blood.

He tells us, "Except a man shall eat My flesh and drink My blood, there is no life in him." We do therefore, after a spiritual sort, drink His blood and He says, "My blood is drink, indeed." Superior drink! Transcendent drink! Strengthening drink—such drink as angels never taste though they drink before the eternal Throne. Oh Beloved, whenever your spirit faints, this wine shall comfort you! When your griefs are many, drink and forget your misery and remember your sufferings no more! When you are very weak and faint, take not a little of this for your soul's sake, but drink a full draught of the wineon the lees, well refined, which was set abroad by the soldier's spike and flowed from Christ's own heart! "Drink to the full. Yes, drink abundantly O Beloved," says Christ to the spouse. And do not linger when He invites. You see the blood has power without to cleanse and then it has power within to strengthen. O precious Blood, how many are Your uses! May I prove them all!

Lastly and twelfth—twelve is the number of perfection. We have brought out a perfect number of its uses—the blood has AN OVERCOMING POWER. It is written in the Revelation, "They overcame through the blood of the Lamb." How could they do otherwise? He that fights with the precious blood of Jesus fights with a weapon that will cut through soul and spirit, joints and marrow—a weapon that makes Hell tremble and makes Heaven subservient and earth obedient to the will of the men who can wield it!

The blood of Jesus! Sin dies at its presence, death ceases to be death—Hell itself would be dried up if that blood could operate there. The blood of Jesus! Heaven's gates are opened! Bars of iron are pushed back. The blood of Jesus! My doubts and fears flee, my troubles and disasters disappear! The blood of Jesus! Shall I not go on conquering and to conquer so long as I can plead that? In Heaven this shall be the choice jewel which shall glitter upon the head of Jesus—that He gives to His people "Victory, victory, through the blood of the Lamb."

And now, is this blood to be had? Can it be got at? Yes, it is FREE, as well as full of virtue—free to every soul that believes. Whoever cares to come and trust in Jesus shall find the virtue of this blood in his case this very morning. Away from your own works! Turn those eyes of yours to the full Atonement made, to the utmost ransom paid! And if God enables you, poor Soul, this morning to say, "I take that precious blood to be my only hope," you are saved and you may sing with the rest of us—

"Now, freed from sin, I walk at large;
The Savior's blood's my full discharge.
At His dear feet my soul I'll lay,
A sinner saved and homage pay."

God grant it may be so, for His name's sake. Amen.

WALKING IN THE LIGHT AND WASHED IN THE BLOOD

"But if we walk in the light, as He is in the light, we have fellowship one with another and the blood of Jesus Christ, His Son, cleanses us from all sin."
1 John 1:7

The light is the evident emblem of the Truth of God. Darkness is the symbol of error. Light represents holiness. Darkness is the appropriate figure for sin. Light represents knowledge, especially of spiritual things, since light reveals. Darkness is the fit token of the ignorance under which the natural mind labors perpetually. By nature we are all born under the dominion of darkness—we grope our way like blind men and when we knew God by the light of His works, we glorified Him not as God, neither were thankful, but became vain in our imaginations and our foolish heart was darkened.

Naturally, spiritual things are not discernible by man—they are spiritual and spiritually discerned and the carnal mind cannot perceive them—for it walks in darkness. The guilt of sin is a thing too high for the carnal mind to understand. The glory of the eternal sacrifice it cannot perceive. The excellence of God, the faithfulness of His promise and the validity of His Covenant—all such things as these are swathed in mist—the carnal mind sees them not. As soon as ever the Grace of God comes into the heart, it makes as great a difference as did the eternal fiat of Jehovah, when He said, "Let there be light," and there was light.

As soon as God the Holy Spirit begins to work upon the soul of man to illuminate him, he perceives at once his own sinfulness. He abhors that sinfulness, he labors to escape from it, he cries out for a remedy—he finds it in Christ—therefore he no longer loves sin, he is not guided any longer by the darkness of policy and selfishness and error, but he walks after the light of the Truth of God, of righteousness, of holiness, of true knowledge. God has brought him into light—he sees now what he never saw before! He knows, feels, believes, recognizes what he never had known anything of before—he is in the light.

Therefore you constantly find the Christian called a child of light and he is warned that he is of the light and of the day. He is told, "You are not of the night nor of darkness." "You were sometime darkness, but now are you light in the Lord: walk as children of light." You perceive in the text, then, that the Christian is spoken of as a man who is in the light. But there is something more said of him than this. He is practically in the light, "if we walk in the light." It is of no use to pretend to have light in the brain—so as to comprehend all knowledge, so as to be sound and orthodox in one's doctrinal opinions—this will be of no vital service so far as the great point of salvation is concerned.

A man may think he has much light, but if it is only notional and doctrinal and is not the light which enlightens his nature and develops itself in his practical walk, he lies when he talks of being in the light, for he is in darkness altogether. Nor is it truthful to pretend or profess that we have light within in the form of experience if we do not walk in it, for where the light is true, it is quite certain to show itself abroad.

If there is a candle within the lantern, its light will stream forth into the surrounding darkness and those who have eyes will be able to see it. I have no right to say I have light unless I walk in it. The Apostle is very peremptory with those who so speak. He says, "He that says I know Him and keeps not His Commandments is a liar and the truth is not in him." The Christian, then, is in the light and he is practically in it—his walk and conversation are regulated by the Truth of God, by holiness—and by that Divine knowledge which God has been pleased to bestow upon him. He walks in the light of faith, in another path than that which is trod by men who have nothing but the light of sense. He sees Him who is invisible and the sight of the invisible God operates upon his soul.

He looks into eternity, he marks the dread reward of sin and the blessed gift of God to those who trust in Jesus and eternal realities have an effect upon his whole manner and conversation—from now on he is a man in the light, walking in that light. There is a very strong description given here—"If we walk in the light as He is in the light." Beloved, the thought of that dazzles me! I have tried to look it in the face, but I cannot endure it. If we walk in the light as God is in the light! Can we ever attain to this? Shall poor flesh and blood ever be able to walk as clearly in the light as He is whom we call "Our Father," of whom it is written, "God is light and in Him is no darkness at all"?

Let us say this much and then commend this wonderful expression to your meditations. Certainly this is the model which is set before us, for the Savior Himself said, "Be you perfect, even as your Father who is in Heaven is perfect." And if we take anything short of absolute perfection as our model of life we shall certainly, even if we should attain to our ideal, fall short of the Glory of God! Beloved, when a schoolmaster writes the copy at the head of the page, he does not expect that the boy will come up to the copy—but then, if the copy is not a perfect one, it is not fit to be imitated by a child.

And so our God gives us Himself as the pattern and copy, "Be you imitators of God as dear children," for nothing short of Himself would be a worthy model. Though we, as life sculptors, may feel that we can never rival the perfection of God, yet we are to seek after it and never to be satisfied until we attain it. The youthful artist, as he grasps his early pencil, can hardly hope to equal Raphael or Michelangelo! But still, if he did not have a noble ideal before his mind, he would only attain to something very mean and ordinary. Heavenly fingers point us to the Lord Jesus as the great Exemplar of His people and the Holy Spirit works in us a likeness to Him.

But what does it mean that the Christian is to walk in light as God is in the light? We conceive it to import likeness, but not degree. We are as truly in the light. We are as heartily in the light. We are as sincerely in the light, as honestly in the light, though we cannot be there in the same degree. I cannot dwell in the sun—it is too bright a place for my residence—unless I shall be transformed, like Uriel, Milton's angel who could dwell in the midst of the blaze of its excessive glory. But I can walk in the light of the sun though I cannot dwell in it. And so God is the Light, He is Himself the Sun and I can walk in the light as He is in the light, though I cannot attain to the same degree of perfection and excellence and purity and truth in which the Lord, Himself, resides.

Trapp is always giving us the Truth of God in a way in which we can remember it–so he says we are to be in the light as God is in the light for quality, but not for equality. We are to have the same light and as truly to have it and walk in it as God does, though as for equality with God in His holiness and perfection–that must be left until we cross the Jordan and enter into the perfection of the Most High.

Having thus briefly sketched the character of the genuine Christian, observe, Beloved, that he is the possessor of two privileges. The first is fellowship with God. "We have fellowship one with another." And the second is complete cleansing from sin–"and the blood of Jesus Christ, His Son, cleanses us from all sin." The first privilege we will have but a word upon–it is fellowship with God. As you read this verse in our translation, it looks very much as if all that was meant was fellowship with your brother Christians. But this, according to able critics, would not convey the sense of the original.

The Arabic version renders it, "God with us and we with Him," and several copies read, "we have fellowship with Him." Our version almost compels you to think of fellowship with other Believers, but such is not the intention of the Spirit. "We have mutual fellowship–between God and our souls there is communion." This is the sense of the passage. God is Light–we walk in light–we agree. "Can two walk together unless they are agreed?" It is clear we are agreed as to the principles which we shall advance–God is the champion of Truth, so are we. God is the promoter of holiness, so are we. God seeks that love may reign instead of selfishness, so does the Christian. God hates error and spares no arrows to destroy it. The Christian also contends earnestly for the faith once delivered to the saints.

God is pure, and the pure in heart shall see God. God is holiness and those who are holy are attracted to God from an affinity of nature, even as the needle is attracted to its pole. If the Lord has visited you and made you to walk in light, you shall surely have fellowship with God your Father. He that is in darkness cannot have fellowship with God. Veiled in ignorance, guided by passion, controlled by error, led astray by falsehood—how can you aspire to talk with your God? Your prayer is but a chattering sound! Your song is the clang of a sounding brass, the noise of a tinkling cymbal! Your devotion bears you no further than the letter which kills!

But oh, poor Soul, if God should take you out of your darkness and make you to see yourself, to see Him and follow after Truth and righteousness and holiness, why then your prayer would be heard in Heaven, your song would mingle with the sweet notes of celestial harps and even your groans and tears would reach your Father's heart, for you would enjoy fellowship with Him! If we walk with God as God is in the light, the secret of God is with us and our secret is with God. He opens His heart to us and we open our heart to Him—we become friends! We are bound and knit together so that being made partakers of the Divine Nature, having escaped the corruption which is in the world through lust, we live like Enoch, having our conversation above the skies.

Upon the second privilege we intend to dwell. I have been driven to this text and yet I have been afraid of it. This text has been handled, the latter part of it, I mean, very often out of its context. Yet it has had such a comforting influence on many souls that I have been half afraid to discourse upon it in its true context. And yet I have felt, "Well, if anything I should say should take away any comfort from any seeking soul, I shall be very sorry, but I cannot help it." I do feel that it is essential to the Christian ministry not to pick passages out of God's Word and rend them away from the context, but to take them as they stand.

As this text stands, it does not seem to me to gleam with the particular ray of comfort which others see in it, but it has another beam of joy even more radiant! God's Word must be taken as God speaks it—we have no right to divide the living child of Divine Truth, or wrest it to make it mean other than it does. According to the text, special pardon of sin is the peculiar privilege of those who walk in the light as God is in the light and it is not the privilege of anyone else. Only those who have been brought by Divine Grace from a state of nature into a state of Grace and walk in the light may claim the possession of perfect cleansing through the blood of Jesus Christ.

In dwelling upon this latter part of the verse, there seemed to me to be seven things in it which any thoughtful reader would be struck with. Considered as the privilege of every man who, however limpingly, is walking in the light, this word, which tells of pardon bought with blood, is very precious—a crown set with jewels! To seven choice pearls I invite your loving gaze.

The first thing that struck me was THE GREATNESS of everything in the text. In some places everything is little. You talk with some men—their thoughts, their ideas are all little. Almost everything is drawn to a scale and aspiring minds generally draw their matters to as great a scale as they can find, but that is necessarily a little one. See to what a magnificent scale everything is drawn in our text! Think, Beloved, how great the sin of God's people is! Will you try and get that thought into your minds? How great is your own sin—your sin before conversion—think that over! Your sin while seeking the Lord in putting confidence in your own works and looking after refuges of lies. Your sins since conversion—turn them over.

Beloved, one sin towers up like an Alp! But we have many sins heaped upon each other, as in the old fable of the giants who piled Pelion upon Ossa, mountain upon mountain! O God, what an aggregate of sin is there in the life of one of Your most pure and most sanctified children! Multiply this. All the sin of one child of God—multiply it by the number of those contained in that word "us." "Cleanses us from all sin! How many are God's children? God's Word shall answer. "A multitude that no man can number, out of all kindreds and peoples and tongues, stood before the Throne." Can you imagine—deep as Hell's bottomless pit! High as Heaven's own Glory—for sin sought to pluck even God out of His Throne! Wide as the east is from the west! Long as eternity is this great mass of the guilt of the people for whom Christ shed His blood! And yet all this is taken away! "The blood of Jesus Christ, His Son, cleanses us from all sin."

Then observe the greatness of the Atonement offered. Will you inwardly digest those words, "the blood of Jesus Christ, His Son"? Blood is at all times precious, but this is no blood of a mere man–it is the blood of an innocent Man! Better still, it is the blood of Man in union with Deity–"His Son!" God's Son! Why, angels cast their crowns before Him! All the choral symphonies of Heaven surround His glorious Throne. "God over all, blessed forever. Amen." And yet He yields His blood! He takes upon Himself the form of a servant and then is scourged and pierced, bruised and torn and at last slain–for nothing but the blood of Deity could make atonement for human sin!

The Atonement must be no man, merely–He must be the God-Man Mediator, the Fellow of Jehovah, co-equal and co-eternal with Him–He must bear the pangs and bitterness of Divine wrath which was due to sin. Think of this–a sacrifice which no human mind can ever properly estimate in the infinity of its value! Here, indeed, we have greatness– great sin, but a great Atonement! Think again–we have here great love which provided such a Sacrifice. Oh, how He must have loved, to have descended from Heaven to earth and from earth to the grave! How He must have loved, to have chosen us, when we were hating Him–when we were enemies! He has reconciled us unto God by His own death!

Dead in trespasses and sins, corrupt–wrapped up in the cerements of evil habits, hateful and hating one another, full of sin and every abomination–yet He loved us so as to yield up His soul unto death for us. We are dealing with great things here, indeed, and we must not forget the greatness of the influence which such an Atonement, the result of such love, must have upon the Christian's heart. Oh, the greatness of the peace which passes all understanding, which flows from this great Atonement! Oh, the greatness of the gratitude which must blaze forth from such a sacred fire as this! Oh, the greatness of the hatred of sin, of the revenge against iniquity which must spring from a sense of such love, when it is shed abroad in the heart!

You are citizens enjoying no mean privilege, oh, you blood-bought citizens of a blood-bought city! God has loved you. You cannot, though I should allot you a whole lifetime—you cannot get to the depth of that love God has loved you and to prove His love He has died in the Person of man for you. He loves you and has overcome the dread result of all your fearful sin! And now, by the love which God has manifested, we do pray you let your holiness, your truthfulness and your zeal prove that you understand the greatness of those things. If your heart can really conceive the greatness of the things here revealed—the great sin, the great Savior offering Himself out of great love that He might make you to be greatly privileged—I am sure your hearts will rejoice!

The next thing which sparkles in the text is its SIMPLE SOLITARINESS— "We have fellowship one with another." And then it is added as a simple, gloriously simple statement, "the blood of Jesus Christ, His Son, cleanses us from all sin." Observe there is nothing said about rites and ceremonies. It does not begin by saying, "and the waters of Baptism, together with the blood of Jesus Christ, His Son, cleanses us." Not a word, whether it shall be the sprinkling in infancy, or immersion of Believers—nothing is said about it—it is the blood, the blood only, without a drop of baptismal water!

Nothing is here said about sacraments—what some call "the blessed Eucharist," is not dragged in here—nothing about eating bread and drinking wine! It is the blood, nothing but the blood—"the blood of Jesus Christ, His Son." And if nothing is said of rites that God has given, rites that man has invented are equally excluded. Not a syllable is uttered concerning celibacy or monasticism! Not a breath about vows of perpetual chastity and poverty! Not a hint about confession to a priest and human absolution! Not an allusion to penance or extreme unction! "The blood of Jesus Christ, His Son, cleanses us from all sin."

It was well done by a poor woman who, as she lay sick, heard for the first time the precious Gospel of her salvation. She was told that the blood alone cleansed from sin. She believed, and then, putting her hand into her bosom, she took out a little crucifix which she had always worn, hanging from a chain about her neck, and said to the preacher, "Then I don't want this, Sir." Ah, truly so! And so may we say of everything that man has devised as a consolation to a poor wounded spirit. "I have found Jesus and I do not want that, Sir." You who want it, keep it–but as for us, if we walk in the light as He is in the light–the blood of Jesus Christ, His Son, so completely purges us from all sin that we dare not look to anything else lest we come into the bondage of the beggarly elements of this world!

You will perceive, too, that nothing is said about Christian experience as a means of cleansing. "What?" says one. "Does not the first sentences of the verse imply that?" Assuredly not, for you perceive that the first sentence of the verse does not interfere, though it is linked, with the other. If I walk in the light as God is in the light, what then? Does my walking in the light take away my sins? Not at all! I am as much a sinner in the light as in the darkness if it were possible for me to be in the light without being washed in the blood.

Well, but we have fellowship with God, and does not having fellowship with God take away sin? Beloved, do not misunderstand me! No man can have fellowship with God unless sin is taken away–but his fellowship with God and his walking in light, does not take away his sin–not at all. The whole process of the removal of sin is here, "And the blood of Jesus Christ, His Son, cleanses us from all sin." I beg to repeat it–the text does not say that our walking in the light cleanses us from sin! It does not say that our having fellowship with God cleanses us from sin–these are the result of cleansing, but they have no connection as cause–it is the blood and the blood alone which purges us from sin! The dying thief looked to Christ and sin was taken away by the blood. And there is a Brother in Christ here who hashad such an experience of Christ's love for sixty years that his heart is now like a shock of corn, ripe for Heaven. He lives in his Master's Presence, he spends the most of his time in his Master's service! But, Beloved, there is not a single atom of difference between him and the dying thief so far as the cleansing away of sin is concerned!

The blood cleansed the thief and the same blood washes this advanced and full-grown Christian, or otherwise he is still unclean.

Observe, yet again, that in the verse there is no hint given of any emotions, feelings, or attainments as co-operating with the blood to take away sin. Christ took the sins of His people and was punished for those sins as if He had been Himself a sinner, and so sin is taken away from us. But in no sense, degree, shape or form is sin removed by attainments, emotions, feelings or experiences! The blood is the only Atonement—the blood, without any mixture of anything else, completes and finishes the work! "For you are complete in Him."

Now I could enlarge for a very long time on this point, but I do not think I shall. I will rather throw in a sentence or two and observe that whereas there are some who urge you to look to your doctrinal intelligence as a ground of comfort. I beseech you Beloved, look only to the blood! Whereas there are others who would set up a standard of Christian experience and urge that this is to be the channel of your consolation. I pray you, while you prize both doctrine and experience, rest not your soul's weight but in the precious blood! Some would lead you to high degrees of fellowship—follow them, but not when they would lead you away from the simple position of a sinner resting upon the blood! There are those who could teach you mysticism and would have you rejoice in the light within. Follow them as far as they have the warrant of God's Word, but never take your foot from that Rock of Ages where the only safe standing can be found!

Certain of my Brethren are very fond of preaching Christ in His Second Coming—I rejoice that they preach the truth concerning Christ Glorified, but, my Beloved, I do beseech you do not place your hope on Christ Glorified, nor on Christ to come, but on "Christ Crucified." Remember that in the matter of taking away sin, the first thing is not the Throne, but the Cross—not the reigning Savior—but the bleeding Savior! Not the King in His Glory, but the Redeemer in His shame. Care not to be studying dates of prophecies if burdened with sin, but seek your chief, your best comfort in the blood of Jesus Christ which cleanses us from all sin—here is the pole star of your salvation—sail by it and you shall reach the port of peace.

A third brilliant flash in the light, viz., THE COMPLETENESS of the cleansing. "The blood of Jesus Christ, His Son, cleanses us from all sin"—not from some sin, but "from all sin." Beloved, I cannot tell you the exceeding sweetness of this Word, but I pray God the Holy Spirit to give you a taste of it. There is original sin, by which we fell in Adam before we were born, and there is inherited sin through which we were born in sin and shapen in iniquity. There is actual sin—the sin of my youth and my former transgressions, the sins of my riper years, the sins which defile the hoary head and make that which should be a crown of Glory to be a crown of grief—and all these sins, original and actual, are all gone! All gone!

Sins against the Law, though it is exceedingly broad so that it makes me a sinner in thought, in word, in deed, in heart—they are all gone! Sins against the Gospel when I kicked against the pricks, when I stifled conscience, when I resisted the Holy Spirit as did also my fathers—when I hated the Truth of God and would not have it because my deeds were evil and I would not come to the light lest my deeds might be reproved. Sins when I would regard none of the sweet invitations of the Gospel—all cleansed away! Sins against Christ Jesus since my conversion when I have backslidden and my heart has been cold towards Him! Sins against the Holy Spirit when I have followed my own impulses instead of the indwelling Deity—all gone!

The Roman Catholic divides sin into venial sins and mortal sins. Be it so—the blood of Jesus Christ cleanses us from all sin, mortal or venial, deadly or pardonable. Sins of commission—here is a long catalogue—think it over! Sins of omission—that is still a larger list! The things which we have left undone which we ought to have done are probably more numerous than the things which we have done which we ought not to have done—all are gone! Some sins are greater than others. There is no doubt whatever that adultery, fornication, murder, blasphemy and such like are greater than the sins of daily life—but whether they are great sins or little sins—they are all gone! That same God who took away the plague of flies from Egypt also took away the plague of thunder and of lightning. All are gone—gone at once!

Pharaoh's chariot is drowned in the Red Sea and the mean Egyptian is drowned in the same way. The depths have covered them. There is not one of them left. There are sins against God—how many there are! Sins of breaking His Day and despising His Word—profaning His name, forgetting Him and not loving Him—but He blots out all! Sins against my friends and my enemies, against my neighbor, against my father, my child, my wife—sins in all relationships—yet all are gone! Then, too, remember there are sins of presumption and sins of ignorance—sins done willfully and unknown sins—the blood cleanses us from ALL sin!

Shall I go on? Surely I need not! But you see the purging is complete. Whether the bill is little or the bill is great, the same receipt can discharge one as the other. The blood of Jesus Christ is as blessed and Divine a payment for the sin of blaspheming Peter as it is for the sin of loving John! Our iniquity is gone, all gone at once and all gone forever. Blessed completeness! What a sweet theme to dwell upon!

The next gem that studs the text is the thought of PRESENTNESS. "Cleanses" says the text—not, "shall cleanse." There are multitudes who think that as a dying hope they may look forward to pardon, and perhaps within a few hours of their dissolution they may be able to say, "My sins are pardoned." Such can never have read God's Word, or, if they have read it, they have read it with unbelieving eyes. Beloved, I would not give the snap of my finger for the bare possibility of cleansing when I come to die!

Oh how infinitely better to have cleansing now! Some imagine that a sense of pardon is an attainment after many years of Christian experience. For a young Christian to say, "My sins are forgiven," seems to them to be an untimely fig, ripe too soon. But, Beloved, it is not so. The moment a sinner trusts Jesus, that sinner is as fully forgiven as he will be when the light of the Glory of God shall shine upon his resurrection countenance. Beloved, forgiveness of sin is a present thing–a privilege for this day, a joy for this very hour! And whoever walks in the light as God is in the light has fellowship with God and has at this moment the perfect pardon of sin.

You perceive that it is written in the present tense as if to indicate continuance–it will always be so with you, Christian. It was so yesterday–it was "cleanses" yesterday, it is "cleanses" today–it will be "cleanses" tomorrow. It will be "cleanses" until you cross the river–every day you may come to this fountain for it "cleanses!" Every hour you may stand by its brim, for it "cleanses." I think there is sanctification here as well as justification. I am inclined to believe that this text has been too much limited in its interpretation and that it signifies that the blood of Jesus is constantly operating upon the man who walks in the light so as to cleanse him from the indwelling power of sin.

And the Spirit of God applies the doctrine of the Atonement to the production of purity till the soul becomes completely pure from sin at the last. I desire to feel every day the constantly purifying effect of the sacrifice of my Lord and Master. Look at the foot of the Cross and I am sure you will feel that the precious drops cleanse from all sin.

Now in the fifth place, the text presents to us very blessedly the thought of CERTAINTY. It is not, "perhaps the blood of Jesus Christ cleanses from sin." The text speaks of it as a fact not to be disputed–it does do so. To the Believer this is matter of certainty, for the Spirit of God bears witness with our spirits that we are born of God. Our spirit in the joy and peace which it receives through believing becomes assured of its being cleansed, and then the Spirit of God comes in as a second Witness and bears witness with our spirit that we are born of God!

My being cleansed from all sin today is to me as much a matter of consciousness as my being better in health. I was conscious of pain when I lay on my sick bed and so, when I was living in sin, as soon as God gave me spiritual life I was conscious that guilt lay heavily upon me. I am conscious now of pain removed and so I am equally conscious of sin removed–I do not hesitate to say it here, that my consciousness of pardoned sin is at this moment as clear and as distinct as my consciousness of removed pain while I look at Jesus Christ, my Lord, by faith.

So is it often with the Christian. It is frequently with him a matter of consciousness most positive and infallible that he is truly and really cleansed from all sin by the blood of Jesus Christ! It is not merely a matter of consciousness, but if you think of it, it is a matter of reasoning. If Jesus Christ did, indeed, take the sins of all who believe, then it follows, necessarily, that I, trusting in Christ, have no longer any sin–for if Christ took my sin–sin cannot be in two places at once! If Christ bears it, then I do not bear it. And if Christ was punished for it, then the punishment of my sin has been endured and I cannot be punished for the sin for which Jesus has been punished–unless God should sovereignly punish men–which would be such an insult to the honesty and justice of God that it must not be tolerated for a moment in our thoughts!

If Jesus Christ has paid the debt it is paid and–

"Justice can demand no more,
Christ has paid the dreadful score."

So the Christian's being cleansed from sin becomes to him a matter of spiritual argument–he can see it clearly and manifestly. Yet more, he is so certain of it that it begins to operate upon him in blessed effect. He is so sure that there is no sin laid to his door that he draws nearer to God than a sinner, defiled with sin, may do. He enters into that which is within the veil–he talks with God as his Father–he claims familiar communion with the Most High God! And though God is so great that the Heaven of heavens cannot contain Him, yet he believes that that same God lives in his heart as in a temple! Now this he could not feel if he did not know that sin is put away. Beloved, no man is capable of virtue in the highest sense of the term till it is a matter of certainty to him that his sin is cleansed.

115

You say, "That is a strong assertion," but I do assert it–all of you who are doing good works with the view to saving yourselves are missing the mark of pure virtue. You say, "Why?" The goodness of an action depends upon its motive. Your motive is to save yourselves–that is selfish–your action is selfish and the virtue of it has evaporated. But the Christian, when he performs good works, does not perform them with any view whatever of merit or self-salvation. "I am saved," he says– "perfectly saved. I have not a sin in God's Book against me–I am clean. Great God, before Your bar I am clean through Jesus Christ–

'Loved of my God, for Him again
With love intense I burn.'

What can I do to prove to all mankind how much, how truly I love my God?" You see, then, that this must be a matter of certainty or else it will never have its right effect upon you. And I pray God that you may suck the certainty out of this text and taste its sweetness to your own soul's inward contentment and be able to say, "Yes, without a doubt, the blood of Jesus Christ, His Son, cleanses us from all sin."

I hope I shall not weary you, but a few words upon the sixth gem which adorns the text, namely, the DIVINITY of it. "Where?" asks one. Does not divinity gleam in this text? Does it not strike you that the verse is written in a God-like style? The God-like style is very peculiar. You can tell the style of Milton from the style of Wordsworth, or the style of Byron. Read a verse and an educated person knows the author by the ring of the sentences. The God-like style is unique in its excellence. You need never put the name at the bottom when the writing is of the Lord. You know it by the very style of it. "Light be! Light was."

Who speaks like that but Deity? Now there is a Divine ring about this sentence–"The blood of Jesus Christ, His Son, cleanses us from all sin." Why, if man were talking of so great an Atonement he would fetch a compass! He would have to go round about! We cannot afford to say such great things as these in a few words. We must adopt some form of

116

speech that would allow us to extol the truth and indicate its beauties. God seems to put away His pearls as if they were but common pebbles. "The blood of Jesus Christ, His Son, cleanses us from all sin"—as if it were as much a matter of every-day work as for a man to wash his hands!

Notice the simplicity of the whole process. It does not seem to take weeks or months—it is done at once! Slowly and by degrees is man's action—we must lay the thing to soak, to fetch the color from it, subject it to many processes and expose it to the wind and rain and frost and sun before it can be cleansed. But here God speaks and it is done! The blood comes into contact with the guilty conscience and it is all over with sin. As if it were but a handful that moves a mountain of sin, He takes up the isles as a very little thing. He counts great oceans of our sin as though they were but a drop in a bucket. Believing in Christ in a moment, by the Divine and majestic process which God has ordained, we get the perfect cleansing of sin.

In the last place, just a hint upon the WISDOM of the text. What a wise way of cleansing from sin the text speaks of! Beloved, suppose God had devised a plan for pardoning sin which did not turn the sinner's face to God? Then you would have a very singular spectacle—you would have a sinner pardoned by a process which enabled him to do without his God— and it strikes me he would be worse off than he was before! But here, before ever the sinner can receive pardon he must say, "I will arise and go unto my Father." And he must come closer into contact with God than he ever came before. He must see God in the flesh of Christ and must look to Him if he would be saved.

I do bless God that I have not to turn my face to Hell to get pardon, but I have to turn my face towards Heaven! That God which was the true root of that disease. It turns the sinner's face in the direction of holiness and bliss. Observe the benefit of this plan of salvation in the fact that it makes the sinner feel the evil of sin. If we were pardoned in a way which did not involve pain to someone, we should say, "Oh, it is easy for God to forgive it." But when I see the streaming veins of Jesus and mark the sweat of His blood fall to the ground and hear Him cry, "They have pierced My hands and My feet," then I understand that sin is a dreadful evil!

If a man should be pardoned without being made to feel that sin is bitter, I do not know that he would be really any the better off—perhaps better unpardoned than pardoned—unless he is led to hate sin. Our gracious God has also chosen this plan of salvation with the wise design of making man glorify God. I cannot see sin pardoned by the substitutionary Atonement of the Lord Jesus without dedicating myself to the praise and glory of the great God of redeeming love. It would be a pity if man could be pardoned and afterwards could live a selfish, thankless life, would it not? If God had devised a scheme by which sin could be pardoned and yet the sinner live to himself, I do not know that the world or the man would be advantaged.

But here are many birds killed with one stone, as the Proverb puts it. Now therefore, at the foot of the Cross, the bands which bound our soul to earth are loosened. We are strangers in the land and therefore, "God forbid that we should glory, save in the Cross of our Lord Jesus Christ, by whom the world is crucified unto us and we are crucified to the world."

I leave this text with the Believer, only adding, if any of you would have it, and joy in it, you must walk in the light. I pray God the Holy Spirit to bring you to see the light of the Glory of God in the face of Jesus Christ! Then you will trust Him and then you shall have fellowship with Him! And by His blood you shall be cleansed from all sin. God bless you for Jesus' sake. Amen.

THE BLOOD OF THE COVENANT

"Now the God of peace, that brought again from the dead our Lord Jesus, that great Shepherd of the sheep, through the blood of the Everlasting Covenant, make you perfect in every good work to do His will, working in you that which is well-pleasing in His sight, through Jesus Christ; to whom be glory forever and ever. Amen."
Hebrews 13:20-21

WHAT we ask others to do we should be prepared to do ourselves. Precept fails unless it is followed up by example. The Apostle had exhorted the Hebrew Believers to pray for him in the words, "Pray for us." And then, as if to show that he did not ask of them what he was not himself willing to give, he utters this most wonderful prayer for them. He may confidently say to his congregation, "Pray for me" who does unfeignedly from his soul pray for them! The prayer of the Apostle, as you observe, is tinged with the subject upon which he had been writing. This Epistle to the Hebrews is full of distinctions between the Old Covenant and the New, the gist of it being to show that the former Covenant was only typical of that abiding dispensation which followed it. It had only the shadow—not the very image of heavenly things.

His subject had been the Covenant and when he prayed, his garments were sweet with the myrrh and aloes and cassia among which his meditations had conducted him. According to the manner of his thoughts was the expression of his desires. He weaved into the texture of his prayer the meditations of his heart. And this is a very right method, especially when the prayer is public, for it ensures variety, it assists others to unite with us and it tends to edification. In fact, as the bee gathers honey from many flowers, and the honey is often flavored with wild thyme or some other special flower which abounds in the region from which it collects its sweets, so does our soul gather dainty stores of the honey of devotion from all sources—but that upon which she longest tarries in her meditations yields a paramount savor and flavor to the expression and the spirit of her prayer.

What was more natural than that a discourse upon the Covenant should be followed by this Covenant prayer—"The God of peace, that brought from the dead our Lord Jesus, that great Shepherd of the sheep, through the blood of the Everlasting Covenant, make you perfect in every good work to do His will"? The subject of the Epistle to the Hebrews is deep, for it passes on from the superficial rudiments to those underlying Truths of God which are more mysterious and profound. It is a book for the higher classes in Christ's school and therefore this prayer is not for babes, but for men of understanding. We could not say to all the saints, "after this manner you should pray," for they would not know what we were asking. They have need to begin with something simpler, such as that sweet, "Our Father, which are in Heaven," which suits all Believers.

Full grown men feed on strong meat, think sublime thoughts and offer mighty prayers. As we may admire in the prayer of the babe its simplicity, and in the prayer of the young man its vivacity, so in the prayer of one who has become a father in Christ and feeds upon the Covenant, we rejoice in its depth, compass and sublimity. All these we find here. I invite those who would understand the deep things of God to ask the Holy Spirit's assistance while we follow the Apostle in this, his Covenant prayer, a prayer of which the Covenant is the thread, the substance and the plea.

The subject of our discourse this morning, therefore, is the Covenant of Grace, as it is here spoken of. And I shall begin by noticing, first, THE COVENANT NAMES which the Apostle uses. He calls the ever-blessed Father, "the God of Peace." And to the Redeemer who has taken the other side of the Covenant, he gives the title, "Our Lord Jesus, that great Shepherd of the sheep." Dear Friends, as many of us as have believed in the Lord Jesus Christ, we are in Christ—and He is our Head and Representative, our Shepherd and Sponsor. On our behalf He made a Covenant with the Father upon this tenor—that we, having sinned, a full recompense should be made to injured Justice—and the Law of God should be fully honored. The Father, on His part, agreeing to grant full pardon, acceptance, adoption and eternal life to us.

Now, the Covenant has been kept on Christ's side. The text assures us of that, for Jesus has, according to His promise, shed His blood. And now the Covenant stands only to be fulfilled on the side of the eternal Father—and under that aspect of the Covenant the Apostle calls the Father, "the God of Peace." What a precious name! Under the Covenant of Works He is the God of Vengeance. To sinners He is the Thrice Holy God, terrible out of His holy places. Even our God is a consuming fire! And yet to us, seeing that the Covenant has been fulfilled on our side by our great Head and Representative, He is "the God of Peace."

All is peace between you and God, Christian! There is no past ground of quarrel remaining, nor any fear that a new one can arise! The Everlasting Covenant secures everlasting peace! He is not the God of a hollow truce, not the God of a patched-up forgetfulness of unforgiven injuries—He is the God of Peace in the very deepest sense—He is, Himself, at peace, for there is a peace of God that passes all understanding. And, moreover, by reason of His mercy, His people are made to enjoy peace of conscience within themselves, for you feel that God is reconciled to you. Your hearts rest in Him. Your sins, which separated you, have been removed—and perfect love has cast out the fear which was torment. While the Lord is at peace with Himself and you are made to enjoy inward peace through Him, He is also at peace with you, for He loves you with a love unsearchable!

He sees nothing in you but that which He delights in, for in the Covenant He does not look at you as you are in yourself, but in your Head, Christ Jesus—and to the eyes of God there is no sight in the universe so lovely as His own dear Son—and His people in His Son. There is beauty enough in Jesus to make Him forget our deformities! There are merits enough in Jesus to swallow up our demerits and efficacy sufficient in the atoning blood of our great High Priest to wash away all our transgressions! As for us, our soul recognizing that blood and perceiving the love of God towards us, feels, now, no war with God. We did rebel once, for we hated Him. And even now, when the old nature champs the bit, and the Lord's will runs cross to our desires, we do not find it easy to bow before Him and say, "I thank You, O Father, Lord of Heaven and earth, because it seemed good in Your sight."

But yet the new nature which comes to the front does rule and govern, and all heart-contest between our soul and God is at an end. To us the Lord is in the widest and most perfect sense, the God of Peace! Oh, how I love that name! He is the peaceful, happy God! He is unruffled, undisturbed! We, within ourselves, are made to enjoy a peace that passes all understanding, which keeps our hearts and minds. God at peace with us, declaring that He will never be angry with us, nor rebuke us! And we, rejoicing in Him, delighting in His Law and living for His Glory. Therefore let us, in every troubled hour, look to the Lord under this cheering name, "the God of Peace," for as such the Covenant reveals Him!

The Apostle had a view of the other great party to the Covenant, and he names Him, "Our Lord Jesus, that great Shepherd of the sheep." We must view our Redeemer in the Covenant, first, as Jesus the Savior who leads us into the Canaan which has been given to us by a Covenant of Salt, even the rest which remains to the people of God. He is also the Lord Jesus in all the dignity of His Nature, exalted far above all principalities and powers–to be obeyed and worshipped by us. And He is our Lord Jesus–ours because He has given Himself to us–and we have accepted and received Him with holy delight to be the Lord whom we cheerfully serve.

He is our Lord Jesus because He saves us. Our Lord Jesus because, by bringing us under His kingdom, He rescues us. And our Lord Jesus because we have a special relation both to His sovereignty and His salvation. We are not generally observant of the appropriateness of our Lord's names. We do not notice the instruction which is intended by the writers who use them, nor do we exercise discretion, enough, ourselves, in the employment of them. Yet there is great force in these titles when appropriately employed. Other names may have small significance, but in the titles of Jesus there is a wealth of meaning.

Further, our Lord is called, "that great Shepherd of the sheep." In the Covenant we are the sheep, the Lord Jesus is the Shepherd. You cannot make a covenant with sheep—they have not the ability to covenant. But you can make a covenant with the Shepherd for them, and so, glory be to God, though we had gone astray like lost sheep, we belong to Jesus, and He made a Covenant on our behalf—and He stood for us before the living God. Now, I have already explained to you that our Lord Jesus, in His death is the good Shepherd—the good Shepherd gives His life for the sheep, and so shows His goodness. In His rising again, He is the great Shepherd, as we have it in the text, for His Resurrection and return to Glory display His greatness. But in His Second Advent He is the chief Shepherd—"when the chief Shepherd shall appear, you, also, shall appear with Him in Glory"—there He shows His superior sovereignty.

Our Lord was good in laying down His life for the sheep—and there are other shepherds whom He makes good—who, in His name, feed His lambs and sheep. When He comes, again, the second time, He will appear with others, the Chief among them all. But in His Resurrection for our justification, in connection with the Covenant, He is alone, and bears the name of the or "that great Shepherd"—that great Shepherd of whom all prophecy was spoken, in whom all the Divine decrees are fulfilled, before whom all others shrink away, who stands alone, as in that Covenant capacity, the sole and only Shepherd of the sheep.

It is very beautiful to trace the shepherds through the Old Testament and to see Christ as Abel, the witnessing shepherd, pouring out that blood which cries from the ground. As Abraham, the separating shepherd, leading out his flock into the strange country where they dwelt alone. As Isaac, the quiet shepherd, digging wells for his flock and feeding them in peace in the midst of the enemies. As Jacob, the shepherd who is surety for the sheep, who earns them all by toil and weariness, who separates them and walks in the midst of them to Canaan, preserving them by his own lone midnight prayers. There, too, we see our Lord as Joseph, the shepherd who is head over Egypt for the sake of Israel, of whom his dying father said, "From thence is the Shepherd, the stone of Israel." He is Head over all things for His Church, the King who governs all the world for the sake of His elect, the great Shepherd of the sheep, who, for their sakes, has all power committed unto His hands.

Then follows Moses, the chosen shepherd who led his people through the wilderness up to the Promised Land, feeding them with manna and giving them drink from the smitten Rock–what a wide theme for meditation here! And then there is David, the type of Jesus, as reigning in the covenanted inheritance over his own people, as a glorious king in the midst of them all. All these together enable us to see the varied glories of "that great Shepherd of the sheep." Beloved, this is a great subject and I can only hint at it. Let us rejoice that our Shepherd is great, because He, with His great flock, will be able to preserve them all from the great dangers into which they are brought–and to perform for them the great transactions with the great God which are demanded of a Shepherd of such a flock as that which Jesus calls His own.

Under the Covenant, Jesus is Prophet, Priest and King–a shepherd should be all this to his flock–and He is great in each of these offices. While we rest in the Covenant of Grace we should view our Lord as our Shepherd and find solace in the fact that sheep have nothing to do with their own feeding, guidance, or protection–they have only to follow their Shepherd unto the pastures which He prepares–and all will be well with them. "He makes me to lie down in green pastures, He leads me beside the still waters."

II. Secondly, the Apostle mentions THE COVENANT SEAL. "The God of peace that brought again from the dead our Lord Jesus, that great Shepherd of the sheep, through the blood of the Everlasting Covenant." The seal of the Covenant is the blood of Jesus. In olden times when men made covenants with each other, they generally used some ceremony to bind the bargain, as it were. Now, under the old dispensation, Covenants with God were always confirmed with blood. As soon as ever blood was shed and the victim died, the agreement made was established.

When our heavenly Father made a Covenant with Jesus Christ on our behalf, that Covenant was true and firm, "according to the sure mercies of David." But to make it stand fast there must be blood. Now, the blood ordained to seal the Covenant was not the blood of bulls or of goats, but the blood of the Son of God, Himself! And this has made the Covenant so binding that sooner may Heaven and earth pass away than one tittle of it fail. God must keep His own promises. He is a free God, but He binds Himself—by two immutable things in which it is impossible for Him to lie—He has bound Himself to bestow Covenant blessings upon the flock which the great Shepherd represented.

Brethren, you and I, as honest men, are bound by our word. If we took an oath, which I trust we would not, we should certainly feel doubly bound by it. And if we had lived in the old times, and blood had been sprinkled on an agreement which we had made, we should regard the solemn sign and never dream of running back from it. Think, for a moment, how impossible it is that the Lord should ever break that Covenant of Grace which He spontaneously made with His own Son— and with us in Him. Now that it has been sprinkled with blood from the veins of His own wellbeloved Son, the Covenant is everlasting. It stands fast, forever, because it is confirmed by blood which is none other than the blood of the Son of God!

Remember, too, that in our case that blood not only confirmed the Covenant, but actually fulfilled it because the Covenant stipulation was on this wise—Christ must suffer for our sins and honor the Divine Law. He had kept the Law in His life, but it was necessary for the complete fulfilling of the Covenant on His part, that He should also be obedient to death, even the death of the Cross. The shedding of His blood, therefore, was the carrying out of His promised obedience to its extremity. It was the actual fulfillment of Christ's side of the Covenant on our behalf, so that now the whole Covenant must stand firm, for that upon which it depended is finished forever. It is not only ratified with that bloody signature, but by that blood it is actually carried out on Christ's part. And it cannot be that the Eternal Father should start back from His side of the compact since our side of it has been carried out to the letter by that great Shepherd of the sheep who laid down His life for us.

By the shedding of the blood, the Covenant is turned into a Testament. In some Bibles, the margin puts it, "testament," and often in other cases we scarcely know how to translate the word, whether to say the New Testament, or the New Covenant. Certainly it is now a Testament, for since Christ has kept His part of the Covenant, He wills to us what is due to Him from God and He makes over to us, by His death, all that comes to Him as His reward—making us His heirs by a Testament which is rendered valid by His death. So you may say, "testament," if you please, or, "covenant," if you will—only never forget that the blood has made both Testament and Covenant sure to all the sheep of whom Jesus is the shepherd.

Dwell with pleasure upon that word, "Everlasting Covenant." Certain men in these days declare that "everlasting" does not mean everlasting, but indicates a period to which an end will come sooner or later. I have no sympathy with them and feel no inclination to renounce the everlastingness of Heaven and other Divine blessings in order to gratify the tastes of wicked men by denying the eternity of future punishment. Human nature leans in that direction, but the Word of God does not. And following its unerring track we rejoice in the Everlasting Covenant which will abide forever and ever! The Covenant of Works is gone. It was based on human strength and it dissolved as a dream. In the nature of things it could not be everlasting. Man could not keep the condition of it and it fell to the ground.

But the Covenant of Grace depended only upon the power, love and faithfulness of Christ who has kept His part of the Covenant and, therefore, the Covenant now rests only upon God, the faithful and true, whose Word cannot fail—

"As well might He His Being quit,
As break His promise, or forget."

"His mercy endures forever, and His Truth throughout all generations." He has said, "I will make an Everlasting Covenant with them, that I will not turn away from them to do them good," and therefore do them good He must, for He is not a man that He should lie, nor the son of man that He should repent. So, then, the Covenant seal makes all things sure.

III. We have now to notice THE COVENANT FULFILLMENT, for the Lord has commenced to fulfill it. "The God of peace that brought again from the dead our Lord Jesus, that great Shepherd of the sheep, through the blood of the Everlasting Covenant." See, then, Jesus Christ has been brought back from the dead through the blood of the Covenant! Here is the story. He was the Covenantor on our behalf. He took our sin upon Himself and undertook to suffer for it. Having been crucified, He yielded up His life, and from the Cross He was taken to the grave and there He lay in vile durance.

Now, it was a part of the Covenant, on God the Father's part, that He would not leave Christ's soul in Hades, nor suffer His Holy One to see corruption. This agreement has been faithfully kept. Christ on the Cross represented all of us who believe in Him—we were crucified in Him. Jesus in the tomb also represented us, for we are buried with Him. Whatever happened to Him happened, also, to the flock. Now, then, what will occur to the body of Jesus? Will God keep His Covenant? Will the worm devour that lovely frame, or will it defy corruption? Will it come to pass that He who has descended into the earth shall never return? Wait. It is the third morning! The promised time has come. As yet no worm has dared to feed upon that God-like form—yet it lies among the dead.

But on the third morning the Slumberer awakes like one that has been refreshed with sleep. He rises! The stone is rolled away. Angels escort Him to liberty. He comes into the open air of the garden and speaks to His disciples. Jesus, who bled, has left the dead, no more to die! He waits for 40 days that He may let His friends see that He is really risen. But He has to rise higher, yet, to be fully brought back to His former honors. Will God be faithful to Him and bring Him back from the dead all the way He once descended? Yes, for on the Mount of Olives, when the time is come, He begins to ascend! Cleaving the ambient air, He mounts from amidst His worshipping disciples till a cloud receives Him! But will He rise fully to the point from which He came?

Will He, in His own Person, gain for His Church a full recovery from all the ruin of the Fall? Ah, see Him as He enters the gates of pearl! How He is welcomed by the Father! See how He climbs aloft and sits upon the Father's Throne, for God, also, has highly exalted Him and given Him a name above every name, that at the name of Jesus every knee should bow. Now note by what means our Lord returned from the dead to all this Glory. It was because He had presented the blood of the Everlasting Covenant! When the Father saw that Jesus had kept all His part of the Covenant, even to death, then He began to fulfill His portion of the contract by bringing back His Son from the grave to life, from shame to honor, from humiliation to Glory, from death to immortality!

See where He now sits till His enemies are made His footstool. And, what has been done to Jesus has been virtually done to all His people, because, you observe, the Lord, "brought again from the dead," not the Lord Jesus as a private Person only, but, "Our Lord Jesus," as "that great Shepherd of the sheep." The sheep are with the Shepherd! Shepherd of the sheep, where is Your flock? We know that You have loved them even to the end. But You are gone! Have You left them in the wilderness? It cannot be, for it is written, "Who can separate us from the love of Christ?" Hear the Shepherd say, "I will that they, also, whom You have given Me, be with Me where I am." "Because I live, you shall live, also." "Where I am there, also, shall My servant be."

Beloved, the sheep never are away from that great Shepherd of the sheep! They are always in His hand and none can pluck them out of it! They were on earth with Him and they are risen with Him. If Jesus had remained in the grave, there must all His sheep have perished. But when the Father brought Him back by the blood, He brought us back by the blood and gave us a lively hope that for our souls they shall never die—and for our bodies the expectation of resurrection—

"For though our inbred sins require
Our flesh to see the dust,
Yet as the Lord our Shepherd rose,
So all His followers must."

Jesus in Heaven is only there as our Representative—His flock is following Him! I wish you could get a picture in your eyes of the hills of Heaven rising up from these lowlands. We are feeding here, awhile, under His watchful eye, and yonder is a river which runs at the foot of the celestial hills and parts us from heavenly pasturage. One by one our beloved ones are being called across the flood by the Good Shepherd's voice—and they cross the river pleasantly at His bidding, so that a long line of His sheep may be seen going over the stream and up the hillside to where the Shepherd stands and receives them.

This line joins the upper flock to the lower and makes them all one company. Do you not see them continually streaming up to Him and passing, again, under the hand of Him that tells them to be fed by the Lamb and made to lie down forever where wolves can never come? Thus the one flock is even, now, with the Shepherd, for it is all one pasture to Him, though to us it seems divided by Jordan's torrent. Every one of the sheep is marked with the blood of the Everlasting Covenant! Every one of them has been preserved because Jesus lived—and as He was brought, again, from the dead by the blood, even so must they be, for so the Covenant stands. Remember, then, dear Friends, that the punishment of the flock was borne by the Shepherd, that the flock died in the Shepherd and that the flock now live because the Shepherd lives!

Consequently their life is a new life and He will bring all His sheep that, as yet, are not called, out of their death in sin, even as He has been brought out of His own death. He will lead onward and upward those that are called, even as He went onward and upward from the grave to the Throne. He will preserve them all their journey through, even as He was preserved by the blood of the Everlasting Covenant. And finally He will perfect them even as He is perfect. Even as the God of Peace has glorified His Son, so also will He bring all His chosen to eternal Glory with Him!

IV. Fourthly, we will view THE COVENANT BLESSING. What is one of the greatest of all the Covenant blessings? The writer of this Epistle here pleads for it. "Now," says he, "the God of peace, that brought again from the dead our Lord Jesus, that great Shepherd of the sheep, through the blood of the Everlasting Covenant, make you perfect in every good work to do His will, working in you that which is well-pleasing in His sight." Notice that one of the chief blessings of

The Old Covenant said, "There are the tables of stone, mind that you obey every word that is written thereon: if you do you shall live, and if you do not you shall die." Man never did obey and consequently no one ever entered Heaven or found peace by the Law. The New Covenant speaks on this wise, "Their sins and their iniquities will I remember no more. I will write My law in their hearts, and on their minds will I write them. I will put My fear in their hearts that they shall not depart from Me." The Prophets enlarge most instructively upon this New Covenant. It is not a Covenant of, "if you will I will," but it runs thus, "I will and you shall." As a Covenant this exactly suits me! If there were something to be performed by me I could never be sure—but as it is finished I am at rest!

God sets us working and we work—but the Covenant, itself, depends wholly upon that great promise, "I will not turn away from them to do them good." So that it was right of Paul to pray that God would make us meet in every good work to do His will, because of old this was the master promise—that those for whom Jesus died should be sanctified, purified and made meet to serve their God. Great as the prayer is, it is asking what the Covenant guarantees! Taking the text, word by word, I perceive that the first blessing asked for by the Apostle is meetness for the Divine service, for the Greek word is not, "Make you perfect," but meet— "fit," "prepared," "able for." I have no reference to the discussion upon the doctrine of perfection in this observation. No one text would decide that controversy—I simply make the observation because it is matter of fact.

The expression should be rendered, "Make you fully complete," or, "fully fitted," to do His will. We ought to request earnestly that we may be qualified, adapted and suited to be used of God for the performance of His will. After the man once dead in sin, is made alive again, the question arises, who shall be his master? We, having died in our great Shepherd, and having been brought again from the dead—to whom shall we yield ourselves? Certainly unto God alone! Our prayer is that we may be made meet to do His will. Our Shepherd did His Father's will, for He cried, "I delight to do Your will, O God." "By which will we are sanctified," and sanctified to the doing of that will, each one of us. It is a grand desire, but it burns in every Christian heart—that now he may be fit to serve his God, he may be a vessel such as God can use—an instrument fit for the Divine hand! We desire that, though weak and feeble, we may not be impure. Unsuitable by reason of lack of native strength, but suitable through having been cleansed by the blood of the Covenant!

Dear Brothers and Sisters, ask for meetness for service! Pray day and night that you may be fully fitted for every good work. But the Apostle asked for an inward work of Divine Grace—not merely meetness for service—but an operation felt. "Working in you that which is well-pleasing in His sight." I long above everything to possess in myself the working of the Holy Spirit more and more clearly. There is so much superficial religion and we are so apt to be content with it that it becomes us to pray for deep heart-work! We need to have our affections elevated, our will subdued, our understanding enlightened and our whole nature deeply spiritualized by the Presence of the Holy Spirit. Now this is the promise of the Covenant—"I will dwell in them and walk in them."

Remember, God worked in Christ in the grave by quickening His body into life. And He must work in us according to the working of that mighty power which He worked in Christ when He raised Him from the dead. Ask the Lord to do it! Do not be satisfied with a little, weak, almost imperceptible pulse of religion, of which you can hardly judge whether it is there or not! Ask to feel the Divine energies working within you, the eternal Omnipotence of God struggling and striving mightily in your spirit until sin shall be conquered and Grace shall gloriously triumph! This is a Covenant Blessing. Seek it! But we need outward as well as inward work. Working in you that which is well-pleasing in His sight—no small matter when you remember that nothing but perfect holiness can please God! Paul would have us made fit for every good work. He wanted us to be many-sided men and women who could do every good work, just as Jesus did.

He wished us to be qualified for any station and every position. When Jesus Christ rose from the dead He was seen—there was not merely a secret quickening in Him—but a visible life! He was seen of angels and of men! And here, below, He lived, for a period of time, the observed of all observers. So, dear Brothers and Sisters, there ought to be in us not only an inner resurrection which we feel, but such a quickening that we shall be manifestly alive to newness of life. We must know the power of our Lord's Resurrection and exhibit it in every action of our lives. May God grant us this! There is much upon this point which time does not permit me to enlarge upon. May you know it all by experience.

Observe, once more, the completeness of this Covenant blessing. Just as Jesus is fully restored to the place from which He came and has lost no dignity nor power by having shed His blood, but rather is exalted higher than ever, so God's design is to make us pure and holy as Adam was at the first—and to add to our characters a force of love which never would have been there if we had not sinned and been forgiven—an energy of intense devotion, an enthusiasm of perfect self-sacrifice which we never could have learned if it had not been for Him who loved us and gave Himself for us. God means to make us the princes of the blood royal of the universe, or, if you will, the bodyguards of the Lord of Hosts. He desires to fashion an order of creatures who will come very near to Him and yet will feel the loveliest reverence for Him.

He will have them akin to Himself, partakers of the Divine Natures and yet the most obedient of servants—perfectly free agents and yet bound to Him by bonds which will never let them disobey in thought, or word, or deed. And this is how He is fashioning this central battalion who shall wait upon His eternal marching orders forever—He is forgiving us great sins! He is bestowing upon us great blessings! He is making us one with His dear Son! And when He has entirely freed us from the cerements of our spiritual death, He will call us up to where Jesus is and we shall serve Him with an adoration superior to all the rest of His creatures!

Angels cannot love so much as we shall, for they have never tasted redeeming Grace and dying love! This high devotion is the Lord's aim. He did not bring up the Lord Jesus from the dead that He might live a common life. He lifted Him up that He might be Head over all things to His Church and that all things might be under His feet. Even so the destiny of Christians is mysteriously sublime—they are not lifted up from their native death to a mere morality. They are destined to be something more than philanthropists and men esteemed by their fellows. They are to exhibit to angels and principalities, and powers, the wonderful Grace of God, showing in their own persons what God can do with His creatures through the death of His Son!

I do but touch, like a swallow, with my wing where it is delightful to dive.

IV. We conclude with THE COVENANT DOXOLOGY, "To whom be glory forever and ever. Amen." If anything in the world can make a man praise his God it is the Covenant and the knowledge that he is in it. I will leave off preaching and ask you to think over the love of God in the Covenant. It does not belong to all of you. Christ is not the Shepherd of the whole herd of men—He is only the Shepherd of the sheep—and He has not entered into any Covenant for all mankind, but for His sheep, alone. The Covenant is for His own people. If you believe in Him, it is a Covenant for you. But if you reject Him, you can have no participation in this Covenant—for you are under the Covenant of Works, which condemns you.

But now, Believer, just sit down for a moment and think over this exceeding mercy. Your God, the everlasting Father, has entered into a solemn Covenant with Christ, on your behalf, that He will save you, keep you and make you perfect. He has saved you! He has performed a large part of the Covenant in you already, for He has placed you in the way of life and kept you to this day, And if, indeed, you are His, He will keep you to the end. The Lord is not as the foolish man who began to build and was not able to finish. He does not commence to carry out a design and then turn from it. He will push on His work till He completes it in you. Can you really believe it? With you, a poor puny mortal, who will soon sleep in the grave—with you He has made an Everlasting Covenant! Will you not say with our text, "To whom be glory"? Like dying David you can say, "Though my house is not so with God, yet has He made with me an EverlastingCovenant ordered in all things and sure"? I am sure you will joyfully add, "Glory be to His name!" Our God deserves exclusive Glory! Covenant theology glorifies God, alone! There are other theologies abroad which magnify men—they give him a finger in his own salvation and so leave him a reason for throwing up his cap and saying—"Well done, I!" But Covenant theology puts man aside and makes him a debtor and a receiver. It does, as it were, plunge him into the sea of infinite Grace and unmerited favor—and it makes him give up all boasting! It stops the mouth that could have boasted by filling it with floods of love—so that it cannot utter a vainglorious word! A man saved by the Covenant must give all the Glory to God's holy name, for to God all the Glory belongs! In salvation worked by the Covenant, the Lord has exclusive Glory. He also has endless Glory. "To whom be glory forever and ever."

Have you glorified God a little, dear Brothers and Sisters, because of His Covenant mercy? Go on glorifying Him! Did you serve Him well when you were young? Ah, not so well as you wish you had? Then serve Him better now in these riper days. Throw yourself into the glorifying of God! The task of saving yourself is not yours—Jesus has done it all! You may sing—

"A charge to keep I have,
A God to glorify!"

But you will never need to add—

"A never-dying soul to save,

And fit it for the sky,"

For that soul of yours is saved—"He has saved us and called us with a holy calling"—and you are fitted for the sky by the blood of the Everlasting Covenant, for Paul says, "Thanks be unto the Father who has made us meet to be partakers of the inheritance of the saints in light." All you have to do is to glorify the Lord who has saved you, set your feet upon a Rock and established your goings.

Now, go at it with all your might! Are you getting gray, dear Brothers and Sisters? With all your experience you ought, now, to glorify the Lord more than ever! You will soon be up yonder in the land of the living! Since you have but a short time to tarry, here, do not praise the Redeemer any longer at a poor dying rate! And, oh, when we ascend above these clouds, how we will magnify our Covenant God! I am sure I shall not feel my powers large enough, even in Heaven, to express my gratitude for His amazing love! I do not wonder that the poet says—

"Eternity's too short
To utter half His praise."

People find fault with that expression, and say it is an exaggeration. How would you have the poets talk? Is not hyperbole allowable to them? I might even plead that it is not an hyperbole, for neither time nor eternity can utter all the praises of the infinite Jehovah!—

"On, for a thousand tongues to sing
Our great Redeemer's praise."

This shall be the sweetest note of all our music—the Covenant—"The Covenant made with David's Lord, in all things ordered well." The Covenant with that great Shepherd of the sheep by which every sheep was preserved and kept—and brought into the rich pastures of eternal Glory! We will sing of Covenant love in Heaven! This shall be our last song on earth and the first in Paradise—"The Covenant, the Covenant sealed with blood." How I wish Christ's ministers would spread more and more of this Covenant doctrine throughout England! He who understands the two Covenants has found the marrow of all theology! But he who does not know the Covenants knows next to nothing of the Gospel of Christ! You would think, to hear some ministers preach, that salvation was all of works, that it was still uncertain who would be saved, that it was all a matter of, "ifs," and, "buts," and "perhaps."

And if you begin to give them, "shalls," and, "wills," and purposes, and decrees, and pledges, and oaths, and blood–they call you Calvinistic! Why, this doctrine was true before Calvin was born or thought of! Calvin loved it as we do, but it did not come from him! Paul had taught it long before–no, the Holy Spirit taught it to us in the Word of God–and therefore we hold it! The bringing back of this Truth of God to the front will be a grand thing for the Church. From the mouth of this cannon the Lord will blow the Pope and all his myrmidons into a thousand shivers! No other doctrine will do it!

By God's good Grace we must live this doctrine as well as preach it, and may He that brought again from the dead our Lord Jesus, that great Shepherd of the sheep, through the blood of the Everlasting Covenant, make you perfect in every good work to do His will. THEN will He have Glory through the Covenant and through you, both now and forever. Amen and amen!

THE BLOOD OF THE COVENANT

"This is the blood of the Testament which God has enjoined unto you."
Hebrews 9:20

THE Apostle declares that whenever God has entered into covenant with man it has not been without the shedding of blood. To a covenant a sacrifice and to a testament a death was evidently necessary. It was so when the arrangements of Israelite worship were first published and established in the wilderness. Paul says, "Neither the first testament was dedicated without blood." He probably had in his mind's eye the 24 th chapter of the book of Exodus where we read that after thetribes had entered into covenant with God and promised to keep His Law, Moses, "sent young men of the children of Israel, which offered burnt offerings and sacrificed peace offerings of oxen unto the Lord. And Moses took half of the blood and put it in basins and half of the blood he sprinkled on the altar. And He took the Book of the Covenant and read in the audience of the people: and they said, All that the Lord has said will we do and be obedient. And Moses took the blood and sprinkled it on the people and said, Behold the blood of the Covenant which the Lord has made with you concerning all these words."

As it was in the old dispensation so is it in the new–there could be no Divine Covenant, even though it was of Grace, without the shedding of blood. Inasmuch as the new Covenant was not the type, but the substance, a more precious sacrifice was needed and nobler blood than any which is found in the veins of bulls or of goats. Jesus, the Son of God must die, or the Covenant would be unsealed, the testament without force. No Covenant blessing comes to us apart from the death of our great Sacrifice, for "without shedding of blood is no remission," and remission is one of the earliest of the gifts of Divine Grace. If we cannot even begin the heavenly life by receiving forgiveness of sins without coming into connection with the blood, we may be sure that no further blessing can come to us apart from it.

It seems to be absolutely necessary that when God comes into communication with guilty man it must be through an atonement and that atonement must be made by blood, or by the sacrifice of a life. I shall not dwell upon the bloodshedding of the old Covenant, for they are only intended to be types of the one great blood-shedding in the death of our Lord Jesus Christ. The death of a chosen victim was the emblem of the death of Christ. The sprinkling of the people with blood was the type of the application of the blood of Christ to the conscience of Believers and every single item of the ceremony, if looked into, would furnish points for edification. But of these we cannot, now, speak particularly, as the Apostle said on a like occasion.

It suffices us to meditate, at this time, upon the blood of our Lord Jesus, once and for all shed on Calvary, trying to understand its relationship to us according to the tenor of the text—"This is the blood of the Testament which God has enjoined unto you." The words which Moses used in the wilderness concerning the typical sacrifice are far more emphatic as we point you to the bleeding Savior on the Cross and say, "Behold, the blood of the covenant which the Lord has made with you." The wisdom of God had many ends to serve in connecting His covenants with blood-shedding and this will be very evident if we think of its effect upon our own hearts. We all feel somewhat of awe in connection with the thought of blood. It is no light thing to see an animal slaughtered—at least it is not so to me—I cannot endure the sight! As to our fellow men, we can scarcely see the tiniest crimson stream issuing from a wound in their flesh without being distressed.

Tender and sensitive natures, such as all should possess, regard the life of men with great care and the blood, as its token, with great reverence. We view a corpse with awe and if we were called to look upon one who had been slain, we would view the body with horror. If any one of us should pass a spot stained with a man's blood, we should tread lightly and hurriedly, feeling, "how dreadful is this place." The Lord God intended that there should be much of awe about every covenant that He made with man, for it is a matter of great solemnity. The Covenant of Works might well be surrounded with dread, for by reason of our sin it was soon turned into a curse. The quaking mountain, the thick darkness and the trumpet voice were fit accompaniments of the Law which brings condemnation and so, also, were the basins filled with blood.

As for the Covenant of Grace, it is also rightly surrounded with awe, even with such awe as that which bows down at Calvary amid the mid-day midnight, the rending of rocks, the opening graves and the groans of the expiring Son of God. The God of Love is, nevertheless, a God of Holiness and the God who passes by transgression, iniquity and sin, is also a God who first vindicates the honor of His broken Law. The Lord intended that pardon and all other Covenant blessings should come to us in such a way that we should never think sin a trifle, nor conclude, from the freeness of Grace that men were free to transgress. The death of Jesus manifests the solemnity of God's dealings with sin and is fitted to bow the soul in the lowest humility before God.

The flowing of the blood and water from the wounded side, the wrapping of the dead body in the grave clothes, the burial in the sepulcher–these are those sad attendants of the Covenant of Grace which make us tender of heart while we rejoice in the Divine favor. With holy trembling we think of every promise, for the shadow of the Cross is over all. Something of aversion and shrinking crosses most minds at the thought of blood. One feels sickened and saddened. The sight of murdered Abel must have been terrible, indeed, to Adam and Eve, unused as they were to gaze on blood. If it would be so to them after the Fall, what would the sight have been to them had they remained pure and perfect beings? In proportion to purity will be the shock to the mind in the presence of death and blood.

Cruel men might gloat over a battlefield, but to the most of us, the sight of a single violent death would be horrible to the last degree. Manhood, till it is brutalized, has the greatest possible aversion to the sight of blood and it is as though God had selected as the token of Atonement that which would show us His hatred of sin. He would move us to flee from evil after a sight of its painful and deadly consequences! He as good as tells us that while a thing is stained with evil, He would sooner destroy it than have it in His sight! Man, the masterpiece of the Divine creation, shall sooner be slain and his life flow out upon the ground than be allowed to wallow in iniquity! It was intended that even while we are being pardoned we should feel horror at having been defiled with sin.

But this aversion must not be used sinfully, as so we have used it. I have heard of persons saying, when we preach of the blood of Christ, "I could not bear to hear so much about blood! It quite disgusted me." I want you to feel shocked because your sin requires such an awful cleansing—but you must not be shocked at the great Sacrifice, itself! That would be grievous, indeed, to me and fatal to you! Can you bear, then, to reject that which, alone, can save you? Are you so delicate that you turn away from the only cleansing that can purge you from soul-destroying stains? Dare you count the blood of the Covenant to be a common, or even a disgusting, thing? I pray you be not so profane! Let a holy tremor seize you as you see the Crucified and watch the pouring forth of His heart's life-stream! Smite on your breast as you look on Him whom you have pierced!

Grieve that your sin should require such a dread Atonement. Lament that you should be guilty of such a horrible thing that even God's own brightest One must bleed before transgression, with all its scarlet dye, could be washed out. Always love and reverence the blood of Jesus Christ, as of a Lamb without blemish and without spot. The types of the old Law were meant to excite horror of sin and awe in the presence of its atonement. It must have been almost a shocking thing to enter into the tabernacle at the time of the great sacrifices and, indeed, at any time, for year after year there never passed a day without blood being sprinkled on the holy curtains. All around, wherever the worshipper came, he saw tokens of the slaughter of bullocks and goats and calves and rams. Everywhere he saw that God could not be approached without atonement—atonement by sacrificial death.

The priests threw the blood of victims in bowls at the foot of the altar and "almost all things were, by the Law, purged with blood"—and all to make man see that God saw something horrible in sin which only death could hide–and that sin was so intolerable to Him that, unless a propitiation had been made, it had not been possible for His pure and holy mind to speak with man at all, or hold amicable conversation with Him. If the aversion which seems natural to us at the sight of blood should lead us to shudder at the cause of its shedding, it will be well.

I beg you, now, to come with me to Calvary and see that great sight, even Jesus Christ, Himself, offered up as a Sacrifice for guilty men! Herein is a marvelous thing! We have heard so often of it that we do not note the miracle of it as we ought to do. But it is the most marvelous thing that ever happened, that ever can happen, or that ever can be imagined to happen–that He who always lives, even God, Himself, should deign to take into union with Himself a body like our own and that, being found in fashion as a man, He should become obedient to death, even the death of the Cross! All former ages are struck dumb with astonishment at this novelty of love–the bleeding Son of God! And all the ages that are yet to come shall look back to Calvary as the center of all the wonders that even the wonder-working God, Himself, has ever worked!

The blood of Christ is the ruby gem of the ring of love. Infinite goodness finds its crown in the gift of Jesus for sinners. All God's mercies shine like stars, but the coming of His own Son to bleed and die for rebel men is as the sun in the heavens of Divine Grace outshining and illuminating all! It surpasses thought–how, then, shall I hope worthily to set it forth in words?

Of that death and of that blood we shall speak in a fourfold way and first, we shall take the verse as it would most accurately be translated–the blood of Jesus Christ is THE BLOOD OF THE EVERLASTING COVENANT. There cannot be much doubt that the word rendered, "testament," should be translated, "covenant." It is the word used for covenant in other passages and though our translators have used the word, "testament," many critics go the length of questioning whether the word can bear that meaning at all. I think they are too rigid in their criticism and that it does bear that meaning in this very chapter but, still,

141

all must admit that the first and most usual meaning of the word is, "covenant."

Therefore, we will begin with that reading and consider the blood of Jesus as the blood of the Covenant. First, looking from the Cross to the Covenant, the blood proves the intense earnestness of God in entering into covenant with man in a way of Grace. The Covenant of Grace is on this wise—the well-beloved Son of God stood as our Representative, as the second Adam, heading up in Himself all those whom the Father gave Him. He covenanted with God on our behalf that He would vindicate the broken Law and that He would also keep it in every jot and tittle on our behalf. As for the Father, He covenanted that because of the Sacrifice which the Son would offer and the obedience which He would render, He would put away the sin of His people and they should be accepted in love.

This is the Covenant of Grace and faithfulness and to show that the august Covenanters were not playing at covenantmaking they sealed the compact with blood. How dreadfully in earnest was God the Father when He gave His Son! How deeply in earnest was the Son when He gave His life! You may play with these things if you dare, but God never will. You may sprinkle this blood upon the threshold where it should never fall and trample on it with careless feet, but God only sees it in the place of honor—on the lintel and the side posts—and looks upon it as something precious beyond all price! Sinner, you, perhaps, think that God will not really forgive you and that His promises may only charm your ears to cheat your heart—but it cannot be so!

God is in real earnest! If He did not mean mercy, He would not have given up His beloved Son. The best possession of all His unsearchable riches was His Only-Begotten and He took Him from His bosom, where He had dwelt serenely always and bade Him come below that He might live and die that we might be saved! God is in death-earnest for the salvation of sinners! Let us speak of the great Atonement which He has provided with earnest hearts, for it is no light thing. I wish that we never thought about these things without the deepest possible solemnity. I wish that never did a preacher speak of them without heart-breaking emotions and that never did we sing a hymn upon the great Sacrifice without prostrating our spirits in the dust before the Most High. Whenever we think of the Atonement, the place whereon we stand is holy ground. The blood of the Everlasting Covenant proved the earnestness of the great Covenant-Maker—let us be in earnest, too.

Next, it displayed the supreme love of God to man. Seeing that He entered into a compact of Grace with man, He would let man see how His very heart went forth with every word of promise and, therefore, He gave up that which was the center of His heart, namely, Jesus Christ. When Jesus wept over the grave of Lazarus, they said, "Behold how He loved him!" But when God gave His Only-Begotten to bleed over the grave of our race, we may more heartily say, "Behold how He loved us!" Brothers and Sisters, we have but a faint idea of how much the Lord our God loves us! "God commends His love toward us in that, while we were yet sinners, Christ died for us."

There was nothing lovable in us—we were enemies to God, polluted and polluting! There was everything in us that was obnoxious to the holy mind of God and yet, because of the riches of His Grace and the supremacy of His mercy, He would love us and He did love us without limit! Passing by fallen angels, the Sovereign Lord looked on the humbler creature, man, and so loved him that He gave up Jesus, Himself, to die on his behalf! Oh that we were touched with some kind of tenderness towards God when we think of this! Man, has God shown such love to man and do you show such coldness to your God? Jesus dies in unutterable agonies that the guilty may be pardoned and do the guilty turn aside as if it were nothing to them that Jesus should die? Can men treat the Cross as if it were either a fiction or a trifle? God has manifested His love in the death of Christ in a way which must have astonished every inhabitant of Heaven—and it ought to ravish every native of this lower globe! May the Holy Spirit enable us, as we think of this blood of the Covenant, to behold the earnestness of God and to admire the intensity of His love.

The blood of the Covenant, next, speaks to us and confirms the Divine faithfulness. The main object of thus sealing the Covenant with blood is to cause it to be "ordered in all things and sure." Men, in old times, when they made compacts that were intended to be solemnly observed, slaughtered certain beasts as a sacrifice and, when blood was thus spilt, there was no drawing back from the engagements. It was a covenant made by cutting or dividing–they split the animals in two and then those who made the covenant passed in between the divided pieces. No revocation was permitted where agreements were thus ratified. It was a sort of registered contract that never could be changed when once there had been a sacrifice to confirm it.

Now it is also so with the Covenant of Grace. It is impossible for God to ever draw back from the Covenant of Grace, or to change it in any of its particulars. He needed not to be held in this manner, for He cannot lie– but that we might have strong consolation who have fled for refuge to Christ Jesus, He has been pleased to give His Covenant this seal. Well do we sing–

"The Gospel bears my spirit up!
A faithful and unchanging God
Lays the foundation for my hope,
In oath and covenant and blood."

It would be blasphemy to suppose that God would be false to a treaty sealed with the blood of His own Son! A doubt about the love of God and about the faithfulness of God is treason against Him, for it impugns His faithfulness and treats Him as a liar, or a covenant-breaker, which He can never be. We may think lightly of the dark mistrusts and suspicions of our hearts, but they are no light things, after all, for they virtually impugn the sealing power of the blood and question the faithfulness of God to the Covenant which has most solemnly been confirmed.

Oh you that seek after peace through Jesus Christ, it is not possible that God should refuse to accept you if you come to Him through the blood of Jesus, for that were to break His Covenant! Oh you who are resting in

Jesus, it is not possible that your Father should ever forsake you, or suffer you to perish, for that were to make the blood-shedding of Christ to be void and His Sacrifice to be of no effect! Oh, blessed Covenant, how sure you are, now that the blood of Jesus is shed! But the blood of the Everlasting Covenant is more than this—it is a guarantee to us of its infinite provision. There can be nothing lacking for a soul redeemed by Christ between here and Heaven, for He that spared not His own Son, how shall He not, with Him, also freely give us all things? All that the Christian needs on the road to Glory will be quite inconsiderable compared with what He has already received in the gift of Jesus Christ!

Do you believe that God will deny you any necessary thing, O Heart, when He has already made His Son bleed for you? If He had held back anything, it would have been that costly alabaster box of His Son's body which contained the most precious ointment that ever perfumed earth or Heaven! But since He broke that precious casket and poured out the priceless contents, He will deny you nothing! No good thing will He withhold from you! He would break up Heaven, itself, if you should require it and pour out the whole creation at your feet if there were need. Already He has given you His angels to be your servitors and His courts to be your dwelling place! Yes, and His Throne to be your shelter—what else do you need? But, if you ask for more, there is more provided, for He gives you Himself to be your portion. Is not this enough? Is not this all? When He gave you His Son, He gave you all, for His Son is One with Him! Oh, the breadth and length, the height and depth of Covenant provisions! That roll of love which has for its seal this precious thing, the blood of Jesus, must contain treasures beyond all estimate. God will supply all our needs according to His riches in Glory by Christ Jesus and the blood of Jesus secures this fact!

I will not dwell longer upon this blood of the Covenant except to say that this blood manifests the depth of the need which the Covenant was meant to meet. Many preachers, nowadays, seem determined to bring everything in God's Word down to their own little scale. They carry a ruler in their pockets with which to measure up eternal things. They have found out that everlasting does not mean unending—they will one day find out, I dare say–that infinite does not mean unlimited! Sin with them is an inconsiderable offense which it is not worth while to make a fuss about. Man, according to their child–the errors of a poor creature who cannot help making mistakes. Of course the punishment of sin, with them, is frittered away and they claim to do this in the name of benevolence, as if it were benevolence to flatter and a good deed to make sin appear less hazardous and to take away the moral sanctions which God has set as barriers against evil.

It follows, in the nature of things, that the Atonement becomes, with them, a very shadowy affair–something or other which in some way or other reconciles us to God, or has some bearing upon our standing with the Divine Being. Nobody knows quite what it is–a misty, hazy, smoky nothing, which they cannot quite deny–but which they forget as much as possible. Brothers and Sisters, I believe in a great Revelation and, to my mind, it is clear that if God, Himself, must become Incarnate and if when He is Incarnate nothing else will do but that He must be nailed to a Cross and die like a felon–there must have been some awful mischief to remove! The race of man must have fallen, indeed, to need such an expedient as this in order to restore it to holiness and God! If I measure the disease by the Remedy, I conclude that the disease must have been deadly! And if, when Christ stood in man's place, being perfectly innocent–if nothing else would do as the substitutionary pain but that He should cry, "My God, My God, why have You forsaken Me?"–then the desert of sin must have been dire, indeed!

In the presence of Calvary and its Christ I am persuaded that sin must be an evil so great that it is not possible to exaggerate its horrors! Oh sons of men, your transgressions are black, indeed, since they can only be expiated by such a sacrifice! Oh sinful creatures, you required a dying God to save you! You cannot be safe for eternity, you cannot be happy with God in this life unless the precious blood of Jesus Christ washes you! Deceive not yourselves with the notion that perhaps your moralities and your outward religiousness may suffice, or that your good intentions may be liberally interpreted! You must, if you would be acceptable with God, feel the sprinkling of the blood of the Son of God, for without shedding of blood there is no remission of sins! This much comes to us as the teaching of the blood of the Everlasting Covenant—if we are in covenant with God we shall know the power of the Atonement of Christ.

II. But now, secondly, you will bear with me while I take our translator's own words—"This is THE BLOOD OF THE TESTAMENT." Upon the whole, our translation is as nearly perfect as we can look for a human work to be. I do not know what the new translation will turn out to be, but the good men will have to have risen up very early and sat up very late if they have produced a version which will surpass that which has so long been used among us. I do not know. I cannot tell because I have not seen it. But this translation very well satisfies me at present and I notice that whenever the translators use a word which is disputed by scholars, they have excellent reasons for it and the more the matter is looked into, the more is their judgment valued.

They thought a good deal before they settled on their expressions and as a rule they came to a sound conclusion. In this case there are reasons and very good reasons, why the word, "testament," should be used. Our translators were not inspired, but they were marvelously guided and directed when they made this version and we may be content to take the text as it stands before us. Jesus Christ has made a will and He has left to His people large legacies by that will. Now, wills do not need to be sprinkled with blood, but wills do need that the testator should be dead, otherwise they are not of force. As it was not possible that Christ should die other than a violent death, seeing He must die as a Sacrifice, the expression, "blood," becomes, in His case, tantamount to, "death."

And so, first of all, the blood of Jesus Christ on Calvary is the blood of the Testament, because it is a proof that He is dead and, therefore, the testament is in force. If there is a question about whether a man is alive or not, you cannot administer to his estate, but when you have certain evidence that the testator has died, then the will stands. So is it with the blessed Gospel—if Jesus did not die, then the Gospel is null and void!

Not without the sprinkled blood does the promise of salvation become yes and amen! Inasmuch as the soldier with a spear pierced His side and forthwith came blood and water, there was the clearest evidence in that blood that Jesus was really dead and that His testament is valid and operative. Therein do we rejoice, for though we sorrow that He died, yet we are glad that His legacy of love is all our own! He has died and lives again, no more to die!

Out of the thick cloud of blackest grief which veils our dying Lord, there falls a silver shower of peace more refreshing than all the brooks of earth can yield–the certainty of our eternal life is proven by the certainty of Jesus' death! His blood is the blood of the Testament because it proves the testator's death. It is the blood of the Testament, again, because it is the seal of His being seized and possessed of those goods which He has bequeathed to us, for, apart from His Sacrifice, our Lord had no spiritual blessings to present to us–His death has filled the treasury of His Grace. He has pardon to bestow and justifying righteousness to give because He died! If He had not shed His blood, He would not have completed His part of the Covenant, nor have fulfilled the will of God. But when He died, with, "It is finished!" upon His lips, then His blood became the seal that Covenant mercies were His own and that they were His to leave to us. Oh treasure up the death of Jesus in your hearts, Believers, for, inasmuch as He has enriched you and given you all things necessary for this life of godliness, He has done this out of His own proper stores which were given Him as the reward of His passion!

The blood of the Testament, again, is a direction as to His legatees. We see who are benefited under His will. To whom did Jesus Christ leave, by will, the blessings of Grace? He must have left them to the guilty because He has left a will that is signed and sealed in blood and blood is for the remission of sin. Jesus has made His testament in the character of a sinatoning Sacrifice and we can only share in it by regarding Him under that character. If I am not a sinner, I have no interest in the legacy of a bleeding Redeemer! The blood-mark proves that the testament was made for those who need atonement by blood and that its legacies are bequeathed to sinners. This is one of the most humbling and yet most blessed of all the Truths of God. It casts down and yet lifts up!

If I have any Grace or any Covenant blessing, it did not come to me because I was heir to it by nature, or because I had purchased it, or because of any intrinsic right in myself—but because Jesus, when He died, had a right to make His will as He pleased and He did so make it that He would give Himself and all that He had to such a poor, needy, empty, lost and guilty sinner as I am! Not because of any good in us do these blessings come to us, but all of our Lord's good will, who made the Testament of Love and sealed it with His heart's blood! Brethren, the legatees in Christ's will are those who come and accept His Atonement. There is nothing in Christ's will for any person who will not trust His blood. I know of no mercy under Heaven for any man who, knowing of the atoning Sacrifice, willfully refuses it!

Certain teachers talk about a "larger hope." I read nothing of this fancy in the Scriptures and I dare not go beyond the Word of the Lord and I am content to say with Moses, "The secret things belong unto the Lord our God; but those things which are revealed belong unto us and to our children forever." "Other foundation can no man lay than that which is laid, which is Jesus Christ." Other hopes, large or small, I know not of from Revelation, except this one—"He that believes in Him is not condemned." "The blood of Jesus Christ, His Son, cleanses us from all sin." "He that believes in Him has everlasting life, but he that believes not is condemned already, because he has not believed in the name of the Only-Begotten Son of God."

Thus, the blood of the Testament is a direction as to the legatees. And, as I said before, what an index it is of the value of the legacies, since even the seal upon the will is no less in value than the heart's blood of the heir of all things! What treasures must be ours under such a Covenant! What riches are yours and mine, my Brothers and Sisters, if we are really trusting in Jesus!

III. But now, in the third place, I must speak for a minute or two upon that blood from another point of view. IT WAS THE BLOOD OF CLEANSING. "This is the blood of the Testament which God has enjoined unto you." Moses sprinkled with blood both the tabernacle and all the vessels of the ministry–the object of the sprinkled blood was to purify so that the Book and the people and all things upon whom the blood fell might be allowed to stand in the Presence of the thrice holy God, being regarded by Him as cleansed. Think of this for a short time. This blood of the Covenant or of the Testament is a blood of purification to us. Wherever it is accepted by faith, it takes away all past guilt. Wonder of wonders! Years of sin vanish in a moment–encrustations of guilt disappear in a single instant and man, up to now guilty and condemned–is rendered perfectly clean in God's sight and accepted in the Beloved because he believes in Christ Jesus!

So priceless a Sacrifice as that of the Son of God is of boundless efficacy for the eternal removal of all evil once and for all. And this is but the beginning of our purification, for that same blood applied by faith takes away from the pardoned sinner the impurity which had been generated in his nature by habit. He ceases to love the sin which once he delighted in–he begins to loathe that which was formerly his choice joy. A love of purity is born within his nature–he sighs to be perfect and he groans to think there should be about him tendencies towards evil. Temptations which once were welcomed are now resisted. Habits which were once most fascinating are an annoyance to his spirit. The precious blood, when it touches the conscience, removes all sense of guilt and when it touches the heart it kills the ruling power of sin!

The more fully the power of the blood is felt, the more does it kill the power of sin within the soul. I hope you are feeling it to be so. We ought to be ashamed, Brothers and Sisters, if we allow those sins to conquer us, now, which overcame us years ago! We ought to possess a growing strength against iniquity, a growing abhorrence of everything that is evil and a growing likeness to Christ–and it will be so if this precious blood is really operating upon our nature and imparting to it a fullness of life–

"The Cross once seen is death to every vice
Else He that died there suffered all His pain,
Bled, groaned, agonized and died in vain."

If you are in any measure failing as to holiness, fly to the blood for help! Perhaps you have not thought enough, of late, of the dying love of your Lord. His death has a living power about it to breed and nourish holiness within you. Remember there is no slaying sin but by nailing it to the Cross. Only the lance which pierced the heart of Jesus can kill the love of sin. You must overcome through the blood of the Lamb—there is no other way for victory!

You will never avoid sin merely by believing it to be your duty to do so—the Law points the way, but cannot bear us along it. A sense of the great love of Christ to you in bearing your sin in His body on the Cross and so removing it from you will give you power to rise superior to temptation. It is charged against some of us, as preachers, that we do not urge men enough to their duties. We deny the charge and yet we claim that we do better, for we touch secret springs that nerve to duty and we point to the strength by which virtuous deeds are done! The acceptance of the Atonement is the great source of virtue. The Grace of God is seen in the Atonement of Jesus, by which sin is put away and thus the heart is won to God and led by gratitude to obey Him. The blood of Jesus is the strongest restraint from transgression.

We say to the pardoned—Will you so dishonor the blood which cleanses you as to go and live in sin? Will you go back to that from which you have been redeemed by the death of your Savior? Will you roll, again, in that foul mire out of which Christ has lifted you and so do despite to the blood which cleanses you and make it to be to you as an unholy thing? It must not be! Let but the heart feel the power of the blood of Jesus and it will growingly aspire after holiness and increasingly seek it! The precious blood is our great security from backsliding, for by it we obtain daily access to God! It keeps the Christian from grievous relapses and preserves him unto the coming of his Lord. Wherever the blood of Jesus Christ is really applied, perfection must be its ultimate result. There will be battling and striving, but there must be victory before long! The holier a man becomes, the more he mourns over his unholiness.

The operations of Grace in his soul make him detect the more readily the motions of sin in his members. There is not the sin within him that there was, but he sees that which is there more clearly and, therefore, he is more than ever grieved about it. No one calls himself so much a wretched man because sin is within him as he does who is also a thankful man, because God gives him the victory. You must not judge that you are not growing in sanctification because you are not increasing in your sense of it. Your sense of your own holiness is a poor test, a very doubtful index of your state. Brothers and Sisters, if you have really fixed your trust in the atoning blood and known its power, you are destined to perfection and all the devils in Hell cannot keep you from it! As sure as you believe, you shall one day stand white-robed among the host that know no discord in their song, no wandering in their walk!

From this spot where I have preached the Word I must, as a Believer, rise to a higher spot where I shall prove the power of Jesus' blood in an immortality of perfection! And from that pew where you sit, believing in the precious blood, you, also, must pass onward through your pilgrimage until you, also, reach the fullness of eternal life, for your Lord has pledged Himself to keep all those whom the Father has given Him and you are among them if, indeed, you believe in Him! Those who are justified shall also be glorified! All Believers shall yet dwell at the right hand of the Majesty in the heavens where there is pleasure forevermore because there is perfection without alloy! May we all, through the Spirit, by the blood of purging be made whiter than snow!

IV. And then, to close, it is THE BLOOD OF DEDICATION. On the day when Moses sprinkled the blood of the Covenant on the people and on the Book, it was meant to signify that they were a chosen people set apart unto God's service. The blood made them holiness unto the Lord. Moses stood upon an elevated place and took the scarlet wool and hyssop and sprinkled the blood on all sides. Try and realize a part of the scene, A man just beneath him is wearing a white robe and a spot of blood has fallen upon it. He sees it. There it is! Will he not prize the crimson sign? I would have preserved that robe as long as I lived and the blood spot, too!

But what would it mean? To the Israelite it meant consecration to God. He would say, "The blood of the Covenant has fallen upon me and I am, therefore, a consecrated man dedicated to God." Now, unless the blood is upon you, my Brother or Sister, you are not saved! But if you are saved, you are, by that very fact, set apart to be God's servant. "You are not your own, you are bought with a price." "You were not redeemed with corruptible things as with silver and gold, but with the precious blood of Christ." A saved man is a bought man—the property of Jesus! Believer, not a hair on your head belongs to you—you belong to Jesus Christ as His servant as surely as you are redeemed by His blood! Now you are set apart! God's own mark is put upon you!

You have believed—that believing has applied the blood to you and you are Christ's. Cannot you see the private token which the Lord has set on you? Do you not feel it? Oh, then, acknowledge its claims in your daily life! Being so set apart, you are, therefore, ordained with due solemnity to be a servant of God, even as Aaron and his sons were consecrated to their priesthood. I have been sometimes asked, "Were you ever ordained?" Yes, I was. Not by the laying on of the hands of any mortal man, but by that precious blood whose purchase-power I feel. When that blood fell upon me and I rejoiced in its cleansing power, I longed, at once, to tell of its efficacy to others. I hope I can say most honestly to my Lord –

"Ever since by faith I saw the stream
Your flowing wounds supply,
Redeeming love has been my theme,
And shall be till I die!"

That same blood has fallen on you, Brother, Sister, and it has ordained you that you should go and bear fruit and that your fruit should remain. Is it not written, "You were slain and have been made unto our God kings

153

and priests"? The slaying of Christ is the ground of our priesthood and the claim for our perpetual service. Let us praise, forever, the Lord who has worked everlasting redemption for us! If we have not Milton's power of song, at least let us come to the same resolve at which he arrived–

"O unexampled love! Love nowhere to be found less than Divine!
Hail, Son of God, Savior of men, Your name
Shall be the copious matter of my song
Henceforth and never shall my harp Your praise
Forget, nor from Your Father's praise disjoin."

Because of all this we are to lead a separated life. It is not for us to live as others live who walk in the vanity of their minds. We are not to seek the world's pleasures. We are not to besmear ourselves with its folly and its selfishness. God's people, if they act as they should, are a separated people. It is written, "The people shall dwell alone, they shall not be numbered among the nations." The Lord has set apart him that is godly for Himself and as the shepherd marks his sheep, so, with the precious blood of Christ applied by faith, has God marked His own elect, that they should abide in Christ and go no more out, no more mingling with the sons of men, nor joying in their joys, nor serving their lusts.

The Lord's portion is His people and His cry to them is, " Come you out from among them and be you separate." God give you to feel this blood of the Covenant, this blood of the Testament, this blood of cleansing, this blood of the setting apart, for Jesus Christ's sake. Amen.

THE SPRINKLING OF THE BLOOD OF THE SACRIFICE

"And the priest shall dip his finger in the blood, and sprinkle of the blood seven times before the Lord, before the veil of the sanctuary. And the priest shall put some of the blood upon the horns of the altar of sweet incense before the Lord, which is in the tabernacle of the congregation; and shall pour all the blood of the bullock at the bottom of the altar of the burnt offering, which is at the door of the tabernacle of the congregation."
Leviticus 4:6, 7

I HAVE preached, before, to you upon the types of our Lord's Sacrifice– the subject is as large as it is important. We began with the laying of the hands upon the offering and we went on to the all-important matter of the slaying of the victim Now we come to the use which was made of the blood of the sacrifice after it had been slain. In thinking upon this subject, I seem to hear a voice saying to me, "Put off your shoes from off your feet, for the place whereon you stand is holy ground." This is the central mystery of our religion. It becomes us to be reverent in heart as we approach it. The Doctrine of Substitution is the heart of the whole matter–our whole heart needs to be awakened while we speak upon it. The Son of God, Himself, assuming human nature and, in that Nature bleeding and dying in our place, is the Revelation of Revelation, the wonder of wonders, the Glory of the glorious God! Solemnity and awe may well fill us while we meditate on such a theme.

Oh, that the Spirit of God may rest upon us now! May His melting power be over this vast assembly! May the speaker feel it and may the hearers experience it, so that we may, with one consent, in spirit and in truth, look to Him who, by the Eternal Spirit, offered up Himself without spot unto God! The sacrifices under the Law of God were varied according to the uppermost thoughts in the offerers' minds and their peculiar conditions before God. A burnt offering, a peace offering, or a sin offering might be brought, according as men wished to give unto the Lord, to have fellowship with Him, or to confess their sin to Him. There was a sacrifice specially arranged for the anointed priest, another for all

155

the congregation, another for a ruler and yet another for one of the common people—in truth the typical sacrifices all pointed to the one Great Sacrifice, but they indicated various marks and characteristics of the undivided Lamb of God.

The victims varied from a bullock or a lamb down to a pair of turtle doves or two young pigeons. We take different views of the Sacrifice of Christ according to our capacity to see it, but all these views may be quite in accordance the Truth of God, for the Atonement is many-sided and operates in many directions. The Levitical types represent the different views which believing minds take of our Lord Jesus Christ. They set forth but one Christ, but that one Christ from various standpoints. The mercy is that the Sacrifice of our Lord Jesus is suitable to you and equally suitable to me—and to all that come to Him by faith. The rich, the poor, the brave, the timid, the amiable and the immoral all find, in Jesus, that which fits their individual case. You may be a person of great mind and profound thought, but you shall find, in Jesus, all that your high intelligence can desire! I may be a person of slender education and of narrow powers of thought, but I shall find the Lord Jesus humbling Himself to my limited capacity.

The manna is said, by the rabbis, to have pleased every man's taste and, even so, the Christ of God is every man's Christ, so that no man who comes to Him shall be disappointed, but each shall find His needs supplied. Each man shall find his case perfectly met by the Savior's Atonement, as much so as if Jesus were prepared for that man, only—as if that man were the only sinner under Heaven—or Jesus a Redeemer sent to him, alone, of all the family of man! Oh, the depth of the wisdom and of the Grace of God in the Person and work of our Lord Jesus Christ! Note particularly, with great interest, that there were sacrifices provided for sins of ignorance under the Law—therefore we safely conclude that a sin of ignorance is a sin. There is not that intensity of evil in a sin of ignorance which is to be seen in willful, deliberate transgression, but still, there is sin in it—for no law can allow ignorance to be an excuse for trespass since it is the duty of the subject to know the law. Even if I do that which is wrong with a sincere wish to do right, still, my wrong act has a measure of sin in it. No amount of sincerity can turn injustice into righteousness, or transform falsehood into truth.

You can illustrate this by the stern facts of Nature. Certain inventors have thought that they could fly and they have, in perfectly honest faith, leaped from a lofty crag. But their honest belief has not saved them from the result of violating the law of gravity–they have fallen to the ground– and have been dashed in pieces just as surely and terribly as if they had felt no real belief in their powers of flight. If a man partakes of a deadly poison believing it to be a health-giving medicine, his sincerity will not hinder the natural course of Nature–he will die in his error. It is precisely so in the moral and spiritual world. Sins committed in ignorance must be, still, sins in the sight of the Lord, or else no expiation would have been provided for them. Without shedding of blood, there is no remission even for sins of ignorance!

Paul persecuted the saints ignorantly, but he thereby incurred sins which required to be washed away–so Ananias told him and so he felt–for he called himself the chief of sinners because he persecuted the Church of God. When the people sinned through ignorance and the thing was hid from the eyes of the assembly, they were to bring an offering as soon as the sin was known. If you have transgressed ignorantly, my Brothers and Sisters, the time may come when you will find out that you were sinning– and it will then rejoice your heart to find that the Lord Jesus has made Atonement for your sins before you knew them to be sins! I am greatly rejoiced to think there should be such a Sacrifice provided, since it may yet turn out that the larger number of our sins are sins of which we have not been aware because our heart has prevented our discovering our error. You may have sinned and have no conscience of that sin at this present time–yes, and you may never have a conscience of that particular offense, in this world–yet it will be sin all the same.

Many good men have lived in an evil habit and remained in it unto death–and yet have not known it to be evil. Now, if the precious blood of Jesus only put away the sin which we perceived in detail, its efficacy would be limited by the enlightenment of our conscience and, therefore, some grievous sin might be overlooked and prove our ruin. But inasmuch as this blood puts away all sins, it removes those which we do not discover as well as those over which we mourn. "Cleanse You me from secret faults" is a prayer to which the Expiation of Christ is a full answer. The Atonement acts according to God's sight of sin and not according to our sight of it, for we only see it in part, but God sees it all and blots it all out.

When we discover our iniquity, it is ours to weep over it with true and deep repentance. But if there are some sins which, in detail, we have not discerned and, consequently, have not, by a specific act of repentance, confessed them separately, yet, for all that, the Lord puts away our sin, for it is written, "The blood of Jesus Christ His Son cleanses us from all sin." Those unknown sufferings of Christ which the Greek Liturgy mentions so wisely, have put away from us those unknown sins which we cannot confess in detail because we have not yet perceived them. Blessed be God for a Sacrifice which cleanses away, forever, not only our glaring faults, but those offenses which the most minute self-examination has not yet uncovered!

After the blood had been spilt by the killing of the sacrifice and thus atonement had been made, three several acts were to be performed by the priest—we have them described in our text—and if you will kindly look, you will see that very much the same words follow in the 17 th verse, where, with somewhat less detail, much the same act is set forth. "And the priest shall dip his finger in the blood and sprinkle it seven times before the Lord, before the veil of the sanctuary. And the priest shall put some of the blood upon the horns of the altar of sweet incense before the Lord, which is in the tabernacle of the congregation; and shall pour all the blood of the bullock at the bottom of the altar of the burnt offering, which is at the door of the tabernacle of the congregation."

All this is symbolic of the work of the Lord Jesus and the manifold effects of His blood. There were three things—first, "the priest shall dip his finger in the blood and sprinkle it seven times before the Lord, before the veil of the sanctuary." This represents the atoning sacrifice in its reference to

God. Next, "The priest shall put some of the blood upon the horns of the altar of sweet incense before the Lord." This sets forth the influence upon the offering of intercessory prayer. Thirdly, we read, "He shall pour all (the rest) of the blood of the bullock at the bottom of the altar of the burnt offering." This displays the influence of the blood of Christ on all our service for the Lord. Oh, for the Spirit's power to us to show the things of Christ!

We begin with THE SACRIFICE OF CHRIST IN ITS RELATION TO THE LORD GOD OF ISRAEL.

In the type before us the prominent thing before God is the blood of atonement. No mention is made of a meat offering, or a drink offering, or even of sweet spices upon the golden altar—the one conspicuous object is blood. This was sprinkled before the Lord before the veil of the Most Holy place. I am well aware that some persons cry out, "The preacher continually talks about blood and, this morning, from the first hymn to the last, he has brought before us constant allusions to blood. We are horrified by it!" I wish you to be horrified for, indeed, sin is a thing to shudder at—and the death of Jesus is not a matter to be treated lightly! It was God's intent to awaken in man a great disgust of sin by making him see that it could only be put away by suffering and death.

In the Tabernacle in the wilderness, almost everything was sanctified by blood. The purple drops fell, even, on the Book and all the people. The blood was to be seen everywhere. As soon as you entered the outer court you saw the great bronze altar—and at the base of it bowls of blood were constantly being poured out! When you passed the first veil and entered the Holy Place, if you saw a priest, he was spattered from head to foot with blood—his snow-white robes bringing the crimson spots most vividly before your eyes. If you looked around, you saw the horns of the golden altar of incense smeared with blood—and the gorgeous veil which hid the innermost sanctuary was bedewed with a frequent sprinkling of the same! The holy tent was by no means a place for sentimentalists—its emblematic teachings dealt with terrible realities in a boldly impressive manner—its ritual was not constructed to gratify the taste, but to impress the mind!

It was not a place for dainty gentlemen, but for broken-hearted sinners. Everywhere, the ignorant eye would see something to displease–but the troubled conscience would read lessons of peace and pardon! Oh, that my words would cause triflers with sin to be shocked at the abominable thing! I would have them filled with horror of that detestable thing which cannot be put away except by that which is infinitely more calculated to shock the instructed mind than rivers of the blood of bulls and of goats–I mean the sacrifice of God's own Son–whose soul was made an offering for sin!

The blood of the sacrifice was sprinkled before the veil seven times, signifying this–first, that the Atonement made by the blood of Jesus is perfect in its reference to God. All through the Scriptures, as you well know, seven is the number of perfection, and in this place it is doubtless used with that intent. The seven times is the same as once and for all–it conveys the same meaning as when we read, "For Christ also has once suffered for sins." And again, "We are sanctified through the offering of the body of Jesus Christ once." It is a complete act. In this text we understand that the Lord Jesus offered unto the justice of God an absolutely complete and satisfactory Atonement by His vicarious suffering and death for guilty men. There is no need of further offering for sin. "It is finished." He has purged our sins! In old times–before the coming of our Lord–the veil hung darkly between the place of God's glorious Presence and His worshipping people. It was only lifted for a moment, once a year, and then that only one of all living men might enter into the Holy of Holies for a brief time–the way into the Holiest not yet being made manifest. But still, the blood was sprinkled towards the place where the Glory of God was pleased to dwell indicating that access to Him could only be by the way of the blood.

Albeit that modern thought will contradict me, I shall not cease to assert perpetually that the greatest result of the death of the Lord Jesus was Godward. Not only does He reconcile us unto God by His death and turn our enmity into love, but He has borne the chastisement of our peace, and thus magnified the Law and made it honorable. God, the Judge of

All, is enabled without the violation of His justice to pass by transgression, iniquity and sin. The blood of the sin offering was sprinkled before the Lord because the sin was before the Lord. David says–"Against You, You only, have I sinned," and the prodigal cries, "I have sinned against Heaven and before you." The Sacrifice of Christ is so mainly a Propitiation before God, so thoroughly a vindication of Divine Righteousness, that this one view of the Atonement is sufficient for any man, even if he obtains no other!

But let him beware of trusting to a faith which does not look to the great Propitiation! This is the soul-saving view–the idea which pacifies conscience and wins the heart! We believe in Jesus as the Propitiation for sin. The lights which stream from the Cross are very varied, but as all the colored rays are found in the white light of day, so all the varied teachings of Calvary meet in the fact that Jesus suffered for sin–the Just for the unjust! Do not your hearts feel glad to think that the Lord Jesus Christ has offered a perfect Atonement, covering all, removing every obstacle to the mercy of God–making a clear way for the Lord most justly to justify the guilty? No man need bring anything more, or anything of his own with which to turn away the anger of God–he may come just as he is–guilty and defiled, and plead this precious blood which has made effectual Atonement for him. O my Soul, endorse the doctrine! Feel the sweet experiences that flow from it and stand, now, in the Presence of God without fear–for seven times has the blood spoken for you unto God!

Note next, that not only is the Atonement, itself, perfect, but that the presentation of that Atonement is perfect, too. The sevenfold sprinkling was typical of Christ, as a Priest, presenting Himself unto the Father as a Sacrifice for sin. This has been fully done. Jesus has, in due order, carried the Propitiation into the sanctuary and appeared in the Presence of God on our behalf. Here are the Apostle's own words, "by His own blood He entered in once into the Holy Place, having obtained eternal redemption for us." It is not our presenting of the blood, but Christ's presenting of the blood which has made the Atonement–even as it is not our sight of the blood, but Jehovah's sight of it which causes us to escape–as it was written concerning the Passover, "When I see the blood, I will pass over you." Jesus at this moment sets His Atonement within view of a righteous God and, therefore, the Judge of all the earth is able to look on the guilty with eyes of mercy! Let us rest perfectly satisfied that all we require to bring us near to God has been done for us–and we may now come boldly unto the Throne of the heavenly Grace–

"No longer far from God, but now,
By precious blood made nigh,
Accepted in the Well-Beloved
Near to His heart we lie."

We now pass on to a few thoughts about ourselves in relation to this type. This sevenfold sprinkling of the blood upon the veil meant that the way of our access to God is only by virtue of the precious blood of Christ. Do you ever feel a veil hanging between you and God? In very truth, there is none, for Jesus has taken it away through His flesh. In the day when His blessed body was offered up, the veil of the Temple was torn in two from the top to the bottom, showing that there is now nothing to divide the Believer from his God. But still, if you think there is such a separating veil; if you feel as if the Lord had hidden Himself; if you are so despondent that you are afraid you will never draw near to the Mercy Seat, then sprinkle the blood towards the Throne of Grace–cast it on the very veil which appears to conceal your God from you! Let your heart go towards God, even if you cannot reach Him, and let this blood go before you, for rest assured nothing can dissolve obstacles and furnish you with an open access to God except the blood of Jesus Christ the Son of God!

Rest assured that you are already come unto God if boldly, yes, even if timidly with trembling finger, you do but sprinkle the blood in the direction which your faith longs to take! If you cannot present the Atonement of Christ, yourself, by the firm hand of an undaunted faith–remember, Christ's own hand has presented the Propitiation long before–and, therefore, the work will not fail because of your feebleness! O that by a simple confidence in the Lord, your Redeemer, you may, this day, by His

Grace, imitate the example of the priest under the Law, for Jesus makes you a priest by the Gospel! You may now look towards the Lord and plead that all-prevailing blood which makes us near, who were once afar off! I have often admired that blessed Gospel precept, "Look unto Me, and be you saved, all the ends of the earth," for suppose I cannot see, yet if I look, I have the promise of being saved! If there should be a mist and a cloud between me and the bronze serpent, yet if I look that way I shall be healed! If I cannot clearly discern all the glories of my Lord and Savior, yet if I look with the glance of trust, blessed be God, He saves me!

Turn, then, your half-opened eyes which only at one corner admit light! Turn them, I say, Godward and Christward—and know that by reason of the atoning blood you are saved! The blood-spattered way is the only one which a sinner's feet can traverse if he would come to God! It is easy, plain and open. See, the priest had the Gospel at his fingertips—at every motion of his hand, he preached it, and the effect of such preaching remained wherever the drops found a resting place!

I further think that the blood was sprinkled on the veil seven times to show that a deliberate contemplation of the death of Christ is greatly for our benefit. Whatever else you treat lightly, let the Sacrifice of Calvary be seriously considered again and again—even unto seven times let it be meditated on! Read the story of our Lord's death in the four Evangelists and ponder every detail till you are familiar with His griefs. I would have you know the story by heart, for nothing will heart about sin—and pray to God for enlightenment that you may see the exceeding greatness of His Grace to us in Christ Jesus! Oh, that you may with all your heart believe in the Lamb of God! Angels desire to look into these things, therefore, I pray you, do not neglect so great a salvation! Think lovingly of the atoning Sacrifice. Earnestly consider it a second time, do it a third time, do it a fourth time, do it a fifth time, do it a sixth time, do it a seventh time!

Remember, too, that this sets out how great our guilt has been, since the blood must be sprinkled seven times before the work of Atonement is fully seen by you. Our guilt has a sevenfold blackness about it and there must be a sevenfold cleansing. If you plead the blood of Jesus once and you do not obtain peace thereby, plead it again! And if the burden still lies upon your heart, still go on pleading with the Lord the one prevailing argument that Jesus bled! If for the present you do not gain peace through the blood of the Cross, do not conclude that your sin is too great for pardon, for that is not the fact since, "all manner of sin and blasphemy shall be forgiven unto men." A fuller acquaintance with Him who has made peace by His blood will calm the tempest of your mind. Christ is a great Savior for great sinners and His precious blood can remove the blackest spots of iniquity. See it sprinkled seven times for a seven-times polluted sinner and rest your soul on Him though seven devils should have entered into you! God, who bids us forgive unto 70 times seven, sets no limit to His own forgiveness.

Reflect that if your case seems to yourself to be very difficult, it is provided for by this sevenfold sprinkling of the blood. If you say, "My heart is so hard! I cannot make it feel." Or if you say, "I am so frivolous and foolish I seem to forget what I once knew," then continue to look to the blood of Jesus and draw hope from it even to seven times. Do not go away from that, I charge you—where else can you go? The devil's desire will be to keep you from thinking about Christ, but remember, thoughts about anything else will do you very little good. Your hope lies in thinking about Jesus, not about yourself! Masticate and digest such a text as this every morning—"He is able to save them to the uttermost that come unto God by Him." Go to bed at night with this verse upon your tongue, "The blood of Jesus Christ His Son cleanses us from all sin." Or this, "Him that comes unto Me I will by no means cast out."

That dear man of God, Mr. Moody Stuart, somewhere tells us that he once talked with a woman who was in great trouble about her sins. She was a well-instructed person and knew the Bible thoroughly, so that he was in a little difficulty what to say to her, as she was so accustomed to the all-saving Truth of God. At last he urged upon her, very strongly, that passage, "This is a faithful saying, and worthy of all acceptation, that Jesus Christ came into the world to save sinners," and he noticed that she seemed to find a quiet relief in a gentle flow of tears. He prayed with her and when she rose from her knees, she seemed much comforted. Meeting her the next day and seeing her smiling face—and finding her full of rest in the Lord—he asked, "What was it that worked you deliverance?" "Oh," she said, "it was that text, 'Jesus Christ came to save sinners.'" "Did you not know that before?" asked Mr. Stuart. Yes, she knew the words before, but she found that in her heart of hearts she had believed that Jesus came to save saints and not sinners!

Do not many awakened persons abide in the same error? Well, I want you, poor troubled heart, yes, and you, also, who are of a joyful spirit, to keep on with this sevenfold presentation of the Sacrifice of Christ unto God. And even if a veil should hang between you and the Lord, I beg you to continue to sprinkle the veil with blood until, before the eyes of your faith, the veil tears in two and you stand in the Presence of your reconciled God, rejoicing in Christ Jesus!

II. Our second head is this—THE BLOOD IN ITS INFLUENCE UPON PRAYER. "The priest shall put some of the blood upon the horns of the altar of sweet incense before the Lord." The priest, in this case, goes from the inside of the Holy Place towards the outer court, having dealt with the veil of the Holy of Holies. He turns round and finds close at his side the altar of incense made of gold and surmounted with a golden crown—to this he goes deliberately and places a portion of the blood upon each of its horns. Horns signify power and the explanation of the symbol is that there is no power in intercessory prayer apart from the blood of expiation.

Remember, first, that the intercession of Christ Himself is based upon His Atonement. He is daily pleading before the Throne of God and His great argument is that He offered Himself without spot unto God. It seems to me most clear and blessed that our Lord Jesus makes this the main plea with the Father on our behalf—"I have finished the work which You gave Me to do." He has suffered in our place and every day He pleads these sufferings for us. His blood speaks better things than that of Abel. He seeks no new plea, but always urges this old one—His blood shed for many for the remission of sins. "It pleased the Father to bruise Him," and now it pleases the Father to hear Him! The bruised spices of His passion are an incense of sweet smell and derive a double acceptance from the blood-smeared altar upon which they are presented.

And now take the type to yourselves. You and I are to offer incense upon this golden altar by our daily intercession for others, but our plea must always be the atoning blood of Jesus. I pray you, dear Friends, to urge this much more than you have been accustomed to do in your prayers. We are to cry to God for sinners and we are to cry to God for saints—but the sacrifice of Jesus must be our strength in petitioning. Intercession is one of the most excellent duties in which a Christian can be engaged—it has about it the honor both of priesthood and kingship. The incense altar ought to be continually smoking before the Lord God of Israel, not only in our public Prayer Meetings, but in our private supplications. We should be continually pleading for our children, for our friends, for our neighbors, for those who are hopeful and those who seem hopeless. But the great plea must always be, "By Your agony and bloody sweat! By Your Cross and passion."

Offer sweet spices of love, faith and hope, and lay on the burning coals of strong desire. But on the horn of your altar smear the blood—

"Blood has a voice to pierce the skies!
'Revenge,' the blood of Abel cries.
But the rich blood of Jesus slain
Speaks, 'Peace' as loud from every vein."

Take care you never advance another plea, or if another, let it be very subsidiary to this master reason. We may say, "O Lord, save men because their immortal souls are precious. Save them that they may escape from endless misery and that they may display the power of Your Grace. Save them, also, that Your Word may not return unto You void, and that Your Church may be built up by their means." But we must never be content with these pleas! We must go on to plead the name of

Jesus, for whatever we ask in that name we shall receive. He who once poured out His soul unto death and now makes intercession for the transgressors, will see to it that our pleas shall not be rejected! In all our intercessions we must remember Calvary–the incense altar, for us, must, on the horn of its strength, be always sprinkled with the blood!

And, dearly Beloved, as this must be the plea of our intercession, so it must be our impulse in making intercession. When we pray, we come, as it were, to this golden altar and we look thereon–what do we see? Stains of blood! We look again, and again see crimson spots, while all the four horns are red with blood. Did my Lord pour out His soul unto death for men and shall not I pour out my soul in living earnest when I pray? Can you now bow your knee to plead with God and not feel your heart set upon the good of men when you see that your Lord has laid down His life that they may be saved? Cold prayers and dull pleas would vanish if we would but remember how Jesus loved–how being in an agony He sweat, as it were, great drops of blood.

Brothers and Sisters, we are sadly blameworthy for neglect of intercessory prayer! I cannot tell how much of a blessing is being withheld because we do not pray importunately for our fellow men! May the Lord awaken us! May He never permit us to neglect the precious use of the Mercy Seat! When the late Dr. Bacchus was ill and near to death, a surgeon visited him. And as he left the room, he was observed to speak to the servant. The good old Divine begged the attendant to tell him what the surgeon said. After some pause, he said, "Dear Sir, he told me not to leave you, for you could not live more than another half-hour." "Then," said the saint, "help me out of bed, let me get upon my knees and spend my last half hour on earth in praying for the Church of God and for the salvation of men."

What a blessed way of spending one's last half-hour! Let me rather say–what a blessed way of spending half-anhour at any time! Try it this afternoon! I do not know any method of benefiting our friends which is more constantly open to us all than that of intercessory prayer. And I cannot give you a better argument for why you should use it than this–

your Lord has sprinkled the golden altar of intercession with His own blood! Where He poured out His blood, will you not pour out your tears? He has given His bleeding heart for men—will not you give your pleading lips?

I think, too, I must say that this smearing of the horns of the altar with blood is meant to give us very great encouragement and assurances whenever we come to God in prayer. Never give anybody up, however bad he may be. If you know a man that is as much like the devil as two peas in a pod, still have hope for him, because when you come to the golden altar to offer your prayers on his behalf what do you see? Why, there is the blood of Christ! What sin is there which it cannot remove? "Oh," you ask, "did Jesus die for sinners like this man and shall I despair of him and, therefore, refuse to pray tion—and this arises out of our narrow views of our Lord Jesus. I pray you enlarge your ideas of God's mercy and of Christ's power to cleanse! Pray not with a phantom hope, but with solid confidence, and say, "Lord, I do but follow with my tears where You have been with Your blood. I am pleading for this man's pardon and You are also making intercession for transgressors. I am pleading for those whom You have bought with Your blood and, therefore, I am confident that my desire is in consonance with Your will and that I shall be heard in Heaven, Your dwelling place."

When we pray, let us with vehement desire plead the blood of Jesus Christ! Perhaps fewer petitions and more urging of the merit of Christ would make better prayers. If we were shorter in what we ask for but longer in pleading the reason why we should obtain it, we might prevail more easily. I suggest that we use fewer nails, but take care that those nails are driven in with Calvary's blood-stained hammer and clenched with this argument—"For Jesus' sake." May this sort of prayer be used by all of us in private and in public—and then we must and shall prevail!

III. Time flies too quickly this morning and, therefore, I must pass over many things I had thought to dwell upon. The last point is, THE BLOOD IN ITS INFLUENCE UPON ALL OUR SERVICE. You see we have been coming outwards from the veil to the golden altar and now we pass

168

outside the Holy Place into the outer court. And there in the open air stands the great bronze altar—the first object that the Israelite saw when he entered the sacred precincts. As soon as he entered into the first enclosure, his eye lighted upon the great altar of brass upon which burnt offerings were burned and oblations were presented unto the Lord. It was at the foot of this bronze altar that the bowls of blood were continually poured out—so that the altar was encrimsoned with it—and the soil around was soaked with the sanguine flood.

That altar represents a great many things and among the rest of them, our Lord Jesus presenting Himself to God as an acceptable Sacrifice. Whenever you think of our Lord as being an offering of a sweet smell unto God, never dissociate that fact in your mind from His being slain for sin, for all our Lord's service is tinged by His atoning death. It is a great mistake, when you are trying to explain any one of the Levitical sacrifices to run entirely upon one line, for there is a blessed union of all of them in Christ. The offerings of a sweet savor were, all of them, in a sense, sin offerings—there are clear indications of this. At the same time the sin offering was not altogether an abomination, but, in part, a sweet savor offering, for the fat, as we have seen in our reading, was presented upon the altar. What God has joined together let no man put asunder. You may look at your Lord under various headings and separately think of His life and of His death—but never stereotype even that division, for His death was the climax of His life—and His life was necessary to His death. Always think of Jesus, in all your meditations upon Him, as presenting Himself to God and pouring out His soul unto death by way of atonement. When I see that great bronze altar, I do not forget how our Lord was accepted of God, but when I see the floods of blood at the foot of the altar, I am reminded of the fact that, "He His own self bore our sins in His own body on the tree."

Viewing the type in reference to ourselves, let us learn that whenever we come to offer any sacrifice unto the Lord, we must take care that we present it by virtue of the precious blood of Christ. The worship of this morning—God knows our hearts—He knows how many have really adored Him. And He knows, out of those who worship, how many of us have presented our sacrifice, thinking only of the merit of Jesus as the reason why it should be received. When you rise from your knees after your morning prayer, have you really pleaded the precious blood? Your petitions will not be acceptable to God if you have not. When you are praying at eventide and speaking with your heavenly Father, have you your eyes upon Christ? If not, your devotion will be rejected.

As it is with worship in the form of prayer, so is it with worship in the form of praise. Sweet sounds are very delightful when we sing the praises of God, but unless the altar is blood-stained upon which we lay our Psalms and hymns, they will not be accepted for all their music! We also bring to God our gifts as He prospers us. I trust we are all ready to give Him a portion of our substance—but do we present it upon the altar which sanctifies the giver and the gift? Do we see the blood of Christ upon it and present our gold and silver through that which is more precious by far? If not, we might as well keep our money. When you go, this afternoon, to your Sunday school classes, or go out into the streets to preach, or go round with your tracts, will you present your holy labor to God through the precious blood? There is but one Altar on which He will accept your services—that Altar is the Person of His dear Son—and in this matter Jesus must be viewed as pouring out His blood for us.

We must view the Atonement as connected with every holy thing. I believe that our testimonies for God will be blessed of God in proportion as we keep the Sacrifice of Christ to the forefront. Somebody asked our Brother, Mr. Moody, how it was that he was so successful. And he is said to have replied, "Well, if I must tell you, it is, I believe, because we come out fair and square upon the Doctrine of Substitution." In that remark he hit the nail on the head. That is the saving doctrine! Keep that before your own mind. Keep it before the minds of those whom you would benefit. Let the Lord see that you are always thinking of His dear Son.

And, Beloved, do you not think that this pouring of the blood at the foot of this bronze altar indicates to us how much we ought to bring there? If Jesus has brought His life, there, and laid Himself thereon, ought we not to bring all that we are and all that we have—and consecrate all to God? Let us not offer a lean, scraggy sacrifice, or one that is half dead, or broken, or diseased—but let us bring our best at its best—and cheerfully present it unto the Most High through the precious blood of Christ. One said of a young man who had lately joined the Church, "Is he O and O?" And another answered, "What do you mean by that?" "Why," said the first, "I mean—Is he out and out for Christ? Does he give himself—spirit, soul and body, to Jesus?" Surely, when we see the altar with Christ Himself upon it and His blood poured out there, we must acknowledge that if we could spend our whole life in zealous labor, and then die a martyr's death, we should not have rendered even half what such amazing love deserves! Let us be stimulated and quickened by the sight of the blood upon the bronze altar!

Lastly, you notice the blood was poured out at the bottom of the altar. What could that mean but this—that the altar of thank offering stood upon and grew out of a basis of blood. So all our deeds for God and our sacrifices for His cause must spring out of the love which He has manifested in the death of His dear Son. We love Him because—you know the "because"—because He first loved us. And how do we know that He loves us? Behold the death of Jesus as the surest proof! I long to put my whole being upon that altar and I should feel, as I did so, that I was not giving my God anything, but only rendering to Him what His dear Son has bought a million times over by once shedding His life-blood! When we have done all, we shall be unprofitable servants and we shall say so. All that we have given to God has been presented out of gratitude for the fact that God so loved us that He gave His only-begotten Son to die for us that we might live through Him.

Load the altar! Heap it high! Let sacrifices smoke thereon, for it is built upon God's unspeakable Gift! When sin is removed, service is accepted—"then shall they offer bullocks upon Your altar." Attempt no offering of your own works till then, for unpardoned sinners bring unaccepted offerings! First, let the blood be recognized and let the full Atonement be rejoiced in. Service rendered to God with a desire for personal merit is abominable in His sight. But when our merit is all found in the Divine Person of His Son, then will He accept us and our offering, too, in Christ Jesus! God grant unto you, dear Hearers, to be accepted in the Beloved. Amen.

THE BLOOD OF SPRINKLING (FIRST SERMON)

"And to Jesus the Mediator of the New Covenant, and to the blood of sprinkling, that speaks better things than that of Abel. See that you refuse not Him who speaks. For if they escaped not who refused Him who spoke on earth, much more shall we not escape, if we turn away from Him who speaks from Heaven."
Hebrews 12:24, 25

WE are joyfully reminded by the Apostle that we have not come to Mount Sinai and its overwhelming manifestations. After Israel had kept the feast of the Passover, God was pleased to give His people a sort of Pentecost and more fully to manifest Himself and His Law to them at Sinai. They were in the wilderness with the solemn peaks of a desolate mountain as their center. And from the top, thereof, in the midst of fire, blackness, darkness, tempest and, with the sound of a trumpet, God spoke to them. "The earth shook, the heavens also dropped at the presence of God: even Sinai itself was moved at the presence of God, the God of Israel." We have not come to the dread and terror of the Old Covenant, of which our Apostle says in another place, "The covenant from the Mount Sinai gave birth to bondage" (Gal 4:24). Upon the Believer's spirit there rests not the slavish fear, the abject terror, the fainting alarm which swayed the tribes of Israel, for the manifestation of God which he beholds, though not less majestic, is far more full of hope and joy! Over us there rests not the impenetrable cloud of apprehension–we are not buried in a present darkness of despair, we are not tossed about with a tempest of horror and, therefore–we do not exceedingly fear and quake. How thankful we should be for this! Israel was privileged in receiving a fiery Law from the right hand of Jehovah, but we are far more favored, since we receive "the glorious Gospel of the blessed God."

Our Apostle next tells us what we have come to. I suppose he speaks of all the saints after the death and resurrection of our Lord and the descent of the Holy Spirit. He refers to the whole Church, in the midst of which the Holy Spirit now dwells. We have come to a more joyous sight

173

than Sinai and the mountain burning with fire. The Hebrew worshipper, apart from his sacrifices, lived continually beneath the shadow of the darkness of a broken Law—he was often startled by the tremendous note of the trumpet which threatened judgment for that broken Law—and thus he always lived in a condition of bondage. To what else could the Law bring him? To convict of sin and to condemn the sinner is its utmost power! The Believer in the Lord Jesus Christ lives in quite another atmosphere. He has not come to a barren crag, but to an inhabited city, Jerusalem above, the metropolis of God! He has left the wilderness for the land which flows with milk and honey and the material mount which might not be touched for the spiritual and heavenly Jerusalem! He has entered into fellowship with an innumerable company of angels who are to him, not cherubim with flaming swords to keep men back from the tree of life, but ministering spirits sent forth to minister to the heirs of salvation!

He is come to the joyous assembly of all pure intelligences who have met, not in trembling, but in joyous liberty, to keep the feast with their great Lord and King. He thinks of all who love God throughout all worlds and he feels that he is one of them, for he has come to "the general assembly and Church of the First-Born, which are written in Heaven." Moreover, he has come "to God the Judge of All," the Umpire and Rewarder of all the chosen citizens who are enrolled by His command, the Ruler and Judge of all their enemies. God is not to them a dreadful Person who speaks from a distance—He is their Father and their Friend in whom they delight themselves—in whose Presence there is fullness of joy for them!

Brothers and Sisters, our fellowship is with the Father, our God! To Him we have come, through our Lord Jesus Christ. Moreover, in the power of the Spirit of God we realize the oneness of the Church both in Heaven and earth—and the spirits of just men made perfect are in union with us. No gulf divides the militant from the triumphant! We are one army of the living God! We sometimes speak of the holy dead, but there are none such—they live unto God—they are perfected as to their spirits even now and they are waiting for the moment when their bodies, also, shall be raised from the tomb to be again inhabited by their immortal souls. We no longer shudder at the sepulcher, but sing of resurrection! Our condition of heart, from day to day, is that of men who are in fellowship with God, fellowship with angels, fellowship with perfect spirits.

We have also come to Jesus, our Savior, who is All and in all. In Him we live! We are joined unto Him in one spirit; He is the Bridegroom of our souls, the delight of our hearts. We are come to Him as the Mediator of the New Covenant. What a blessed thing it is to know that Covenant of which He is the Mediator! Some in these days despise the Covenant, but saints delight in it. To them the Everlasting Covenant, "ordered in all things, and sure," is all their salvation and all their desire. We are covenanted ones through our Lord Jesus! God has pledged Himself to bless us. By two Immutable things wherein it is impossible for Him to lie, He has given us strong consolation and good hope through Grace, even to all of us who have fled for refuge to the Lord Jesus. We are happy to live under the Covenant of Grace, the Covenant of Promise, the Covenant symbolized by Jerusalem above which is free and the mother of us all!

Then comes the last thing of all, mentioned last, as I shall have to show you, for a purpose. We have come "to the blood of sprinkling." On that first day at Sinai no blood of sprinkling was presented, but afterwards it was used by Divine order to ratify the national Covenant which the tribes made with Jehovah at the foot of the hill. Of that Covenant the Lord says, "which My Covenant they broke, although I was an husband unto them." He never broke His Covenant, but they broke it, for they failed to keep that condition of obedience, without which a Covenant founded upon works falls to the ground. We have come to the blood of sprinkling which has fallen upon a Covenant which never shall be broken, for the Lord has made it to endure though rocks and hills remove! This is called by the Holy Spirit, "a better Covenant which was established upon better promises." We have come to the Covenant of Grace, to Jesus the Mediator of it and to His blood which is the seal of it!

Of this last we are going to speak at this time—"The blood of sprinkling which speaks better things than that of Abel." I shall need, this morning, to occupy all the time with what I regard as only the first head of my discourse. What is it? "The blood of sprinkling." It will be our duty, afterwards, to consider where we are—"we have come unto this blood." And, thirdly, to remember, what then? "See that you refuse not Him who speaks."

FIRST, WHAT IS IT? What is this "blood of sprinkling?" In a few words, "the blood of sprinkling" represents the pains, the sufferings, the humiliation and the death of the Lord Jesus Christ which He endured on the behalf of guilty man. When we speak of the blood, we wish not to be understood as referring solely or mainly to the literal material blood which flowed from the wounds of Jesus. We believe in the literal fact of His shedding His blood, but when we speak of His Cross and blood, we mean those sufferings and that death of our Lord Jesus Christ by which He magnified the Law of God. We mean what Isaiah intended when he said, "He shall make His soul an offering for sin." We mean all the griefs which Jesus vicariously endured on our behalf at Gethsemane, Gabbatha and Golgotha—and especially His yielding up His life upon the tree of scorn and doom. "The chastisement of our peace was upon Him, and with His stripes we are healed." "Without shedding of blood there is no remission of sins" and the shedding of blood intended is the death of Jesus, the Son of God!

Remember that His sufferings and death were not only apparent, but true and real—and that they involved an incalculable degree of pain and anguish. To redeem our souls, cost our Lord an exceedingly sorrowfulness, "even unto death." It cost Him the bloody sweat, the heart broken with reproach and especially the agony of being forsaken of His Father till He cried, "My God, My God, why have You forsaken Me?" Our Mediator endured death under the worst possible aspects, bereft of those supports which are, in all other cases of godly men, afforded by the goodness and faithfulness of God. His was not merely a natural death, but a death aggravated by supernatural circumstance which infinitely intensified its woe! This is what we mean by the blood of Christ–His sufferings and His death.

These were voluntarily undertaken by Himself out of pure love to us and in order that we might, thereby, be justly saved from deserved punishment. There was no natural reason on His own account why He should suffer, bleed and die. Far from it–"He, only, has immortality." But out of supreme love for us, that man might be forgiven without the violation of Divine rectitude, the Son of God assumed human flesh and became in very deed, a Man, in order that He might be able to offer in man's place a full vindication to the righteous and unchangeable Law of God. Being God, He thus showed forth the wondrous love of God to man by being willing to personally suffer rather than the redeemed should die as the just result of their sin! The matchless majesty of His Divine Person lent supreme efficacy to His sufferings. It was a Man that died, but He was also God and the death of Incarnate God reflects more Glory upon Law than the deaths of myriads of condemned creatures could have done. See the yearning of the great God for perfect righteousness! He had sooner die than stain His Justice even to indulge His Mercy! Jesus the Lord, out of love to the Father and to men, undertook willingly and cheerfully, for our sakes, to magnify the Law and bring in perfect righteousness. This work was so carried out to the utmost that not a jot of the suffering was mitigated, nor a particle of the obedience foregone– "He became obedient unto death, even the death of the Cross." Now He has finished transgression, made an end of sin and brought in everlasting righteousness, for He has offered such an Expiation that God is just and the justifier of him that believes. God is at once the righteous Judge and the infinitely loving Father through what Jesus has suffered.

Brothers and Sisters, though I have said that there was no reason why the Son of God should bleed and die on His own account, yet towards us there was a reason. Our Lord, from of old, in the Everlasting Covenant was constituted the Head and Representative of all who were in Him. And so, when the time came, He took the place, bore the sin and suffered the penalty of those whom the Father gave Him from before the foundations of the world! He is as much the representative Man as the first Adam was the representative man. And, as in Adam the sin was committed which ruined us, so in the second Adam the Atonement was made which saves us. "As in Adam all die, even so in Christ shall all be made alive." There was no other Person so fit to undertake the enterprise of our redemption as this second Man, who is the Lord from Heaven! He properly, but yet most generously and spontaneously, came and shed His precious blood in the place of sinners to bring the guilty near to God.

But the text does not merely speak of the blood shed, which I have explained to you, but of, "the blood of sprinkling." This is the Atonement applied for Divine purposes and especially applied to our own hearts and consciences by faith. For the explanation of this sprinkling we must look to the types in the Old Testament. In the Old Testament the blood of sprinkling meant a great many things. In fact, I cannot just now tell you all that it meant. We meet with it in the Book of Exodus, at the time when the Lord smote all the first-born of Egypt. Then the blood of sprinkling means preservation. The basin filled with blood was taken, a bunch of hyssop was dipped into it and the lintel and the two side posts of every house tenanted by Israelites were smeared with the blood. And when God saw the blood upon the house of the Israelite, He bade the destroyer pass that family by and leave their first-born unharmed. The sprinkled blood meant preservation—it was Israel's Passover and safeguard.

The sprinkled blood very frequently signified the confirmation of a covenant. So is it used in Exodus 24, which I read to you just now. The blood was sprinkled upon the Book of the Covenant and also upon the people, to show that the Covenant was, as far as it could be, confirmed by the people who promised, "All that the Lord has said will we do." The blood of bulls and of goats in that case was but a type of the sacrificial blood of the Lord Jesus Christ. The lesson which we learn from Exodus 24 is that the blood of sprinkling means the blood of ratification or confirmation of the Covenant, which God has been pleased to make with men in the Person of our Lord Jesus Christ. Since Jesus died, the promises are Yes and Amen to all Believers and must assuredly be fulfilled. The Covenant of Grace had but one condition and that condition Jesus has fulfilled by His death, so that it has now become a Covenant of pure and unconditional promise to all the seed.

In many cases the sprinkling of the blood meant purification. If a person had been defiled, he could not come into the sanctuary of God without being sprinkled with blood. There were the ashes of a red heifer laid up and these were mixed with blood and water. And by their being sprinkled on the unclean, his ceremonial defilement was removed. There were matters incident to domestic life and accidents of outdoor life which engendered impurity—and this impurity was put away by the sprinkling of blood. This sprinkling was used in the case of recovery from infectious disease, such as leprosy. Before such persons could mingle in the solemn assemblies, they were sprinkled with the blood and thus were made ceremonially pure. In a higher sense this is the work of the blood of Christ. It preserves us, it ratifies the Covenant and wherever it is applied, it makes us pure, for "the blood of Jesus Christ, His Son, cleanses us from all sin." We have our hearts sprinkled from an evil conscience, for we have come unto the obedience and sprinkling of the blood of Jesus Christ.

The sprinkling of the blood meant, also, sanctification. Before a man entered upon the priesthood, the blood was put upon his right ear, on the big toe of his right foot and on the thumb of his right hand, signifying that all his powers were thus consecrated to God. The ordination ceremony included the sprinkling of blood upon and round about the altar. Even thus has the Lord Jesus redeemed us unto God by His death and the sprinkling of His blood has made us kings and priests unto God forever. He is made of God unto us, sanctification, and all else that is needed for the Divine service.

One other meaning of the blood of the sacrifice was acceptation and access. When the High Priest went into the Most Holy Place once a year, it was not without blood, which he sprinkled upon the Ark of the Covenant and upon the Mercy Seat, which was on the top thereof. All approaches to God were made by blood. There was no hope of a man drawing near to God, even in symbol, apart from the sprinkling of the blood! And now, today, our only way to God is by the precious Sacrifice of Christ. The only hope for the success of our prayers, the acceptance of our praises, or the reception of our holy works is through the ever-abiding merit of the atoning Sacrifice of our Lord Jesus Christ! The Holy Spirit bids us enter into the Holy of Holies by the blood of Jesus—there is no other way!

There were other uses besides these, but it may suffice to put down the sprinkling of the blood as having these effects, namely, that of preservation, satisfaction, purification, sanctification and access to God. This was all typified in the blood of bulls and of goats, but actually fulfilled in the great Sacrifice of Christ.

With this as an explanation, I desire to come still closer to the text and view it with great care, for to my mind it is singularly full of teaching. May the Holy Spirit lead us into the Truth of God which lies herein like treasure hid in a field!

First. The blood of sprinkling is the center of the Divine Manifestation under the Gospel. Observe its innermost place in the passage before us. You are privileged by almighty Grace to come first to Mount Zion, to climb its steeps, to stand upon its holy summit and to enter the city of the living God, the heavenly Jerusalem. In those golden streets, surrounding the hallowed shrine, you behold an innumerable company of angels. What a vision of Glory! But you must not rest here, for the great general assembly, the festal gathering, the solemn convocation of the enrolled in Heaven is being held and all are there in glad attire, surrounding their God and Lord! Press onward to the Throne of God, itself, where sits the Judge of all, surrounded by those holy spirits who have washed their robes and, therefore, stand before the Throne of God in perfection.

Have you not come a long way? Are you not admitted into the very center of the whole Revelation? Not yet. A step further lands you where stands your Savior, the Mediator, with the New Covenant. Now is your joy complete! But you have a further object to behold. What is in that innermost shrine? What is that which is hidden away in the Holy of Holies? What is that which is the most precious and costly thing of all, the last, the ultimatum, God's grandest Revelation? The precious blood of Christ, as of a lamb without blemish and without spot—the blood of sprinkling! This comes last—it is the innermost truth of the dispensation of Grace under which we live. Brothers and Sisters, when we climb to Heaven, itself, and pass the gate of pearl, and wend our way through the innumerable hosts of angels and come even to the Throne of God and see the spirits of the just made perfect and hear their holy hymn—we shall not have gone beyond the influence of the blood of sprinkling! No, we shall see it there more truly present than in any other place.

"What?" you say, "the blood of Jesus in Heaven?" Yes. The earthly sanctuary, we are told, was purified with the blood of bulls and of goats, "but the heavenly things themselves with better sacrifices than these"(Heb 9:23). When Jesus entered, once and for all, into the Holy Place, He entered by His own blood, having obtained eternal redemption for us—so says the Apostle in the 9

th chapter of this Epistle. Let those who talk lightly of the precious blood correct their
view before they are guilty of blasphemy, for the Revelation of God knows no lower deep—this is the heart and center of all. The manifestation of Jesus under the Gospel is not only the Revelation of the Mediator, but especially of His Sacrifice! The appearance of God, the Judge of all, the vision of hosts of angels and perfect spirits do but lead up to that Sacrifice which is the source and focus of all true fellowship between God and His creatures!

This is the character which Jesus wears in the innermost shrine where He reveals Himself most clearly to those who are nearest to Him. He looks like a lamb that has been slain! There is no sight of Him which is more full, more glorious, more complete, than the vision of Him as the great Sacrifice for sin! The Atonement of Jesus is the concentration of the Divine Glory—all other Revelations of God are completed and intensified here. You have not come to the central sun of the great spiritual system of Grace till you have come to the blood of sprinkling–to those sufferings of Messiah which are not for Himself, but are intended to bear upon others, even as drops when they are sprinkled exert their influence where they fall. Unless you have learned to rejoice in that blood which takes away sin, you have not yet caught the keynote of the Gospel dispensation! The blood of Christ is the life of the Gospel! Apart from Atonement, you may know the skin, the rind, the husk of the Gospel–but its inner kernel you have not discovered.

I next ask you to look at the text and observe that this sprinkling of the blood, as mentioned by the Holy Spirit in this passage, is absolutely identical with Jesus, Himself. Read it. "To Jesus the Mediator of the New Covenant, and to the blood of sprinkling, that speaks better things than that of Abel. See that you refuse not Him who speaks." He says it is the blood that speaks and then he proceeds to say, "See that you refuse not Him who speaks." This is a very unexpected turn which can only be explained upon the supposition that Jesus and the blood are identical in the writer's view. By what we may call a singularity in grammar, in putting Him for it, the Spirit of God intentionally sets forth the striking Truth of God that the Sacrifice is identical with the Savior! "We are come to the Savior, the Mediator of the New Covenant, and to the blood of sprinkling that speaks; see that you refuse not Him."

Beloved Friends, there is no Jesus if there is no blood of sprinkling! There is no Savior if there is no Sacrifice! I put this strongly because the attempt is being made, nowadays, to set forth Jesus apart from His Cross and Atonement. He is held up as a great ethical teacher, a self-sacrificing spirit who is to lead the way in a grand moral reformation and, by His influence, to set up a kingdom of moral influence in the world! It is even hinted that this kingdom has never had prominence enough given to it because it has been overshadowed by His Cross! But where is Jesus apart from His Sacrifice? He is not there if you have left out the blood of sprinkling which is the blood of Sacrifice! Without the Atonement, no man is a Christian and Christ is not Jesus! If you have torn away the sacrificial blood, you have drawn the heart out of the Gospel of Jesus Christ, and robbed it of its life! If you have trampled on the blood of sprinkling and counted it a common thing, instead of putting it above you upon the lintel of the door and all around you upon the two side posts, you have fearfully transgressed! As for me, God forbid that I should glory save in the Cross of our Lord Jesus Christ, since to me that Cross is identical with Jesus, Himself!

I know no Jesus but He who died, the Just for the unjust. You can separate Jesus and the blood materially, for by the spear-thrust and all His other wounds, the blood was drawn away from the body of our Lord. But spiritually this "blood of sprinkling" and the Jesus by whom we live, are inseparable! In fact, they are one and indivisible, the same thing, and you cannot truly know Jesus, or preach Jesus, unless you preach Him as slain for sin! You cannot trust Jesus except you trust Him as making peace by the blood of His Cross. If you have done with the blood of sprinkling, you have done with Jesus altogether—He will never part with His mediatorial Glory as our Sacrifice—neither can we come to Him if we ignore that Character! Is it not clear in the text that Jesus and the blood of sprinkling are one? What God has joined together, let no man put asunder. Note this right carefully.

Thirdly, observe that this "blood of sprinkling" is put in close contact with "the New Covenant." I do not wonder that those who are lax in their views of the Atonement have nothing honorable to say concerning the Covenants, Old or New. The Doctrine of the Covenants is the marrow of divinity, but these vain-glorious spirits choose to despise it. This is natural, since they speak slightingly of the Atonement. What covenant is there without blood? If it is not ratified, if there is no sacrifice to make it sure, then is it no covenant in the sight of God or of enlightened men. But, O Beloved, you who know your Lord and follow on to know Him yet better, to you the Covenant of promise is a heritage of joy and His Atonement is most precious as the confirmation of it! To us the sacrificial death of our Lord is not a Doctrine, but the Doctrine! It is not an outgrowth of Christian teaching, but the essence and marrow of it! To us, Jesus, in His Atonement, is Alpha and Omega. In Him, the Covenant begins and ends! You see how it was confirmed by blood. If it is a man's covenant, if it is confirmed, it stands. But this is God's Covenant, confirmed with promises, oaths and blood—and it stands fast forever and ever! Every Believer is as much interested in that Covenant as was Abraham the father of Believers, for the Covenant was made with Abraham and his spiritual seed. And in Christ it is confirmed to all that seed forever by His most precious blood! That, also, is evident enough in the text—fail not to consider it well.

But, fourthly, I want you to notice that according to the text, the blood is the voice of the new dispensation. Observe that on Sinai there was "the sound of a trumpet, and the voice of words, which voice they that heard entreated that the word should not be spoken to them anymore." You look, therefore, under the new dispensation, for a voice, and you do not come to any till you reach the last object in the list—and there, see, "the blood of sprinkling that speaks." Here, then, is the voice of the Gospel! It is not the sound of a trumpet, nor the voice of words spoken in terrible majesty, but the blood speaks and, assuredly, there is no sound more piercing, more potent, more prevailing! God heard the voice of Abel's blood and visited Cain with deserved punishment for killing his brother. And the precious blood of Jesus Christ, the Son of God, cries in the ears of God with a voice which is always heard. How can it be imagined that the Lord God should be deaf to the cry of His Son's Sacrifice? Lo, these many ages the blood has cried—"Forgive them! Forgive them! Accept them! Deliver them from going down into the pit, for I have found a ransom!"

The blood of sprinkling has a voice of instruction to us even as it has a voice of intercession with God. It cries to us, "See the evil of sin! See how God loves righteousness! See how He loves men! See how impossible it is for you to escape from the punishment of sin except by this great Sacrifice in which the Love and the Justice of God equally appear! See how Jehovah spared not His own Son, but freely delivered Him up for us all!"

What a voice there is in the Atonement!—a voice which pleads for holiness and love, for justice and Grace, for truth and mercy. "See that you refuse not Him who speaks."

Do you not hear it? If you take away the blood of sprinkling from the Gospel, you have silenced it! It has no voice if this is gone. "Oh," they say, "the Gospel has lost its power!" What wonder when they have made it a dumb gospel! How can it have power when they take away that which is its life and speech? Unless the preacher is always preaching this blood and sprinkling it by the Doctrine of Faith, his teaching has no voice either to awaken the careless or to cheer the anxious! If ever there should come a wretched day when all our pulpits shall be full of modern thought and the old Doctrine of a Substitutionary Sacrifice shall be exploded, then will there remain no word of comfort for the guilty or hope for the despairing! Hushed forever will be those silver notes which now console the living and cheer the dying! A dumb spirit will possess this sullen world and no voice of joy will break the blank silence of despair. The Gospel speaks through the Propitiation for sin and if that is denied, it speaks no more. Those who preach not the Atonement exhibit a dumb and dummy gospel–a mouth it has, but speaks not–they that make it are like unto their idol!

Let me draw you nearer, still, to the text. Observe, that this voice is identical with the voice of the Lord Jesus, for it is put so. "The blood of sprinkling that speaks. See that you refuse not Him who speaks." Whatever the Doctrine of the Sacrifice of Jesus may be, it is the main teaching of Jesus, Himself. It is well to notice that the voice which spoke from Sinai was also the voice of Christ. It was Jesus who delivered that Law, the penalty of which He was, Himself to endure! He that read it out amidst the tempest was Jesus! Notice the declaration–"Whose voice then shook the earth." Whenever you hear the Gospel, the voice of the precious blood is the voice of Jesus, Himself, the voice of Him that shook the earth at Sinai! This same voice shall, by-and-by, shake not only the earth, but also Heaven! What a voice there is in the blood of sprinkling since, indeed, it is the voice of the eternal Son of God who both makes and destroys! Would you have me silence the Doctrine of the Blood of Sprinkling? Would any one of you attempt so horrible a deed? Shall we be censured if we continually proclaim the Heaven-sent message of the blood of Jesus? Shall we speak with bated breath because some affected person shudders at the sound of the word, "blood?" or some "cultured" individual rebels at the old-fashioned thought of sacrifice? No, verily, we will sooner have our tongue cut out than cease to speak of the precious blood of Jesus Christ! For me there is nothing worth thinking of or preaching about but this grand Truth of God which is the beginning and the end of the whole Christian system, namely, that God gave His Son to die that sinners might live! This is not the voice of the blood, only, but the voice of our Lord Jesus Christ, Himself! So says the text and who can contradict it?

Further, my Brothers and Sisters, from the text I learn another Truth of God, namely, that this blood is always speaking. The text says not, "the blood of sprinkling that spoke," but "that speaks." It is always speaking, it always remains a plea with God and a testimony to men. It never will be silenced, either one way or the other. In the intercession of our risen and ascended Lord, His Sacrifice always speaks to the Most High. By the teaching of the Holy Spirit, the Atonement will always speak in edification to Believers still upon the earth. It is the blood that speaks, according to our text–this is the only speech which this dispensation yields us. Shall that speech ever be still? Shall we decline to hear it? Shall we refuse to echo it? God forbid! By day, by night, the great Sacrifice continues to cry to the sons of men, "Turn from your sins, for they cost your Savior dearly! The times of your ignorance God winked at, but now commands all men everywhere to repent, since He is able to forgive and yet be just. Your offended God has, Himself, provided a Sacrifice–come and be sprinkled with its blood and be reconciled once and for all."

The voice of this blood speaks wherever there is a guilty conscience, wherever there is an anxious heart, wherever there is a seeking sinner, wherever there is a believing mind. It speaks with a sweet, familiar, tender, inviting voice. There is no music like it to the sinner's ear–it charms away his fears. It shall never cease its speaking so long as there is a sinner yet out of Christ–no, so long as there is one on earth who still needs its cleansing power because of fresh backslidings. Oh, hear its voice! Incline your ears and receive its blessed accents! It says, "Come, now, and let us reason together, says the Lord; though your sins are as scarlet, they shall be as white as snow; though they are red like crimson, they shall be as wool."

This part of my discourse will not be complete unless I bid you notice that we are expressly told that this precious blood speaks "better things than that of Abel." I do not think that the whole meaning of the passage is exhausted if we say that Abel's blood cries for vengeance and that Christ's blood speaks for pardon. Dr. Watts puts it–

"Blood has a voice to pierce the skies!
'Revenge!' the blood of Abel cries!
But the dear stream when Christ was slain
Speaks peace as loud from every vein."

That is quite true, but I conceive that it is not all the sense and, perhaps, not even the sense here intended. Revenge is scarcely a good thing, yet Abel's blood spoke good things, or we should hardly read that Christ's blood speaks "better things." What does the blood of Abel speak? The blood of Abel speaks to a complete and believing obedience to God. It shows us a man who believes God and, notwithstanding the enmity of his brother, brings to God the appointed sacrifice of faith, strictly following up, even to the bitter end, his holy obedience to the Most High. That is what the blood of Abel says to me. And the blood of Jesus says the same thing most emphatically. The death of Jesus Christ was the crown and close of a perfect life. It was a fit completion of a course of holiness. In obedience to the Great Father, Jesus even laid down His life. But if this is all the blood of Jesus speaks, as some say that it is, then it does not speak better things than the blood of Abel, for it only says the same things in a louder voice. The martyrdom of any saint has a voice for obedience to God as truly as the martyrdom of Jesus. But the death of our Lord says far more, infinitely more than this! It not only witnesses to complete obedience, but it provides the way by which the disobedient may be forgiven and helped to obedience and holiness. The Cross has a greater, deeper, gladder Gospel for fallen men than that of a perfect example which they are unable to follow!

The blood of Abel said this, too—that he was not ashamed of his faith, but witnessed a good confession concerning his God, even to the death. He put his life in his hands and was not ashamed to stand at the altar of God and avow his faith by obediently offering the ordained sacrifice. Now, I grant you that the blood of Jesus also declares that He was a faithful and true Witness who willingly sealed His witness with His blood. He proved, by shedding His blood, that He could not be turned aside from truth and righteousness, even though death stood in His way. But if that is all that the blood of sprinkling speaks, it says no better things than the blood of Abel. "Be faithful unto death," is the voice of Abel as well as of Jesus. Jesus must have said more than this by his blood-shedding.

The blood of Abel said good things. That is implied in the fact that the blood of Jesus Christ says better things. And no doubt the blood of Abel rises to the dignity of teaching self-sacrifice. Here was a man, a keeper of sheep, who, by his mode of life, laid out his life for the good of those committed to his charge. And at the last, in obedience to God, he yielded himself up to die by a brother's hand. It was the first draught of a picture of self-sacrifice. Our Lord Jesus Christ also made a complete self-sacrifice. All His life He gave Himself to men. He lived never for Himself. The Glory of God and the good of men were united in one passion which filled His whole soul. He could say, "The zeal of Your House has eaten Me up." His death was the completion of His perfect self-sacrifice. But if that were all, the blood of Jesus says no better thing than Abel's death says, though it may say it more emphatically.

Our Lord's blood says "better things than that of Abel." And what does it say? It says, "There is redemption through His blood, the forgiveness of sins according to the riches of His Grace." "He, Himself, bore our sins in His own body on the tree, that we, being dead to sins, should live unto righteousness: by whose stripes we were healed." "He has made Him to be sin for us, who knew no sin; that we might be made the righteousness of God in Him." The voice of the more." "The blood of Jesus Christ, His Son, cleanses us from all sin." Now, my Brothers and Sisters, these are better things than Abel's blood could say and they are what the blood of Jesus speaks to everyone upon whom it is sprinkled by faith! It must be applied to each one of us by faith, or it says nothing to us. But when it falls on each believing individual, it says to him words of blessing which pacify his conscience and delight his soul!

The Apostle says that "You have come to the blood of sprinkling." Is it so? Has that blood of sprinkling ever been applied to you? Do you feel it? Are you preserved? Are you cleansed? Are you brought near to God? Are you sanctified unto God's service by the atoning Sacrifice? If so, then go out and, in firm confidence that never can be shaken, make your glory in the blood of sprinkling! Tell every sinner whom you meet, that if the Lord Jesus washes him, he shall be whiter than snow! Preach the atoning sacrifice of the Lamb of God and then sing of it! Remember that wondrous threefold song in the 5 th chapter of Revelation, where, first of all, the elders and living creatures round about the Throne ofGod sing a new song, saying, "You were slain and have redeemed us to God by Your blood out of every kindred, and tongue, and people, and nation." Then ten thousand times ten thousand and thousands of thousands of angels take up the strain and cry, "Worthy is the Lamb that was slain."

Nor is this all, for the Apostle tells us, "Every creature which is in Heaven, and on the earth, and under the earth, and such as are in the sea, and all that are in them, heard I, saying, Blessing, and honor, and Glory, and power, be unto Him that sits upon the Throne, and unto the Lamb forever and ever." See you not that they all extol the Lord Jesus in His sacrificial Character as the Lamb slain? I have scant patience with those who dare to put this great Truth of God into the background and even sneer at it or misrepresent it on purpose. Sirs, if you would be saved, you must have the blood of Jesus sprinkled upon you! He that believes not in Christ Jesus, in Jesus the Atoning Sacrifice, must perish!

The eternal God must repulse with infinite disgust the man who refuses the loving Sacrifice of Jesus! Inasmuch as he counted himself unworthy of this wondrous Sacrifice, this marvelous Expiation–there remains no other Sacrifice for sin–and nothing for him but that eternal blackness and darkness and thunder which were foreshadowed at Sinai! Those who refuse the Atonement which Wisdom devised, which Love provided and which Justice has accepted, have signed their own death warrant—and none can wonder that they perish!

The Lord lead us to Glory in Christ Crucified! Amen.

THE BLOOD OF SPRINKLING (SECOND SERMON)

"You have come…to Jesus, the Mediator of the New Covenant, and to the blood of sprinkling, that speaks better things than that of Abel. See that you refuse not Him who speaks."
Hebrews 12:24, 25

IN the former part of this sermon the text grew upon me so largely that it was quite impossible to express all its meaning. In as condensed a manner as possible, I explained what was meant by, "the blood of sprinkling," and I also enlarged upon the high position which this precious blood occupies in the Gospel dispensation. But I was obliged to leave, for this second occasion, two practical questions which the text is sure to raise if it is carefully thought upon.

The doctrinal portion of our meditation was greatly blessed to our hearts, for God the Holy Spirit refreshed us thereby—may He now fulfill His sacred office with equal power by revealing the things of Christ to us in a way which shall cause self-examination—and awaken us to give more earnest heed than ever to the voice of Him who speaks from Heaven. No theme can excel in value and excellence that of the precious blood of Jesus! Unless the Holy Spirit shall prepare our hearts, even with such a topic as this before us, we shall not be profited. But if He will show these choice Truths of God to us, we shall be comforted, quickened, edified and sanctified by them.

It is a considerable disadvantage to some of you that you have not heard the former part of the sermon [Sermon #1888, "The Blood of the Sprinkling (First Sermon)] but I hope you will read it at your leisure, and then, if you read this in connection with it, the whole subject will be before you. Not that I can set it all out in words—I only mean that it will be before you as the ocean is before us when we sit on the beach—or as the heavens are before us when we gaze upon Arcturus with his sons. Finite language fails to convey the Infinite and if ever there was a text which deserved to be called Infinite, it is that which is now before us!

Having touched, as with a swallow's wing, the surface of our great theme under the first division of the sermon, I have now to speak with you upon the second, which is this—Where are we with reference to this blood of sprinkling? The text says, "You have come." We have not come to Mount Sinai, but we have come to Mount Zion, to angels and their God, to saints and their Mediator—and to the blood of sprinkling. This having had its share of our thoughts, we are to conclude with the question, What then? If we have come to this blood of sprinkling, what then? The answer is, "See that you refuse not Him who speaks." Let us give to the wondrous Truths of God revealed to us by the sacrifice of Jesus the most earnest heed, that our souls may hear and live. May the Holy Spirit enable us to hear the heavenly voice at this hour! "Faith comes by hearing"—may it come at this time by our reverently hearing the voice of the blood of sprinkling!

II. My business under the second head of my discourse is to answer the question, WHERE ARE WE? I have to explain what is meant by the expression which is found in the 22 nd ndverse with this 24 th and read, "You have come to the blood of sprinkling."

Well, first, you have come to the hearing of the Gospel of the atoning Sacrifice. The Israelites left Egypt and, having passed the Red Sea, they entered the desert and, at length, came to the mount of God, even to Sinai, that terrible mountain! In the valley around that Throne of God they were gathered together in their thousands. What a sight that vast multitude must have been! Probably two millions or more were encamped before the mount. Then, "The Lord came from Sinai and rose up from Seir unto them; He shined forth from Mount Paran; and He came with ten thousands of His saints; from His right hand went a fiery Law for them." Israel crouched in the valley below, subdued by the terrible majesty of the scene and overawed by the trumpet Voice which pealed forth from the midst of the thick darkness. The Lord spoke with them, but their uncircumcised ears could not bear His glorious voice, and they entreated that Moses might act as mediator and speak in God's place.

You and I have not come to such a terrible sight at this hour. No quivering mountain smokes before you, no terrible lightning appalls you, no thunder distresses you—

"Not to the terrors of the Lord,
The tempest, fire, and smoke.
Not to the thunder of that Word
Which God on Sinai spoke.
But we have come to Sion's hill
The city of our God,
Where milder words declare His will
And spread His love abroad."

Among the great things which you are called upon to consider under the Gospel is, "the blood of sprinkling." Count yourselves happy that you are privileged to hear of the divinely appointed way of reconciliation with God! You have come to hear, not of your sin and its doom, not of the last judgment and the swift destruction of the enemies of God—but of love to the guilty, pity for the miserable, mercy for the wicked, compassion for those who are out of the way! You have come to hear of God's great expedient of Wisdom by which He, by the same act and deed condemns sin and lets the sinner live—by which He honors His Law and yet passes by transgression, iniquity and sin! You have come to hear, not of the shedding of your own blood, but of the shedding of His blood who, in His infinite compassion, deigned to take the place of guilty men—to suffer, that they might not suffer—and die, that they might not die!

Blessed are your ears that they hear of the perfect Sacrifice! Happy are your spirits, since they are found where Free Grace and boundless love have set forth a great Propitiation for sin! Divinely favored are you to live where you are told of pardon freely given to all who will believe on the name of the Lord Jesus, as the Lamb of God which takes away the sin of the world! You hear at this hour not Law, but Gospel! Not the sentence of judgment, but the proclamation of Grace! "See that you refuse not Him who speaks." It is no small thing for the Kingdom of God to have come so near unto you. Awake to a sense of your privilege! You

do not sit in heathen midnight, nor in Popish gloom, nor in Jewish mist–
but day has dawned on you–do not refuse the Light of God!

In a better sense, going a little further, we have not only come to the
blood of sprinkling by hearing about it, but we have come to it because
the great God now deals with us upon methods which are founded and
grounded upon the atoning Sacrifice of Christ. If God were to deal with
us upon the terms laid down at Sinai, He need not be long in finding the
"two or three witnesses" to prove that we have broken His Law! We
would be, ourselves, compelled to plead guilty! No witnesses would be
required. Truly, He has not dealt with us after our sins! We are so faulty
that we can draw no comfort from the prospect of judgment by the Law
of God–we appeal to mercy, alone, for on any other ground our case is
hopeless! "This do and you shall live" is a Covenant which brings us no
ray of comfort, for its only word to us is that thunderbolt–"The soul that
sins, it shall die."

By the works of the Law, none can be justified, for by that Law we are all
condemned. Read the Ten Commandments and pause at each one–and
confess that you have broken it either in thought, word or deed.
Remember that by a glance we may commit adultery! By a thought we
may be guilty of murder! By a desire we may steal. Sin is any lack of
conformity to perfect holiness and that lack of conformity is justly
chargeable upon every one of us! Yet the Lord does not, under the
Gospel dispensation, deal with us according to Law. He does not, now,
sit on the Throne of Judgment, but He looks down upon us from the
Throne of Grace! Not the iron rod, but the silver scepter is held over us!
The long-suffering of God rules the age and Jesus, the Mediator, is the
gracious Lord-Lieutenant of the dispensation. Instead of destroying
offending man from off the face of the earth, the Lord comes near to us
in loving condescension and pleads with us by His Spirit, saying, "You
have sinned, but My Son has died. In Him I am prepared to deal with
you in a way of pure mercy and unmingled Grace."

O Sinner, the fact that you are alive proves that God is not dealing with
you according to strict justice, but in patient forbearance! Every moment

you live is another instance of Omnipotent long-suffering. It is the Sacrifice of Christ which holds back the axe of Justice which otherwise must execute you! The barren tree is spared because the great Dresser of the vineyard, who bled on Calvary, intercedes and cries, "Let it alone this year, also." O my Hearer, it is through the shedding of the blood and the mediatorial reign of the Lord Jesus that you are, at this moment, on praying ground and pleading terms with God! Apart from the blood of Atonement you would now be past hope, shut up forever in the place of doom! But see how the great Father bears with you! He stands prepared to hear your prayer, to accept your confession of sin, to honor your faith and to save you from your sin through the Sacrifice of His dear Son!

Through our Lord Jesus, Sovereign Grace and Infinite Love find a free way to the most undeserving of the race! Through the Divine Sacrifice, the Lord says, "Come now and let us reason together: though your sins are as scarlet, they shall be as white as snow." "Believe on the Lord Jesus Christ and you shall be saved." Thus the rebel is treated as a child and the criminal as a beloved one! Because of yonder death on Calvary's cruel tree, God can invite guilty men to come to Him and He can receive them to the bosom of His love. O my dear Hearers, do remember this! I am not sent to scold you, but to woo you! I am not sent to thunder at you, but to let the soft cleansing drops from the heart of Jesus fall upon you! I beg you not to turn away, as men may well do when the tidings are heavy, but listen diligently, for the message is full of joy!

You are now in the house of prayer, addressed by one of the Lord's ambassadors, and the tidings are of peace through a Propitiation which God, Himself, has provided and accepted. We cry not to you, "Prepare for vengeance," but we proclaim, "a God ready to pardon!" We do not threaten that He will no more have mercy upon you, but we tell you that He waits to be gracious. If I had to say, "You have provoked Him past bearing and He now means to destroy you," what a miserable man I would be! How could I bring such evil tidings to my fellow creatures? Then would it have been woe to me that my mother bore me for so hard a fate! Thank God, it is not so! By virtue of the blood of sprinkling the language of boundless Love is heard among our apostate race and we are entreated to acquaint ourselves with God and be at peace!

No, my Hearer, the day of Grace is not over—you have not come to Sinai. No, you are not yet condemned past all hope, for you are still within reach of Jesus, the Mediator! There is forgiveness. The fountain which was opened of old for sin and for uncleanness is still open. If you have sinned like David, if you will but accept the sprinkling of the blood of Jesus, I am able to speak to you as Nathan did to the guilty king and say, "The Lord has put away your sin; you shall not die." At any rate, God is now dealing with you on Gospel terms—he sits on Zion—not on Sinai! He pronounces invitations of Grace and does not utter the stern sentence of Justice!

Further, there is a far more effectual way of coming to the blood of sprinkling than this—when, by faith, that blood is sprinkled upon our souls. This is absolutely needed—the blood shed must become, to each one of us, the blood sprinkled. "How can I know," says one, "that the blood of Christ is upon me?" Do you trust yourself with Christ? Do you believe that He made an atonement on the Cross and will you venture your eternal destiny upon that fact, trusting in what Jesus did and in that, alone? If you do thus trust, you shall not trust in vain! Do you apply your heart to the precious blood of Jesus? Then that precious blood is applied to your heart! If your heart bleeds for sin, bring it to the bleeding heart of Jesus and it shall be healed!

I showed, in the early part of this discourse, that the blood sprinkled on the lintel and the two side posts of the door preserved the Israelites on the night of the Passover—it shall also preserve you. The blood sprinkled upon the defiled made them ceremonially clean—it shall cleanse you. Have I not often quoted those blessed words, "The blood of Jesus Christ, His Son, cleanses us from all sin"? That blood put upon the sons of Aaron dedicated them to God! And if it is applied to you, it shall consecrate you to God and you shall become the accepted servant of the Most High! Oh, what a blessed thing to assuredly know that we have come to the blood of sprinkling by a true and humble faith! Can you say that you rely only on Jesus for salvation? Can you call Heaven and earth to witness that you have no other confidence? Then remember the Words of the Lord—"He that believes in Him has everlasting life. He that believes in Him is not condemned." "Therefore, being justified by faith, we have peace with God."

Are not these words full of strong assurance? Indeed, we have not come to Mount Sinai, the place of trembling, but to Zion, the place which is beautiful for situation, the joy of the earth, the vision of peace, the home of infinite blessedness! Conscience no longer thunders at you for your sins, for your sins are gone! The Expiation has covered them—the sprinkling of the blood has put them all away! Your iniquities are cast into the depths of the sea—God has cast them behind His back! The handwriting of ordinances that was against you, Christ has taken away, nailing it to His Cross, as a record in which there is no more condemning force! The debt is paid, the bill is receipted! Who can lay anything to the charge of God's elect? O Beloved, it is a most blessed thing to come to the blood of sprinkling!—

"The terrors of Law and of God
With me can have nothing to do!
My Savior's obedience and blood
Hide all my transgressions from view."

The act of faith whereby we accept and trust in the Lord Jesus as our Mediator and Sacrifice is the true and effectual coming to the blood of sprinkling. May none of us forget to come! He is the Lamb of God which takes away the sin of the world—and those who come to Him shall be led into full salvation. Have you thus come? If you have not, why do you delay? He says, "Him that comes to Me I will in no wise cast out." Come to Him, for He is calling you! Come to Him, even as you now are, and He will receive you without fail!

Further, to come to this blood of sprinkling means thankfully to enjoy all that comes to us through the blood of sprinkling. I have intruded upon this, somewhat, already. Brothers and Sisters, if you have come to the blood of sprinkling, believe in the full pardon which God has given you and in your consequent peace with God. It is a blessed word in the Creed, "I believe in the forgiveness of sins." Do you believe in the forgiveness of sins? I have seen some of the children of God who have believed in Jesus, but it has been with a faith which did not realize the full blessing promised to them—for they were as troubled about their sins as if they had never been forgiven! Now, a man who receives a free pardon from the Queen and goes his way out of prison, rejoices in that pardon as a reality and, therefore, walks abroad without fear. You must believe in the pardon of God as a reality and act accordingly. If He has absolved you for Jesus' sake, then you are absolved! Why tremble like a guilty wretch waiting for the verdict? Why talk about fearing Divine wrath? If you are pardoned, the deed of Grace is done and can never be undone, for the gifts and calling of God are without repentance on His part. His remission of sin is a clear jail delivery, a sure plea, a full acquittal!—

"Oh, how sweet to view the flowing
Of our Lord's atoning blood,
With Divine assurance knowing
He has made my peace with God!"

I want every child of God, in his inmost soul, to come to the blood of sprinkling by full assurance of his justification and then to go on to enjoy constant access to the Mercy Seat and communion with the Lord God! We may now, with holy boldness, speak with God in prayer, for the Mercy Seat is sprinkled with the blood! O pardoned one, be not backward to enjoy your liberty of fellowship! You are clean through the blood and, therefore, you may enter into the closest communion with the Divine Father! You are consecrated by the blood and, therefore, you may abound in the service of your God! Seeing your sin is pardoned, treat your God as a child would treat a father and be not so awed by His majesty as to be cast down and distressed because of past sin! Take the good that God provides you. Enjoy the peace the blood has bought you. Enter into the liberty that your ransom price has ensured you. Do not stand in feelings, fears and dreams, but come unto this blood of sprinkling and rest there—and be filled with joy and peace through believing! With such a ransom found for you, dream not of going down into the Pit, but ascend with gladness unto the hill of the Lord and stand in His Holy Place!

I think, once more, that this coming to the blood of sprinkling means, also, that we feel the full effect of it in our lives. The man who knows that Jesus shed His blood for him—and has had that blood applied to his conscience—becomes a sin-hating man, consecrated to Him who has cleansed him. "The love of Christ constrains us because we thus judge that if One died for all, then were all dead: and that He died for all, that they which live should not from this day on live unto themselves, but unto Him which died for them, and rose again." I believe that there is no fruitful source of virtue like faith in the precious blood of Jesus! I hope your conduct will always support me in this assertion. Those who are debtors for salvation to their dying Lord should be the most holy of men. You people who think that you will get to Heaven by some other way than by "the blood of sprinkling" have no sure bonds to hold you to holiness. You trust partly to your own works and partly to what Jesus has done. Well, you do not owe Him much and, therefore, you will not love Him much! And, therefore, you will not feel bound to live strict, holy, gracious lives.

But the man who knows that his many sins are all washed away through the blood of Jesus and that thus he is saved—he is the man who will serve the Lord with all his heart! He who has received a finished righteousness and complete salvation is under boundless obligations of gratitude—and the force of these obligations will urge him to a consecrated life. Over him the supreme power of gratitude will exert its sacred influence and he will not only be carefully obedient, but ardently zealous in the service of his Redeemer. We know it is so and we mean to prove it by our daily conduct! Brothers and Sisters, I would have you exhibit more and more of the influence of the precious blood in sanctifying your lives. Are there not Christians who hold the Doctrine of the Atoning Blood and yet are no better than others? Alas, it is so! But it is one thing to hold to a doctrine and another thing for that doctrine to take hold upon your heart and influence your life! Oh, if we believed practically what we profess to believe, what manner of persons should we be in all holy conversation and godliness!

Hear me, my Brothers and Sisters, and answer the appeals I make to you as in the Presence of the Lord. Bloodbought, can you live for yourself? Blood-washed, can you defile your garments? Marked with the King's own name, in the King's own blood—how can you yield yourself to other rulers? God grant that we may come unto the blood of sprinkling till it shall purify our nature and fill us with an all-consuming enthusiasm for Him whose heart was pierced for us!

I ask you, then, to put the question closely home, "Have I come unto this blood of sprinkling? If not, why should I not come at once?" I read the other day an imaginary story which describes the need of looking well to this great business. Receive it as a parable—A little daughter of the house of Israel had heard the commandment concerning the Passover night and, as she lay ill in her bed she cried, "Father, have you sprinkled the blood upon the lintel and the two side posts?" Her father answered, "Not yet, my child. It shall be done." The daughter was distressed and filled with fear. After waiting a little while she again cried, "Father, Father, have you sprinkled the blood upon the door?" He answered carelessly, "Child, I have told Simeon to sprinkle it and I have no doubt it is done." "But, Father," she cried, "it is near midnight and the destroying angel will soon be abroad. Are you sure that the blood is over the door? Jehovah our God has said that we must sprinkle the blood upon the lintel and the two side posts, or else the Destroyer will not pass over us. Father, are you sure it is done?" The father passed over her enquiry. He had been eating of the lamb with his friends and thought that this was sufficient. He did not care to give too much prominence to the ghastly idea of blood. He was of a liberal mind and would not believe that a merciful God would smite his household for so small an omission.

Then his daughter arose from her bed, made strong by the God of Israel. Nothing would content her until she had been outside and seen, for herself, whether the saving mark was over the door of her father's house. It was almost midnight, but by the light of the moon she looked and no blood-mark was there! How great was her distress! "Father," she cried, "make haste and bring the basin." There it stood, filled with blood, for the Paschal Lamb had been slain. The father, at her entreaty, dashed the hyssop into it, struck the lintel and the two side posts and shut the door—and as he did so, the midnight hour arrived. They were saved so as by fire! The daughter's obedient care and reverence of the Lord had warded off the sword of the Destroyer.

Oh that the holy anxiety of someone now present would work the same blessing for other households! Ask, dear child, ask the question, "Father, have you come to the blood of sprinkling? Is the blood of the Lamb above your head, between you and God? Is it on both sides of you, when you come in and go out?" O Soul, be thus anxious about yourself and rest not till you have, by faith, been purged with hyssop and cleansed by the blood of the one Sacrifice for sin!

III. The last part of our subject is this—WHAT THEN? According to our text, the blood of Jesus is the Voice of the new dispensation. It is the blood which speaks and it speaks better things than the blood of Abel. What, then, is our duty? How does the Apostle express our obligation? "See that you refuse not Him who speaks."

I would have a quarter of an hour's very quiet talk with you, without excitement or quibbling debate. Lend me your ears, for I speak in all love for your souls. I want, dear Friends, that this great Truth of the Atonement which I so often preach may have a fair hearing and not be left to lie among the number of forgotten things.

Do not refuse the voice of Jesus by cold indifference. God was made flesh and dwelt among men and, in due time, He took upon Himself our sin and suffered for it in His own body on the tree, that sin might be put away by the Sacrifice of Himself. By His death upon the Cross, our Lord made atonement for the sin of man—and those who believe in Him are delivered from evil and its consequences. The main point is that Jesus died for us, the Just for the unjust. His atoning blood has a voice—"See that you refuse not Him who speaks." The text says see to it; look to it; make sure of it; be careful about it. Do not miss the salvation of your Lord through neglect, for he who dies by neglecting the healing medicine will as surely perish as he who stabs himself! Be in earnest to accept the Savior–I beseech you to do so, for I am afraid that many refuse Him who speaks because they never think of Him, or of His Sacrifice. It seems to me that if I were a young man I would give this matter very early notice. However deeply I might be engaged in business, I would feel that my first concern ought to be to set myself right with God. Other matters would be sure to drop into order if I could be right with the Lord of All! If I heard it said that salvation came by the blood of Christ, I think I would pull myself together and resolve to understand this amazing statement. I would not let it go by me, but would endeavor to reach the bottom of it and understand it practically. I would meditate much upon teaching so wonderful as this–that the Son of God, in man's stead, honored the justice of God by death and so put away sin.

When I was a youth I had a great longing to begin life on right principles. I longed to find deliverance from sin. I would wake up with the sun in summer time to read my Bible and such books as Bunyan's, "Grace Abounding," Baxter's, "Call to the Unconverted," Alleine's, "Alarm" and Doddridge's, "Rise and Progress of Religion in the Soul." In these books I tried to discover the way of salvation, but the chief thing I longed to know was, "How can man be just with God? How can God be just with man and yet put away his sin?" Do you not think that these questions are of high importance? I beg that they may not have the cold shoulder from you. Give this question due space. I know that a great many things demand your attention nowadays, but I claim for this, which is the innermost Revelation of God, that it should have an early and earnest hearing. God Incarnate in Christ Jesus–bleeding and dying for human sin–is a marvel of love too great to be passed over without thought! I pray you, therefore, "refuse not Him who speaks." Do not say, "I pray you, have me excused." I do not suppose that you will become an infidel or act as a blasphemer towards this grand Truth of God. I will not accuse you of denying the fact of the Atonement, but my great fear is lest you should be indifferent to it! If it is so, that God, Himself, has come to earth to bleed and die to save guilty man, it is the greatest, gladdest news that ever came to our poor erring race–and every member of that race should receive it with hopeful attention!

When you resolve to study the Doctrine, do not approach it with prejudice through misapprehension. Those that hate the Gospel of Christ are very busy in caricaturing the Doctrine of the Atonement. They assert that we preach that God was not merciful by nature, but must be appeased by the blood of His own Son. They charge us with saying that Jesus, by His death, made God loving. We distinctly teach the very opposite of that statement! What we do say is this, that God is infinitely loving–that, in fact, God is Love–but that love does not cause Him to be unjust or unholy, for that, in the long run, would not be love. God is the Judge of all the earth and He must do right. The Lord, as the great moral Governor, if He makes a Law and threatens a penalty, must execute that penalty, or else His Law will lose its authority. If the penalty threatened is not executed, there is a tacit acknowledgment that it was threatened in error. Could you believe in a fallible God? The Lord has made a Law which is perfect, just and good.

Would you rather be without Law? What reasonable person desires anarchy? God has backed up that Law with a threat. What is the use of a Law if to break it involves no evil consequences? A government that never punishes offenders is no government at all! God, therefore, as moral Ruler, must be just and must display His indignation against wrong and evil of every kind. It is written on the conscience of men that sin must be punished. Would you have it go unpunished? If you are a just man, you would not. To meet the case, therefore, the Lord Jesus Christ, by Himself bearing the penalty of death, has honored the Divine Law. He has shown to all intelligences that God will not wink at sin, that even His infinite mercy must not come in the way of His justice.

This is the Doctrine–do not listen to those who twist and pervert it. It is the love of God which has provided the great Atonement by which, in a judgment better than ours, the Law finds a glorious vindication and the foundation of moral government is strengthened! Consider this matter and judge it fairly, with candid minds. We assure you from God's Word that apart from the Atonement of our Lord Jesus, you can never be saved either from the guilt or power of evil. You will find no peace for your conscience that is worth having, no thorough and deep peace, except by believing in this atoning Sacrifice! Neither will you meet with a motive strong enough to rescue you from the bonds of iniquity. Therefore, "See that you refuse not Him who speaks." Hear, and your soul shall live! Quibble, and you will die in your sins.

Do not refuse the voice of the Lord Jesus by rejecting the principle of expiation. If God is content with this principle, it is not for us to raise objection. The Lord God is infinitely more concerned to fix matters on a right foundation than we ever can be and if He feels that the Sacrifice of Jesus meets the case in all points, why should we be dissatisfied with it? If there were a flaw in the proceedings, His holy eyes would see it. He would not have delivered up His own Son to die unless that death would perfectly fulfill the design intended by it. A mistake so expensive He would never have perpetrated! Who are you to raise the question? If God is satisfied, surely you should be! To refuse the Atonement because we are too wise to accept so simple a method of mercy is the utmost height of folly! What? Will you refuse Him who speaks because the present phase of human madness dares to dispute the Divine way of human redemption? I pray you, do not!

Once more. Do not refuse this voice of mercy by preferring your own way of salvation. You have, no doubt, a way of salvation in your own mind, for few men have given up all hope. Perhaps your chosen hope is that you will be saved by doing your best. Alas, no man does his best– and the best acts of a rebel must be unaccepted of his king! So long as he is a rebel, his acts are those of a rebel and of no esteem with his prince. Perhaps your hope lies in saying so many prayers, going to church, or attending chapel–or are you so unwise as to trust to a minister or priest? Now, we beseech you, hear the Witness of God which He has given us in this Book and learn that other foundation can no man lay than that which is laid, which is Jesus Christ the Righteous! There is one salvation and there can be no other! All other hopes are lying vanities and arrogant insults to Jesus. God has set forth Christ to be a Propitiation for sin. There is no other propitiation, or atonement, or way of acceptance–and if you reject this way–you will die in your sins!

I cannot help it if you do not like this teaching, although I shall be grieved if you refuse it. I can only tell you the Truth of God and leave it with your own hearts. Do not willfully refuse it. When I meet you face to face in that last day, to which we all must come, I shall not be clear of your blood unless I tell you what is assuredly the Truth of God–that in the precious blood of Christ is the only cleansing from sin–and the only acceptance with God. By believing in Jesus, as slain for you, you shall be saved! But do what you may, pray as you may, fast as you may, give alms as you may–you shall not enter Heaven by any other road! The way to Glory is by the way of the Cross. "Without shedding of blood there is no remission." Look to Him whom you have pierced and mourn for your sins. Look not to any other, for no other is needed, no other is provided, no other can be accepted! Jesus is the only Messenger of the Covenant of life and peace. "See that you refuse not Him who speaks."

"See that you refuse not." Then there is a choice about it! If you had never heard the Gospel, you could not have refused it–but now that you have heard the message, it lies within your power–and it is an awfully dangerous power to refuse Him who speaks! Oh, can you, will you, dare you refuse my bleeding Savior–refuse the Lord of Love? I see Him now. The crown of thorns is about His brow. He is hanging on His Cross, expiring in unutterable agony! Can you refuse Him while He presents such a spectacle of sacrifice? His eyes are red with weeping–have you no tears for such sorrow? His cheeks are all stained with the brutal soldiers' spit–have you no love and homage for Him? His hands are fastened to the wood–His feet the same–and there He hangs to suffer in the sinner's place. Will you not yield yourselves to Him? I could joyfully bow before the foot of the Cross to kiss His dear feet Stained with blood! What a charm He has for me! And you–do you refuse Him?

He is no mere man! It is God, Himself, who hangs upon the Cross! His body is that of a man, but it is in union with the Godhead. He who died at

Calvary is God over all and this makes His death so effectual. He whom you have offended, in order to be justly able to pardon you, hangs there and dies for you–and do you turn your back on Him? O Sirs, if you are wise, you will come, as I said I gladly would come, and kiss those bleeding feet and look up and say, "My Lord, I am reconciled to You– how could I be otherwise? My enmity is dead. How can I be an enemy to Him that died for me? In shame, scorn and misery Jesus dies that I may live! O Lord Jesus, You have worked in me not merely reconciliation, but full submission and hearty love. I joy to sink myself in You and to be Yours forever." See that you refuse not my Lord. May the sweet Spirit who loves the Cross and, like a dove, hovers round it now, descend upon you all who hear my message! May the Holy Spirit apply the blood of sprinkling to you and may you feel that instead of refusing Him who speaks, you will rejoice in His name!

When the text says, "See that you refuse not," it tacitly and pleadingly says, "See that you accept Him." Dear Hearers, I trust you will receive my Lord into your hearts! When we read of refusing, or receiving, we perceive an action of the will. Jesus must be willingly received–He will not force Himself upon any man. Whoever accepts Jesus is, himself, accepted of Jesus. Never was there a heart willing to receive Him to whom Jesus denied Himself. Never! But you must be willing and obedient. Grace works this in you–and in you this must be. Till the heart entertains Jesus gladly, nothing is done. All that is short of a willing hearing of Jesus and a willing acceptance of His great Atonement, is short of eternal life. Say, will you have this Savior, or do you decline His love? Will you give Him a cold refusal? Oh, do not but, on the contrary, throw open the doors of your heart and entreat your Lord and Savior to come in!

I do not wonder that the Israelites asked that they might no longer hear the Voice of thunder from the top of Sinai–it was too terrible for human ears–but you have no such excuse if you refuse Him who speaks, for Jesus speaks in notes more sweet than music, more tender than a mother's sonnet to her babe! Let me remind you that He was known to say, "Come unto Me, all you that labor and are heavy laden, and I will give you rest. Take My yoke upon you and learn of Me, for I am meek and lowly in heart, and you shall find rest unto your souls." He declared that all manner of sin and of blasphemy should be forgiven unto men. He stood and cried, on the last day of the feast, "If any man thirsts, let him come unto Me and drink." I am telling you no fables, for Christ, who was born at Bethlehem and died on Calvary, by His own blood which He shed for many, assures you that there is forgiveness for every one of you who, confessing his sin, will come and put his trust in Him!

"See that you refuse not Him who speaks," for though you hear only my poor feeble voice pleading with you, with an honest, loving heart at the back of it, yet God the Holy Spirit is speaking and Jesus Christ, Himself, is speaking to you! Refuse me if you please, but do not refuse my Lord! The blood of Jesus says, "I was poured out for the guilty. I was shed to manifest Divine Love. I am sprinkled to cleanse from sin." Each drop, as it falls, creates peace of heart. Stand where that blood is falling! Let it sprinkle you!

Thus the blood speaks. Will you not answer, "Lord, we come to You, for You have drawn us. Your wounds have wounded our hearts. Your death has killed our enmity. Sprinkle us unto Yourself. Bedew us with Your blood. Let us be accepted in the Beloved." Amen. So may God hear us!

THE BLOOD SHED FOR MANY

"For this is My blood of the new testament, which is shed for many for the remission of sins."
Matthew 26:28

THE Lord Jesus Christ was then alive, sitting at the table and yet, pointing to the cup filled with red wine, He said, "This is My blood, which is shed for many." This proves that He could not have intended that the wine was literally His blood. Surely it is no longer necessary to refute the gross and carnal dogma of transubstantiation which is obviously absurd! There sat the living Lord at the supper, with His blood in His veins and, therefore, the wine could not literally be His blood! Value the symbol, but to confound it with the thing symbolized would draw into the idolatrous worship of a piece of bread!

Our Lord spoke of His blood as shed when as yet the nails had not pierced His hands and feet. And the spear had not broached His side. Is not this to be accounted for by the fact that our Lord was so taken up with the thought of our redemption by His death that He speaks of that as done which He was so resolved to do? Enjoying loving communion with His chosen disciples, He spoke freely. His heart did not study accuracy so much as feeling and so, in speech as in feeling, He antedated His great work of Atonement and spoke of it as done. To set forth the future intent of the blessed ordinance of the Lord's Supper He must, of necessity, treat His death as an accomplished fact. And His complete absorption in His work made it easy and natural for Him to do so. He ignores moods and tenses. "His work is before Him."

By the use of such language, our Lord also shows us the abiding presence of the great Sacrifice as a power and an influence. He is the "Lamb slain from the foundation of the world" and, therefore, He speaks of His blood as shed. In a few hours it would be literally poured forth, but long ages before, the Lord God had regarded it as done. In full confidence in the great Surety, that He would never draw back from the perfect fulfillment of His engagements, the Father saved multitudes in virtue of the future Sin-Offering! He communed with myriads of saints on the strength of the purification which would, in the fullness of time, be presented by the great High Priest. Could not the Father trust His Son? He did and by this act set us a great example of faith. God is, in very deed, the Father of the faithful, seeing that He, Himself, reposed the utmost confidence in Jesus! And because of what He would yet do in the pouring out of His soul unto death, He "opened the Kingdom of Heaven to all Believers." What, My soul? Can you not trust the Sacrifice, now that it has been presented? If the foresight of it was enough for God, is not the consummation of it enough for you? "Behold the Lamb of God," who even before He died was described as taking away the sin of the world! If this was so before He went to Calvary, how surely is it so now that He has said in verity and truth, "It is finished"!

Dear Friends, I am going to preach to you again upon the cornerstone of the Gospel. How many times will this make, I wonder? The doctrine of Christ Crucified is always with me. As the Roman sentinel in Pompeii stood to his post even when the city was destroyed, so do I stand to the truth of the Atonement though the Church is being buried beneath the boiling mud showers of modern heresy. Everything else can wait, but this one Truth of God must be proclaimed with a voice of thunder! Others may preach as they will, but as for this pulpit, it shall always resound with the Substitution of Christ. "God forbid that I should glory save in the Cross of our Lord Jesus Christ." Some may continually preach Christ as an example and others may perpetually discourse upon His coming to Glory—we also preach both of these, but mainly we preach Christ Crucified, to the Jews a stumbling block and to the Greeks foolishness—but to them that are saved Christ the Power of God and the Wisdom of God!

You have before you a cup, filled with wine, which Jesus has just blessed and presented to His disciples. As you look into its rosy depths, hear Him speak of the cup as His blood, for thus He would teach us a solemn lesson!

Note, first, THE IMPORTANCE OF THE PRECIOUS BLOOD OF CHRIST. The vital importance of the great Truth of God of the death of Christ as a vicarious Sacrifice is set before us in this cup, which is the memorial of His blood shed for many.

Blood represents suffering, but it goes further and suggests suffering unto death. "The blood is the life thereof" and when blood is too copiously shed, death is suggested. Remember that in the sacred Supper you have the bread as a separate emblem of the body and then the wine as a separate symbol of the blood–thus you have a clear picture of death, since the blood is separated from the flesh. "As often as you eat this bread and drink this cup, you do show the Lord's death." Both acts are essential.

Upon the death of Christ you are invited to fix your attention and upon that only. In the suffering of our Lord unto death we see the boundless stretch of His love. "Greater love has no man than this, that he lay down his life for his friends." Jesus could not be more loving to us than to yield Himself unto death, even the death of the Cross. O My Lord, in Your bloody sweat and in the piercing of Your hands and feet and side, I see the highest proof of Your love! Here I see that Jesus "loved me and gave Himself for me." Beloved, I beg you to consider often and lovingly the sufferings of your Redeemer unto the pouring out of His heart's blood. Go with Him to Gethsemane and then to the house of Caiaphas and Annas. And then to Pilate's hall and Herod's place of mockery! Behold your Lord beneath the cruel scourges and in the hands of the executioners upon the hill of shame. Forget not one of the sorrows which were mingled in the bitter cup of His crucifixion–its pain, its mockery, its shame. It was a death reserved for slaves and felons. To make its deep abysses absolutely bottomless, He was forsaken, even, of His God! Let the darkness of, "Eloi, Eloi, lama Sabachthani," bear down upon your spirit till, as you sink in awe, you also rise in love! He loved you better than He loved Himself! The cup means love, even to the shedding of His blood for you.

It means something more. We have called our Lord, in our hymn, "Giver of life for life," and that is what this cup means. He gave up His life that we might live! He stood in our place and stead in the day of Jehovah's wrath, receiving into His bosom the fiery sword which was unsheathed for our destruction! The pouring out of His blood has made our peace with God. Jehovah made the soul of His Only-Begotten an offering for sin, that the guilty might be cleared. "He has made Him to be sin for us, who knew no sin; that we might be made the righteousness of God in Him." That is what the wine in the cup means—it means the death of Jesus in our place. It means the blood poured out from the heart of the Incarnate God that we might have fellowship with God—the sin which divided us being expiated by His death.

Our blessed Savior would have us hold His death in great reverence—it is to be our chief memory. Both the emblems of the Lord's Supper set forth the Savior's death. This peculiarly Christian ordinance teaches nothing if it does not teach this. Christ's death for men is the great doctrine of the Church. We profess ourselves partakers of the merit of His death when we come to this table. Our Lord's death is then remembered, shown, declared, testified and trusted in. Evidently the Lord Jesus means us to treat the fact of His death as a Truth of God to be made pre-eminently prominent—He would not have instituted an ordinance especially to remind us of the shedding of His blood if He had not regarded it as the forefront of His whole earthly career.

The other ordinance of our holy faith also sets forth our Lord's death. Are we not, "Buried with Him by baptism into death?" Is not Baptism an emblem of His being immersed beneath the waves of sorrow and death? Baptism shows us that participation in Christ's suffering by which we begin to live—the Lord's Supper shows us that participation in Christ's suffering by which that life is sustained. Both institutions point to His death.

Besides, Beloved, we know from Holy Scripture that this doctrine of the death of Christ is the very core of Christianity. Leave out the Cross and you have killed the religion of Jesus. Atonement by the blood of Jesus is not an arm of Christian truth—it is the heart of it! Even as the Lord said of the animal, "The blood is the life thereof," so is it true of the Gospel—the sacrificial death of Jesus is the vital point of our profession. I know nothing of Christianity without the blood of Christ. No teaching is healthy which throws the Cross into the background.

The other day, when I was enquiring about the welfare of a certain congregation, my informant told me that there had been few additions to the church, although the minister was a man of ability and industry. Furthermore, he let me see the reason for failure, for he added, "I have attended there for several years and during all that time I do not remember hearing a sermon upon the Sacrifice of Christ. The Atonement is not denied, but it is left out." If this is so, what is to become of our churches? If the light of the Atonement is put under a bushel, the darkness will be dense. In omitting the Cross you have cut the Achilles tendon of the Church—it cannot move, nor even stand when this is gone. Holy work falls to the ground! It faints and dies when the blood of Jesus is taken away. The Cross must be put in the front more than ever by the faithful, because so many are unfaithful. Let us endeavor to make amends for the dishonor done to our Divine Master by those who deny or dishonor His vicarious Sacrifice. Let us abide steadfast in this faith while others waver! Let us preach Christ Crucified if all others forbear. Grace, mercy and peace be to all who exalt Christ Crucified!

This remembrance of the death of Christ must be a constant remembrance. The Lord's Supper was meant to be a frequent feast of fellowship. It is a grievous mistake of the Church when the communion is held but once in the year, or once in a quarter of a year—and I cannot remember any Scripture which justifies once in the month. I should not feel satisfied without breaking bread on every Lord's Day. It has come to me even more often than once a week, for it has been my delight to break bread with many a little company of Christian friends. Whenever this Supper is celebrated, we declare that "Christ died for our sins according to the Scriptures." We cannot think of that death too often! Never was man blamed in Heaven for preaching Christ too much, no, not even on earth to the sons of God was the Cross ever too much spoken of!

Outsiders may say, "This man harps only upon one string." Do you wonder? The carnal mind is enmity against God and it specially shows its hatred by railing at the Cross. Saintly ones find here, in the perpetual monotony of the Cross, a greater variety than in all other doctrines put together. Preach Christ, and Christ, and Christ, and Christ and nothing else but Christ–and opened ears shall find in your ministry a wondrous harmony of linked sweetnesses, a charming perfectness of all manner of delicious voices! All good things lie within the compass of the Cross–its outstretched arms overshadow the whole world of thought–from the east even unto the west it sheds a hallowed influence. Meanwhile, its foot is planted deep in the eternal mysteries and its top pierces all earth-born clouds and rises to the Throne of the Most High. Christ is lifted up upon the Cross that He may draw all men unto Him. And if we desire to draw them, this must be our magnet.

Beloved, the precious blood of Christ should be had by us in vivid remembrance. There is something to me most homely about that cup filled with the fruit of the vine. The bread of the Supper is the bread of our common meal and the wine is the usual attendant of feasts. That same pure blood of the grape which is set on our sacramental table I drink with my friends. Look at those ruby, ruddy drops, suggesting your Lord's own blood. I had not dared to invent the symbol, nor might any man of mortal mold have ventured on such a thing, lest he should seem to bring that august death down to our lowly level! But in infinite condescension Jesus, Himself, chooses the symbol and while by its materialism He sets forth the reality of the Sacrifice, by its commonness He shows how freely we may partake of it! He would not have us know Him after the flesh and forget the spiritual nature of His grief. And yet He would have us know that He was in a real body when He bled–and that He died a real death and became most truly fit for burial and, therefore, He symbolizes His blood, not by some airy fancy, or mystic sign–but by common wine in the cup! Thus would He reach us by our eyes and by our taste, using two gates of our nature which lead up to the castle of the heart, but are not often the King's roadway thereto. O blessed Master, do You arrange to teach us so forcibly? Then let us be impressed with the reality of the lesson and never treat Your passion as a thing of sentiment, nor make it a myth, nor view it as a dream of poetry. You shall be in death most real to us, even as is that cup of which we drink.

The dear memorials of our Lord's blood-shedding are intended for a personal remembrance. There is no Lord's Supper except as the wine touches the lips and is received into the communicant's own self. All must partake. He says, "Drink you all of it." You cannot take the Lord's Supper by deputy or representative–you must each of you approach the table and personally eat and drink. Beloved, we must come into personal contact with the death of Christ. This is essential. We must, each one, say, "He loved me and gave Himself for me." In His blood you must be personally washed. By His blood you must be personally reconciled to God. Through His blood you must personally have access to God and by His blood you must personally overcome the enemy of your souls. As the Israelite's own door must be smeared with the blood of the Paschal lamb, so must you individually partake of the true Sacrifice and know, each one for himself, the power of His redemption.

As it is personal, it is a charming fact that it is a happy remembrance. Our remembrance of Christ is chastened with repentance, but it is also perfumed with faith. The Lord's Supper is no funeral meal, but a festival! Most fitly do we begin it with the giving of thanks and close it with a hymn. It is called by many the "Eucharist," or the giving of thanks. It is not a fast, but a feast. My happiest moments are spent with the King at His table when His banner over me is love. The death of Christ is a wellspring of solemn joy. Before our great Sacrifice died, the best token of His death was the blood of bulls and of goats. See how the victims writhe in death! The sacrificial knife does terrible work at the foot of the altar. It is hard to stand by and see the creatures bleed. After our Lord's death was over, the blood of animals was not the type, but the blood of the grape. That which was terrible in prospect is joyous in remembrance! That which was blood in the shedding is wine in the receiving! It came from Him with a wound, but it comes to us with a blessing. His blood is our song in the house of our pilgrimage and it shall add the best music to our heavenly harmonies as we sing before the throne, "Unto Him that has loved us, and washed us from our sins in His own blood; to Him be glory forever and ever." If our Lord Jesus has made the memory of His love to be more sweet than wine, let us never turn from it as though it had become a distasteful theme. Let us find our choicest pleasures at the Cross!

Once more, our Savior meant us to maintain the doctrine of His death and the shedding of His blood for the remission of sins, even to the end of time, for He made it to be of perpetual remembrance. We drink this cup "until He comes." If the Lord Jesus had foreseen with approbation the changes in religious thought which would be brought about by growing "culture," He would surely have arranged a change of symbols to suit the change of doctrines! Would He not have warned us that towards the end of the 19 th Century men would become so "enlightened" that the faith of Christendom must of necessity take a new departure and, therefore, would He have appointed a change of sacramental memorials? But He has not warned us of the coming of those eminently great and wise men who have changed all things and abolished the old-fashioned Truths of God for which martyrs died!

Brethren, I do not believe in the wisdom of these men and I abhor their changes, but had there been any ground for such changes, the Lord's Supper would not have been made of perpetual obligation. The perpetuity of ordinances indicates a perpetuity of doctrine! But hear the moderns talk–"The Apostles, the Fathers, the Puritans–they were excellent men, no doubt, but then, you see, they lived before the rising up of those wonderful scientific men who have enlightened us so much." Let me repeat what I have said. If we had come to a new point as to believing, should we not have come to a new point as to the ordinances in which those beliefs are embodied? I think so. The evident intent of Christ in giving us settled ordinances and especially in settling this one which so clearly commemorates His shedding of His blood, was that we might know that the truth of His Sacrifice is forever fixed and settled–and must unchangeably remain the essence of His Gospel!

Neither 19 centuries, nor 19,000 centuries can make the slightest difference in this Truth of God, nor in the relative proportion of this Truth to other Truths of God so long as this dispensation lasts. Until He comes a second time without a sin offering unto salvation, the grand work of His first coming must be kept first and foremost in all our teaching, trusting and testifying! As in the southern hemisphere the cross is the mariner's guide, so, under all skies is the death of our Redeemer the polestar of our hope upon the sea of life. In life and in death we will glory in the Cross of Christ and never be ashamed of it, be we where we may!

II. Secondly, note well THE CONNECTION OF THE BLOOD OF CHRIST WITH THE COVENANT. Read the text again—"This is My blood of the new testament." The translation would be better, "This is My blood of the Covenant."

What is this Covenant? The Covenant is that which I read to you just now in Jeremiah 31:33—"This shall be the Covenant that I will make with the house of Israel. After those days, says the Lord, I will put My Law in their inward parts, and write it in their hearts; and will be their God, and they shall be My people." See also Jeremiah 32:40—"And I will make an everlasting Covenant with them, that I will not turn away from them, to do them good; but I will put My fear in their hearts; that they shall not depart from Me." Turn also to Ezekiel 11:19—"I will put a new spirit within you; and I will take the stony heart out of their flesh, and will give them an heart of flesh." Look in the same prophecy at 36:26—"A new heart also will I give you, and a new spirit will I put within you: and I will take away the stony heart out of your flesh, and I will give you an heart of flesh." What a Magna Charta is this! The old Covenant says, "Keep the Law and live." The new Covenant is, "You shall live and I will lead you to keep My Law, for I will write it on your heart." Happy men who know their standing under this Covenant!

What has the blood of Jesus Christ to do with this Covenant? It has everything to do with it, for the Covenant could never have been made, apart from the blood of Jesus! Atonement was taken for granted in the establishment of the Covenant. No one else could have stood as our Representative to fulfill our side of the Covenant, except the Lord Jesus Christ. And even He could only have performed that Covenant by

216

shedding His blood. In that cup you see the emblem of the blood which made the Covenant possible.

Moreover, the blood of Jesus makes the Covenant sure. His death has fulfilled man's side of the Covenant and God's part stands sure. The stipulation of the Covenant is fulfilled in Christ and now the tenor of it is pure promise. Note how the "shalls" and "wills" follow each other in quick succession. An arrangement of absolute Grace on God's part towards the undeserving sons of men is now in full action through the Sacrifice of Christ!

This Covenant of Grace, when rightly understood, exerts a blessed influence over the minds of men conscious of sin. The chaplain of a jail, a dear Friend of mine, once told me of a surprising case of conversion in which a knowledge of the Covenant of Grace was the chief instrument of the Holy Spirit. My friend had under his charge a man most cunning and brutal. He was singularly repulsive, even in comparison with other convicts. He had been renowned for his daring and for the utter absence of all feeling when committing acts of violence. I think he had been called "the king of the garrotters." The chaplain had spoken to him several times, but had not succeeded, even, in getting an answer. The man was sullenly set against all instruction. At last he expressed a desire for a certain book, but as it was not in the library, the chaplain pointed to the Bible which was placed in his cell and said, "Did you ever read that Book?"

He gave no answer, but looked at the good man as if he would kill him. The question was kindly repeated, with the assurance that he would find it well worth reading. "Sir," said the convict, "you would not ask me such a question if you knew who I was. What have I to do with a book of that sort?" He was told that his character was well known to the chaplain and that for this very reason he recommended the Bible as a book which would suit his case. "It would do me no good," he cried, "I am past all feeling." Doubling up his fist he struck the iron door of the cell and said, "My heart is as hard as that iron! There is nothing in any book that will ever touch me." "Well," said the chaplain, "You need a new heart. Did you ever read the Covenant of Grace?" To which the man answered sullenly by enquiring what he meant by such talk. The chaplain replied, "Listen to these words—'A new heart also will I give you, and a new spirit will I put within you.'" The words struck the man with amazement, as well they might!

He asked to have the passage found for him in the Bible. He read the Words again and again and when the chaplain came back to him the next day, the wild beast was tamed. "Oh, Sir," he said, "if He gives me a new heart it will be a miracle of mercy and yet I think," he said, "He is going to work that miracle upon me, for the very hope of a new nature is beginning to touch me as I never was touched before." That man became gentle in manner, obedient to authority and childlike in spirit! Though my friend has nothing left of the sanguine hopes he once entertained of converted criminals, he yet believes that in this case no observer could have questioned the thorough nature of the work—and yet the only means was the Doctrine of the Covenant!

My rebellious heart is not affected by the fact that God commands me to do this or that, but when He declares free and full forgiveness and goes on to promise love and favor and renewal of nature, I feel broken down! How can I rebel against One who does such wonders in me and designs such great things for me?—

"Dissolved by His goodness, I fall to the ground
And weep to the praise of the mercy I've found."

How dear and precious this makes the blood of Christ, since it is the blood of the Everlasting Covenant! Coming under this blessed Covenant, we henceforth adore the fullness of that Grace which, at the cost of the most precious of all lives, has made this arrangement for unworthy men!

You will perhaps say to me, "Why did our translators use the word, 'testament' in our Authorized Version? "They were hardly so wise as usual in this instance, for, "covenant" is the better word of the two to set

218

forth the original, but the idea of a testament is there also. The original may signify either or both. The word, "settlement," which has dropped out of use, nowadays, was often employed by our Calvinistic forefathers when they spoke of the everlasting arrangement of Grace. The word, "settlement," might take in both covenant and testament–there is a Covenant of Grace, but the Covenant stipulation being fulfilled by our Lord Jesus, the arrangement becomes virtually a testament through which, by the will of God, countless blessings are secured to the heirs of salvation. The blood of Jesus is the seal of the Covenant and transforms its blessings into bequests of love entailed upon Believers. The settlement or arrangement by which God can be just and yet the Justifier of the ungodly–and can deal with Believers, not on terms of Law, but on terms of pure Grace–is established by the Sacrifice of our Lord. O my Brothers and Sisters, as God's covenanted ones, drink of the cup with joy and renew your pledge with the Lord your God!

III. A third point comes up in the text very manifestly–THE BLOOD HAS AN INTIMATE CONNECTION WITH REMISSION. The text says, "This is My blood of the new Covenant, which is shed for many for the remission of sins." Jesus suffering, bleeding, dying, has procured for sinners the forgiveness of their sins!

Of what sins? Of all sins of every sort and kind, however heinous, aggravated and multiplied! The blood of the Covenant takes every sin away, be it what it may. There was never a sin believingly confessed and taken to Christ that ever baffled His power to cleanse it! This Fountain has never been tried in vain. Murderers, thieves, liars, adulterers and what not, have come to Jesus by penitence and faith–and through the merit of His Sacrifice their sins have been put away.

Of what nature is the remission? It is pardon, freely given, acting immediately and abiding forever, so that there is no fear of the guilt ever again being laid to the charge of the forgiven one! Through the precious blood our sins are blotted out, cast into the depths of the sea and removed as far from us as the east is from the west. Our sins cease to be–they are made an end of–they cannot be found against us any more forever. Yes, hear it, hear it, O wide earth! Let the glad news startle your darkest dens of infamy—there is absolute remission of sins! The precious blood of Christ cleanses from all sin! Yes, it turns the scarlet into a whiteness which exceeds that of the newly-fallen snow—a whiteness which never can be tarnished! Washed by Jesus, the blackest of sinners shall appear before the Judgment Seat of the all-seeing Judge without spot!

How is it the blood of Jesus effects this? The secret lies in the vicarious or substitutionary character of our Lord's suffering and death. Because He stood in our place, the justice of God is vindicated and the threats of the Law are fulfilled. It is now just for God to pardon sin. Christ's bearing the penalty of human sin instead of men has made the moral government of God perfect in justice, has laid a basis for peace of conscience and has rendered sin immeasurably hateful, though its punishment does not fall upon the Believer. This is the great secret, this is the heavenly news, the Gospel of salvation—that through the blood of Jesus sin is justly put away! Oh, how my very soul loves this Truth of God! Therefore do I speak it in unmistakable terms.

And for what end is this remission of sins secured? My Brothers and Sisters, if there were no other end for the remission of sins but its own self, it would be a noble purpose and it would be worth preaching every day of our lives! But it does not end here. We are mistaken if we think that the pardon of sins is God's ultimatum. No, no! It is but a beginning, a means to a further purpose. He forgives our sins with the design of curing our sinfulness. We are pardoned that we may become holy! God forgives the sin that He may purify the sinner. If He had not aimed at your holiness, there had not been so imperative a necessity for an Atonement—but to impress you with the guilt of sin, to make you feel the evil which sin has worked, to let you know your obligation to Divine Love—the Lord has not forgiven you without a Sacrifice. Ah, what a Sacrifice! He aims at the death of your sinfulness, that you may henceforth love Him, serve Him and crucify the lusts which crucified your Lord. The Lord aims at working in you the likeness of His dear Son! Jesus has saved you by His self-sacrificing obedience to Justice, that you may yield your whole soul to God and be willing to die for the upholding of the Kingdom of Love and Truth.

The death of Christ for you pledges you to be dead to sin, that by His Resurrection from the dead you may rise into newness of life and so become like your Lord. Pardon by blood aims at this. Do you catch the thought? If you believe in the Lord Jesus Christ, God's intent is to make you like the Firstborn among many brethren and to work in you everything that is comely and of good report. But this is not all—He has a further design to bring you into everlasting fellowship with Himself. He is sanctifying you that you may behold His face and that you may be fit to be a comrade of His only-begotten Son throughout eternity! You are to be the choice and dear companion of the Lord of Love. He has a throne for you, a mansion and a crown for you—and an immortality of such inconceivable glory and blessedness that if you did but form even a distant conception of it, no golden apple of earth would turn you aside from pursuing the prize of your high calling! Oh, to be forever with the Lord! Forever to behold His face! I fail to reach the height of this great argument! See, my Brothers and Sisters, to what the blood of your Lord destines you! O my Soul, bless God for that one cup which reminds you of the great Sacrifice and prophesies to you your glory at the right hand of God forever!

IV. I cannot forget to notice, in closing, THE CONNECTION OF THE BLOOD WITH MEN. We are told in the text that this blood is shed "for many for the remission of sins." In that large word, "many," let us exceedingly rejoice. Christ's blood was not shed for only the handful of Apostles. There were but eleven of them who really partook of the blood symbolized by the cup. The Savior does not say, "This is My blood which is shed for you, the favored eleven," but "shed for many." Jesus did not die only for the clergy! I recollect in Martin Luther's life that he saw, in one of the Roman churches, a picture of the Pope, the cardinals, bishops, priests, monks and friars all on board a ship. They were all safe, every one of them. As for the laity, poor wretches, they were struggling in the sea and many of them drowning! Only those were saved to whom the good men in the ship were so kind as to hand out a rope or a plank. That is not our Lord's teaching! His blood is shed "for many," and not for the few. He is not the Christ of a caste, or a class, but the Christ of all conditions of men. His blood is shed for many sinners, that their sins may be remitted.

Those in the upper room were all Jews, but the Lord Jesus Christ said to them, "This blood is shed for many," to let them see that He did not die only for the seed of Abraham, but for all races of men that dwell upon the face of the earth. "Shed for many." His eyes, I doubt not, glanced at these far-off islands and at the vast lands beyond the western sea. He thought of Africa, India and the land of Sinim. A multitude that no man can number gladdened the far-seeing and foreseeing eyes of the Redeemer! He spoke with joyful emphasis when He said, "shed for many for the remission of sins." Believe in the immeasurable results of Redemption! Whenever we are making arrangements for the preaching of this precious blood, let us make them on a large scale. The mansion of love should be built for a large family. Let us not sing–

"We are a garden walled around
Pray keep the walls most tight and sound,"

But let us expect to see large numbers brought within the sacred enclosure! We must yet break forth on the right hand and on the left. The masses must be compelled to come in! This blood is shed for many.

A group of half-a-dozen converts makes us very glad and so it should, but oh, to have half-a-dozen thousand at once! Why not? This blood is shed "for many." Let us cast the great net into the sea. You young men, preach the Gospel in the streets of this crowded city, for it is meant for many! You who go from door to door, do not think you can be too hopeful, since your Savior's blood is shed for many and Christ's, "many," is a very great many! It is shed for all who ever shall believe in Him– shed for you, Sinner, if you will now trust Him! Only confess your sin and trust Christ–and be assured that Jesus died in your place! It is shed for many so that no man or woman born shall ever trust Christ in vain, or find the Atonement insufficient for him. Oh, for a large-hearted faith, so that by holy effort we may lengthen our cords and strengthen our stakes, expecting to see the household of our Lord become exceedingly numerous! He shall see of the travail of His soul and shall be satisfied! By His righteousness shall He justify many, for He shall bear their iniquities! Dwell on that word, "many," and let it nerve you for far-reaching labors.

Now note THE CONNECTION OF THE BLOOD WITH OURSELVES. Dear Hearer, are you among the many? Why are you not? May His Grace bring you to trust in Him and you may not doubt that you are among the many. "Ah," you say, "that is what I am listening for! How can I partake in the effect of this Sacrifice?" Do you see that wine cup which I set before you just now? How are you to enjoy that wine which fills the cup? Its ruddy drops—how are they to be yours? The matter is very simple. I think I see you take the chalice in your hand and raise it to your mouth. You drink and the deed is done! This is no mystery. Bread and wine are ours by eating and drinking. Christ is ours by our receiving Him. The merit of His precious blood becomes ours by that simple childlike faith which accepts Jesus to be our All. We say, "Here it is. I believe in it. I take it. I accept it as my own." It is yours. No man can take from you that which you have eaten and drunk. Christ is yours forever if you receive Him into your heart.

If you have any question as to whether you have drunk, I will tell you how to solve it—drink again! If you have been eating and you have really forgotten whether you have eaten or not—such things do occur to busy men who eat but little—if, I say, you would be sure that you have eaten, eat again! If you will be assured that you have believed in Jesus, believe again! Whenever you have any doubt about whether Christ is yours, take Him again! I like to begin again. Often I find the best way of going forward is to go back to my first faith in Jesus and, as a sinner, renew my confidence in my Savior. "Oh," says the devil, "you are a preacher of the Gospel, but you do not know it yourself." At one time I used to argue with the accuser, but he is not worth it and it is by no means profitable to one's own heart. We cannot convert or convince the devil—it is better to refer him to our Lord. When he tells me I am not a saint, I answer, "Well, what am I, then? "A sinner," he says. "Well, so are you!" "Ah," he says,

"You will be lost!" "No," say I, "that is why I shall not be lost, since Jesus Christ came into the world to save sinners and I, therefore, trust in Him to save me." This is what Martin Luther calls cutting the devil's head off with his own sword and it is the best course you can follow!

You say, "If I take Christ to myself as a man takes a cup and drinks the contents, am I saved?" Yes, you are. "How am I to know it?" Know it because God says so! "He that believes in Him has everlasting life." If I did not feel a pulse of that life, (as I did not at first), I, nevertheless would believe that I had it simply on the strength of the Divine Assurance. Since my conversion I have felt the pulsing of a life more strong and forcible than the life of the most vigorous youth that ever ran without weariness—but there are times when it is not so. Just now I feel the heavenly life joyously leaping within me, but when I do not feel it, I fall back on this—God has said, "He that believes in Him has everlasting life." God's Words against all my feelings! I may get into a fainting fit and my circumstances may operate upon my heart as this hot weather operates upon my body and make me feel dull and sleepy, but this cannot make the Word of God of no effect! I go back to the Book and believe the bare Word of the Lord, "He that believes in Him has everlasting life." That is enough for me! I believe and, therefore, I live! Our inward experience is fine corroborative evidence, but God's testimony is the best foundation our confidence can have!

I recollect a story told of William Dawson whom our Wesleyan friends used to call Billy Dawson, one of the best preachers that ever entered a pulpit. He once gave out as his text, "Through this Man is preached unto you the forgiveness of sins." When he had given out his text he dropped down to the bottom of the pulpit, so that nothing could be seen of him—only there was a voice heard saying, "Not the man in the pulpit, he is out of sight, but the Man in the Book! The Man described in the Book is the Man through whom is preached unto you the forgiveness of sins."

I put myself and you and everybody else out of sight, and I preach to you the remission of sins through Jesus only! I would sing with the children, "Nothing but the blood of Jesus." Shut your eyes to all things but the Cross. Jesus died and rose again–and went to Heaven–and all your hope must go with Him! Come, my Hearer, take Jesus by a distinct act of faith this morning! May God the Holy Spirit grant you Grace to do so and then you may go on your way rejoicing! So be it in the name of Jesus!

THE BLOOD OF SPRINKLING AND THE CHILDREN

"Then Moses called for all the elders of Israel, and said unto them, Draw out and take you a lamb according to your families, and kill the Passover lamb. And you shall take a bunch of hyssop, and dip it in the blood that is in the basin, and strike the lintel and the two side posts with the blood that is in the basin; and none of you shall go out at the door of his house until the morning. For the Lord will pass through to smite the Egyptians, and when He sees the blood upon the lintel, and on the two side posts, the Lord will pass over the door, and will not suffer the destroyer to come in unto your houses to smite you. And you shall observe this thing for an ordinance to you and to your sons forever. And it shall come to pass, when you come to the land which the Lord will give you, according as He has promised, that you shall keep this service. And it shall come to pass, when your children shall say unto you, What mean you by this service? that you shall say, It is the sacrifice of the Lord's Passover, who passed over the houses of the children of Israel in Egypt, when He smote the Egyptians, and delivered our houses."
Exodus 12:21-27

I WANTED, dear Friends, earnestly wanted, to continue the subject of last Lord's-Day morning, for I felt it important that we should bear again and again our witness to the doctrine of the vicarious Sacrifice of Jesus Christ our Lord. But, at the same time, I promised that I would endeavor to keep "the feast of the children" and have a sermon which should be specially addressed to Sunday school teachers. I could not preach a school sermon at the appointed time, so as to open your children's week, but thought a discourse might come in, none the less suitably, if I brought up the rear by closing your meetings. How am I to fulfill both my purposes? I think the subject before us will enable me to do so. We shall preach of the sprinkled blood and of Jesus, the great Sacrifice for sin— and then we shall press upon all who know the value of the great Redemption that they teach the young in their earliest days what is meant by the death of Jesus and salvation through His blood.

The Paschal lamb was a special type of our Lord Jesus Christ. We are not left to gather this from the general fact that all the ancient sacrifices were shadows of the one true and real Substance—we are assured in the New Testament that "Christ our Passover is sacrificed for us" (1 Cor 5:7). As the Paschal lamb must be without blemish, so was our Lord, and its killing and roasting with fire were typical of His death and sufferings. Even as to time our Lord fulfilled the type, for the time of His Crucifixion was the Passover. As the impression answers to the seal, so does the Sacrifice of our Lord correspond with all the items of the ceremonial Passover. We see Him "drawn out" from among men and led as a lamb to the slaughter. We see His blood shed and sprinkled. We see Him roasted in the fire of anguish. By faith we eat of Him and flavor the feast with the bitter herbs of penitence. We see Jesus and salvation where the carnal eye sees only a slaughtered lamb and a people saved from death.

The Spirit of God in the ceremonial Passover lays special emphasis upon the sprinkling of the blood. That which men so greatly oppose, He as diligently sets forth as the head and front of Revelation. The blood of the chosen lamb was caught in a basin and not spilled upon the ground in wastefulness, for the blood of Christ is most precious. Into this bowl of blood a bunch of hyssop was dipped. The sprays of that little shrub would hold the crimson drops, so that they could be easily sprinkled. Then the father of the family went outside and struck with this hyssop the lintel and the two side posts of the door—and so the house was marked with three crimson streaks. No blood was put upon the threshold. Woe unto the man that tramples upon the blood of Christ and treats it as an unholy thing! Alas, I fear that many are doing so at this hour, not only among the outside world, but among those who profess and call themselves Christians.

I shall endeavor to bring forward two things. First, the importance attached to the sprinkled blood and, secondly, the institution connected with it, namely, that the children should be instructed in the meaning of sacrifice, so that they also may teach their children and keep afire the memory of the Lord's great deliverance.

First—THE IMPORTANCE ATTACHED TO THE BLOOD OF SACRIFICE is here made very plain. Pains are taken to make the sacrifice observable, yes, to force it upon the notice of all the people! I note, first, that it became and remained the national mark. If you had traversed the streets of Memphis or Rameses on the night of the Passover, you could have told who were Israelites and who were Egyptians by one conspicuous token. There was no need to listen under the window to hear the speech of the people within the house, nor to wait till any came into the street so that you could observe their attire. This one thing, alone, would be a sufficient guide—the Israelite had the blood mark upon his doorway—the Egyptian had it not. Mark you, this is still the great point of difference between the children of God and the children of the Wicked One. There are, in truth, but two denominations upon this earth—the Church and the world—those who are justified in Christ Jesus and those who are condemned in their sins. This shall stand for a never-failing sign of the "Israelite, indeed." He has come to the blood of sprinkling, which speaks better things than that of Abel. He that believes in the Son of God as the one accepted Sacrifice for sin, has salvation and he that believes not in Him will die in his sins.

The true Israel are trusting in the Sacrifice once offered for sin—it is their rest, their comfort, their hope. As for those who are not trusting in the atoning Sacrifice, they have rejected the counsel of God against themselves, and thus have declared their true character and condition. Jesus said, "You believe not because you are not of My sheep, as I said unto you"—and lack of faith in that shedding of blood, without which there is no remission of sin—is the damning mark of one who is a stranger to the commonwealth of Israel. Let us make no question about it—"Whoever goes onward and abides not in the teaching of Christ, has not God." (See 2 John 9 in the Revised Version). He that will not accept the Propitiation which God has set forth must bear his own iniquity! Nothing more just and yet nothing more terrible can happen to such a man than that his iniquity should not be purged by sacrifice nor offering forever. I care not what your supposed righteousness may be, nor how you think to commend yourselves to God—if you reject His Son, He will reject you!

If you come before God without the atoning blood, you have neither part nor lot in the matter of the Covenant inheritance and you are not numbered among the people of God! The Sacrifice is the national mark of the spiritual Israel and he that has it not is an alien—he shall have no inheritance among them that are sanctified—neither shall he behold the Lord in Glory.

Secondly, as this was the national mark, it was also the saving token. That night the Angel of Death spread His wings on the blast and as He flew down the streets of Egypt He smote high and low, the first-born of princes and the first-born of beasts, so that in every house and in every stall there was one dead. Where He saw the blood-mark He entered not to smite, but everywhere else the vengeance of the Lord fell on the rebellious. The words are very remarkable—"The Lord will pass over the door, and will not suffer the destroyer to come in unto your houses to smite you." What holds back the sword? Nothing but the bloodstain on the door! The lamb has been slain and they have sprinkled their houses with the blood and, therefore, they are secure. The sons of Jacob were not richer, nor wiser, nor stronger, nor more skilled than the sons of Ham—but they were redeemed by the blood and, therefore, they lived, while those who knew not the redeeming token died. When Jericho fell down, the one house that stood was that which had the scarlet line in the window—and when the Lord visits for sin—the man that shall escape is he who knows Jesus, "in whom we have redemption through His blood, the forgiveness of sin according to the riches of His Grace."

I call your very special attention, however, to the words that are used in the 23 rd verse—"The Lord will pass through to smite the Egyptians; and when He sees the blood upon the lintel, and on the two side posts, the Lord will pass over the door." What an instructive expression! "When He sees the blood." It is a very comforting thing for you and for me to behold the Atonement, for thus we gain peace and enter into rest. But, after all, the grand reason of our salvation is that the Lord Himself looks upon the Atonement and is well pleased for His righteousness' sake. In the 13 th verse we hear theLord, Himself, say—"When I see the blood I will pass over you." Think of the holy eyes of God being turned to Him that takes away the sin of the world–and so fixed on Him that He passes over us! He is of purer eyes than to behold iniquity, but He looks upon the face of His Anointed and forgives the sin. He accepts us with our Sacrifice. Well does our hymn writer pray–

"Him and then the sinner see;
Look through Jesus' wounds on me."

It is not our sight of the sprinkled blood which is the basis of salvation, but God's sight of it! God's acceptance ofChrist is the sure guarantee of the salvation of those who accept His Sacrifice. Beloved, when your eyes of faith are dim; when your eyeballs swim in a flood of tears; when the darkness of sorrow hides much from your vision, then Jehovah sees the blood of His Son and spares you! In the thick darkness, when you cannot see at all, the Lord God never fails to see in Jesus that with which He is well pleased and with which His Law is honored. He will not suffer the destroyer to come near you to harm you, because He sees in Christ that which vindicates His justice and establishes the necessary rule of Law. The blood is the saving mark! At this moment this is the pressing question for each one in the company gathered in this house– Do you trust the Divine Propitiation or do you not? Bring to me what you will to prove your own personal excellence. I believe in no virtue which insults the Savior's blood which alone cleanses us from all sin! Rather, confess your multiplied transgressions and shortcomings–and then take heart and hope–for there is forgiveness large and free for the very chief of sinners through Him who has made peace by the blood of His Cross!

O my Hearer, guilty and self-condemned, if you will now come and trust in Jesus Christ, your sins, which are many, shall be all forgiven you and you shall love so much in return that the whole bent and bias of your mind shall be turned from sin to gracious obedience! The Atonement applied to the conscience saves from despair and then, acting upon the heart, it saves from the love of evil. But the Atonement is the saving sign! The blood on the lintel and on the two side posts secured the house of the poorest Israelite. But the proudest Egyptian, yes, even

Pharaoh on the throne, could not escape the destroyer's sword. Believe and live! Reject the Atonement and perish!

Note, next, that the mark of the blood was rendered as conspicuous as possible. The Israelites, though they ate the Paschal lamb in the quiet of their own families, yet made no secret of the sacrifice. They did not make the distinctive mark upon the wall of some inner chamber, or in some place where they could cover it with hangings, that no man might perceive it. No, they smote the upper part of the doorway and the two side posts of the door so that all who passed by the house must see that it was marked in a peculiar manner—and marked with blood! The Lord's people were not ashamed to have the blood thus put in the forefront of every dwelling—and those that are saved by the great Sacrifice are not to treat the doctrine of Substitution as a hole-and-corner creed, to be secretly held, but not openly avowed. The death of Jesus in our place is not a redemption of which we are ashamed to speak in any place! Call it old-fashioned and out of date—our critics may—but we are not ashamed to publish it to the four winds of Heaven and to avow our confidence in it! He that is ashamed of Christ in this generation, of him will Christ be ashamed when He comes in the Glory of His Father and all His holy angels with Him!

There is a theology abroad in the world which admits the death of Christ to a certain indefinable place in its system, but that place is very much in the rear. I claim for the Atonement the front and the center—the Lamb must be in the midst of the throne! Atonement is not a mystery to be scarcely spoken of, or if spoken of at all, to be whispered. No, no, it is a sublime simplicity, a fact for a child to know, a truth for the common people to rejoice in! We must preach Christ Crucified whatever else we do not preach! Brothers and Sisters, I do not think you ought to hear a minister preach three sermons without learning the doctrine of Atonement! I give wide latitude when I say this, for I would desire never to preach at all without setting forth salvation by faith in the blood of Jesus! Across my pulpit and my tabernacle shall be the mark of the blood—it will disgust the enemy—but it will delight the faithful! Substitution seems to me to be the soul of the Gospel, the life of the Gospel, the essence of the Gospel! Therefore must it be always in the front.

Jesus, as the Lamb of God, is the Alpha, and we must keep Him first and before all others. I charge you, Christian people, do not make this a secondary doctrine! Keep your perspective right and have this always in the foreground. Other Truths of God are valuable and may most worthily be placed in the distance, but this is always to be in the foreground. The center of Christianity is the Cross and the meaning of the Cross is Substitution—

"We may not know, we cannot tell,
What pains our Jesus bore,
But we believe it was for us"

The great Sacrifice is the place of gathering for the chosen seed—we meet at the Cross, even as every family in Israel met around the table whereon was placed the lamb—and met within a house which was marked with blood. Instead of looking upon the vicarious Sacrifice as placed somewhere in the remote distance, we find in it the center of the Church. No, more—it is the vital, all-essential center, that to remove it is to tear out the heart of the Church! A congregation which has rejected the Sacrifice of Christ is not a church, but an assembly of unbelievers! Of the Church I may truly say, "The blood is the life thereof." Like the doctrine of Justification by Faith, the doctrine of a vicarious Sacrifice is the article of standing or falling to each Church—Atonement by the substitutionary Sacrifice of Christ means spiritual life—and the rejection of it is the reverse. Therefore we must never be ashamed of this all-important Truth of God, but make it as conspicuous as possible. "For the preaching of the Cross is to them that perish foolishness; but unto us which are saved it is the power of God."

Further, the sprinkled blood was not only most conspicuous, but it was made very dear to the people, themselves, by the fact that they trusted in it in the most implicit manner. After the doorposts had been smeared, the people went inside their houses and shut the door, never to open it again till the morning. They were busy inside—there was the roasting of the lamb, the preparing of the bitter herbs, the girding of their loins, the getting ready for their march and so forth—but this was done without fear of danger, though they knew that the destroyer was abroad. The command of the Lord was, "None of you shall go out at the door of his house until the morning." What is going on in the street? You must not go to see. The midnight hour has come. Did you not hear it? Hark, that dreadful cry! Again a piercing shriek! What is it? The anxious mother asks, "What can it be?" "There was a great cry in Egypt." The Israelites must not heed that cry so as to break the Divine Word which shut them in for a little moment till the tempest was passed.

Perhaps persons of doubtful mind, during that dread night, may have said, "Something awful is happening. Hear those cries! Listen to the tramping of the people in the streets, as they hurry to and fro! It may be there is a conspiracy to slay us in the dead of night." "None of you shall go out at the door of his house until the morning" was sufficient for all who truly believed! They were safe and they knew it, and so, like the chicks beneath the wings of the hen, they rested in safety. Beloved, let us do the same! Let us honor the precious blood of Christ not only by speaking of it boldly to others, but by a calm and happy trust in it for ourselves. In full assurance let us rest. Do you believe that Jesus died for you? Then be at peace! Let no man's heart fail him, now that he knows that Jesus died for our sins according to the Scriptures. Let the Cross be the pillar of our confidence, unmoved and immovable. Do not be agitated about what has been or what is to be—we are housed in safety in Christ Jesus both from the sins of the past and the dangers of the future! All is well, since love's atoning work is done! In holy peacefulness let us proceed with our household work, purging out the old leaven and keeping the feast. And let no fear or doubt disturb us for an instant.

We pity those who die without Christ, but we cannot quit our Lord under the pretence of saving them—that would be folly. I know there are terrible cries outside in the streets—who has not heard them? Oh, that the people would but shelter beneath the blood-mark! It pierces our heart to think of the doom of the ungodly when they perish in their sins. But, as Noah did not quit the ark, nor Israel leave her abode, so our hope is not larger than the Cross will warrant. All who shelter beneath the blood of the Atonement are secure! But as for those who reject this great salvation, how shall they escape? There are great and sad mysteries in this long night, but in the morning we shall know as much of God's dealings with men as it will be good for us to know. Meanwhile, let us labor to bring our fellows within the pale of safety, but yet let us be, ourselves, peaceful, composed, restful and joyful. "There is therefore now no condemnation to them which are in Christ Jesus." "Therefore being justified by faith, we have peace with God through our Lord Jesus Christ." "And not only so, but we also joy in God through our Lord Jesus Christ, by whom we have now received the Atonement."

Possess your souls in patience. Oh, rest in the Lord and wait patiently for Him! Feed upon the Lamb, for His flesh is meat, indeed. That same Jesus who has preserved your life from destruction will be the sustenance of that life evermore. Be happy beneath the saving blood-mark! Make a feast of your Passover. Though there is death outside, let your joy within be undisturbed.

I cannot stay long on any one point and, therefore, notice, next, that the Paschal blood shedding was to be had in perpetual remembrance. "You shall observe this thing for an ordinance to you and to your sons forever." As long as Israel remained a people, they were to keep the Passover—as long as there is a Christian upon earth, the sacrificial death of the Lord Jesus must be kept in memory! No progress of years or advance of thought could take away the memory of the Paschal sacrifice from Israel. Truly it was a night to be remembered when the Lord brought out His people from under the iron yoke of Egypt. It was such a wonderful deliverance, as to the plagues which preceded it and the miracle at the Red Sea which followed it, that no event could possibly excel it in interest and glory! It was such a triumph of God's power over the pride of Pharaoh and such a manifestation of God's love to His own people, that they were not merely to be glad for one night, nor for one year, nor even for a century—they were to remember it forever!

Might there not come a time when Israel would have achieved further history? Might not some grander event eclipse the glory of Egypt's overthrow? Never! The death of Egypt's first-born and the song of Moses at the Red Sea must remain forever woven into the tapestry of Hebrew history. Evermore did Jehovah say, "I am the Lord your God, which have brought you out of the land of Egypt, out of the house of bondage." Beloved, the death of our Lord Jesus Christ is to be declared and showed by us until He comes. No Truth of God can ever be discovered which can put His sacrificial death into the shade. Whatever shall occur, even though He comes in the clouds of Heaven, yet our song shall be forever, "Unto Him that loved us and washed us from our sins in His own blood."

Amid the splendor of His endless reign He shall be "the Lamb in the midst of the Throne." Christ, as the Sacrifice for sin, shall always be the subject of our hallelujahs—"For You were slain." Certain vainglorious minds are advancing—advancing from the Rock to the abyss! They are making progress from truth to lies. They are thinking, but their thoughts are not God's thoughts, neither are their ways His ways. They are leaving the Gospel! They are going away from Christ and they know not where. In denying the substitutionary Sacrifice, they are denying the only hope of man! As for us, we hear the Lord saying to us, "You shall observe this thing for an ordinance to you and to your sons forever"—and so we will! "Jesus Christ, the same yesterday, today, and forever," is our boast and Glory! Let others wander where they will, we abide with Him who bore our sins in His own body on the tree.

Notice next, dear Friends, that when the people came into the land where no Egyptian ever entered, they were still to remember the Passover. "It shall come to pass, when you have come to the land which the Lord will give you, according as He has promised, that you shall keep this service." In the land that flowed with milk and honey there was still to be the memorial of the sprinkled blood! Our Lord Jesus is not for the first day of our repentance, only, but for all the days of our lives—we remember Him as well at our highest spiritual joys as in our deepest spiritual griefs. The Paschal lamb is for Canaan, as well as for Egypt, and the Sacrifice for sin is for our full assurance as well as for our trembling hope. You and I will never attain to such a state of Grace that we can do without the blood which cleanses from sin! If we should ever reach perfection, then would Christ be even more precious than He is today, or, if we did not find Him so, we might be sure that our pretended attainment was a wretched delusion! If we walk in the Light as God is in the Light, and have constant fellowship with Him, yet still the blood of Jesus Christ His Son cleanses us from all sin!

Moreover, Brothers and Sisters, I want you to notice carefully that this sprinkling of the blood was to be an allpervading memory. Catch this thought–the children of Israel could not go out of their houses–and they could not come in, without the remembrance of the sprinkled blood. It was over their heads–they must come under it. It was on the right hand and on the left–they must be surrounded by it. They might almost say of it, "Where shall we go from Your Presence?" Whether they looked on their own doors, or on those of their neighbors, there was the same threefold streak, and it was there both by day and by night. Nor was this all. When two of Israel married and the foundation of a family was laid, there was another memorial. The young husband and wife had the joy of looking upon their first-born child and then they called to mind that the Lord had said, "Sanctify to Me all the first-born." As an Israelite, he explained this to his son and said, "By strength of hand, the Lord brought us out from Egypt, from the house of bondage. And it came to pass, when Pharaoh would hardly let us go, that the Lord slew all the first-born in the land of Egypt, both the firstborn of man and the first-born of beast! Therefore I sacrifice to the Lord all that opens the matrix, being males, but all the first-born of my children I redeem."

The commencement of every family that made up the Israelite nation was thus a time of special remembrance of the sprinkling of the blood, for then the redemption money must be paid, and thus an acknowledgment made that they were the Lord's, having been bought with a price. In many ways and everywhere present, the people were reminded of the need of sacrifice! To the thoughtful, every going down of the sun reminded them of the night to be remembered, while the beginning of each year in the month Abib brought home to them the fact that the beginning of their nation dated from the time of the killing of the lamb. The Lord took means to keep this matter before the people, for they were wayward and seemed bent upon forgetting—even like this present age.

In the 13 th chapter, in verse 9, we read, "It shall be for a sign unto you upon your hand, and for a memorial betweenyour eyes." And again, in verse 16, we read, "And it shall be for a token upon your hand, and for frontlets between your eyes: for by strength of hand the Lord brought us forth out of Egypt." By this is meant that they were, from then on, to do everything with regard to redemption—and they were from then on to see everything in connection with redemption. Redemption by blood was to consecrate each man's hand so that he could not use it for evil, but must employ it for the Lord. He could not take his food, or his tools in his hand, without remembrance of the sprinkled blood which had made his food and his labor a blessing. All his acts were to be under the influence of atoning blood! Oh, what service you and I would render if it were always redeemed labor that we gave! If we went to our Sunday school class, for instance, feeling, "I am bought with a price," and if we preached with redeemed lips the Gospel of our own salvation, how livingly and lovingly we would speak! What an effect this would have on our lives!

You would not dare, some of you, to do what you now do if you remembered that Jesus died for you! Many a thing which you have left undone would at once be minded if you had a clearer consciousness of redeeming love. The Jews became superstitious and were content with the letter of their law—and so they wrote out certain verses upon little strips of parchment called "tephillin," which they enclosed in a box—and then strapped upon their wrists. The true meaning of the passage did not lie in any such childish action—it taught them that they were to labor and to act with holy hands, as men under overwhelming obligations to the Lord's redeeming Grace. Redemption is to be our impulse for holy service, our check when we are tempted to sin. They were also to wear the memory of the Passover as frontlets between their eyes, and you know how certain Jews actually wore phylacteries upon their foreheads! That could be no more than the mere shell of the thing! The essence of the command was that they were to look on everything in reference to redemption by blood!

Brothers and Sisters, we should view everything in this world by the light of redemption—and then we shall view it aright. It makes a wonderful change whether you view Providence from the standpoint of human merit or from the foot of the Cross. We see nothing truly till Jesus is our light! Everything is seen in its reality when you look through the glass, the ruby glass of the atoning Sacrifice. Use this telescope of the Cross and you shall see far and clear. Look at sinners through the Cross! Look at saints through the Cross! Look at sin through the Cross! Look at the world's joys and sorrows through the Cross! Look at Heaven and Hell through the Cross! See how conspicuous the blood of the Passover was meant to be and then learn from all this to make much of the Sacrifice of Jesus, yes, to make everything of it, for Christ is All.

One thing more—we read in Deuteronomy, in the 6 th verse, concerning the Commandments ofthe Lord, as follows—"And you shall bind them for a sign upon your hand, and they shall be as frontlets between your eyes. And you shall write them upon the posts of your house, and on your gates." See, then, that the Law of God is to be written hard by the memorials of the blood. In Switzerland, in the Protestant villages, you have seen texts of Scripture upon the doorposts. I half wish we had that custom in England. How much of Gospel might be preached to wayfarers if texts of Scripture were over Christian people's doors! It might be ridiculed as Pharisaical, but we could get over that. Few are liable to that charge in these days through being too religious. I like to see texts of Scripture in our houses, in all the rooms, on the cornices and on the walls. But outside on the door—what a capital advertisement the Gospel might get at a cheap rate! But note that when the Jew wrote upon His doorposts a promise, or a precept, or a doctrine, he had to write upon a surface stained with blood! And when the next year's

Passover came round he had to sprinkle the blood with the hyssop right over the writing.

It seems to me so delightful to think of the Law of God in connection with that atoning Sacrifice which has magnified it and made it honorable. God's commands come to me as a redeemed man. His promises are to me as a blood-bought man. His teaching instructs me as one for whom Atonement has been made. The Law in the hand of Christ is not a sword to slay us, but a jewel to enrich us! All the Truths of God taken in connection with the Cross are greatly enhanced in value! Holy Scripture, itself, becomes dearer to a sevenfold degree when we see that it comes to us as the redeemed of the Lord—and bears upon its every page marks of those dear hands which were nailed to the tree for us.

Beloved, you now see how everything was done that could well be thought of to bring the blood of the Paschal lamb into a high position in the esteem of the people whom the Lord brought out of Egypt. And you and I must do everything we can think of to bring forward and keep before men forever the precious doctrine of the atoning Sacrifice of Christ! He was made sin for us though He knew no sin, that we might be made the righteousness of God in Him.

II. And now I will spend a short time in reminding you of THE INSTITUTION THAT WAS CONNECTED WITH THE REMEMBRANCE OF THE PASSOVER. "It shall come to pass, when your children shall say unto you, What mean you by this service? that you shall say, It is the sacrifice of the Lord's Passover."

Inquiry should be excited in the minds of our children. Oh, that we could get them to ask questions about the things of God! Some of them enquire very early, but others of them seem diseased with much the same indifference as older folks. With both orders of mind we have to deal. It is well to explain to children the ordinance of the Lord's Supper, for this shows forth the death of Christ in symbol. I regret that children do not more often see this ordinance. Baptism and the Lord's Supper should both be placed in view of the rising generation, that they may then ask us, "What mean you by this?"

Now, the Lord's Supper is a perennial Gospel sermon and it turns mainly upon the Sacrifice for sin. You may banish the doctrine of the Atonement from the pulpit, but it will always live in the Church through the Lord's Supper. You cannot explain that broken bread and that cup filled with the fruit of the vine without reference to our Lord's atoning death! You cannot explain "the communion of the body of Christ" without bringing in, in some form or other, the death of Jesus in our place! Let your little ones, then, see the Lord's Supper, and let them be told most clearly what it sets forth. And if not the Lord's Supper—for that is not the thing, itself, but only the shadow of the glorious fact—dwell much and often in their presence upon the sufferings and death of our Redeemer. Let them think of Gethsemane, Gabbatha and Golgotha—and let them learn to sing in plaintive tones of Him who laid down His life for us. Tell them who it was that suffered, and why. Yes, though the hymn is hardly to my taste in some of its expressions, I would have the children sing—

"There is a green hill far away,
Without a city wall."

And I would have them learn such lines as these—

"He knew how wicked we had been,
And knew that God must punish sin—
So out of pity Jesus said,
He'd bear the punishment instead."

And when attention is excited upon the best of themes, let us be ready to explain the great transaction by which God is just and yet sinners are justified. Children can well understand the doctrine of the expiatory Sacrifice—it was meant to be a Gospel for the youngest. The Gospel of Substitution is a simplicity, though it is a mystery. We ought not to be content until our little ones know and trust in their finished Sacrifice. This is essential knowledge and the key to all other spiritual teaching. May our dear children know the Cross and they will have begun well. With all their getting may they get an understanding of this and they will have the foundation rightly laid.

This will necessitate your teaching the child his need of a Savior. You must not hold back from this necessary task. Do not flatter the child with delusive rubbish about his nature being good and needing to be developed. Tell him he must be born again! Don't bolster him up with the fancy of his own innocence, but show him his sin! Mention the childish sins to which he is prone and pray the Holy Spirit to work conviction in his heart and conscience. Deal with the young in much the same way as you would with the old. Be thorough and honest with them. Flimsy religion is neither good for young nor old. These boys and girls need pardon through the precious blood as surely as any of us. Do not hesitate to tell the child his ruin—otherwise he will not desire the remedy. Tell him, also, of the punishment for sin and warn him of its terror. Be tender, but be true. Do not hide from the youthful sinner the Truth of God, however terrible it may be! Now that he has come to years of responsibility, if he believes not in Christ, it will go ill with him at the Last Great Day. Set before him the Judgment Seat and remind him that he will have to give an account of things done in the body. Labor to awake the conscience and pray God the Holy Spirit to work by you till the heart becomes tender and the mind perceives the need of the great salvation.

Children need to learn the doctrine of the Cross that they may find immediate salvation. I thank God that in our Sunday school we believe in the salvation of children as children! How very many has it been my joy to see of boys and girls who have come forward to confess their faith in Christ! And I again wish to say that the best converts, the clearest converts, the most intelligent converts we have ever had have been the young ones! And, instead of there being any deficiency in their knowledge of the Word of God and the Doctrines of Grace, we have usually found them to have a very delightful acquaintance with the great cardinal Truths of Christ. Many of these dear children have been able to speak of the things of God with great pleasure of heart and force of understanding. Go on, dear teachers, and believe that God will save your children! Be not content to sow principles in their minds which may possibly develop in later years, but be working for immediate conversion! Expect fruit in your children while they are children! Pray for them that they may not run into the world and fall into the evils of outward sin—and then come back with broken bones to the Good Shepherd. Pray that they may, by God's rich Grace, be kept from the paths of the Wicked One and grow up in the fold of Christ—first as lambs of His flock—and then as sheep of His hand.

One thing I am sure of, and that is that if we teach the children the Doctrine of the Atonement in the most unmistakable terms, we shall be doing ourselves good. I sometimes hope that God will revive His Church and restore her to her ancient faith by a gracious work among children. If He would bring into our Churches a large influx of young people, how it would tend to quicken the sluggish blood of the supine and sleepy! Child Christians tend to keep the house alive. Oh, for more of them! If the Lord will but help us to teach the children, we shall be teaching ourselves. There is no way of learning like teaching—and you do not know a thing till you can teach it to another. You do not thoroughly know any Truth of God till you can put it before a child so that he can see it. In trying to make a little child understand the Doctrine of the Atonement you will get clearer views of it yourselves and, therefore, I commend the holy exercise to you.

What a mercy it will be if our children are thoroughly grounded in the doctrine of redemption by Christ! If they are warned against the false gospels of this evil age, and if they are taught to rest on the eternal Rock of Christ's finished work, we may hope to have a generation following us which will maintain the faith and will be better than their fathers! Your Sunday schools are admirable, but what is their purpose if you do not teach the Gospel in them? You get children together and keep them quiet for an hour-and-a-half, and then send them home—but what is the good of it? It may bring some quiet to their fathers and mothers and that is, perhaps, why they send them to the school. But all the real good lies in what is taught the children! The most fundamental Truth of God should be made most prominent—and what is this but the Cross? Some talk to children about being good boys and girls and so on. That is to say, they preach the Law to the children, though they would preach the Gospel to grown-up people!

Is this honest? Is this wise? Children need the Gospel, the whole Gospel, the unadulterated Gospel! They ought to have it and, if they are taught of the Spirit of God, they are as capable of receiving it as persons of ripe years. Teach the little ones that Jesus died, the Just for the unjust, to bring us to God! Very, very confidently do I leave this work in the hands of the teachers of this school. I never knew a nobler body of Christian men and women, for they are as earnest in their attachment to the old Gospel as they are eager for the winning of souls. Be encouraged, my Brothers and Sisters–the God who has saved so many of your children is going to save many, many more of them! And we shall have great joy in this Tabernacle as we see hundreds brought to Christ. God grant it, for His name's sake! Amen.

THE BLOOD OF THE LAMB, THE CONQUERING WEAPON

"And they overcame him by the blood of the Lamb and by the word of their testimony. And they loved not their lives unto the death."
Revelation 12:11

WHEREVER evil appears, it is to be fought with by the children of God in the name of Jesus and in the power of the Holy Spirit. When evil appeared in an angel, straightway there was war in Heaven. Evil in mortal men is to be strived against by all regenerate men. If sin comes to us in the form of an angel of light we must still war with it. If it comes with all manner of deceivableness of unrighteousness we must not parley for a single moment but begin the battle at once—if we belong to the armies of the Lord. Evil is at its very worst in Satan himself—with him we fight. He is no mean adversary. The evil spirits which are under his control are, any one of them, terrible foes. But when Satan himself personally attacks a Christian, any of us will be hard put to it.

When this dragon blocks our road, we shall need heavenly aid to force our passage. A pitched battle with Apollyon may not often occur. But when it does you will know it painfully—you will record it in your diary as one of the darkest days you have ever lived. And you will eternally praise your God when you overcome him. But even if Satan were ten times stronger and more crafty than he is, we are bound to wrestle with him—we cannot for a moment hesitate, or offer him terms. Evil in its highest, strongest and proudest form is to be assailed by the soldier of the Cross and nothing must end the war but complete victory.

Satan is the enemy, the enemy of enemies. That prayer of our Lord's, which we usually render, "Deliver us from evil," has the special significance of "Deliver us from the Evil One," because Satan is the chief embodiment of evil and in him evil is intensified and has come to its highest strength. That man had need have Omnipotence with him who hopes to overcome the enemy of God and man. He would destroy all godly ones if he could. And though he cannot, such is his inveterate hate that he worries those whom he cannot devour with a malicious eagerness.

In this chapter the devil is called the "great red dragon." He is great in capacity, intelligence, energy and experience. Whether or not he was the chief of all angels before he fell I do not know. Some have thought that he was such and that when he heard that a man was to sit upon the Throne of God, out of very jealousy he rebelled against the Most High. This also is conjecture. But we do know that he was and is an exceedingly great spirit as compared with us. He is a being great in evil–the Prince of Darkness–having the power of death. He shows his malice against the saints by accusing the Brethren day and night before God. In the Prophets we have the record of Satan standing to accuse Joshua the servant of God. Satan also accused Job of serving God from mercenary motives–"Have not You made an hedge about him and all that he has?"

This ever active enemy desires to tempt as well as accuse–he would have us and sift us as wheat. In calling him the dragon, the Holy Spirit seems to hint at his mysterious power and character. To us a spirit such as he is must ever be a mystery in his being and working. Satan is a mysterious personage though he is not a mythical one. We can never doubt his existence if we have once come into conflict with him. Yet he is to us all the more real because so mysterious. If he were flesh and blood it would be far easier to contend with him. But to fight with this spiritual wickedness in high places is a terrible task. As a dragon he is full of cunning and ferocity.

In him, force is allied with craft. And if he cannot achieve his purpose at once by power, he waits his time. He deludes, he deceives. In fact, he is said to deceive the whole world. What a power of deception must reside in him, when under his influence the third part of the stars of Heaven are made to fall and myriads of men in all ages have worshipped demons and idols! He has steeped the minds of men in delusion so that they cannot see that they should worship none but God, their Maker. He is styled "the old serpent." And this reminds us how practiced he is in every evil art.

He was a liar from the beginning, and the father of lies. After thousands of years of constant practice in deception he is much too cunning for us. If we think that we can match him by craft we are grievous fools for he knows vast more than the wisest of mortals. And if it once comes to a game of policies, he will certainly clear the board and sweep our tricks into the bag. To this cunning he adds great speed so that he is quick to assail at any moment, darting down upon us like a hawk upon a poor chick. He is not everywhere present. But it is hard to say where he is not.

He cannot be omnipresent—but yet by that majestic craft of his—he so manages his armies of fallen ones that, like a great general, he superintends the whole field of battle and seems present at every point. No door can shut him out, no height of piety can rise beyond his reach. He meets us in all our weaknesses and assails us from every point of the compass. He comes upon us unaware and gives us wounds which are not easily healed.

But yet, dear Friends, powerful as this infernal spirit certainly must be, his power is defeated when we are resolved never to be at peace with him. We must never dream of terms or truce with evil. To suppose that we can let him alone and all will be well is a deadly error. We must fight or perish—evil will slay us if we do not slay it. Our only safety will lie in a determined, vigorous opposition to sin, whatever shape it assumes, whatever it may threaten, whatever it may promise. The Holy Spirit, alone, can maintain in us this enmity to sin.

According to the text it is said of the saints, "They overcame him." We are never to rest until it is said of us also, "They overcame him." He is a foeman worthy of your steel. Do you refuse the conflict? Do you think of turning back? You have no armor for your back. To cease to fight is to be overcome. You have your choice between the two—either to gird up the loins of your minds for a life-long resistance—or else to be Satan's slave forever. I pray God that you may awake, arise, and give battle to the foe. Resolve once and for all that by the Grace of God you will be numbered with those who overcome the archenemy.

Our text brings before us a very important subject for consideration What is the conquering weapon? With what sword did they fight who have overcome the great red dragon? Listen! "They overcame him by the blood of the Lamb." Secondly, how do we use that weapon? We do as they did who overcame "by the word of their testimony. And they loved not their lives unto the death."

First, WHAT IS THIS CONQUERING WEAPON? They overcame him by "the blood of the Lamb."

The blood of the Lamb signifies, first, the death of the Son of God. The sufferings of Jesus Christ might be set forth by some other figure but His death on the Cross requires the mention of blood. Our Lord was not only bruised and smitten but He was put to death. His heart's blood was made to flow. He of whom we speak was God over all, blessed forever. But He condescended to take our manhood into union with His Godhead in a mysterious manner. He was born at Bethlehem a babe. He grew as a child, He ripened into manhood and lived here among us, eating and drinking, suffering and rejoicing, sleeping and laboring as men do. He died in very deed and was buried in the tomb of Joseph of Arimathea.

That death was the grand fact which is set forth by the words "the blood of the Lamb." We are to view Jesus as the Lamb of God's Passover—not merely separated from others, dedicated to be Israel's memorial and consecrated to Divine service but as the Lamb slain. Remember that Christ viewed as living and not as having died, is not a saving Christ. He Himself says, "I am He that lives and was dead." The moderns cry, "Why not preach more about His life and less about His death?" I reply, Preach His life as much as you will but never apart from His death. For it is by His blood that we are redeemed.

"We preach Christ." Complete the sentence—"We preach Christ crucified," says the Apostle. Ah, yes, there is the point. It is the death of the Son of God which is the conquering weapon. Had He not poured forth His soul unto death, even to the death of the Cross–had He not been numbered with the transgressors and put to a death of shame–we should have had no weapon with which to overcome the dragon prince. By "the blood of the Lamb," we understand the death of the Son of God. Hear it, O men! Because you have sinned, Jesus dies that you may be cleared from your sin. "He His own Self bare our sins in His own body on the tree" and died that He might redeem us from all unrighteousness.

The point is His death and, paradoxically, this death is the vital point of the Gospel. The death of Christ is the death of sin and the defeat of Satan and hence it is the life of our hope and the assurance of His victory. Because He poured out His soul unto death, He divides the spoil with the strong.

Next, by "the blood of the Lamb" we understand our Lord's death as a substitutionary sacrifice. Let us be very clear here. It is not said that they overcame the archenemy by the blood of Jesus, or the blood of Christ, but by the blood of the Lamb. And the words are expressly chosen because, under the figure of a lamb, we have set before us a sacrifice. The blood of Jesus Christ, shed because of His courage for the truth, or out of pure philanthropy, or out of self-denial conveys no special Gospel to men and has no peculiar power about it. Truly it is an example worthy to beget martyrs. But it is not the way of salvation for guilty men.

If you proclaim the death of the Son of God but do not show that He died the Just for the unjust to bring us to God, you have not preached the blood of the Lamb. You must make it known that "the chastisement of our peace was upon Him," and that "the Lord has laid on Him the iniquity of us all," or you have not declared the meaning of the blood of the Lamb. There is no overcoming sin without a substitutionary sacrifice. The lamb under the old Law was brought by the offender to make atonement for his offense and in his place it was slain.

This was the type of Christ taking the sinner's place, bearing the sinner's sin and suffering in the sinner's place and thus vindicating the justice of

God and making it possible for Him to be just and the Justifier of Him that believes. I understand this to be the conquering weapon—the death of the Son of God set forth as the propitiation for sin. Sin must be punished—it is punished in Christ's death. Here is the hope of men.

Furthermore, I understand by the expression, "The blood of the Lamb," that our Lord's death was effective for the taking away of sin. When John the Baptist first pointed to Jesus, he said, "Behold the Lamb of God, which takes away the sin of the world." Our Lord Jesus has actually taken away sin by His death. Beloved, we are sure that He had offered an acceptable and effectual propitiation when He said, "It is finished." Either He did put away sin, or He did not. If He did not, how will it ever be put away? If He did, then are Believers clear. Altogether apart from anything that we do or are, our glorious Substitute took away our sin, as in the type, the scapegoat carried the sin of Israel into the wilderness.

In the case of all those for whom our Lord offered Himself as a substitutionary sacrifice, the justice of God finds no hindrance to its fullest flow—it is consistent with justice that God should bless the redeemed. Near nineteen hundred years ago Jesus paid the dreadful debt of all His elect and made a full atonement for the whole mass of the iniquities of them that shall believe in Him, thereby removing the whole tremendous load and casting it by one lift of His pierced hand into the depths of the sea. When Jesus died, an atonement was offered by Him and accepted by the Lord God so that before the high court of Heaven there was a distinct removal of sin from the whole body of which Christ is the Head.

In the fullness of time each redeemed one individually accepts for himself the great atonement by an act of personal faith but the atonement itself was made long before. I believe this to be one of the edges of the conquering weapon. We are to preach that the Son of God has come in the flesh and died for human sin and that in dying He did not only make it possible for God to forgive but He secured forgiveness for all who are in Him. He did not die to make men savable but to save them. He came not that sin might be put aside at some future time but to put it away then and there by the sacrifice of Himself. By His death He "finished transgressions, made an end of sin and brought in everlasting righteousness."

Believers may know that when Jesus died they were delivered from the claims of Law and when He rose again their justification was secured. The blood of the Lamb is a real price which did effectually ransom His elect. The blood of the Lamb is a real cleansing which did really purge away sin. This we believe and declare. And by this sign we conquer. Christ crucified, Christ the Sacrifice for sin, Christ the effectual Redeemer of men—we will proclaim everywhere, and thus put to rout the powers of darkness.

II. I have shown you the sword. I now come, in the second place, to speak to the question, How DO WE USE IT? "They overcame him by the blood of the Lamb."

When a man gets a sword, you cannot be quite certain how he will use it. A gentleman has purchased a very expensive sword with a golden hilt and an elaborate scabbard—he hangs it up in his hall and exhibits it to his friends. Occasionally he draws it out from the sheath and he says, "Feel how keen is the edge!" The precious blood of Jesus is not meant for us merely to admire and exhibit. We must not be content to talk about it and extol it and do nothing with it. But we are to use it in the great crusade against unholiness and unrighteousness, till it is said of us, "They overcame him by the blood of the Lamb."

This precious blood is to be used for overcoming and consequently for holy warfare. We dishonor it if we do not use it to that end. Some, I fear, use the precious blood of Christ only as a quietus to their consciences. They say to themselves, "He made atonement for sin, therefore let me take my rest." This is doing a grievous wrong to the great sacrifice. I grant you that the blood of Jesus does speak better things than that of Abel and that it sweetly cries, "Peace! Peace!" within the troubled conscience. But that is not all that it does. A man who wants the blood of Jesus for nothing but the mean and selfish reason, that after having been forgiven through it he may say, "Soul, take your ease, eat, drink and be merry—hear sermons, enjoy the hope of eternal felicity, and do nothing"—such a man blasphemes the precious blood and makes it an unholy thing.

We are to use the glorious mystery of atoning blood as our chief means of overcoming sin and Satan—its power is for holiness. See how the text puts it—"They overcame him by the blood of the Lamb"—these saints used the doctrine of atonement not as a pillow to rest their weariness but as a weapon to subdue their sin. O my Brothers, to some of us, atonement by blood is our battle-ax and weapon of war by which we conquer in our struggle for purity and godliness—a struggle in which we have continued now these many years. By the atoning blood we withstand corruption within and temptation without. This is that weapon which nothing can resist.

Let me show you your battlefield. Our first place of conflict is in the heavenlies and the second is down below on earth. First, then, my Brothers and Sisters who believe in the blood of Jesus, have to do battle with Satan in the heavenlies. And there you must overcome him "by the blood of the Lamb." "How?" you say. I will lead you into this subject. First, you are to regard Satan this day as being already literally and truly overcome through the death of the Lord Jesus. Satan is already a vanquished enemy. By faith grasp your Lord's victory as your own since He triumphed in your nature and on your behalf.

The Lord Jesus Christ went up to Calvary and there fought with the Prince of Darkness, utterly defeated him and destroyed his power. He led captivity captive. He bruised the serpent's head. The victory was the victory of all who are in Christ. He is the representative seed of the woman and you who are of that seed and are in Christ actually and experimentally, you then and there overcame the devil by the blood of the Lamb. Can you get a hold of this tog? Do you not know that you were circumcised in His circumcision, crucified on His Cross, buried with Him in Baptism and therein also risen with Him in His resurrection? He is your federal Head and you, being members of His body, did in Him what He did.

Come, my Soul, you have conquered Satan by your Lord's victory. Will you not be brave enough to fight a vanquished foe and trample down the enemy whom your Lord has already thrust down? You need not be afraid, but say, "Thanks be to God which gives us the victory through our Lord Jesus Christ." We have overcome sin, death and Hell in the Person and work of our great Lord. And we should be greatly encouraged by that which has been already worked in our name. Already we are more than conquerors through Him that has loved us. If Jesus had not overcome the enemy, certainly we never should have done so. But His personal triumph has secured ours.

By faith we rise into the conquering place this day. In the heavenlies we triumph, as also in every place. We rejoice in our Lord Jesus Christ, the Michael of the angels, the Redeemer of men. For by Him we see Satan cast out and all the powers of evil hurled from their places of power and eminence.

This day I would have you overcome Satan in the heavenlies in another sense—you must overcome him as the Accuser. At times you hear in your heart a voice arousing memory and startling conscience. A voice which seems in Heaven to be a remembrance of your guilt. Hark to that deep, croaking voice, boding evil! Satan is urging before the Throne of Justice all your former sins. Can you hear him? He begins with your childish faults and your youthful follies. Truly a black memory. He does not let one of your wickednesses drop out. Things which you had forgotten he cunningly revives. He knows your secret sins, for he had a hand in most of them.

He knows the resistance which you offered to the Gospel and the way in which you stifled conscience. He knows the sins of darkness, the sins of the bedchamber, the crimes of the inner chambers of imagery. Since you have been a Christian he has marked your wickedness and asked, in fierce sarcastic tones, "Is this a child of God? Is this an heir of Heaven?" He hopes to convict us of hypocrisy or of apostasy.

The foul fiend reveals the wanderings of our hearts, the deadness of our desires in prayer, the filthy thoughts that dropped into our minds when we have been at worship. Alas, we have to confess that we have even tolerated doubts as to eternal verities and suspicions of the love and faithfulness of God! When the Accuser is about his evil business he does not have to look far for matter of accusation, nor for facts to support it. Do these accusations stagger you? Do you cry, "My God, how can I face You? For all this is true and the iniquities now brought to my remembrance are such as I cannot deny. I have violated Your Law in a thousand ways and I cannot justify myself."

Now is your opportunity for overcoming through the blood of the Lamb. When the Accuser has said his say and aggravated all your transgressions, be not ashamed to step forward and say, "But I have an Advocate as well as an Accuser. O Jesus, my Savior, speak for me!" When He speaks, what does He plead but His own blood? "For all these sins I have made atonement," says He, "all these iniquities were laid on Me in the day of the Lord's anger and I have taken them away." Brethren, the blood of Jesus Christ, God's dear Son, cleans us from all sin. Jesus has borne the penalty due to us—He has discharged for us upon the Cross all our liabilities to the justice of God and we are free forever, because our Surety suffered in our place.

Where is the Accuser now? That dragon voice is silenced by the blood of the Lamb. Nothing else can ever silence the Accuser's cruel voice but the voice of the blood which tells of the infinite God accepting, in our behalf, the sacrifice which He Himself supplied. Justice decrees that the sinful shall be clear, because the accepted Substitute has borne his sin in His own body on the tree. Come, Brother or Sister, the next time you have to do with Satan as an accuser in the heavenly places, take care that you defend yourself with no weapon but the Atonement. All comfort drawn from inward feelings or outward works will fall short.

The bleeding wounds of Jesus will plead with full and overwhelming argument and answer all. "Who shall lay anything to the charge of God's elect? It is God that justifies. Who is he that condemns? It is Christ that died, yes rather, that is risen again, who is even at the right hand of God, who also makes intercession for us." Who, then, shall accuse the child of God? Every accuser shall be overcome by the invincible argument of the blood of the Lamb.

Still further, the Believer will have need to overcome the enemy in the heavenly places in reference to access to God. It may happen that when we are most intent upon communing with God, the Adversary hinders us. Our heart and our flesh cry out for God, the living God. But from one cause or another we are unable to draw near unto the Throne. The heart is heavy, sin is rampant, care is harassing and Satanic insinuation is busy. You seem shut out from God and the Enemy triumphs over you. You feel very near the world and very near the flesh and very near the devil—you mourn your miserable distance from God. You are like a child who cannot reach his father's door because a black dog barks at him from the door.

What is the way of access? If the foul Fiend will not move out of the way, can we force our passage? By what weapon can we drive away the Adversary so as to come to God? Is it not written that we are made near by the blood? Is there not a new and living way consecrated for us? Have we not boldness to enter into the Holiest by the blood of Jesus? We are sure of God's love when we see that Christ died for us. We are sure of God's favor when we see how that Atonement has removed our transgressions far from us. We perceive our liberty to come to the Father and therefore we each one say—

"I will approach You—I will force
My way through obstacles to You;
To You for strength will have recourse,
To You for consolation flee!"

254

Pleading the propitiation made by the blood of the Lamb, we dare draw near to God. Behold, the evil spirit makes way before us. The sacred name of Jesus is one before which he flees. This will drive away his blasphemous suggestions and foul insinuations better than anything that you can invent. The dog of Hell knows the dread name which makes him lie down—we must confront him with the authority and especially with the Atonement of the Lamb of God. He will rage and rave all the more if we send Moses to him—for he derives his power from our breaches of the Law and we cannot silence him unless we bring to him the great Lord who has kept the Law, and made it honorable.

We next must overcome the enemy in prayer. Alas, we cannot always pray as we would! Do you ever feel, when you are in prayer, as if something choked your utterance—and, what is worse—deadened your heart? Instead of having wings as of an eagle to mount to Heaven, a secret evil clips your wings and you cannot rise. You say within yourself, "I have no faith and I cannot expect to succeed with God without faith. I seem to have no love. If I have any, my heart lies asleep and I cannot stir myself to plead with God. Oh, that I could come out of my closet, saying, 'Vici! Vici!'—'I have overcome! I have overcome!' But, alas, instead I groan in vain and come away unrelieved. I have been half dead, cold and I cannot hope that I have prevailed with God in prayer."

Whenever you are in this condition fly to the blood of the Lamb as your chief remedy. When you plead this master argument you will arouse yourself and you will prevail with God. You will feel rest in pleading it and a sweet assurance am utterly unworthy and I admit it. But, I beseech You, hear me for the honor of Your dear Son. By His agony and bloody sweat, by His Cross and passion, by His precious death and burial, I beseech You hear me! O Lord, let the blood of Your Son prevail with You! Can You put aside His groans, His tears, His death, when they speak on my behalf?"

If you can thus come to pleading terms with God upon this ground, you must and will prevail. Jesus must be heard in Heaven. The voice of His blood is eloquent with God. If you plead the atoning sacrifice, you must overcome through the blood of the Lamb.

Thus have I spoken of overcoming in the heavenlies. But I shall have to show you how you must contend against the Evil One in a lower sphere, even on this earth. You must first overcome in the heavenly places before the Throne. And when you have been thus triumphant with God in prayer, you will have Divine Grace to go forth to service and to defeat evil among your fellow men. How often have I personally found that the battle must first be fought above! We must overcome in order to service. Many a score of times of late I should not have ventured into this pulpit had it not been for power at the Mercy Seat. Those who know the burden of the Lord are often bowed down and would not be able to bear up at all were it not for having in secret battled with their enemy and won the day.

I have been bowed down before the Lord and in His Presence I have pleaded the precious blood as the reason for obtaining help and the help has been given. Faith, having once made sure that Jesus is hers, helps herself out of the treasury of God to all that she needs. Satan would deny her but in the power of the blood she takes possession of Covenant blessings. You say to yourself, "I am weak but in the Lord, my God, there is power—I take it to myself. I am hard and cold but here is tenderness and warmth and I appropriate it. It pleased the Father that in Jesus should all fullness dwell and by virtue of His precious blood, I take out of that fullness what I need and then with help thus obtained I meet the enemy and overcome him."

Satan would hinder our getting supplies of Divine Grace wherewith to overcome him. But with the blood mark on our foot we can go anywhere. With the blood mark on our hand we dare take anything. Having access with confidence, we also take with freedom whatsoever we need and thus we are provided against all necessities and armed against all assaults through the atoning sacrifice. This is the fountain of supply and the shield of security—this, indeed, is the channel through which we receive strength for victory.

When we really feel the power of the precious blood of Christ we overcome the great enemy by laying hold upon the all-sufficiency of God. Thus, being victorious in the heavenlies, we come down to the pulpit or to the Sunday school class made strong in the Lord and in the power of His might. Having overcome Satan at the Throne of Grace, we see him like lightning fall from Heaven even before our feeble instrumentality. We speak and God speaks with us. We long for souls and God's great heart is yearning with us. We entreat men to come and the Lord also pleads with them to come so that they no longer resist. Spiritual power of a holy kind rests upon us to overcome the spiritual power of an evil kind which is exerted by Satan, the world and the flesh.

The Lord scatters the power of the enemy and breaks the spell which holds men captive. Through the blood of the Lamb we become masters of the situation and the weakest among us is able to work great wonders. Coming forth to the service of God in the power of our victory in Heaven gained by pleading the blood of the Lamb we march on conquering and to conquer and no power of the enemy is able to stand against us.

It is time that I now showed you how this same fight is carried on on earth. Among men in these lower places of conflict saints overcome through the blood of the Lamb by their testimony to that blood. Every Believer is to bear witness to the atoning sacrifice and its power to save. He is to confirm the doctrine. He is to emphasize it by earnest faith in it. And he is to support it and prove it by his experience of the effect of it. You cannot all speak from the pulpit but you can all speak for Jesus as opportunity is given you. Our main business is to bear witness with the blood in the power of the Spirit. To this point we can all testify. You cannot go into all manner of deep doctrines or curious points but you can tell to all those round about you that "There is life in a look at the Crucified One."

You can bear witness to the power of the blood of Jesus in your own soul. If you do this you will overcome men in many ways. First, you will arouse them out of apathy. This age is more indifferent to true religion than almost any other. It is alive enough to error but to the old faith it turns a deaf ear. Yet I have noticed persons captivated by the Truth of Substitution who would not listen to anything else. If any discourse can hold men, as the ancient mariner detained the wedding guest, it is the story of Divine Love, incarnate in the Person of Jesus, bleeding and dying for guilty men. Try that story when attention flags. It has a fascination about it. The marvelous history of the Son of God, who loved His enemies and died for them—this will arrest them.

The history of the Holy One who stood in the sinners' place and was in consequence put to shame and agony and death—this will touch them. The sight of the bleeding Savior overcomes obduracy and carelessness. The doctrine of the blood of the Lamb prevents or scatters error. I do not think that by reasoning we often confute error to any practical purpose. We may confute it rhetorically and doctrinally but men still stick to it. But the doctrine of the precious blood—when it once gets into the heart— drives error out of it and sets up the throne of Truth. You cannot be clinging to an atoning sacrifice and still delight in modern heresies.

Those who deny inspiration are sure to get rid of the vicarious atonement because it will not allow their errors. Let us go on proclaiming the doctrine of the great sacrifice and this will kill the vipers of heresy. Let us uplift the Cross and never mind what other people say. Perhaps we have taken too much notice of them already. Let the dogs bark, it is their nature to. Go on preaching Christ crucified. God forbid that I should glory, save in the Cross of the Lord Jesus Christ!

We also overcome men by softening rebellious hearts. Men stand out against the Law of God and defy the vengeance of God. But the love of God in Christ Jesus disarms them. The Holy Spirit causes men to yield through the softening influence of the Cross. A bleeding Savior makes men throw down their weapons of rebellion. "If He loves me so," they say, "I cannot do other than love Him in return." We overcome men's obduracy by the blood, shed for many for the remission of sins.

How wonderfully this same blood of the Lamb overcomes despair. Have you ever seen a man shut up in the iron cage? It has been my painful duty to talk with several such prisoners. I have seen the captive shake the iron bars but he could not break them, or break from them. He has implored us to set him free by some means. But we have been powerless. Glory be to God, the blood is a universal solvent and it has dissolved the iron bars of despair, until the poor captive conscience has been able to escape. How sweet for the desponding to sing–

"I do believe, I will believe,
That Jesus died for me"!

Believing that, all doubts and fears and despairs fly away and the man is at ease.

There is nothing, indeed, dear Friends, which the blood of the Lamb will not overcome. For see how it overcomes vice and every form of sin. The world is foul with evil like a stable which has long been the lair of filthy creatures. What can cleanse it? What but this matchless Stream? Satan makes sin seem pleasurable, but the Cross reveals its bitterness. If Jesus died because of sin, men begin to see that sin must be a murderous thing. Even when sin was but imputed to the Savior it made Him pour out His soul unto death. It must, then, be a hideous evil to those who are actually and personally guilty of it. If God's rod made Christ sweat great drops of blood, what will His axe do when He executes the capital sentence upon impenitent men! Yes, we overcome the deadly sweetness and destructive pleasures of sin by the blood of the Lamb.

This blood overcomes the natural lethargy of men towards obedience. It stimulates them to holiness. If anything can make a man holy, it is a firm faith in the atoning sacrifice. When a man knows that Jesus died for him, he feels that he is not his own but bought with a price and therefore he must live unto Him that died for him and rose again. In the Atonement I see a motive equal to the greatest heroism–yes, a motive which will stimulate to perfect holiness. What manner of persons ought we to be for whom such a sacrifice has been presented! Now are we quickened into intensity of zeal and devotion. See, dear Brothers, how to use the blood of the Lamb in this lower sphere while contending with evil among men.

But I must close with this. It is not merely by testimony that we use this potent Truth. We must support that testimony by our zeal and energy. We need concentrated, consecrated energy. For it is written, "They loved not their lives unto the death." We shall not overcome Satan if we are fine gentlemen, fond of ease and honor. As long as Christian people enjoy the world, the devil will suffer little at their hands. They that overcame the world in the old days were humble men and women, generally poor, always despised. They were never ashamed of Christ. They only lived to tell of His love and died by tens of thousands rather than cease to bear testimony to the blood of the Lamb.

They overcame by their heroism. Their intense devotion to the cause secured the victory. Their lives to them were as nothing when compared with the honor of their Lord. Brethren, if we are to win great victories we must have greater courage. Some of you hardly dare speak about the blood of Christ in any but the most godly company. And scarcely there. You are very retiring. You love yourselves too much to get into trouble through your religion. Surely you cannot be of that noble band that love not their own lives unto the death!

Many dare not hold the old doctrine nowadays because they would be thought narrow and bigoted and this would be too galling. They call us old fools. It is very likely we are. But we are not ashamed to be fools for Christ's sake and the Truth's sake. We believe in the blood of the Lamb, despite the discoveries of science. We shall never give up the doctrine of atoning sacrifice to please modern culture. What little reputation we have is as dear to us as another man's character is to him. But we will cheerfully let it go in this struggle for the central Truth of Revelation. It will be sweet to be forgotten and lost sight of, or to be vilified and abused, if the old faith in the substitutionary sacrifice can be kept alive.

This much we are resolved on, we will be true to our convictions concerning the sacrifice of our Lord Jesus. For if we give up this, what is there left? God will not do anything by us if we are false to the Cross. He uses the men who spare not their reputations when these are called for in defense of the Truth of God. Oh to be at a white heat! Oh to flame with zeal for Jesus! O my Brothers and Sisters, hold to the old faith and say, "As for the respect of men, I can readily forfeit it. But as for the Truth of God, that I can never give up." This is the day for men to be men. For, alas, the most are soft creatures. Now we need backbones as well as heads. To believe the Truth concerning the Lamb of God and truly to believe it—this is the essential of an overcoming life. Oh for courage, constancy, fixedness, self-denial, willingness to be made nothing for Christ! God give us to be faithful witnesses to the blood of the Lamb in the midst of this ungodly world!

As for those of you who are not saved, does not this subject give you a hint? Your hope lies in the blood of the Lamb—

"Come, guilty souls and flee away,
Like doves, to Jesus' wounds."

The atoning sacrifice, which is our glory, is your salvation. Trust in Him whom God has set forth to be the propitiation for sin. Begin with this and you are saved. Every good and holy thing which goes with salvation will follow after. But now, this morning, I pray you accept a present salvation through the blood of the Lamb. "He that believes in Him has everlasting life."

REDEMPTION THROUGH BLOOD—THE GRACIOUS FORGIVENESS OF SINS

"In whom we have redemption through His blood, the forgiveness of sins, according to the riches of His Grace."
Ephesians 1:7

READ the chapter and carefully note how the Apostle goes to the back of everything and commences with those primeval blessings which were ours before time began. He dwells on the Divine love of old and the predestination which came out of it–and all that blessed purpose of making us holy and without blame before Him in love, which was comprehended in the Covenant of Grace. It does us good to get back to these antiquities–to these eternal things. You shake off something of the dust of time, as you no longer walk down its restless ages, but traverse the glorious eternity where centuries seem no more than fallen leaves by the way. Thousands of years are less than a drop of a bucket compared with the lifetime of the Almighty! How sublime a thing to climb, in contemplation, to the everlasting God and the eternal council chamber–and to see the heart of love beating towards the chosen people before all time–and the infinite mind of God devising and purposing their good! This is an exceedingly great refreshment and the wonder is that so few Believers dare to ascend this sublime hill of the Lord, there to commune with Him who Was and Is, and is to come!

After the Apostle had briefly touched upon that subject, he then began to speak of present blessings–matters of actual experience–and he commenced by saying, "In whom we have redemption." The Grace of the eternal past is a matter of faith, but here is something which is within our grasp and enjoyment. The other we believe, but this we actually and literally receive. "We have redemption through His blood, the forgiveness of sins."

And here let me say what a charming thing it is to deal with experimental divinity–not with theories, but with matters of fact–great facts which are dear to you because they have been worked in you, and you have not been merely a delighted spectator of them, but you have been the subject and object of them! "In whom we have redemption." Whether others have it or not, we have "redemption through His blood, the forgiveness of sins." We do not hope for it, but we have it. We do not merely think so, but we know that we have it. We are redeemed! We are free from bondage! We are forgiven and are no longer under condemnation!

At this time, as God shall help me, I shall dwell upon the forgiveness of sins. We have not time to plunge into the deeps of the eternal purpose, nor even to dive into the full Doctrine of Redemption, but, as the swallow with his wing touches the brook and then is up and away, so must it be with my thoughts at this time—a mere touch of the river of the Water of Life will be a blessing to myself and, as I cast a little spray over you, I hope it will refresh you, also. May the Holy Spirit help our meditation!

The first observation, taken distinctly from the text, is this—THAT THE FORGIVENESS OF SINS IS A GRAND BLESSING. The Apostle has mentioned it, if you notice, among the great things of God—His electing love, His adoption of us by Jesus Christ, His acceptance of us in the Beloved. Side by side with these colossal mercies, he puts this one, that we have "the forgiveness of sins, according to the riches of His Grace." This is a blessing of no mean stature, for it marches with the giants of Election and Adoption. Let it stand prominently out before us at this time. What is this "forgiveness of sins"? Too often, in popular talk, it is supposed that the chief and main thought of the forgiven sinner is that he has escaped from Hell. Salvation means much more than this and what it further means is too much kept in the background, but yet I will begin with rescue from punishment, for if sin is pardoned, the penalty is extinguished. It would not be possible for God to forgive and yet to punish. That would be a forgiveness quite unworthy of God. It would, indeed, be no forgiveness at all! We are certain that the everlasting punishment of sin declared in Scripture will never happen to the man who is forgiven. When transgression is removed, the soul stands clear at the bar of God, and there can be no further penalty. "I absolve you," says the great Judge—and that carries with it weight, so that a man that is forgiven is cleared of the punishment which he must otherwise have borne. "Blessed is he whose transgression is forgiven, whose sin is covered." "There is therefore now no condemnation to them which are in Christ Jesus."

Yet Divine favor restored is a still brighter result of forgiveness to many. Speaking from my own experience, while I was under conviction of sin I had less apprehension of the punishment of sin than I had of sin, itself. I do not know that I very frequently trembled at the thought of Hell—I did so whenever it came before my mind. But when I was in the hands of the Holy Spirit, as a Spirit of bondage convincing me of sin, my great trouble was that God was angry with me—properly and rightly so. I mourned that I had offended my Maker, that I had grieved the living God, that I had sinned against His righteous will and that I could not rejoice in His favor, nor sun myself in His smile. I felt that it was right on the part of the holy God to be displeased with me. I believe that the great joy of forgiveness, to the Believer, is that God has taken away His anger from him. That sweet hymn, which we often sing, is a paraphrase of a passage in Isaiah—

"I will praise You every day,
Now Your anger's turned away;
Comfortable thoughts arise
From the bleeding Sacrifice."

"Though You were angry with me, Your anger is turned away and You comforted me."

Forgiveness means this among men. A person has grieved and wronged me. I feel hurt in my mind about it. When I forgive him, I no longer feel grieved or angry with him—I think of him as before—and we are on good terms. If my forgiveness is genuine—and in God's case it is emphatically so—then there is no resentment left. The offense is as though it had never been committed. I say to the person who did me wrong, "I take a sponge and I wipe it all off the slate. Give me your hand, let us stand as we stood before." The pardon of sin by God is after such a fashion. He blots out the sin as the Oriental erases with his pencil the record made upon his waxen tablet so that no trace of it remains. He smiles where otherwise he must have frowned. He gives complacent love where otherwise there must have been indignation and wrath. Do you not think that this is the sweetest way of looking at the forgiveness of sin? If you are, at this time, under legal work, feeling the tortures of a guilty conscience, you will appreciate such a pardon very highly. In the case of the poor penitent prodigal, it was the kiss of his father's lips, it was his restoration to his father's heart, it was the cheering words of his father's love that constituted to him the sweetest fragrance of the rose of forgiveness. Yes, the Lord Jesus Christ has come, that we poor guilty ones may be restored to the favor of God and walk consciously in the light of His Countenance because sin is removed!

This pardon of sin, being of this full and sweet character, involving both the reversal of the penalty of sin and the ending of the distance that intervened between us and God, brings with it the removal of much distress and sorrow from the heart! I do not think that there can be any grief outside of Hell that is more terrible to bear than the wounds of conscience. We read that, "David's heart smote him" and, believe me, the heart can smite as with an iron mace and smite where the bruise is intensely felt. Give me into the power of a roaring lion, but never let me come under the power of an awakened, guilty conscience! Yes, shut me up in a dark dungeon, among all manner of loathsome creatures–snakes and reptiles of all kinds–but, oh, give me not over to my own thoughts when I am consciously guilty before God! This, surely, is the worm that dies not and the fire that is not quenched!

I do not speak, now, what I have merely heard of, though, if you will read Mr. Bunyan's, "Grace Abounding," you will find a striking account of it there. I speak of what I have felt in my own soul. No pains of body can rival, for a moment, the agonized feeling of the heart when the hot irons of conviction burn their way through the soul. When God sets up the conscience and makes it a target for His arrows, they drink up the life blood of our spirit till we cry out and wonder how such anguish can come to a creature so insignificant. Our soul seems too small a cup to contain such an ocean of misery—too narrow a field for so cruel a battle. It is not the Lord that is the author of the misery, but He is giving us up, for a while, that we may be filled with our own ways and learn the bitterness of our own sin. When the Lord comes to us with a forgiving word, these sorrows are gone like the mists of the morning when the sun arises. We still grieve to think that we have sinned, but that gnawing remorse, that vulture eating up the liver, is smitten with death and the man breathes hopefully again. Though the penitence remains, the torment is removed from me, when God has forgiven me.

Let me say, here, that full forgiveness of sin, consciously enjoyed, will not only lift an enormous weight from off the soul, but it will breathe into the heart a great joy. When you know that sin is forgiven, you cannot be sad as before. The thought of perfect pardon, if it does but fill the spirit, will thrust out gloom and remove apathy. It will make the lame man leap as a hart—he may still be lame, but he will leap as if he were not! And the tongue of the dumb, even though untrained to speech, shall be made to sing concerning Free Grace and dying love. When the thoughts are concentrated upon the enjoyment of complete forgiveness, full reception into the Divine favor and the blotting out of sin, then is the heart lifted into the suburbs of Heaven! My dear Hearers, do you know what I am talking about? Some of you do, blessed be the name of the Lord, but I am afraid that some of you do not—and you never will know the sweetness of mercy until you have first tasted the bitterness of sin! You will never know how Divine Grace can heal until you have felt how sin can wound. There is no clothing you till you are stripped. There is no making you alive till you are killed. There is no filling you till you are empty.

The Lord fills the hungry with good things, but the rich He sends away empty. God Himself will never comfort you till you are driven to self-despair—and if you have already come to that, it is a great privilege to me to be allowed to tell you that the fact of forgiveness of sin is not only a doctrine of the creed, but it is a promise of God's Word! "I believe in the forgiveness of sins"—this is no mere formula, but a realized fact with me. Removal of the penalty, removal of God's offense against us, the clearing away of all the turbid waters within the heart and the creation of joy and peace through perfect reconciliation to God–this is a summary account of the forgiveness of sin. It is a vast and rich blessing!

II. And now, secondly, THE FORGIVENESS OF SINS IS BOUND UP WITH REDEMPTION BY BLOOD. Take the text, "In whom we have redemption through His blood, the forgiveness of sins." Redemption and forgiveness are so put together as to look as if they were the same thing. Assuredly they are so interlaced and intertwisted that there is no having the one without the other.

Do you ask–"How is it that there should always need to be redemption by blood in order to the forgiveness of sin?" I call your attention to the expression, "Redemption through His blood." Observe, it is not redemption through His power, it is through His blood. It is not redemption through His love, it is through His blood. This is insisted upon emphatically, since, in order to the forgiveness of sins, it is redemption through His blood, as you have it over and over again in Scripture. "Without shedding of blood is no remission." But they say– they say–that Substitution is not just! One said, the other day, that to lay sin upon Christ and to treat Him as guilty–and let Him die for the unjust– was not just! Yet the objector went on to say that God forgave men freely without any atonement at all! Of this wise critic I would ask–Is that just? Is it just to pass by breaches of the law without a penalty? Why any law at all? And why should men care whether they keep it or break it? It was stated by this critic that God, out of His boundless love, treated the guilty man as if he were innocent. I would ask–if that is right, where is the wrong of God's treating us as innocent because of the righteousness of Christ?

I venture to affirm that pardon is needless, if not impossible, upon the theory that the man, though guilty, is treated as if he were not guilty. If all are treated alike, whether guilty or not guilty, why should anyone desire pardon? It were easy to answer quibblers, but they really are not worth the answering! It is to me always sufficient if I find a Truth of God taught in Scripture–I ask no more. If I do not understand it, I am not particularly anxious to understand it! If it is in the Scriptures, I believe it. I like those grand, rocky Truths of the Bible which I cannot break with the hammer of my understanding, for on these I lay the foundations of my soul's confidence! Redemption by blood is here linked with forgiveness of sins and, in many other Scriptures we find it plainly stated. It is so. Let that stand for a sufficient answer to all objectors.

And it is so, if we come to think of it, because this reflects great honor upon God. They say, "Let God simply forgive the sin and have done with it." But where, then, is His justice? "Shall not the Judge of the earth do right?" He threatened sin with punishment. If He does not execute His threats, what then? Can we be sure that He will fulfill His promises? If He breaks His Word one way, might He not break it another? If the Lord should not execute the penalty which He has threatened for sin, would it not look as if He made a mistake in threatening a penalty at all? Would it not seem as if He had been too severe, at first, and then had to catch Himself up and revise His own judgment afterwards? And shall that be? Might it not be supposed that, after all, God made much ado about nothing and that He was really jesting with men when He threatened them with fearful punishment on account of sin? Shall God say, "Yes," and, "No"? Shall He speak and not speak?

This is according to the folly of man! Sometimes it may even be wisdom in a fallible man to reverse his word and retract his declaration, but with God this cannot be! It is necessary for the vindication of His own justice, His wisdom and His holiness, that He shall not forego one of His threats any more than one of His promises! And, since it is just that sin should be punished and that, though the sinner should, in wondrous mercy be permitted to go free, it is wise and just that Another should step in—God Himself should step in—and bear for the sinner what is due to the justice of the Most High. The Substitution of our Lord in our place is the central Doctrine of the Gospel and it greatly glorifies the name of God.

Besides that, Beloved, that sin should not be pardoned without an Atonement is for the welfare of the universe. This world is but a speck compared with the universe of God. We cannot even imaging the multitudes of beings over which the great Lawgiver has rule. And if it could be whispered anywhere in that universe that, on this planet, God tampered with law, set aside justice, or did anything, in fact, to save His own chosen, so that He threw His own threats behind His back and disregarded His own solemn ordinance—why, this report would strike at the foundations of the Eternal Throne! Is God unjust in any case? Then how can He judge the universe? What creatures, then, would fear God, when they knew that He could play fast and loose with justice? It were a calamity even greater than Hell, itself, that sin should go unpunished! The very reins of moral order would be snatched from the hand of the great Charioteer—and I know not what of mischief would happen! Evil would then have mounted to the high Throne of God and would have become supreme throughout His domains. It is for the welfare of the universe, throughout the ages, that in the forgiveness of sins there should be redemption by blood. Let lovers of anarchy cavil at it, but let good men accept the Sacrifice of the Son of God with joy as the great establishment of law and justice.

Moreover, this also is arranged for our comfort and as assurance of heart. I declare before you all that if I had been anywhere assured, when I was under conviction of sin, that God could forgive me outright without any atonement, it would have yielded no sort of satisfaction to me, for my conscience was sitting in judgment upon myself and I felt that if I were on the Throne of God, I must condemn myself to Hell. Even if I could have derived a temporary comfort from the notion of forgiveness apart from atonement, the question would afterwards have come up—how is this just? If God does not punish me, He ought to do so—how can He do otherwise? He must be just, or He is not God! It must be that such sin as mine should bring punishment upon itself. Never, until I understood the great Truth of God of the substitutionary death of Christ, could my conscience get a moment's peace! If an atonement was not necessary for God, it certainly was necessary for me—and it seems to me necessary to every conscience that is fairly instructed as to the absolute certainty that sin involves deserved sorrow—and that every transgression and every iniquity must have its just recompense of reward. It was necessary for the perpetual peace of every enlightened conscience that the glorious Atonement should have been provided.

Besides that, the Lord meant to save us in a safe way for the promotion of our future reverence for the Law. Now, if sin had been blotted out so readily and nothing more said of it, what effect would that have had on us in the future? I think that everyone who has felt the burden of sin, has stood at the foot of the Cross, heard the cries of the great Sacrifice and read God's wrath against sin written in crimson lines upon the blessed and perfect Person of the innocent Savior—every such person feels that sin is an awful thing! You cannot trifle with transgression after a vision of Gethsemane. You cannot laugh at it and talk about the littleness of its demerit, if you have once stood on Golgotha and heard the cry, "Eli, Eli, lame Sabachthani?" The death of the Son of God upon the Cross is the grandest of all moral lessons because it is a lesson that affects the very soul of the man and changes his whole idea of sin. The Cross straightens him from the desperate twist which sin gave him at the first. The cure of the first Adam's fall is the second Adam's death—the second Adam's Grace, which comes to us through His great Sacrifice! We love sin till we see that it killed our best Friend—and then we loathe it forevermore.

I say, again, that if the great Father forgave you and said, "There is nothing in it. Go your way, it is all over," you would have lacked that grand source of sanctified life which now you find in the wounds of Him who has made sin detestable to you—and has made perfect obedience, even unto death—the subject of your soul's admiration. Now you long to be unto the great Father, in your measure, what your great Redeemer was to Him when He magnified the Law and made it honorable. This is no mean benefit.

O Beloved Friends, I do bless the Lord, at this time, for the forgiveness of sins through redemption by blood! There is something worth preaching in this Truth of God. You can live on it—you can die on it. I am constantly—almost every week—at the deathbeds of our members here— we are so large a Church that one or two, every week, are going Home.

When we begin to talk about the precious blood of Jesus–the blood of the Everlasting Covenant, you should see the brightness of dying eyes! I mark the quiet of the departing spirit and, as my dear Friends grip my hand, their testimony is unvaryingly, "Jesus is the Rock of our confidence and all is well."

O Lord Jesus, hold Your Cross before my closing eyes! O blessed Redeemer, what will a man do in death who has not Your death to be the death of his sin? How can a man live who has never seen You lay down Your life in His place, "the Just for the unjust, to bring us to God"? Whatever others may say, let us repeat our text with solemn assurance, "In whom we have redemption through His blood, the forgiveness of sins."

III. But now, thirdly–and the text is very clear upon this, as upon the other two points–THE FORGIVENESS OF SIN IS STILL A MATTER OF GRACE–AND OF RICH GRACE. "We have redemption through His blood, the forgiveness of sins, according to the riches of His Grace."

I admit that the forgiveness of sins, on God's part, is a matter of justice, now that the redemption by blood has been completed. The man believes. The man confesses his sin. And it is written, "If we confess our sins, He is faithful and just to forgive us our sins." The Sacrifice is so great that it justly puts away the sin and it is righteously forgiven. But observe this–the act of God in forgiving is not one atom the less gracious, because, in His infinite wisdom, He has so contrived that it is unquestionably just. If any make this assertion, they will be called upon to prove it–and they can prove it.

Pardon is the more gracious to us that it does not come to us in an unrighteous way. We see God's great prudence and wisdom in planning the method by which He may "be just, and the Justifier of him that believes." Those thoughts and plans on God's part are all tokens of great love to us. Beloved, it is only by Divine Grace that we are justified, yet that this Grace is exercised in a way of justice causes the Grace to be not less, but even manifestly more gracious!

The death of Christ, the redemption by blood, instead of veiling the Grace of God, only manifests it. Put the thing before your own minds. Suppose that somebody has offended you and you say, "Think no more of it. It is all forgiven"? Very well. That is kind of you and commendable. It shows the graciousness of your character. But suppose, on the other hand, you were in office as a judge and felt compelled to say, "I am willing to forgive you, but your offense has resulted in such great mischiefs and all these things have to be cleared away. I will tell you what I will do. I will clear them away myself. I will bear the result of your sin in order that my pardon may be seen to be most sure and full. I will pay the debt in which you have involved yourself. I will go to the prison to which you ought to go as the consequence of what you have done. I will suffer the effect of your wrongdoing instead of condemning you to suffer it"?

Well, now, the forgiveness that costs you so much would manifest your graciousness much more than that which costs you nothing beyond a kind will and a tender heart! Oh, if it is so, that God, the Divine Ruler, the Judge of all the earth, says to guilty man, "I will pardon you, but it is imperative that My Law be carried out. And this cannot be done except by the death of My dear Son, who is One with Me, who is very God of very God, who Himself wills to stand in your place and vindicate My justice by suffering the penalty due to you"–then I say that the Grace of God is a thousandfold more clearly shown than by the free forgiveness which "modern thought" pleads for! Pardon which has cost God more than it cost Him to make all worlds–which has cost Him more than to manage all the empires of His Providence–which has cost Him His Only-Begotten Son and has cost that Only-Begotten Son a life of sorrow and a death of unutterable and immeasurable anguish–I say that this pardon is pre-eminently gracious! Love is more displayed in this, infinitely more, than by a mere word and a wave of the hand which would dismiss the sinner without any attempt at an atoning sacrifice.

Besides, Beloved, let this always be remembered, that it is in the application of redemption and the personal pardon of any sinner, through the blood of Jesus, that the Grace of God is best seen by that sinner. To each one, that pardon through the Lord Jesus comes, not only according to Grace, but "according to the riches of His Grace." I can understand that God should forgive you, all of you. I could hear it with full belief and it would not astonish me. But that He should pardon me–that I should have the forgiveness of sins and redemption by blood–that truly astonishes me! And I believe that any person, under a sense of sin, sees more of the Grace of God in His own salvation than in the salvation of anybody else. He may be quite conscious that he has never been a thief, or a drunk, or a murderer and yet, when he comes to look at it, he may see reasons why the pardon of sin in his case should be more remarkable than even in the case of a drunk, or a thief, or a murderer! There may be elements in his own case which may make him seem to have sinned even more grievously than open transgressors because he transgressed against greater light, with less temptation and with a direr presumption of rebellion against the Most High. That Jesus died is unutterable Grace–but that He loved me and gave Himself for me–this is overwhelming Grace and makes the heir of Heaven say with emphasis, "Blessed be God that, in Jesus, I have redemption through His blood, the forgiveness of sins, according to the riches of His Grace!"

Do you not feel at this time, you that have been pardoned, that nothing but the riches of God's Grace could ever have pardoned you? No scanty Grace could have provided an atonement equal to your iniquities! Poverty of Grace would have left you ruined by your debt of sin! Riches of Grace were needed and riches of Grace were forthcoming in redemption by blood and in the full, perfect, irreversible forgiveness which God gave you in the day when you believed on Jesus Christ your Savior! Oh, that the Holy Spirit would help you to sing of the Grace of God today and every day!

IV. Thus far have I brought you, then, in three remarks. Kindly follow me in the fourth one, upon which I will not be long.

Fourthly, THIS FORGIVENESS OF SINS IS ENJOYED BY US NOW. "In whom we have"–we have–"redemption through His blood, the forgiveness of sins, according to the riches of His Grace." I remember the astonishment with which I felt as I sat in a ministers' meeting and heard one who professed to be a preacher of the Gospel, assert that he did not think that any of us could be sure that he was forgiven. I ventured at once to say that I was sure—and I was pleased, but by no means surprised, to find that others dared to say the same. I hope I have hundreds before me who enjoy the same assurance!

Brothers and Sisters, if there is no consciousness of the forgiveness of sins possible, how can there be any rest for the conscience? Yet Jesus says, "Come unto Me, all you that labor and are heavy laden, and I will give you rest." What rest is possible to the condemned? Can you go to bed tonight with your sins unforgiven? Some of you may have the foolhardiness to do that, but I would not dare to do it! Look where you are. Within a moment you may be dead. Within that moment you will be in Hell, past all hope. In a single instant you may be eternally lost—can you endure the thought? Our breath has but to stop, or the heart to cease beating and instantly life is over! How can you be at peace while sin is unforgiven? Unless sin had made men mad, they would never rest till they were cleared from their sins. There cannot be any true rest without a consciousness of forgiveness. Yet that rest is promised—therefore the present enjoyment of an assurance of forgiveness must be possible!

And, next, where could there ever be that great love in the hearts of men and women which we read of in Scripture? She that washed the Savior's feet with her tears and wiped them with the hairs of her head—would she have done so if she had not known that she was forgiven? She loved much because she had had much forgiven her! And the stimulus, the zeal, the fervor that spurs on a man in his service and suffering for the Lord Jesus must arise out of the consciousness that the Lord has done great things for him—and the conclusion that, therefore, he must do great things for his Lord. Surely, you have robbed Christianity of its highest moral force if you have denied the possibility of knowing that you are pardoned!

Moreover, where is there any testimony of the power of Grace? We that come and preach to you would be liars if we, ourselves, have never tasted and handled pardoning Grace. We do, at any rate, but preach to you a second-hand Gospel, which we have never tested and proved for ourselves. If I did not know, in my very soul, that the blood of Jesus Christ, His Son, cleanses us from all sin, how could I dare to face you with the Gospel message? I have not impudence enough to tell you of what is, or is not the Truth of God, about which I am uncertain myself! God grant me Grace to break stones, or sweep chimneys sooner than come and tell you a cunningly-devised fable, or a tale about which I have no assured certainty, derived from personal knowledge! Could I say to you, "I dare say there is bread, but I myself am hungry and I have never eaten a mouthful of the provision which I offer you"? Think of my saying to one perishing of thirst, "There is Living Water flowing from the Rock, but personally I am thirsty." You might say to me at once, "Then go home to your house and next time you appear, be sure of the truth of what you tell us. If you do not believe it, how should we believe it?" Beloved, there are thousands, there are still tens of thousands on earth who know that the Son of God has power on earth to forgive sins! And there are myriads in Heaven who passed to their happiness confident that they had been forgiven—and they sang on earth the same song that they sing in Heaven, "Worthy is the Lamb that was slain." They have washed their robes and made them white in the blood of the Lamb! They know it, they have no doubt about it! Many of us know it here and rejoice therein at this moment.

Dear Friend, what would you give to have this assurance? You may have it—"Believe on the Lord Jesus Christ, and you shall be saved." "He that believes and is baptized shall be saved." "Whoever believes in Him is justified from all sin." "He that believes in Him has everlasting life." Oh, that God's Grace may lead you to cast away all other confidences and to lay your guilty spirit down at Jesus' feet! Then shall you go your way rejoicing that you, also, with us, can say, "In whom we have redemption through His blood, the forgiveness of sins."

Fifthly–and this is only a brief head, but it is a point that must not be left out–THE FORGIVENESS OF SINS BINDS US TO OUR LORD JESUS CHRIST. Let us read the text again. "In whom we have redemption through His blood." We have nothing apart from Jesus! Every blessing of the Covenant binds us to Christ. Covenant gifts are so many golden chains to fasten the soul of the Believer to his Lord. Our wealth of mercy is all in Christ. There is nothing good outside of Christ. When are we pardoned, Brothers and Sisters? When have we forgiveness? Why, when we are in Him, "in whom we have redemption through His blood, the forgiveness of sins." O son of Adam, living without Jesus, hear and take warning! So long as you are out of Christ, you must bear your own burden till it crushes you to the dust! But as soon as you have touched the hem of His garment there is a link of connection–and if you can rise from that to holding Him by the feet–the union is closer! And if you can, from that, become like Simeon, who took Him up in his arms, then may you cry, "My eyes have seen Your salvation!" When you have Christ to the fullest, you have Grace to the fullest! It is as you are in Christ–in connection and communion with Christ–that you receive the pardon of sin, for all the pardon is in Him. Do you see that?

"In whom we have redemption through His blood, the forgiveness of sins." The forgiveness is not so much in His office and in His work, as in Himself. When you get Christ, you have redemption, for He is Redemption. When you get Christ, you have forgiveness of sins, for He is the Propitiation for our sins. He has put the sin away by the Sacrifice of Himself. Get Christ and you have the proof, the evidence, the sum, the substance of perfect pardon. If you accept the Beloved, you are "accepted in the Beloved." When you are in Him, then you are forgiven, but your forgiveness is only in Him. In Him you have redemption–out of Him you are in bondage.

Beloved, every day, as we go afresh to God for a sense of pardon, let us know that we can never get it unless we come viewing Jesus. I notice that some Believers, when they get rather dull and cold, begin the work of self-examination. This may appear very proper, but it is dreary work. I do not believe, dear Friends, if you are very poor, that you will ever get rich by looking through all your empty cupboards. If it is very cold and you have no coals in the cellar, you will not become warm by going into the cellar and seeing that there is nothing below but an empty coal hole. No, no–if our Graces are to be revived we must begin with a renewed consciousness of pardon through the precious blood–and the only way to get that sense of pardon is to go to the Cross, again, even as we went at first! I sometimes wonder that you do not get tired of my preaching because I do nothing but hammer away on this one nail. I have driven it in up to the head and I have gone round to the other side to clinch it–but I still keep at it. With me it is, year after year, "None but Jesus! None but Jesus!" Oh, you great saints, if you have outgrown the need of a sinner's trust in the Lord Jesus, you have outgrown your sins! But you have also outgrown your Grace and your saintship has ruined you! He that has the mind of Christ within him must still come to his Lord, just as he came at the first.

I frankly confess that still I cry to my Lord Jesus–

"Nothing in my hands I bring,
Simply to Your Cross I cling."

Still, to this day, I have no redemption in myself, but only in Jesus! I am not an inch forwarder as to the ground of my trust. Is it not so with you? Do we not still say of Jesus–"In whom we have redemption through His blood"? To this day we find no reason for forgiveness in ourselves. The precious blood is still our one plea! Lost and condemned are we apart from the one offering of our Great High Priest. But cleansed and justified are we in Him–

"Oh, how sweet to view the flowing
Of His sin-atoning blood!
He has made my peace with God."

You know the story of the poor bricklayer who fell from a scaffold, and when they took him up, he was so much injured that they fetched a minister to him, who, stooping over him, said, "My dear Man, you have a very short time to live. I entreat you to make your peace with God." To the surprise of the minister, the man opened his eyes and said, "Make my peace with God, Sir? It was made for me nearly 1,900 years ago, upon the Cross of Calvary, by Him that loved me and gave Himself for me." Oh, the joy which this creates in the heart! Yes, it is in Jesus that the peace is made–effectually made, made for me, made for you, made for all Believers! In Jesus is perfect redemption! In Jesus pardon is provided, proclaimed, presented and sealed upon the conscience! Go and live on Jesus; live with Jesus; live in Jesus; never go away from Jesus and may He be dearer to you every day of your lives! Blessed be His adorable name! Amen, and Amen.

BLOOD EVEN ON THE GOLDEN ALTAR

"And the priest shall put some of the blood upon the horns of the altar of sweet incense before the LORD, which is in the Tabernacle of the Congregation."
Leviticus 4:7

ALL through Holy Scripture you constantly meet with the mention of "blood." "Without shedding of blood is no remission." "The blood of Jesus Christ, His Son, cleanses us from all sin." "You were not redeemed with corruptible things, as silver and gold, from your vain conversation received by tradition from your fathers, but with the precious blood of Christ." The word, "blood," is recorded over and over again, and if any complain of the preacher that he frequently uses this expression, he makes no kind of apology for it–he would be ashamed of himself if he did not often speak of the blood! The Word of God is as full of references to blood as the body of a man is full of life and blood.

But what does, "the blood," mean in Scripture? It means not merely suffering, which might very well be typified by blood, but it means suffering unto death. It means the taking of a life. To put it very briefly, a sin against God deserves death as its punishment, and what God said by the mouth of the Prophet Ezekiel still stands true, "The soul that sins, it shall die." The only way by which God could fulfill His threatening sentence and yet forgive guilty men was that Jesus Christ, His Son, came into the world and offered His life instead of ours. His life, because of the dignity of His Person, and the majesty of His Nature, was so vast in its value that He could give it not only for one man, but for the whole multitude of men who should believe in Him! Now, that by which men are saved is the suffering of Jesus Christ even unto death, as Peter writes, "Christ, also, has once suffered for sins, the Just for the unjust, that He might bring us to God." Paul puts it, "Christ has redeemed us from the curse of the Law, being made a curse for us: for it is written, Cursed is everyone that hangs on a tree." And again, "He has made Him to be sin for us, who knew no sin; that we might be made the righteousness of God in Him."

All the sacrifices under the Law of God, when their blood was poured out, were typical of the life of Christ given for men as a Sacrifice in the place of those who had offended unto death against the Law of God and, therefore, were doomed to die. You who hear me constantly know very well what I mean. Have I ever given any uncertain sound about this great central Truth of God? There is no way of salvation under Heaven but by faith in the Substitutionary Sacrifice of Jesus Christ! And the way by which we are redeemed from eternal wrath is by Christ having stood as Substitute for us and having died in our place, as it is written, "The chastisement of our peace was upon Him, and with His stripes we are healed."

It is worthy of note that in the death of Christ, the shedding of blood was made very conspicuous, as if to refresh our memories about the teaching of the types of the Mosaic Law. Jesus was scourged unto bleeding. His temples were pierced and lacerated with a crown of thorns. His hands and feet were nailed with iron to the Cross. His side was opened by the soldier's spear and forthwith there flowed blood and water. There are many ways by which men may die without the shedding of blood—the capital punishment of our own country is free from this accompaniment—but our Savior was ordained to die by a death in which the shedding of blood was conspicuous, as if to link Him forever with those sacrifices which were made as types and symbols of His great atoning work! My dear Brother, Mr. Pearce, in his prayer, seemed to set forth Christ evidently crucified among you. I wish that even though you have to use your imaginations a little, you would think that you see Jesus on the Cross. Picture Him here, tonight, and lovingly watch Him. You will need few words from me if you do but catch sight of Him. Behold your Savior pouring out His life's blood that He might bear your guilt away, dying for you that you might live forever!

In the verse before our text we read that the priest was to take of the blood of the bullock of the sin offering and sprinkle it seven times "before the Lord, before the veil of the sanctuary." The veil concealed the inner dwelling place of God and this veil was to be sprinkled seven times, that is, perfectly. There was to be a perfect presentation of the precious blood before the place where God was concealed. After that was done, the priest was to take some of the blood of the bullock and smear with it the four horns of the golden altar which stood just in front of the veil, and near the golden candlesticks. This altar was intended for the burning of sweet incense upon it and the priest was to smear with blood the four horns of it. What was meant by that act? Let me read the text again and then at once seek to explain it. "The priest shall put some of the blood upon the horns of the altar of sweet incense before the Lord."

My first observation is this–THE ATONEMENT WAS PRESENTED WITH A VIEW TO THE LORD.
Have you not often heard it said that all the Atonement accomplished was something in relation to us? We think upon the death of Christ and it stirs our affections, but some teachers say that is the only result–it brings us to God, but it does not bring God to us! That is what they say, but when we turn to Holy Scripture we find that the blood shedding was with reference to God, Himself, as well as with reference to us, because in the text it is distinctly said, "The priest shall put some of the blood upon the horns of the altar of sweet incense before the Lord."

Its place was where the Lord would especially see it. I would like the young people, when they get home, to take a pencil and mark in the first chapters of the Book of Leviticus how often the expression is used, "before the Lord." The bringing of the bullock, the killing of the sacrifice, the sprinkling of the blood–all was to be done, "before the Lord." Whether any man saw it or not, was of small account, for it was, "before the Lord." True, it was done in the presence of the congregation, but it is specified over and over, again, that it was, "before the Lord." I would remind you that in the memorable type of the paschal lamb, the Lord gave special instructions as to where the blood was to be sprinkled. Was it to be within the house? Remember that all the people were inside the house–on the Passover night there was not a man outside! Where, then, was the blood put? Upon the interior walls of the house where they could see it? Might it not tend to comfort them if they could look upon it? That was not the Lord's plan–the blood was not put where the people could see it–it was sprinkled outside the house! And the Inspired account tells us that the Lord, Himself, said to Moses and Aaron, "And they shall take of the blood, and strike it on the two side posts and on the upper door post of the houses…and when I see the blood, I will pass over you." It was put where God could see it, and, as if to show that that was the main point, it was put where the people could not see it–that it might be distinctly said to them, "It is, after all, God's sight of the great sacrifice which saves you."

Next, the place of the blood is where the Lord sees it in reference to us. Understand where the Lord sees it with reference to us. They charge us with teaching that the Atonement in some way changes the Nature of God. We have never said so and we never dreamed anything of the kind! Above all things, we have always taught that God is Immutable and cannot be changed either in His Nature or in His purpose. They tell us that we teach and, they tell others that we teach, that the Sacrifice of Christ was offered to make God love His people. We have, over and over and over again, denied this, and declared that–

"'Twas not to make Jehovah's love
Towards the sinner flame,
That Jesus, from His Throne above,
A suffering Man became!
'Twas not the death which He endured,
Nor all the pangs He bore,
That God's eternal love procured,
For God was love before."

Christ in His Sacrifice is the result of God's love, not the cause of it! Yet, dear Friends, we do confess, without any hesitation, to this fact, that the death of Christ has a reference to God's dealing with us in this way–the claims of Divine Justice must be met. The Judge of all the earth must do right and He cannot suffer sin to go unpunished! Our own conscience confirms that Truth of God–there is no sinner, even when he is most hardened, who deep down in his soul does not know that to be true! And when he lies dying, it causes him great trouble to think that he is going where God must visit his sin upon him!

Now, what Christ has done is this—the Father has given us, in Christ, that which satisfies the claims of Infinite Justice. God can be just and yet the Justifier of him that believes. Executing the death penalty upon our Surety, He declares that whoever believes on Him shall not perish, but have everlasting life! Oh, dear Friends, it is God's looking on and seeing in His Son the vindication of His law, the honoring of His holiness—it is this which is the very essence of Christ's Sacrifice as to its result upon us!

I believe that the great Lord, the just Judge of all, looks on Jesus Christ with extreme delight as having suffered for His people. He sees in the sufferings of Christ the honoring of His own holiness. Jesus loved holiness so much that He would sooner die than that holiness should be impugned. He was so true, so upright, so just, that He would rather suffer to the death on the tree than that God should, in the least degree, violate His Word, or infringe His Justice. The Father looks on Christ's great Sacrifice and He takes great delight in it because He sees in it His own holiness honored and glorified!

And what a delight He must take in the love of Christ when He sees that Jesus loved us with a love which many waters could not quench, and which death, itself, could not drown! The great Father looks to the death of Christ and sees Christ's love triumphant on the tree, and He is charmed with it. I do not think that you and I can ever tell what pleasure the Father has in the finished work and Sacrifice of His dear Son. We read that He "smelled a savor of rest" in what was only a typical sacrifice—but what a savor of rest must the great heart of the Infinite Jehovah find in the Infinite Sacrifice of His Well-Beloved! You look upon it with bleared and bedimmed eyes, yet you see enough to make you wonder and adore. But what does God see in the Atonement of Jesus? Ah, Beloved, we cannot fully answer you, but we know that He sees there that which He eternally looks upon with infinite complacency and, for the sake of it, He looks upon us, poor guilty ones as we are, with complacency, too! He loves us because of what Christ has done in reference to us!

That is my first remark and though I have but feebly set it forth, yet, Beloved, it is a great and glorious Truth of God! The Atonement has a bearing towards the Lord, Himself, and, therefore, in this ancient type, the blood was smeared upon the altar of sweet incense before the Lord.

II. But now, secondly, coming to the very heart of the text–THE ATONEMENT GIVES POWER TO THE ITERCESSION OF THE LORD JESUS CHRIST.

That altar of sweet incense was the type of Christ pleading for men, making intercession for the transgressors. The horns of the altar signify the power of His intercession and the power of Christ's intercession lies in His Sacrifice–lies in the blood. If I might be allowed to picture such a scene, I seem to see the Divine Son pleading with His Father and He pleads the merit of His own blood.

The Father sees it, first, as a reason why the Son should plead with Him, for the blood shows His nearness of kin to man. Has Jesus blood? "Forasmuch, then, as the children are partakers of flesh and blood, He, also, Himself, likewise took part of the same." Here is the token to His Father that He is truly Man! Here is the sure testimony of His identification with His people for whom He makes intercession! The mark is made by His own blood upon the horns of the altar and its presence there proves that He is qualified to plead for men, seeing that, while He is God, His blood shows that He is evidently also Man!

I hear Him begin to plead and if Justice would stay Him and say, "How can You plead for the guilty? Before this Great White Throne, unsullied by a stain, how can You ask that God should bless the impure and foul?" Jesus points to His own blood as the token of His removal of impeding sin. "The Lamb of God, that takes away the sin of the world," has taken it away by the shedding of His own blood! "The blood of Jesus Christ, His Son, cleanses us from all sin." "Hear Me, My Father," He cries, "hear My plea on behalf of the penitent sinner! I have put away his sin. Answer My prayer and bless him, for I have taken away the sin that cursed him. I have borne its penalty and made expiation for it by My death."

Do you not think, also, that this blood, which is the very power of Christ's intercession, signifies His fulfillment of Covenant engagements? We read of "the blood of the Everlasting Covenant." Jesus had engaged with His Father "to finish the transgression and to make an end of sins, to make reconciliation for iniquity and to bring in everlasting righteousness," and He has done so! By His death, He could say, of His work as the Messiah, "It is finished!" By that death He had fulfilled His Suretyship engagement to His Father in connection with the Covenant of Grace and this, Beloved, is the very sinew of His strength in interceding for His people–this is the very essence of His pleading! He has done all that He agreed to do, therefore He asks the Father to fulfill His part of the Everlasting Covenant and to save the people redeemed by the blood shed on Calvary.

And, it seems to me, that Christ also uses His blood as the great power of His pleading in His claim of reward. "Have I not died for My people? Then will You not let them live, O My Father? Behold, O Justice, with uplifted sword, if you seek Me, let these go their way." Jesus seems to say, "My Lord, My God, I have become Your Servant. I took upon Myself the form of a Servant and was made in the likeness of sinful flesh. And I have performed all the service You did lay upon Me. Reward Me, then, for all My toil. Let Me see of the travail of My Soul. Let Me be satisfied according to the promise which You did make to Me when I undertook this work."

Do you not see, then, my Brothers and Sisters, that the blood on the horns of the altar means this–that Christ's blood is the very strength of His pleading with God? Because He died for guilty men, therefore, today, when He asks for the sinner's salvation, He will have it granted to Him, for the blood prevails with God, speaking better things than that of Abel!

III. And now, in the last place, I want to say to you that THIS BLOOD GIVES ACCEPTANCE TO OUR WORSHIP.

We bring to God sweet incense through Jesus Christ our Savior. Our prayers, our praises, our services are like the mixture of sweet perfumes which were burnt of old upon the altar before God. But it is the blood-mark on the altar that makes the incense acceptable. It is the atoning Sacrifice of our Lord Jesus Christ that gives prayer, praise and service acceptance in the sight of God.

In beginning to speak upon this point, I want you to notice that the blood is on the altar before we begin to pray. It was the blood that gave acceptance to the incense burnt upon the altar—it was not the stacte, onycha and galbanum—those, "sweet spices with pure frankincense," that, by themselves, ascended with fragrance unto the Lord. There must be the blood of the sacrifice sprinkled on the horns of the altar! What does this mean? Why, Beloved, that God accepts us in Christ because of Christ, Himself, and Christ, alone! It is true that we are to bring forth good works, for faith without works is dead. Still, the reason of our acceptance with God is not our good works, but Christ and His atoning Sacrifice, alone! As we come to Him, we sing—

"Nothing in my hand I bring,
Simply to Your Cross I cling."

Before you have performed a single work of holiness, before you have felt any of those sweet emotions which come out of the possession of Divine Love shed abroad in your heart, if you believe in the Lord Jesus Christ, you are accepted with God—Christ has saved you! Therefore is it that a man is justified by faith without works, for it is the faith that justifies him as it lays hold on Christ. There shall be an abundance of sweet spices on the altar, by-and-by, but apart from them, and before there has been a living coal smoking there, the altar has been consecrated unto God by the sprinkling of the blood of the Sacrifice! I like to think of that glorious fact! Let your good works be multiplied, but keep all of them at a distance from the Sacrifice of Christ! Never dream of adding them to

Christ's Sacrifice to make it complete, for it is perfect without anything of yours. When you repent of sin, if you begin to trust in your repentance, away with your repentance! When you serve God, if you begin to trust in your service, away with it! Away with it! It becomes an antichrist if it takes the place that should be occupied by Jesus, only, for His precious blood, alone, can put away sin!

But now I want you to note, dear Friends, that whenever you come to God with your worship, you must take care that you notice the blood on the altar, because it removes the sin of our worship. The best worship that we ever render to God is far from perfect. Our praises, ah, how faint and feeble they are! Our prayers, how wandering, how wavering they are! When we get nearest to God, how far off we are! When we are most like He, how greatly unlike He we are! This I know, that my tears need be wept over, and my faith is so mingled with unbelief that I have to repent of that sad admixture! Brothers and Sisters, keep your eyes fixed on the blood of Jesus! There is no prayer, no praise that can come before God, of itself, for it is so imperfect. Therefore, keep your eyes on the blood of Jesus, that even the sin of your holy things may be put away by the Sacrifice once offered on Calvary.

Do you not think, also, that we would pray a great deal better if we thought more of the blood on the altar as our plea in prayer? I remember a Primitive Methodist Prayer Meeting at which a Brother could not get on with his supplication. He was very earnest and fervent, but he could not make any progress. He did not seem as if he had power to pray. He shouted, as Methodists do, but there is not much in that—yet he could not get on with real praying till a friend at the back end of the room cried out, "Plead the blood, Brother! Plead the blood!" He did so and then he began to pray with mighty power! Here lies the force of all your pleas in prayer—if you can plead for Jesus' sake and in His name, by His agony and bloody sweat, by His Cross and passion—then you have discovered the great secret of prevailing with God! Your hand is on the lever and you can move the world if you will!

Should we not, also, make the precious blood of Jesus the highest note of our praises? When we are praising God, we think a great deal of the music. I do not blame anybody for doing that, especially if he is the leader of the Psalmody, but, Brothers and Sisters, we may come to think more of the melody and the harmony than we do of the heart and soul of praise! Keep your eyes on the crucified Christ and then sing as loudly as you like. Fix your gaze on those five precious wounds–they shall help you to praise Christ better than all the notes of the scales, for what higher note can we ever reach than this, "Unto Him that loved us, and washed us from our sins in His own blood"? Now you have sounded out the very highest note in the scale! Oh, the precious blood, the atoning Sacrifice, the great Substitution of our Lord Jesus Christ! The Hallelujah Chorus of all the redeemed shall have no nobler note than this, "He loved us and saved us. He loved us and died for us and we are washed in His blood."

Let me here say that every sort of worship, not only prayer and praise, but every kind of worship that we can render to the Lord, will be acceptable with God in proportion as we exhibit, with it, the blood upon the altar. I find it a very sweet way of worshipping God to sit down and meditate. I hope you feel the same. You do not need any words at such seasons. You have been reading a chapter of the Bible and God has spoken to you and you, perhaps, have knelt in prayer and have spoken with Him. Now you sit down and meditate. I like to sit quite still and look up, or sit quite still with closed eyes, and just think. Now, the thinking, the meditating, the contemplation which will be best for you and most acceptable with God is that which keeps close to the Cross and near the precious sacrifice. Do you notice what holy men and women say when they come to die? You stand at their bedside and talk to them. If they are in any trouble and distress of conscience, what do they begin to talk about? Why, about the precious Sacrifice of Christ upon the Cross! It does not matter to what sect they belong, or to what denomination they have been joined in life–they always come back to this point at the last. There is no passing out of this life with comfort–there is no hope of entering into Heaven with delight–except as we are resting upon the precious blood of Christ!

Ah, dear Friends, there may be some here who do not think much of this theme. There always were such. It is nothing to you that Jesus should die. But if there is anything that sanctifies, any Truth of God that digs deep into the heart and puts the Seeds of Life into the very center of our being—if there is anything that makes the Christian devout, humble, holy—it is the Doctrine of the Cross! I can almost gauge your piety to a certainty by what you think of the bleeding Savior. If He is nothing to you, you are not in the blessed secret. But if Jesus Christ is first and last with you. If you preach Christ crucified—if you love Christ crucified—in that proportion God dwells in you and you dwell in Him! This is not theory that I am talking—this is no Truth of God that lies upon the borders of the Christian religion and may, or may not be accepted! This is the very heart of the Gospel and if you take this away, you have killed it!

You are no Christian if you disbelieve this Truth of God! If you are not saved by the precious blood of Christ, you are damned! There is but one gate of life and that is sprinkled with the blood of Christ. If you turn away from that door, you have chosen the broad road that leads to destruction. O you who feel your guilt, come to my Lord for pardon! O you who confess your sin, come to His blood for cleansing! It is still true that—

"There is life for a look at the Crucified One!
There is life at this moment for you."

How many years have I come to this pulpit, telling this old, old story, telling it very poorly and very imperfectly, and yet you are not tired of hearing it! Look how the crowds still throng this house! I might have given you some pretty novelties every now and then, but had I done so, I believe I would have lost you! But this old Truth of God, even if you do not accept it, commands your attention. You cannot help coming to hear it—oh, that you would also believe it! It has made me supremely happy. I was about to say that it has given me an angel's happiness and, sometimes, I could even say without exaggeration it gives me solid peace with which I can live, and with which, by-and-by, I hope to die!

It enables me to stand alone against unnumbered foes and feel as happy as if everybody were with me, for, in this great Truth that Jesus died for me, that Jesus bore my sins in His own body on the tree, there is a rock beneath my feet! He who is on that rock may stand there and defy even death and Hell! Oh, that you would come and trust my Lord, you restless ones, you who do not know what peace means! Trust Him! Believe that He died for you! Trust Him and you shall have peace like a river—and righteousness like the waves of the sea!

May we now come to the Communion Table thinking much of the precious blood once shed for many for the remission of sins!

WITH OR WITHOUT SHEDDING OF BLOOD

"Without shedding of blood is no remission."
Hebrews 9:22

WEEK after week, standing before this congregation to preach the things concerning the Kingdom of Christ, I sometimes say to myself, "I wonder how much longer I shall have to point out to some of these people the way of salvation before they will walk in it–I wonder how many times I shall have to preach to them the Doctrine of Justification by Faith in the Crucified Christ of Calvary and how often I shall have to urge them to an immediate decision for Christ, the renunciation of their self-confidence and the forsaking of their sins?" It seems to me that after I have done this, the right thing for me to do is to keep on asking you, "Have you given due attention to these Truth of God? Do you know them in your soul?" For, "if you know these things, happy are you if you do them," but the very opposite of happy are you if you leave them undone!

I am going to try to enlist the attention of any earnest, thoughtful persons who are here, any of those who are still unconverted, but who have begun to consider their ways and to turn unto the Lord. To you, dear Friends, I mean to preach nothing but the simple Gospel of Jesus Christ–and not to preach it as though I were addressing the settlers in Australia or the pundits of Hindustan–but to preach it distinctly to you and to urge you to accept it here and now. Ifyou have not accepted it by the time the sermon is done, it shall be through no fault of mine–the blame must lie at your own door, that you have been directed to the way of salvation, but have not walked in it–or that, having heard the Gospel and taken some interest in it, you have willfully rejected it.

The subject of my discourse is to be the remission–the putting away and getting rid of sin–and that concerns every one of us, from the youngest child to the oldest man or woman, for we are all sinners. It is very common for people to say, "Oh, yes, we are all sinners!" But I do not use that expression as they do. I mean that you have done wrong and that I have done wrong and that we have, all of us, done wrong! "We have done the things which we ought not to have done and we have left undone the things which we ought to have done, and there is no health in us." We have chosen the wrong instead of the right. We have chosen to please ourselves rather than to please God. We have even lived as if there were no God! If there had really been no God, our conduct might not have been materially affected. We have all sinned in some way or other–

"Each wandering in a different way,
But all the downward road."

And, dear Friends, we all of us need to be cleansed from this sin. There is not one among us who can afford to live in sin, or who can afford to die in sin. We may find a temporary pleasure in it, but it must end in eternal loss to us unless there comes a time when God's Grace saves us from it–we cannot be truly happy while we are out of gear with God. And since we are immortal beings and our soul will not die, but will live on forever, there will come a time in which the sin which is unforgiven will be a sore plague to us. So it is vitally important that we should enquire whether, being sinners, we have been forgiven or not!

I hope I shall be able to reach the conscience of each person here while I try to talk to you about two contrasts. First we have, in our text, sin unremitted and sin remitted. without shedding of blood and withshedding of blood.

So, first, we will consider these two things which are so opposite to each other–SIN UNREMITTED AND SIN REMITTED.

The Apostle says, "Without shedding of blood is no remission." I do not like the sound of those words, " noremission." They seem to me like a funeral knell–"no remission." That might have been the sound in the ears of every sinner from the time of Adam until now–"no remission." It would have made this world a dreadful prison if everywhere, when we sat down to think of our sin, there stared us in the face the words, "no remission." This is, indeed, one of the inscriptions across the vault of Hell–"no remission," "no remission." I say that I cannot bear the sound of those words, yet they must be sounded aloud, for there are still some persons to whom they apply. I trust that the sounding of those words in their ears may be the means of their awakening!

What does it mean when we say that a man has sinned and that there is no remission for him? It means, first, that he is the object of the daily anger of God. God has a benevolent regard for him as one of His creatures and is not willing that he should perish. God would infinitely prefer that the sinner should turn to Him and live, but, viewing him as an impenitent sinner, we read that "God is angry with the wicked every day." I have learned not to take much notice of other people's opinions, yet I do not like to make anybody angry if I can help it. If I have ever done so—and sometimes it has happened unintentionally—I have had no pleasure in reflecting that someone was angry with me. And if it was somebody who would not be angry without a cause, it has been a very painful thing to live under a consciousness of his displeasure. I want you whose sins are unforgiven, to reflect that God is angry with you every day. When He looks upon you, He cannot regard you as a father regards a dear child who has done everything he can to please him, but He must look upon you as a rebel—as one who has revolted against Him and defied Him to His face. When He looks upon your sin, His anger must flame forth. A man who is not angry with sin must be a guilty man and, in proportion to the holiness of God must be his abhorrence of evil.

Reflect, then, upon what a sad condition you are in. If God should never smite you in His righteous wrath—if He should continue to give you the mercies of this life every day just as He has done, I think, dear Friend, that it ought to trouble you all the more that you are still provoking Him by your continued sin. If you really are of the noble spirit that I hope you are, you will not be so ungenerous as merely to regret your faults because of the suffering it will bring to yourself, but you will lament it because it offends so loving, so good, so tender, so gracious a Being as the God of the whole earth! Were He vindictive—had He no heart of compassion—if He had made no proclamation of mercy and no terms of Grace—I could understand how you could brazen your forehead and defy

Him. But how can you live in enmity against the God who has been so gracious to you? Let the thought of the mercy of God make your unremitted sin such a burden upon your conscience that you will not rest until you have repented of it and been forgiven!

Remember, dear Friends, that, in addition to being the object of the daily anger of God, you are in constant peril ofsuffering that anger to the fullest. A single step may cause you to fall—and that fall may lead to the grave. Who among us can tell all the perils of this mortal life? I remember reading a work in which there were collected together numerous instances of the simple means by which men have died, such as the swallowing of a fruit stone, or the sticking of a small bone in the throat, the breathing of some invisible noxious gas, or the failure of some almost imperceptible organ in the body to perform its usual functions. How suddenly death often comes! A friend said to me, this morning, "Do you know that So-and-So is dead?" He was a dear fellow servant of Christ, an eminent preacher of the Gospel. I had no idea, when I saw him a little while ago in robust health, that he and I should never speak to each other again in this world! You, also, must often have heard of the death of friends—and someday people will tell the survivors that you, too, are gone. With unremitted sin upon you, you know where you will go, do you not? I need not tell you where they are driven whose sin has never been forgiven—and whose sin never will be forgiven—as they have passed out of this world unwashed in theprecious blood of Jesus!

May I very earnestly put to all of you who are still unsaved, this question—"How will you be able to die with unremitted sin upon you?" There are some of us who believe that there is a spot on this earth where our mortal remains are to lie—and it is possible that the tree of which the planks will form our coffin has already been cut down. We expect to die unless the Lord shall soon come and that will amount to much the same thing. And, expecting to die, we would like to be ready to die and to have our house in order. I like to meet a sensible man who insures his life so as not to leave his wife and family in poverty, or who, when he has means at his disposal, lays by for a rainy day that should he be out of work, he will not need to go and beg. Now, if such provision as this is commendable—and who will say that it is not—is it not much more commendable with regard to eternal things? Are we to be careful about lesser matters and yet to make no preparation for that last moment in which we must pass out of this world to undergo the solemn testing in the scales of unerring Justice? If unremitted sin is upon you—and it is to be fearful that it is upon very many of you—I pray you to consider what you will do in that dread hour when the immortal tenant of your house of clay makes her fatal leap without a wing to buoy her up—and sinks into despair and into yet deeper despair in the bottomless abyss! God grant that none of our spirits may ever know what it is to be found disembodied with unforgiven sin and afterwards to hear the trumpet of the great Day of Judgment ring out—and to go back into our risen bodies with sin unforgiven—and to be cast, body and soul, into the lake that burns forever and ever!

This is, surely, enough for me to say upon that sorrowful theme, so let us now think upon the brighter theme of remission. Our text seems to me to be musical with hope—"Without shedding of blood is no remission." Then it is clearly implied that, with remission! In the Gospel we always have glad news to tell.Unconverted Sinner with your unremitted sin, we have glad news to tell you! And this is it—your sin may be remitted! There is no sin of which you can repent, which may not be forgiven you! There lives not a mortal man who, if he repents of his sin, shall not find mercy! There is a sin which is unto death, but those who commit it never ask for mercy, or desire it. They are dead even while they live, their conscience is seared as with a hot iron, and they rush to Hell willingly. But never has a man sincerely anxious for salvation committed that sin! Let no penitent man despair, for there is remission forevery sin of which any man truly repents and for which he exercises faith in the precious blood of the Lord Jesus Christ!

The remission of sin which God gives to His people is complete. That is to say, it wipes out all his sins, whatever they may have been. Now look, Believer, there is the list of your sins, it is a huge roll! If I were to unroll it, how long would it be? Would it not belt the globe and reach from the earth to the sun and back again? Can you see all the sin that is recorded there? Yet the moment that the blood of Jesus is applied to that roll, the whole record is blotted out and there shall never be any more sin inscribed there, for Jesus Christ never yet divided a man's sins, forgiving some, and leaving others unforgiven! He deals with sin in the mass, takes it all up and flings it into the sea, or buries it in His own sepulcher! And never shall it have a resurrection, for, says the Lord, "the iniquity of Israel shall be sought for, and there shall be none; and the sins of Judah, and they shall not be found." In the Epistle from which our text is taken, the Lord says, "I will put My Laws into their hearts, and in their minds will I write them; and their sins and iniquities will I remember no more." King Hezekiah said to the Lord, "You have cast all my sins behind Your back." And King David wrote, "As far as the east is from the west"–and that is an infinite distance–"so far has He removed our transgressions from us." So you see that God completely sweeps away our sins when He remits them!

Further, the man who gets remission of sin, gets a clearance from all danger of any penalty resulting from sin, so thathe can sing–

"If sin is pardoned, I'm secure,
Death has no sting beside!
The Law gave sin Its damning power,
But Christ, my Ransom, died."

In dying, Christ bought my pardon so that I have no cause to fear the punishment of my sin! What a blessing it is that the sin is gone and the penalty is gone too! When a man's sin is remitted, he comes to the position which would have been his if he had never sinned. We fell, federally, in Adam, and we fell, actually, by our own sin. But Christ has put us back whereAdam was in his state of innocence. No, He has done more than that for us, for man was but man before he fell, but now man is linked to the Eternal in the Person of the God-Man, Christ Jesus, so we are nearer to God than Adam was before he fell! I said, Sinner, that God was angry with you, but if your sin is remitted, His anger is gone! What does a forgiven sinner say to God? "Though You were angry with me, Your anger is turned away and You comforted me." "Like as a father pities his children, so the Lord pities them that fear Him." Jeremiah wrote, "The Lord has appeared of old unto me, saying, Yes, I have loved you with an everlasting love; therefore with loving-kindness have I drawn you." It is sin that separates us from God—when that is put away, there is no longer any separation—but we are one in blessed amity, sacred relationship, holy concord and near and dear communion!

Do all of you, dear Friends, know what this remission of sin is? There are some of us who could boast of this—not that we could boast of anything that we are to us, the very chief of sinners! There are many here who could join with me in this declaration, "We were guilty and Helldeserving, but, having believed in the Lord Jesus Christ, we know that our sins, which were many, are all forgiven. We are 'clothed in the righteousness of Christ and are accepted in the Beloved!' And we know it and there is, therefore, now no condemnation to us who are in Christ Jesus. And we are not afraid of any, for, 'being justified by faith, we have peace with God through our Lord Jesus Christ.' The peace we have, through believing in Jesus, is so full, so rich, so deep, that it cannot be broken! Death itself will only deepen it. We are not afraid to die—why should we be? With the robe of His righteousness upon us, we shall stand boldly even in the great Day of Judgment—and with the name of Jesus upon us, He will welcome us and say to us, 'Come, you blessed of My Father, inherit the kingdom prepared for you from the foundation of the world.'"

I wish with all my heart and soul that every one of you had received the remission of your sin! I bless God that there are many in this place who are humbly resting on the great atoning Sacrifice. My Brothers and Sisters in Christ, do not question the remission of your sins, for, to question that is to question the Word of God itself! God Himself declares that every believer in Christ is justified and saved. But many of you who have heard the Gospel, have not believed it. "This is the condemnation, that light is come into the world, and men loved darkness rather than light, because their deeds were evil." This is your greatest sin—that you have not believed on Jesus Christ, whom God has sent! Oh, that God the Holy Spirit would convince you of the sin of unbelief and enable you to repent of it and to lay hold on Jesus Christ by a act of childlike faith, that you might live through Him!

II. This brings me to the second point of my discourse, which divides itself into two parts–WITHOUT SHEDDING OF BLOOD–AND WITH SHEDDING OF BLOOD.

"Without shedding of blood," says the Apostle–wherever that is the case, there is no remission. It is not possiblethat any sin should ever be forgiven to any man without shedding of blood. This has been known from the very first. As soon as man had sinned, God taught him that he needed a sacrifice. Adam and Eve, after they had sinned, tried to clothe themselves with fig leaves, but that was not a sufficient covering. God must kill some animals, shedding their blood and, in their skins our first parents must be clothed. When Cain and Abel had grown up, the only sacrifice that God would accept was the slain lamb. To Cain and his sacrifice of the fruits of the earth, God had no respect. Job is, perhaps, the earliest of the Patriarchs, but he offered sacrifices for his children lest they should have offended God while they were feasting. He did not think nor did any of those ancient men who feared God think of finding acceptance with Him and remission of sin–without shedding of blood.

This belief has been almost universally held. There is scarcely to be found a tribe of men who have not believed in this. Wherever explorers go, they find that wherever there is any conception of God, there is a sacrifice in some form or other. Many people have thought it necessary to make very great sacrifices and some have even imagined that they could only expiate their guilt by offering up their own children, so deeply-seated is the thought in our humanity that there must be a sacrifice for sin! I scarcely know of any religion, except Socinianism, without a sacrifice. Humanity craves for it and cannot do without it. If anyone should proclaim a religion without a sacrifice, you would soon see how quickly this building would be emptied, or any other place of worship! There are always more spiders than people where the Atonement is left out. Men must have a sacrifice–in their inmost hearts they know their absolute need of it when they seek to approach the Lord.

The old Mosaic Law revealed this need of a sacrifice for sin. The most prominent thing about it—that which must have stuck everybody—was the blood. I do not know whether you have ever realized that the Tabernacle, which waspraised for its beauty, must have looked like a veritable shambles and the gorgeous Temple, itself, must have needed abundant arrangements for its cleansing because of the continual sacrifices offered there—because so much of the service consisted in the shedding and sprinkling of blood. The most prominent idea that a worshipper would get would be that there was something for which an atonement was needed and that this involved the presentation of life before God. And that is just the thought that God would have us still retain in our minds, for, "without shedding of blood is no remission."

Do not quarrel with this Truth of God, dear Friends, for you cannot alter it. It is not for me to stand here to justify the ways of God to men, or to propound any theories of atonement. I have no theory. I simply say what the Apostle says, "Without shedding of blood is no remission." And there is no remission otherwise. You may stand and weep for sin till you become a very Niobe, or be transformed into a dripping well, or waste away in one continual shower of penitential lamentation, but no sin will ever be washed away so! To repent of sin is a part of your natural duty. And attention to one part of duty cannot atone for the neglect of another part.

"Oh, but!" you say, "in addition to this weeping and lamentation, I mean to amend." Well, suppose you do? If, from this time forth, you never sin again—if a wrong thought, or word, or act should never again stain your character, you will have done no more than it was your duty to do! And the fulfillment of your duty will be no atonement for the faults of the past—all your tears and all your efforts cannot put away the guilt of the past, for "without shedding of blood isno remission." And repentance and good works are not shedding of blood!

Suppose you add to these things what you call religiousness? Very well. Do so. Attend the House of Prayer, join in the petitions of the saints as far as you can, sing with them, but, all the while mind what you are doing, for you may be adding to your sin instead of decreasing it, by relying upon such things as those! I repeat the declaration that you have only done what you ought to have done and that cannot make amends for your previous misdeeds and neglects, so that there, too, you rest upon a broken reed.

Are you so foolish as to hope that sin can be put away by some sleight of hand that may be practiced by so-called "priests"? A plague upon them! They swarm on the face of this earth—these men who say that they are endued with some strange power by which they can remit human guilt by the muttering of certain words and by passing you through certain performances which are generally attended with the transference of some part of your substance to the pockets of the so-called "priests!" O Sirs, be not deceived by them! Open your eyes and see for yourselves what there can be in one of your fellow men just because there have been laid upon his head the hands of a man wearing lawn sleeves, that he should have the power to put away your sins! If this folly is to be believed, do not let us hear any more about "the enlightened 19 th century to believe in such a transparent lie as that! Go to theliving God for pardon, for He alone can give it! Make your confessions at His feet— only there they will be valid! And when you have confessed your sin to God, do not in any degree rely on sacramental efficacy, or on priestly power, but trust wholly to the shedding of blood! There is your hope! But without shedding of blood, priest or no priest, sacrament or no sacrament, you will be lost as surely as you are a human being and a sinner!

My last point is to be with the shedding of blood there is remission. That is a much more delightful topic. If God hadnot provided the Sacrifice for sin, my text would have sounded the death-knell of all our hopes. "Without shedding of blood—no remission," would have been like the flaming sword of the cherubim keeping us back from the Tree of Life. "My son, God will provide Himself a lamb for a burnt offering," was the sweet assurance of Abraham to Isaac. But to us there is a still sweeter assurance—God has Lamb for a burnt offering! Listen to this, you who would haveremission! God Himself came into this world. He who was offended by man's sin, condescended to become the Sacrifice to put away that sin! And coming here, He took upon Himself a human body, spotless and without taint of original sin. And here He lived as Man, perfect Man, yet just as truly very God of very God. When He had reached the appointed time, He offered Himself upon the altar as the one Sacrifice for human sin and, by the shedding of His blood, there is remission for sin! Think of this great Truth of God! Here was an innocent Sufferer, the value of whose life was worth more than an innumerable number of ours. It did more for the honor of God's Law for Christ to die than if we had all died, for allcreated beings will see how just God is when He will not let His own Son escape even when guilt is only imputed to Him.

Jesus Christ has died. The Son of God has offered Himself as a Sacrifice for sin! So now, whoever believes on Him shall have immediate remission of sin. It hardly matters how I tell you this great Truth so long as I make it clear to you. If I spoke it ungrammatically, if I uttered it so that you had to lean forward and strain your ears to catch the message, it would not matter as long as you were able to understand it. You are bound to lay hold of this Truth of God, for it is your life! If you do not grasp it, whose fault will it be? If I stood in the midst of a company of criminals condemned to die and told them that a free pardon could be obtained in a certain way, there would not be one of them who would criticize my voice or my manner because, if they really wanted pardon, they would all be taken up with the thought of getting it! It does not matter to me what criticism you may happen to make about me. I shall sleep just as well, I daresay, for all that—and live as long!

But I beseech you not to let any remarks or thoughts about me, or the place, or anything else drive any of you from this conviction—that you must either be saved or lost! That you must have your sins forgiven or else you will be ruined forever! That the only way of getting them forgiven is through the shedding of blood and that the only way of availing yourselves of the efficacy of the shedding of blood of Christ is by simple confidence in Him! Does anybody misunderstand that expression? Then I put it thus—give yourself up deliberately into the hands of Christ to save you from the consequences of your sin. As one who is falling, drops because he must, but drops cheerfully because another stands with outstretched arms to catch him, so drop into the Savior's arms! We are all prone to sin, but if we give ourselves up to Christ, He will change our natures and make us love holiness. He will renew our hearts so that we shall seek after that which is good, pure, lovely and excellent in the sight of God. Salvation from the propensity to sin, as well as from the guilt of sin, will be given at once to everyone who believes in the Lord Jesus Christ!

"But I do not feel right," one says. Feeling right is not the all-important matter. "Believe on the Lord Jesus Christ, and you shall be saved."

"I will go home and pray," says another. That is not what I urge you to do first. First, believe, and then pray. To putprayer in the place of faith is to suggest to God that He should change the plan of salvation, which is, as I just reminded another Friend, "Believe on the Lord Jesus Christ, and you shall be saved." "What am I to do, then? Am I to believe that Jesus Christ died for me in particular?" I did not say that. You are to trust Jesus Christ whether you have any particular interest in Him or not. You will find out your particular interest in Christ In due time. Just now, look at Christ upon the Cross. That is a spectacle that is well worthy of your careful observation! There He hangs, He who made all worlds! With hands and feet fastened to the accursed tree, He hangs there to die the death of a slave—the death that the Romans would scarcely inflict upon slaves unless they had committed some extraordinary crimes. He whom the angels worship, hangs there to die, "the Just for the unjust, that He might bring us to God." Can you not trust your soul with Him? Will you not believe that God, for Christ's sake, can forgive you? Will you not now rush into His arms and confess your sins, yet look up and say, "I know that You can forgive, for Christ has died, and I do rest my soul on His atoning Sacrifice"?

I remember—though it was many years ago—when first I really understood that I was simply to look to Jesus Christ and that, doing so, I would be saved. I felt in my heart that I wished I had known it long before, for I had been for years seeking rest and finding none–I only needed to be told that there was nothing for me to do but simply look to Christ! Oh, how I did leap at that message! It was the best sermon I ever heard, yet it was, in itself, a very poor one. But it had in it that which was the means of saving my soul. I trusted Christ then with my soul and now I have nothing else to rest on. I have preached some thousands of times since that day and God has given me many souls, but I have not found any improvement as to the way of salvation. I trusted wholly in Christ, then, and well I might, for I had nothing else to trust to! And I trust in nothing but Jesus Christ, now, and well I may, for I still have nothing else to trust to!

If there is a poor sinner here who sees the lifeboat of faith come close up to him and he is afraid to step in, if it is any comfort to you, Sinner, let me tell you that if you step into that lifeboat and are lost, I must be lost, too, for I do not know of any other way of escape! If there is anyone who trusts in Jesus Christ and is damned, I must be damned with him–I am perfectly willing to go with him to prison and to death. If my Lord Jesus Christ is not able to save a sinner just as he is, then He is not able to save me. And if the blood of Jesus Christ cannot wash out sin, then mine will never be washed out, for I have nothing but the blood of Jesus Christ to trust to, and I say to Him–

"Other refuge have I none–
Hangs my helpless soul on You."

O Sinner, you can hang where I can hang and where all God's people are hanging! "Ah," you say, "you do not know what a great sinner I am." No, and you do not know what a great Savior He is! "Ah, but I have such a hard heart!" But His heart was broken and He can break yours! "Yes, but it will be an amazing thing if He ever saves me." Ah, there you are right, and so it is when He saves anybody–and He delights to work wonders of Grace! I wonder which will be the biggest wonder in Heaven–you or I–or someone else here or elsewhere? Well, we shall see when we get there, but mind that you get there! God bless you, for His dear Son's sake! Amen.

FREEDOM THROUGH CHRIST'S BLOOD

"As for you also, by the blood of your covenant I have set forth your prisoners out of the pit wherein is no water. Turn you to the stronghold, you prisoners of hope: even today do I declare that I will render double unto you."
Zechariah 9:11, 12

THIS morning, I tried to show that in consequence of the blood of the Covenant having been shed and theCovenant having so been fulfilled, Jesus Christ was brought back out of the prison of the grave, set at liberty and exalted to indescribable Glory in the highest Heaven. I then showed that Jesus Christ is the Representative of all His people–that when He was set free, they were virtually set free, and that when He returned into Glory, He went there as their Representative, taking possession of the heavenly places in their name, so that, in due time, where He is, there they may also be. I had not time, this morning, to make a fitting application of our subject. But happily for us, here stands another text, an older one, and yet most suitable to come after the other, so I will use it now.

Jesus Christ has been delivered from the bondage of the grave and I have to remind you, first, that there are other prisoners who have been set free through the blood of the Covenant. there are other persons yet to be set free through the blood of the Covenant. in honor of the secret reason of their liberation–the blood of the Covenant.

First, then, dear Friends, we have to notice that THERE ARE SOME PERSONS WHO HAVE BEEN ALREADY SET FREE THROUGH THE BLOOD OF THE COVENANT.

This leads us to consider where they were prisoners and to what they were prisoners. We are told, in the text, thatthey were in "the pit." That is where all God's people were once. You know that, in the East, they did not always take the trouble to build prisons–an empty well, or a place where they had been accustomed to hide their corn, or an underground,

305

unused reservoir would serve for a prison. The poor prisoner was let down by ropes and the mouth of the pit or well was covered with a big stone–and there he was left to die. Generally the place was noisome and foul, a living grave rather than anything else. The position of a poor captive, sitting down on a stone at the bottom of a deep, dirty pit, is a very apt picture of the state of man by nature. When he is really awakened to a sense of his true position, he finds that this is the very image of where he is. He is put in that prison by the Law of God. He feels that he has broken the Law and that the Law must punish him. Conscience builds huge walls harder than granite around him–and when he tries to find a way of escape, there is none that he can discover. He realizes that the Judge of all the earth must abhor iniquity and must punish sin. In addition to that, sin has put him in that prison, for, though he has mourned over his sin since he was even partly awakened, yet he cannot cease from sin any more than the Ethiopian can change his skin or the leopard his spots! Like the big stone over the mouth of the well, his tendency to sin and his corruptions shut him in. He cannot lift that stone–he is a prisoner to his own evil desires and depraved heart and, at the same time, a prisoner lawfully detained, under a warrant from the High Court of Heaven by the officers of Divine Justice.

Many of you, my Brothers and Sisters in Christ, can recollect the time when you were in that pit. I remember being in it for years and, oh, what a happy day it was for me when I was lifted right up out of it! It is a horrible place, that pit reconciled God–to see sin, yet not to see the Savior–to behold the deadly disease in all its loathsomeness, but not to trust the Good Physician and so to have no hope of ever being healed of our malady! Of all the miseries that can be endured in this life, this is one of the greatest.

This poor prisoner, shut up in a pit out of which he could not escape, could find no comfort. The text says it was a pit in which there was no water. I saw the Mamertine Dungeon, which might very well be likened to a pit–the entrance to the first vault is through a narrow hole, then another narrow hole from the bottom of that vault into the second one. But in the floor of the lower dungeon, in which Paul is said to have been confined, there is a spring which continually bubbles up–and I drank of the water–as cold and fresh and clear as any I ever drank. There was at least one source of comfort there, for, in the stifling heat of that horrible dungeon, there was some water. But when we were shut up in the pit by our own sin and by Divine Justice, there was no water there. Do you remember when you tried to drink at the cistern of human ceremonies and found that it was filled with brine which increased your thirst instead of slaking it? You sought next to drink of what you thought was the water of your self-righteousness–but you were like a pilgrim on the desert sands who sees the deceptive mirage–limpid streams and crystal fountains before his eyes, but when he presses forward to drink of them, he finds nothing there but the burning sand! Some of us were duped and deluded, for a while, with the vain hope of accomplishing our own salvation, but it all turned to nothing and we were still in the pit wherein was no water. Oh, what numerous devil's agents there are about trying to cheat poor souls who are in this pit with the notion that they can supply them with water in the pit and that they can remain there–that they can continue unforgiven and unrenewed–and still enjoy true comfort! But that is an idle tale! No, more–it is a fatal delusion! There might as well be found water in Hell as true comfort for a soul that realizes its guilt and fears the thunders of the wrath of God, yet is not reconciled to God by the death of His Son. Apart from that Living Water which Jesus came to bring, such a soul is truly in "the pit wherein is no water."

And, dear Friends, there was a still worse point about our bondage. It was a thoroughly hopeless one, for we were not merely shut up in that pit for a short time, but we were shut up there to die! When a man is cast into a deep pit and the mouth of it is covered over with a stone–and his captors give him neither food nor water–he knows at once what that harsh treatment means. If they meant him to live, they would at least put him down with a crust of bread and a pitcher of water. But we were in a pit wherein was no water and we felt that there was nothing before us but "a certain fearful looking for of judgment and fiery indignation." I have known what it is to wake in the morning and wonder that I was not in Hell, and to go to my bed at night afraid to fall asleep lest I should sleep myself into eternity! When a man is in such a state as that, he feels that life is hardly worth living, and he could almost say with Job, "My soul chooses strangling and death rather than my life."

This is the position into which many who are the true children of God are brought–they are not all tried alike, for all are not made equally sensitive of sin and to some, faith comes much sooner than to others. But there are many persons who were thus shut up, but concerning whom the text now says, "By the blood of your covenant, I have sent forth your prisoners out of the pit wherein is no water." Notice that expression, "I have sent forth your prisoners." That is theblessing–we who have believed in the Lord Jesus Christ are in prison no longer. We are trusting in the blood of theCovenant and, therefore, there are no fetters upon us now, no stone walls, or prison bars, or terrors of conscience, or convictions of sin to frighten us now, for the Lord has said, "Their sins and their iniquities will I remember no more." There are thousands in this Tabernacle who were once in this prison, but they are out of it, now, and they can say, "Therefore being justified by faith, we have peace with God through our Lord Jesus Christ."

We are out of this pit by right. We did not break out of prison contrary to the Law of God–we have the right to be out because the debts for which we were imprisoned, are all paid–a full Atonement has been offered for the sins for which we were put in prison! There has been a complete expiation made, wide as the sin of all the Lord's people, and as vast as the demands of infinite and inflexible Justice. Every child of God is justly saved! It would bean eternal injustice if any soul for whom the Savior stood as a Substitute could die by the sword of Divine Justice. But that can never be–

"Payment God cannot twice demand,
First at my bleeding Surety's hand,
And then again at mine."

No, my blessed Savior–

"Complete Atonement You have made,
And to the utmost farthing paid,
Whatever Your people owed–
Nor can His wrath on me take place,
If sheltered in Your righteousness,
And sprinkled with Your blood."

But, dear Friends, we are free by might, as well as by right, for that same Jesus who bought our liberty for us, has secured it to us. Those grim prison walls He has thrown down by His own pierced hands. Those black shades of darkness that surrounded us, He has chased away by His own glorious manifestation as our Sun of Righteousness! It is the Lord, the Liberator, who has set His people free! Therefore, if you are among them, rend the heavens with your joyful shouts, you liberated ones! By the blood of the Covenant you are set free by the almighty "Breaker" who has come to break down your prison walls and to make you "free indeed."

And, Beloved, we are now free forever, for the Lord says–" I have sent forth your prisoners." And when God sendsus forth out of prison, who can send us back? When He says, "Let there be light," who can create darkness? When He says to me, "Be free," who can chain me up again? Let all the hosts of Hell surround me–as the Philistines surrounded poor blind Samson–my soul shall say with David, "They compassed me about; yes, they compassed me about; but in the name of the Lord I will destroy them." When Christ makes a man free, it is not with a temporary liberty, to last for a month, or a year–but Christ's emancipated slaves can never be enslaved again! Redeemed by His precious blood, the Redemption is not temporary, but eternal!

And, blessed be God, that freedom is freedom indeed! If you know what it is to be a Christian to the fullest, believing the true Gospel, not clouding its beauty, not putting upon yourself the old yoke of bondage, not mixing Judaism with Christianity, not bringing in human ordinances to make you the cramped and fettered slave of man–if you are the Lord's free men, then you are "free indeed!" "O Lord," said David, "truly I am

Your servant; I am Your servant, and the son of Your handmaid: You have loosed my bonds." He who loves holiness and walks in the fear of the Lord all the daylong is the only true free man! He is the free man whom God's Grace makes free—all others are slaves! No earthly power can bring real freedom to the soul—it is Grace and Grace, alone, that brings it by the blood of the Covenant! And where that freedom comes, no form of bondage can make a man a slave. He may be owned by some cruel master and whipped to his work, but his soul is free! He may be shut up in a damp, dark dungeon, but he can sing there, as others have done before him—

"Stone walls do not a prison make,
Nor iron bars a cage."

I cannot further enlarge upon this tempting theme, but I want every true child of God, everyone who has been set free by the great Liberator, to act and live like Christ's free man—not to go about fawning and crouching like a slave who dreads his master's lash, but to walk uprightly, in both senses of that word, as a free man should, in the Presence of the Lord who has bought His servant's freedom at the incalculable cost of His own most precious blood. May the Lord graciously grant to you "access by faith into this Grace wherein we stand, and rejoice in hope of the Glory of God!"

II. Secondly, and briefly, THERE ARE OTHER PERSONS WHO SHALL YET BE SET FREE THOUGH THE BLOOD OF THE COVENANT. Some of them are, I fully believe, going to be set free tonight! This is the favored hour in which the Lord is going to save them and set them free forever! They did not know this when they came in here, but the Lord had designs of love towards them in moving them, by His Spirit, to enter this House of Prayer an hour or so ago.

To those who are going to be set free I have to say this. By nature, you are in the state that I have been describing, though perhaps you are hardly aware of it. You are prisoners in the pit without water. If unrenewed in heart, you are ina state of alienation from God and of spiritual danger, destitution and misery! But, dear Souls, though this is the case with all of you who have not been born-again, there is this cheering Truth of God–though you are prisoners, you are "prisoners of hope." Wherever the Gospel is preached, there is hope for sinners and whoever hears it may take heart of hope. I am not now speaking merely about outwardly moral people, but I am speaking of any who have strayed in here and who have sinned grossly–drunkards, swearers, harlots–the very worst and lowest of persons. You are prisoners to your sins, but you are prisoners of hope, for you are within reach of One who sets free from sin! The Lord Jesus Christ, whom we preach to you, saves His people from their sins! And I pray that He may come to you, in all the plenitude of His liberating power and set you free from your sins this very hour!

Though you are in this prison, there is a Divine command given to you–"Turn you to the stronghold." If youwould obtain liberty from your sin, both in its guilt and in its power, you must look to Jesus, who is the Stronghold to which captive sinners are to turn! "Oh," you say, "this pit is truly horrible." I know it is, but the Lord Jesus Christ has come to roll away the stone from the mouth of it and, looking down to you, He says, "Turn you to Me, your only Stronghold. There is hope for you, you prisoners of hope, if you will but turn unto Me." "But," you say, "we have looked all around, but we have found no consolation. No man cares for our souls." There is One in Heaven who cares for your souls and who, because He does, has come to tell you that there is hope for the worst, the most hardened, the most despairing of you all! He bids you escape for your life and look not behind you, nor tarry in all the plain, but press on till you reach the Stronghold where you will be safe even when the wrath of God pursues you! "Christ Jesus came into the world to save sinners." "The Son of Man is come to seek and to save that which was lost." Whoever turns to Him shall live, whoever he or she may be!

"But I am so feeble," says someone. Then turn away from your feebleness to His strength. "But I am so sinful," says another. Then turn away from your sinfulness to His blood–the blood of the Covenant which washes black sinners whiter than driven snow! You are not to turn to yourself, nor to a human priest, nor to your own works, nor even to your prayers or your tears—all these are full of sin and worthless to give you acceptance in God's sight. But the Lord Jesus Christ is Divine—so look to Him and to what He has done—and especially to His great atoning Sacrifice upon the Cross, for if you trust to that by a sincere and humble faith, you will certainly be saved!

This declaration of hope in the Gospel is for the present moment. do I declare that I will render double unto you." You are getting very old, but "even today" mercy is declared to you! You have been, perhaps, wasting the former part of this Sabbath, but "even today" is mercy declared to you. It is seldom that you go to a place of worship, but you are here tonight—and "even today" is mercy proclaimed to you! You had so provoked God that you thought He had cast you away. Well, you have probably gone to the full length of your tether, but "even today" does God proclaim that there is still hope for you—that hope which He has laid up in Jesus on whom He has laid all necessary help for you!

And what is it that He tells you today? Why, that He will render double to you! Do notice that. He will renderdouble to you. You have committed great sin, but He will give you double mercy to wash out that double sin. But your heart is doubly hard—then He will give you a double portion of His Holy Spirit to soften it! But you feel a double tendency to sin—then He will doubly write His Law on the new heart that He will give you! But you are so desponding. Then He will give you double comfort. But you say that you feel so weak in prayer. Then He will give you double strength. But your faith is so feeble. Then He will give you double Grace to increase it. O Soul, if God says that He will give you all that you need, that ought to satisfy you! But when He says that He will give you double— double for all your sins—what wondrous Grace is that! If you put down a sin, God puts down two mercies. Put down another sin and He puts down two more mercies. "Ah," you say, "but I can keep on putting down sins forever, they are so many!" And my Lord can put down mercies forever and ever for, however many your sins may be, they can be counted—but His mercies are innumerable! I know that your sins can be counted, for they are all written in a book, but God's mercies cannot be written in a book–they are altogether countless. His mercy is immeasurably greater than your sin. David laid hold of that great Truth of God when he prayed, "Have mercy upon me, O God, according to Your loving kindness: according unto the multitude of Your tender mercies blot out my transgressions." I tell you, Sinners, if you are lost, it will not be for lack of mercy! If your sins destroy you, it will not be because the blood of the Covenant has not power to wash away your sins. If you perish, it will not be because Jesus Christ is not able to save you. Why will it be, then? It will be because you have not believed on the Lord Jesus Christ, for "he that believes not is condemned already, because he has not believed in the name of the only begotten Son of God."

I do pray the Lord that you may have reason enough and Grace enough given you to know that your eternal interests depend upon your believing on the Lord Jesus Christ. You have not to go and spin a righteousness which you are so fond of doing, but to come and take the spotless robe that Christ has woven. You have not to bring the money for your own ransom, though you would like to do that, but you are to take the liberty which has been bought by Christ's precious blood and which is freely presented to every believing sinner, "for God so loved the world that He gave His only begotten Son, that whoever believes in Him should not perish, but have everlasting life." We who have escaped from the noisome pit, would, if we could, tempt you to also escape–we long that you may share the blessed liberty that we enjoy! Dear children, will you not follow your father and mother into Gospel liberty? Dear husbands, do you not desire to experience the holy joy that throbs in your wives' bosom? Good wives, do you not wish to have your husbands' Christ to be your own Christ? Brothers, would you like your sisters to be without you in Heaven? Will you not share with them in the blessings of eternal life? Oh, that we might all together come to Christ right now! For after all, whatever God has done for us, saints are still sinners, so we will come down to your level and each one, taking the hand of some poor fellow sinner who has never come to Christ, we will try to come together, now, and look up to Him. There is the Cross of Calvary and there is the Savior who hung there. O You blessed Jesus, we have no hope but in You! And these poor souls whom we have brought along with us, Lord, help them to look to You just now, even as we ourselves looked to You long ago! Clear their eyes even more than ours are cleared and may they, as they look unto You, find that–

"There is life for a look at the Crucified One"– life for them, life for them just now, life from the death of sin, life from condemnation, life to be had at once, by a glance at Your wounds and by simple faith in You! You wear the thorn-crown and it seems to us as if all Your thoughts were hedged about with thorns that they might be fixed on sinners. And Your hands are fastened wide open, as if You would never close them again, but hold them always open to welcome poor sinners! And Your feet are fastened as if You would always graciously receive all who come to bow before You. Yes, and Your dear heart was opened by the soldier's spear as if to make a way for guilty souls into Your inmost affection. Jesus, by Your Grace we come to You! Spirit of the living God, draw this whole houseful of sinners and saints and enable each one of us to say–

"There is a fountain filled with blood,
Drawn from Immanuel's veins
And sinners, plunged beneath that flood,
Lose all their guilty stains!
I do believe, I will believe,
That Jesus died for me,
That on the Cross He shed His blood
From sin to set me free."

III. My last words–and they shall be very few–are to be IN HONOR OF THE BLOOD OF THE COVENANT.

To you who have believed in Jesus and who are now coming to His table, let me say–As we come to the Communion, let us think of the blood of the Covenant. If we are free men and women in Christ Jesus, it is because the blood of Jesus ratified the Covenant of our liberty. It is because God saw the blood and delivered us. Let me remind youof that beautiful verse in the Book of Exodus, from which I have preached more than once. The blood of thepaschal lamb, as you know, was to be sprinkled on the lintel and the two side posts of the houses of all the children of Israel. And what did God say about it? Did He say, "When you stand outside your house and look up at the blood I will save you"? No, He did not say that, but, "When I see the blood, I will pass over you." It is God's sight of the blood ofChrist which, at bottom, is the reason for the salvation of the redeemed! How I rejoice to think that although my faith sight of the blood gives me peace, still, if that eye of mine ever gets dim, it does not imperil my salvation, for God's eye is not dim and it is always fixed on the blood of His Son! In sacred contemplation the Father surveys the Sacrifice of His Son with supreme satisfaction—and as He sees the blood, He spares us for His Son's sake!

But, then, dear Friends, the blood of the Covenant is also to be extolled because it is our sight of it that brings usp eace. When we realize that Jesus died for us, there is peace in our soul. I do not know whether you are like me in this respect, but there are times when I, as it were, take the fact of my eternal safety for granted. But there comes a severe sickness, or deep depression of spirit. There comes a time when death has to be looked in the face and the sense of past sin rises vividly before me—and then it is a blessed thing to stand once more at the foot of the Cross and to look up to Jesus hanging there, and to say—

"My faith does lay her hand
On that dear head of Yours,
While like a penitent I stand,
And there confess my sin."

And as I meditate upon that theme, despondency goes, pain is forgotten and I say, "Yes, yes, yes! I am safe! I am saved by the precious blood of Jesus! I do love Him and I would fall down at His dear feet and weep with mingled repentance and gratitude—repentance because I have sinned—gratitude because I have such a gracious Savior to put my sin away." Brothers and Sisters in Christ, let us praise the blood because God sees it—and praise the blood because we also see it by faith!

Praise the blood, too, because when we really trust in it, it gives us liberty. If you get away from the blood of theCovenant, you get into slavery. But keep close to that and you are at liberty. In prayer, mind that you plead the blood, for that is the way to get the "double" spoken of in the text. The double blessing comes by the blood of the Covenant. If you need more Grace, plead the blood for it. There is one talisman that will open every vault in the treasury of God–the blood of the Covenant! You cannot be denied if you plead the atoning Sacrifice of Jesus Christ! Knock at Heaven's gate with the crimson token in your hand and as surely as God loves Jesus Christ–and He loves Him more than all of us put together love Him–He will honor His Son's great Sacrifice and He will say to you, "According to your desire and your faith, so be it unto you." There are some preachers who cannot or do not preach about the blood of Jesus Christ–I have one thing to say to you concerning those–Never go to hear them! Never listen to them! A ministry that has not the blood in it, is lifeless, "for the blood is the life thereof"–and a dead ministry is no good to anybody! Leave out the atoning Sacrifice and it would be better for the people that the places in which a Christless, bloodless Gospel is preached, should be all burnt to the ground, for the atoning Sacrifice is the soul and life and marrow of Christianity! Rest in that and you are saved! But get away from that and you have wandered where peace and life and safety can never come! God Almighty bless you, for Jesus Christ's sake! Amen.

THE BLOOD OF CHRIST'S COVENANT

"As for you, also, by the blood of your Covenant I have sent forth your prisoners out of the pit wherein is no water."
Zechariah 9:11.

THE LORD is here speaking to His ancient people, Israel. That nation had always been preserved, although other nations had been destroyed—and the reason was that God had entered into a Covenant with Abraham on their behalf. Circumcision was the sign and seal of the Covenant, so that God could truly speak of "the blood of your Covenant." The Jews have never ceased to be a nation, though they have been scattered, peeled and delivered over into the hand of their adversaries because of their sins. They may enjoy various rights and privileges in the different countries where they sojourn for a while, but they cannot be absorbed into the nationalities by which they are surrounded. They must always be a separate and distinct people—but the day shall yet come when the branches of the olive tree, which have been so long cut off, shall be grafted in again. Then shall they, as a nation, again behold the Messiah, the true and only King of the Jews—and their fullness shall be the fullness of the Gentiles, also!

All Believers have some share in that Covenant made with Abraham, for he is the father of the faithful. We who believe in Jesus are of the seed of Abraham, not according to the flesh, but according to the promise, and we are pressed by a Covenant which like that made with Abraham, is signed and sealed with blood even "the blood of the Everlasting Covenant." We, too, are saved and kept as a separate and distinct people, not because of any natural goodness in us, or because of our superiority over others, but solely and entirely because the Lord has made an Eternal Covenant concerning us, which is "ordered in all things and sure," because Jesus Christ is, Himself, the Surety on our behalf that its guarantees and pledges shall all be carried into effect.

So, applying our text to the Covenant people of God in all ages, we have first to consider THEIR NATURAL AND YET PRIVILEGED CONDITION.

By nature they are like prisoners in a pit wherein is no water, but by Grace they are in Covenant relationship to God!

Brothers and Sisters in Christ, when we were in our natural state, we were like prisoners. A prisoner is one who haslost his liberty–and that was our condition before Jesus met with us and set us free. We were "carnal, sold under sin," in bondage to our own lusts and held captive by the devil at his will. No doubt we boasted of our free will, but our will, itself, was enslaved with all the rest of our powers. There is no greater mockery than to call a sinner a free man. Show me a convict toiling in the chain gang and call him a free man if you will! Point out to me the galley slave chained to the oar and smarting under the taskmaster's lash whenever he pauses to draw a breath–and call him a free man if you will–butnever call a sinner a free man, even in his will, as long as he is the slave of his own corruptions! In our natural state wewore chains, not upon our limbs, but upon our hearts–fetters that bound us and kept us from God, from rest, from peace, from holiness–from anything like freedom of heart and conscience and will! The iron entered into our soul and there is no other slavery as terrible as that. As there is no freedom like the freedom of the spirit, so is there no slavery that is at all comparable to the bondage of the heart!

A prisoner is also one who feels that he cannot escape from his prison– and that is how we felt. We began to have longings after better things. A heavenly Visitor came to us and dropped a new and strange thought into our minds–and we began to pant after something higher and nobler than this poor world could give us–but we could not reach it, for we were prisoners. We could not escape from the cruel grip of our captor and it became quite clear to us that we could never be delivered from the house of bondage by any power of our own. Do you not remember, my Brothers and Sisters, when you used to sorrowfully say–

"I would but cannot pray
I would but can't repent"–

and when you could use Paul's words as your own and sadly cry, "To will is present with me; but how to perform that which is good I find not?" You were still a prisoner, yet you were beginning to be one of the "prisoners of hope."

That is a strange kind of prison that is mentioned in the text—"the pit wherein is no water." In the East, pits were frequently used as prisons. When a tyrant king wished to keep anyone in safe custody and also in ignominy and shame, and sorrow, he would have him cast into one of these waterless pits where the poor prisoner would be beyond human sight or hearing—and with no possible hope of deliverance from his doleful dungeon. Such was our sad state by nature, and well do we remember our first efforts to obtain release! We were in dense darkness and we felt all round the walls of our prison to try to find a door, or window, or ladder by which we might escape, but all in vain. We tried to look up, but we seemed to have been thrust, like Paul and Silas, into some inner prison where no ray of light could penetrate. The fact that there was "no water" in our prison-pit made our agonies all the more terrible! Those of you who have passed through that state of deep conviction of sin know that in such circumstances there is no comfort for the present and no hope for the future—as to the past, there is nothing to look back upon but sin—and as to the future, there is nothing "but a certain fearful looking for of judgment and fiery indignation." To a sinner in that condition, there seems nothing within but a heart as hard as stone, nothing beneath but a gapping Hell and nothing around but thick darkness. How dreary and dreadful is the state of man by nature—and how painfully conscious he is of his true condition when the Holy Spirit reveals it to him! Then is he, indeed, like a prisoner in a "pit wherein is no water."

This is the actual state, by nature, of all the elect—they are prisoners, just as other men are—and they are in as dark and dismal a pit and they have as little comfort in it as the very worst of mankind have. Yet, by Divine Grace, they are inan altogether different condition from that of others, for they are in Covenant with God though they are not yet aware of that blessed and comforting Truth! God's election of His people took place long before their creation. Those whom He has chosen unto eternal life were given to Christ in the Covenant of Grace, in that eternity of which we can form so slight a conception. And when they were born into this world, though they were born in sin and grew up to be the children of disobedience—enemies to God by wicked works—yet the Covenant made with Christ on their behalf remained unbroken all the while!

"Well," says someone, "that is strange." Yes, it is strange, but it is true. We must never forget that we were under a Covenant of Works long before we were born. Adam stood as our federal head and representative in that Covenant. You, my Sister, never put out your hand to pluck the forbidden fruit—and you and I, my Brother, never partook of it, yet we all have to share the consequences of Adam's transgression because he was our Covenant head. Do you object to that and say that it was unjust to visit upon us the sin of another? If you do, then you must equally object to the Gospel plan of salvation by the righteousness and death of Another, even Jesus Christ, our Lord and Savior, the one great federal Head and Representative of all who believe in Him! He took the place of the countless myriads of His elect who had been given to Him by His Father, and died on Calvary's Cross in their place, although great numbers of them had not then been born and, consequently, could not have any virtue or merit of their own! Through His substitutionary Sacrifice, they were even then "accepted in the Beloved" and, in the fullness of time, they become Believers in Him and so enter consciously into the enjoyment of the Covenant privileges which had been conferred upon them from eternity! The Covenant is not made with them when they believe in Jesus—it was made on their behalf by the Father and the Son in the eternal council chamber long before the daystar knew its place or planets ran their round!

See, then, the twofold condition of the chosen—they are like prisoners in a pit wherein is no water, yet is there an eternal Covenant concerning them which guarantees that they shall be brought out of the bondage of their sins and shall be set at liberty forever! Does someone here say, "I trust that such a blessed Covenant as that has been made on my behalf"? Dear Brother or Sister, if you have a sincere longing to be a sharer in the blessings of the Covenant of Grace, methinks that is a proof that you have an interest in it already! And if you will, at this moment, put your soul's trust in that precious blood that is their sign and seal of the Covenant, then you may rest assured that Grace has inscribed your name from all eternity in God's eternal book!

II. Now let us turn to the second part of our subject which is THE MEANS OF THE DELIVERANCE OF THESE COVENANTED ONES– AND THE EVIDENCES OF THEIR DELIVERANCE.

The text says, " By the blood of your Covenant I have sent forth your prisoners out of the pit wherein is no water." I think this means, first, that the blood of our Lord Jesus Christ is the essential matter of the Covenant. In order to make the conditions of the Eternal Covenant effective for His people, it was necessary that Christ should be obedient unto death and that His blood should be shed for many for the remission of their sins. When, by faith, I look upon the blood of Jesus–whether I see it streaming down in the bloody sweat of Gethsemane or flowing in the crimson rivulets at Gabbatha or in the sacred streams of Golgotha, I see in that precious blood of Christ the essential matter of the Covenant, and I sing, with sadness on His account, but with rejoicing on my own–

"Oh, how sweet to view the flowing
Of His sin-atoning blood!
By Divine assurance knowing
He has made my peace with God!"

Yes, O blessed Jesus, You have fulfilled on our behalf Your part of the Eternal Covenant! You have met all the demands of Infinite Justice even to the uttermost farthing! Your Father justly requires perfect obedience to His holy Law and You have rendered it in Your pure and spotless life. The offended Majesty of that Law demands adequate punishment for man's multiplied violations of its just requirements–and Your one Infinite Sacrifice has fully paid the penalty, so that Divine Justice is completely satisfied and the dishonored Law is magnified and glorified. Thus it is that God can "be just and the Justifier of him which believes in Jesus," for in the Person, life and death of Christ, their Covenant Head and Representative, all claims upon Believers have been discharged forever!

Further, the blood of Jesus is also the Seal of the Covenant. Speaking after the manner of men, until the blood ofJesus had been shed, the Covenant was not signed, sealed and ratified. It was like a will that could only become valid by the death of the testator. It is true that there was such perfect unity of heart between the Father and the Son, and such mutual foreknowledge that the Covenant would be ratified in due time— that multitudes of the chosen ones were welcomed to Heaven in anticipation of the redemption which would actually be accomplished by Christ upon the Cross. But when Jesus took upon Himself the likeness of men and in our human nature suffered and died upon the accursed tree, He did, as it were, write His name in crimson characters upon the Eternal Covenant and thus sealed it with His blood. It is because the blood of Jesus is the Seal of this Covenant that it has such power to bless us and is the means of lifting us up out of the prison-pit wherein is no water. Let me put it thus to some of you who have long been under conviction of sin. You have been trying in your poor way to keep the Law of God, but you have utterly failed to do so. You know that there are many precious promises in God's Word, but you get no comfort from them. Why is that? You feel that you are like a prisoner in a pit—and that you are shut away from the Presence of the thrice-holy God—and that His awful attribute of Justice bars your way like the flaming sword at the gate of Paradise, so that you cannot come near to Him. Then you listen to the Gospel, of which the sum and substance is this—that Jesus Christ has fully atoned for the sins of all His people, that He has suffered everything that they deserved to suffer and that God has accepted His substitutionary Sacrifice as a sufficient Atonement for all who believe in Him. As soon as you trust Him, you are lifted up out of the prison-pit, your feet are set upon a rock and a mug of grateful praise is put into your mouth! You are not afraid of the sword of Divine Justice now—no, you go and stand beneath the flashing blade and trust to it to defend you against all your adversaries! You rightly say, "As Jesus suffered in my place, Justice demands that I should go free! He has discharged all my liabilities. The Law has no longer any terror to me." So you see, Beloved, how the blood of Christ's Covenant brings the poor, trembling, despairing soul up out of that dread prison "wherein is no water."

Now I want, dear Friends, to ask you all to answer honestly one or two questions that I am about to put to you. The first is–Do you know what it means to be delivered from that pit by the blood of Christ's Covenant ? Perhaps I ought first of all to ask–Do you know what it means to be a prisoner in that pit wherein is no water? Have you ever moaned and groaned under the weight of your sin? Have you ever smarted under the lash of that ten-thonged whip of the Law? Has your conscience, itself, been sufficiently awakened as to condemn you? Have you ever been brought to such a state of self-despair that you could see nothing but death and damnation written upon everything that pertains to you? Was your comeliness withered, your strength dried up and your pride humbled so that you had to sit in sackcloth and ashes and cry, "Unclean! Unclean!" as the leper of old had to warn others to keep away from him? If not, I fear that you have never proved the power of the blood of the Covenant, for he who has never been humbled has never been exalted!

I feel sure that some of us here can answer, "Oh, yes! We remember well when we were humbled so that we felt ourselves to be less than nothing and vanity–and we realized that, by nature, we were totally ruined and undone–and blessed be God, we also recollect the time when a Power infinitely above our own, drew us up out of the pit in which we were imprisoned." But, my dear Hearers, have you also been conscious of the working of this Almighty Power? Have you felt a mysterious influence, which you could not comprehend, drawing you out of your natural state and giving you new thoughts, new desires, new hopes, new joy and also new pains? Certainly you have never been delivered from this waterless prison by any power less than the Divine, so if God's hand has not yet been stretched out on your behalf, you are still in the pit! Or, as Peter said to Simon the sorcerer, you are still "in the gall of bitterness, and in the bond of iniquity." Is there anyone here who is in that pit, yet who earnestly longs to escape from it? Is your soul yearning to be delivered, not only from the consequences of sin, but from the sin, itself? Are you panting after reconciliation with God and acceptance in the Beloved? Do you hunger and thirst after righteousness? Then you are already among those whom the Savior calls blessed and to whom He has given that gracious promise, "they shall be filled." Such longings as these grow not in Nature's soul–they are the product of Divine Grace. Therefore, be very thankful for them, for they are at least hopeful indications of the Holy Spirit's working within you! And you may rest assured that where He has begun a good work, He will continue it until He brings it to perfection. He will never lift you part of the way out of the pit and then let you fall back again into the prison–He will bring you right out, even as the children of Israel were brought out of Egypt with a high hand and a stretched-out arm!

If you have been delivered, I feel sure that you will prize your deliverance. I would give little for what you call your grace if you would not willingly part with all else that you have rather that part with that! A slave who has been set free will value his liberty beyond all price. The man who can talk lightly of being free, never knew what bondage meant. I fear that none of us think highly enough of what the Lord has done for us. We get to worrying ourselves because He has not done more for us, because we are not yet perfect–how much better it would be if we would praise and bless Him for all that He has done for us! Remember that you are a free man even though some links of your chain are still clinging to you. Thank God that the chain is broken and that the last links shall soon be snapped–and you shall be perfectly delivered from the badge of bondage! Therefore be of good courage, prize your deliverance and praise Him who has done such great things for you!

Surely, too, if you have been drawn out of this pit wherein is no water, you will love your Deliverer and you will desire above everything else to live to Him and to labor for Him all your life!

I hope you can truthfully say to your Lord–

"Have You a lamb in all Your flock
I would disdain to feed?
Have You a foe, before whose face

I fear Your cause to plead?
You know I love You, dearest Lord,
But oh, I love to soar
Far from the sphere of mortal joys,
And learn to love You more."

I trust that you have dedicated yourself wholly to your Lord–perhaps not in writing, yet just as truly as if you had set your signature to such a covenant as some have felt moved to leave upon record. If you have resolved thus in your heart, you can say with me at the moment, "Lord Jesus, I am Yours–body, soul and spirit–wholly Yours, only Yours, always Yours. You have bought me for Yourself, not with corruptible things such as silver and gold, but with Your own most precious blood and, therefore, You shall have me with all my powers, all my possessions, all my possibilities in life and in death, in time and in eternity! I give all up to You absolutely without reserve, that You may do with me whatever You please and whatever will bring most Glory to Your holy name. I fear there is much dross still remaining in me–in all the gold You have given me in Your wondrous Grace. If it seems good in Your sight, put me into the hottest furnace, but O Lord, do take away all the dross and then fashion me into a vessel meet for Your own use!" The man who can truthfully talk thus to the Lord Jesus is in the Covenant! And by the blood of the Covenant he has been brought forth out of the prison wherein is no water!

Perhaps you are afraid to say as much as this, lest it should seem to be presumption on your part. Well then, possibly you can say, "I dare not talk as some do about their attainments in spiritual things, but I do trust in the Lord Jesus Christ. My sole reliance is upon His perfect righteousness and His one great Sacrifice for all." Then, my Brother or my Sister, you are among those who have built upon the Rock and you shall be preserved in the greatest storm that can ever beat upon you! You are no longer a prisoner in the pit wherein is no water! Faith in Jesus is not the heritage of the slaves of sin and Satan–it is the portion of those who are free men and free women in Christ Jesus–and if He has made you free, you are free, indeed, and you can never be enslaved again! You are at liberty to walk wherever you will on all the holy land which is the purchase possession of the children of the King! Every promise that He has given to His chosen people is a promise to you, so take full advantage of all your privileges as a Believer in the Lord Jesus Christ! You are now His and you shall be His when this world is on fire and when all things that are of time and sense shall perish in the last great conflagration! You shall be His amid the pomp and terrors of that tremendous day and you shall be His amidst the splendor and Glory of eternity!

If any here are still prisoners in the pit wherein is no water, may the Lord even now bring them forth by the blood of His Covenant, that they may share with all the chosen ones, all the blessings of that Covenant now and to all eternity! And too Him shall be the praise and the Glory forever and ever. Amen.

BY WATER AND BLOOD

"This is He that came by water and blood, even Jesus Christ–not by water only, but by water and blood."
1 John 5:6

BY the terms "water" and "blood" we understand the purifying and the pardoning effects of Christ's work for His people. He came to purify them from the power of sin, that they might no longer live in it. This is indicated by the declaration that He "came by water." He also came to put away the guilt of their sin, that they might not be condemned for it. This is set forth by the intimation that He also came "by blood." We might say that all the Lord's Prophets who came before Christ, in a certain sense, "came by water." That is to say, they all sought the purification of the Lord's people. Whether it was Isaiah, whose lips had been touched with the live coal from the altar, or Jeremiah, whose eyes were fountains of tears as he wept over sinners, or Amos, who spoke as a herdsman, or Ezekiel, whose message was one of grandeur and sublimity, the objective of every one of them was to purge the people from their sins. It was against sin that they all lifted up their voices, yet none of them could pardon sin and no one of them ever professed to be able to do so! Of the whole of them it must to said that they came by water only, and not by blood.

But Jesus Christ does what the Prophets could not do. It is true that He does seek to make His people holy, but it is by His blood that all their sins are forever put away. John the Baptist was the last and the greatest of all the Prophets who came before Christ yet he had to say, "He that comes after me is mightier than I, whose shoes I am not worthy to bear." John never spoke of his own blood having any power to take away sin, but he pointed to Christ and said, "Behold the Lamb of God, which takes away the sin of the world." So far as our Lord's first disciples were concerned, He certainly "came by water," for contact with His unique Personality must have tended to purify their lives. Yet He also came "by blood" as well as by water, for it was by virtue of His atoning Sacrifice that their sins were blotted out and that they became "accepted in the Beloved."

The two ordinances of our holy religion were intended, I take it, to sum up the teaching of Christ. The one is Baptism, which represents the cleansing of the conscience as the body is washed with water, the death of the soul to the old carnal life, its burial with Christ and its resurrection to a life of holiness. Then comes the ordinance of the Lord's Supper which sets forth, in the broken bread and the poured-out wine, the great Truth of Christ's Atonement—the fact that He has, by His death, perfected forever all those who have been set apart unto Him.

It is very important that we should always carry in our minds the remembrance of these two Truths of God—first, that Jesus Christ "came by water," that is, it was His Divine purpose to purify His people and make them holy. And, secondly, that Jesus Christ "came by blood," that is, it was His grand aim and objective to deliver His people from the guilt of sin. These are the two topics upon which I am going to speak to you as the Holy Spirit shall graciously guide me.

So, first, JESUS CHRIST "CAME BY WATER"—it was His Divine purpose to purify His people.
It is manifest that there was an urgent necessity for this purification, for all of us had become as an unclean thing in the sight of God. Even our righteousnesses were as filthy rags. We could not cleanse ourselves, neither could we obtain cleansing through the works of the Law. Yet it was imperatively necessary that we should be made holy—otherwise, where God is and where His holy angels dwell, we could never be—and, therefore, what we ourselves could not do, and what the Law could not do, "God sending His own Son in the likeness of sinful flesh" has perfectly accomplished!

If any of you ask me how Christ makes His people holy, I would remind you that when the Spirit of God reveals Jesus Christ to our heart, we then begin to perceive the exceeding sinfulness of sin. What? Did sin stab my Savior to the heart? Did sin nail my Best-Beloved to the Cross?

Then I hate sin with a perfect hatred and will be revenged upon it! The Atonement of Christ gives such an exhibition of the guilt of sin as is not to be seen anywhere else—no, not even in the flames of Hell! And when a soul sees Christ despised, rejected, wounded, bleeding and dying because of sin, it realizes how foul and vile a thing sin is and so is moved to hate it, not only because of its foulness and blackness, but also out of gratitude to Christ who has put it away. Did my Savior love me so much as to bear the dread penalty of my sin? Then I will give sin no quarter, but seek to utterly destroy it—

"The dearest idol I have known,
Whate'er that idol is"—

shall be cast down from the throne which it has usurped that I may worship my gracious God, and Him alone!

This gratitude to Christ begets a more and more intense love to Christ and the more we love Him, the more we become like He—and becoming like He is, sin is cast out and virtue is nourished. Ask any Christian whether he has not found that the best weapon with which to smite his sins has been a nail from Christ's Cross or the spear that pierced His side! Men have tried to overcome sin by the reasoning of philosophy, or by arguments fetched from common sense—but those blunt wooden swords have been powerless to destroy it! It is only the sharp two-edged sword of the Spirit—the grand Doctrine of the love and Grace of our Lord and Savior Jesus Christ that can pierce our sin to the heart and lay it in the dust! You have, Beloved, but to meditate upon His passion to receive the virtue of the water which flowed from His side, and that shall enable you to trample upon your lusts and to consecrate all your powers and passions to His service.

I appeal to the experience of every Christian here to confirm what I have said—my Brother or Sister in Christ, was there not great need for Christ to come "by water" to you? For, first, what was your nature? No, what is it? If you were left to yourself, what might you not become? If circumstances put temptation in your way and God's Grace did not restrain you, what sin might you not commit? Have you not, sometimes, when your feet have almost gone and your steps have well-near slipped, looked down into the depths of the horrible pit of human corruption and shuddered with alarm at the discovery of possibilities of evil which you had scarcely suspected? Well, then, if you have such a nature as this, you do indeed need the purifying streams from the heart of Christ to make it clean, and you may well pray to Him, with Toplady–

"Let the water and the blood,
From Your split side which flowed,
Be of sin the double cure,
Cleanse me from its guilt and power."

Then, next, what about our thoughts? As I walked to this House of Prayer tonight and tried to concentrate my meditations upon the Person and work of the Lord Jesus Christ, I could not help feeling how mysterious it is that the more we try to guide our thoughts into right channels, the more determined they seem to be to run towards evil. Have you not sometimes found that even in your most hallowed moments, some unchaste and vile thought which you abhor as you hate the very fiend, himself, will suddenly come into your mind? Does not blasphemy at times intrude into your prayers? Does it not occasionally happen that the hymn you are singing suggests something the very reverse of praise to God and that the text of the sermon, or some part of the discourse, itself, becomes a peg upon which the devil hangs a temptation to sin? Alas, alas, our thoughts, if left to themselves, are as a cage of unclean birds or a den of wild beasts! And as Hercules needed to turn a stream of water to clean the Augean stable, our Lord Jesus Christ needed to pour rivers of water out of His own heart to cleanse the foul stable of our corrupt thoughts!

Then think of our words. I am not now speaking of carnal man–I am talking of professing Christians!. Would any of us like to have all our words printed for a single week? If any of you would, I can honestly say that I would not. One does earnestly try to keep the tongue from evil and the lips from speaking guile, but oh, how many idle words, how many frivolous words, how many sharp, angry, hot, unkind words fly from our lips almost before we are aware of it! God forgive us for the sins of the tongue! If we had nothing else for which to praise Christ, we ought to bless Him to all eternity that He came "by water" to cleanse that tongue which is naturally so foul!

Then look at our actions. John writes truly, "Whoever is born of God does not commit sin, for His seed remains in him and he cannot sin, because he is born of God"–that is to say, he does not sin willfully, he does not continue sinning, yet he does sin. Need I try to prove that he does? O Beloved, look at your lives since you have known the Lord, and see my life this week has been perfectly pure"? You know that you cannot! Well then, if with the utmost possible guard upon your own conduct, with the most diligent check upon your conversation, with the greatest watchfulness concerning your thoughts, you are still made to feel that there is a corrupt nature within you and that the flesh still lusts against the Spirit, how thankful you ought to be that Jesus Christ "came by water" that He might purge your nature and make it clean!

Thus have I shown you the necessity for this purification. Now let me try to set before you the power of this "water"which makes the Christian clean. It is not a matter of speculation as to whether Christ makes sinners into saints–He is constantly performing this blessed work, which no power but that which is Divine could ever accomplish! Think for a minute or two of the forces which it has to overcome. There is the old nature of which I have been speaking, and that is not an enemy that can be easily overthrown. Have you ever tried to bind it fast with fetters and to keep it in chains? That "old Adam" is very strong–and even in aged Christians who sometimes seem to fancy that their corruptions have grown as aged and as feeble as they are, it has been, alas, only too sadly proved that the "old Adam" does not become weak as easily as the old man does! The opposition of our carnal nature to the Grace and work of Christ is so strong that nothing but Omnipotence, itself, can overcome it, yet Jesus Christ so gloriously "came by water" that He completely conquers the flesh!

Then there is the enmity of the world, which is always in antagonism to Christ and to His people, too. Worldlings are always ready to turn us aside to sin, and they will never help us to walk the narrow way that leads unto life. The way of the world is always towards evil—the habits and customs of the world are evil, only evil, and that continually! As the Apostle John says, "All that is in the world, the lust of the flesh, and the lust of the eyes, and the pride of life, is not of the Father, but is of the world."All these evils continually beset us and powerful, indeed, must be that stream which can counteract and overcome them! Yet Jesus Christ does this through coming "by water" as well as by blood!

There is also the devil to be overthrown and we must never think lightly of his powers. He has overcome many mighty men and he would easily overpower us if we were left to contend with him in our own unaided strength. Bunyan's pilgrim found it to be no child's play to fight with Apollyon, nor shall we! "We wrestle not against flesh and blood, but against principalities, against powers, against the rulers of the darkness of this world, against spiritual wickedness in high places." But, blessed be God, we go not to this warfare at our own charges! And greater is He who is with us than all that can be against us!

Yes, that awful trinity of evil—the world, the flesh and the devil—shall not be able to overcome even one Believer in the Lord Jesus Christ! Think of this, Beloved, and let your eyes sparkle with the delight of anticipation—you shall one day have no tendencies to sin—you shall then be as pure in nature as the holy angels! You shall then be fit to consort with cherubim and seraphim and the glorified spirits that day without night circle the Throne of God! And even the Lord God, Himself, the Infinitely Pure and Holy One, shall not disdain to dwell among you, for then you shall be perfectly free from sin, "without fault before the Throne of God." Not even the all-piercing eyes of God shall be able to discover in you any thought of wrong, any word of evil, any act of sin, any corruption of nature, any sloth, or pride, or lust, or temper, or anything contrary to His holy will! Free from all sin forever are all those who shall stand "before the Throne and before the Lord, clothed with white robes, and palms in their hands." And I shall be there and you shall be there, if here we are trusting in Him who "came by water" to "purify unto Himself a peculiar people, zealous of good works." Have no doubt concerning it, my Brother or Sister in Jesus! Strong are your foes, but far stronger is your glorious Helper! Many and mighty are your enemies, but Almighty is your Friend! Stern is the conflict that has to be faced, but sure is the victory that shall, in due time, be won! So press on bravely day by day, and moment by moment, resisting even unto blood, striving against sin!

How many of us have already proved the purifying power of this "water" by which Christ came? Of course, I need hardly point out to you that there is no support here for the unscriptural doctrine of baptismal regeneration! The water that flowed from Christ's side is typical of the cleansing work of the Truth that He has revealed, even as He said to His disciples, "You are clean through the Word which I have spoken unto you." Have you, Beloved, felt the cleansing power of the Truth as it is in Jesus? If not, God grant that you may realize it now—and to Him shall be the praise forever!

II. Now, secondly, I have to remind you that JESUS CHRIST CAME BY BLOOD AS WELL AS BY WATER. Not by water only, but by water and blood—that is to say, it was His grand aim and objective, by His atoning Sacrifice, to deliver His people from the guilt of sin!

There are some who are continually trying to get the Doctrine of the Atonement out of the Bible. Certain philosophical divines, who have just a smattering of theological knowledge, and who seem to forget the couplet—

"A little learning is a dangerous thing
Drink deep, or taste not the Pierian spring"—

try to hold up Christ for our admiration as a great Teacher, as a mighty Prophet, and as our perfect Exemplar—but as to the idea of Christ shedding His blood to wash away sin, they cry, "Away with it! Away with it!" And yet, my dear Friends, Christ cannot be of the slightest service to any of us if He did not come "by blood" to put away the guilt of our sin as well as "by water" to purify us from its defilement! For, supposing you and I could, by some mysterious influence, become from this time forth perfectly holy—what would be the good of that to us? I do not know that it would be any benefit to us at all if there were no Atonement! I think that it would be a curse rather than a blessing, for we would still be under condemnation on account of the sins which we have already committed! We are even now in the position of condemned criminals—and if there is no atoning Sacrifice of Christ to put away the guilt of our many transgressions—and we have to pay the penalty which is the inevitable consequence of our past sins, how intense and, indeed, intensified mustbe our anguish as after being made holy, we have to suffer for the iniquities which we committed before that great change was worked upon us! I have only to state the matter thus for you to see that such a condition of things is utterly impossible. Oh, no! If I must be lost, I will remain as I am! If there is no pardon for my past transgressions, it is of no use for me to have purity for the future! If I could become perfectly holy for a time, but would, after all, be cast away from God's Presence, I do not want a temporary holiness of that sort, for I do not see how it could be of the slightest possible use to me! And my very nature recoils against even a good thing which would only increase my misery to an intolerable degree.

But, Beloved, I have only been supposing for the sake of argument, what is not true, for Jesus Christ did come "byblood" as well as "by water." Paul truly wrote to the Hebrews, "Once in the end of the world has He appeared to put away sin by the sacrifice of Himself." And He has forever put away all the sin of everyone who believes in Him. That great Sacrifice was once and for all completed on Calvary—and it is made efficacious to each one of the innumerable host for whom Christ died as soon as, by faith, he appropriates the blessing to himself! As Joseph Hart sings—

"The moment a sinner believes,
And trusts in his crucified God,
His pardon at once he receives,
Redemption in full through His blood."

It was by virtue of Christ's atoning Sacrifice that Paul was able to say at Antioch what we can truthfully repeat in your hearing today, "Be it known unto you, therefore, men and brethren, that through this Man is preached unto you the forgiveness of sins: and by Him, all that believe are justified from all things, from which you could not be justified by the Law of Moses." The precious blood of Jesus Christ, God's Son, cleanses from all sin all those who put their trust in Him! It is no sooner applied by the Holy Spirit to the heart and conscience than every sin that a man has ever committed ceases to be! And the virtue in Christ's blood is so great that it covers all the sin that the man will ever commit, as John Kent sings—

"Here's pardon for transgressions past,
It matters not how black their cast!
And, oh, my Soul, with wonder view,
For sins to come here's pardon too!"

A Believer in Jesus has no record against him in God's Book of Remembrance. The Lord says to him as He said to Israel of old, "I have blotted out, as a thick cloud, your transgressions and, as a cloud, your sins." They are as completely obliterated, annihilated and destroyed as if they had never been committed! It is this glorious Truth of God which sets Christ apart from all the Prophets that came before Him—and all His servants who have or will come after Him—they all "came by water," seeking to make their message the means of purification to the Lord's people. But Christ came "not by water, only, but by water and blood," for He came both to purify His people and to put away the guilt of their transgression!

Those who deny the Atonement of Christ must have very low views of what God is and of what is due to His offended Majesty. According to them, God is to be insulted, His Throne is to be attacked, His crown is to be assailed and His honor is to be impugned—and yet no adequate recompense is to be made to Him! Such persons must also have very low views of sin. They make it out to be a mere trifle which God is to forgive without exacting any penalty for it. They seem to think that in His mercy, He can put away sin without any reparation to His broken Law and without any satisfaction being rendered to His offended Justice! But he who reads his Bible aright knows that all such notions are altogether erroneous! He has learned from the Scriptures that God is inflexibly stern in His Justice although He is supremely gracious in His Love. God hates sin so much that He had to turn away His face even from His well-beloved Son when He was, by imputation, bearing the sins of His people upon Calvary! And it was that desertion by His Father that wrung from Christ that saddest of all the cries from the Cross, "My God, My God, why have You forsaken Me?" But now that Christ has endured the full penalty for His people's sin, God can "be just and the Justifier of him who believes in Jesus." God's love can be displayed to the utmost without in any way infringing the rightful claims of His Justice. And all His attributes remain absolutely unsullied after the vindication they have received through the atoning Sacrifice of Christ.

All this has been accomplished because Jesus Christ came "not by water only, but by water and blood." Oh, the power of the precious blood of Jesus! Did you ever feel it, dear Friends? If so, you will never doubt the truth of the Atonement, for it will be very real to you. Never can I forget the day when I first felt in my soul the power of the blood of Jesus! Christ's blood has the power to put away sin from the sight of the all-seeing Jehovah, but it also has the power, so far as man is concerned, to give peace to the troubled conscience, rest to the weary heart, joy to the miserable life! No one could ever have been more wretched and sad than I was, when under a sense of sin, life had become almost unbearable though I was but a lad. But oh, what a leap my soul gave from the very depths of despair up to the heights of overflowing joy when I realized that Christ had come to me—"not by water only, but by water and blood"—and that He had put away my sins as far as the East is from the West, so that they should be remembered against me no more forever!—

"Ever since by faith I saw the stream
His flowing wounds supply,

Redeeming love has been my theme,
And shall be till I die."

Remember, my dear Hearer, that Jesus Christ must come to you "by blood" or else He will never come to you "by water." Christ never gives a man holiness of life unless that man accepts Him as the great Propitiation for sin. Do you ask, "How can Christ come to me by water and by blood?" The only way that I know is the one that I have pointed out to you over and over again. It is this—you are a sinner, lost and undone. Jesus Christ came to seek and to save the lost. To do this, He had to take the sinner's place—to bear the sinner's guilt and to suffer the penalty that the sinner deserved to suffer. "He was wounded for our transgressions, He was bruised for our iniquities: the chastisement of our peace was upon Him and with His stripes we are healed." Have you faith enough to appropriate His work? Perhaps you question whether you may do so. Well, rest assured of this—there never was a sinner who trusted Christ and then was told that he had no right to trust Him. Oh, no! He, Himself, said, "Him that comes to me I will in no wise cast out," and He will not cast you out if you come to Him! Can you believe that His blood was shed for you? Dare you rest your soul's salvation upon the great work of which He said, "It is finished," before He bowed His head and gave up the ghost? Will you now trust Christ as your Substitute and Savior? You know the verses that we often sing—

"Just as I am—without one plea
But that Your blood was shed for me,
And that You bid me come to You,
O Lamb of God, I come.
Just as I am—and waiting not
To rid my soul of one dark blot,
To You, whose blood can cleanse each spot,
O Lamb of God, I come."

Is this the language of your heart? Then I venture to say that Christ has come to you, "not by water only but by water and blood," that Christ died for your sins according to the Scriptures and that God will never punish you for your transgressions as Christ has borne the full penalty for them all! Then if you have received Christ, thus, as coming to you by blood, I feel sure that you will also believe that He has come to you by water, to purify you from all defilement and, therefore, you will not any longer knowingly and willfully continue in sin! The gratitude which you must feel in your heart for all that Christ has done for you will constrain you to walk before Him in holiness and humility, and to seek to obey His will at all times!

Now, many of us are coming to the Table of our Lord to commune with Him and with one another—and there we must especially think of how He came to us, "not by water only, but by water and blood." The broken bread will remind us of His body broken for us, and the wine in the cup will bring to our remembrance His precious blood of the New Covenant shed for us for the remission of our sins. Oh, what a wonder it is that we, who once were as the prodigal son in the far country, wasting our substance in riotous living, or perhaps even herding among the swine— are now welcomed at our Father's board among His happy forgiven children! A few years ago, no, even a few months ago, some of us would not have been spending the Sabbath evening among the Lord's people in a House of Prayer—and it would never have entered into our thoughts that we should be found sitting as honored guests at His Table! Our ideas of enjoyment, then, were very different from what they are now. The laughter of fools was then in our mouth and perhaps the song of the drunkard issued from our lips. But now, by God's Grace, a blessed change has been worked in us, for we are washed, we are sanctified, we are justified in the name of the Lord Jesus and by the Spirit of our God! So, as we come to this Table of Communion, let us come humbly remembering what we once were, thankfully recollecting what Christ has done for us and earnestly entreating Him to continue and complete His good work in us by purifying us with water even as He has already put away our guilt by His blood! And to Him shall be the Glory forever and ever! Amen.

THE BLOOD OF THE TESTAMENT

"For when Moses had spoken every precept to all the people according to the Law, he took the blood of calves and of goats, with water, and scarlet wool, and hyssop, and sprinkled both the book, and all his people, saying, This is the blood of the testament which God has enjoined unto you."
Hebrews 9:19, 20

Blood is always a terrible thing. It makes a sensitive mind shudder even to pronounce the word. But to look upon the thing, itself, causes a thrill of horror. Although by familiarity men shake this off, for the seeing of the eyes and the hearing of the ears can harden the heart, the instinct of a little child may teach you what is natural to us in reference to blood. How it will worry if its finger bleeds ever so little–shocked at the sight, even if there is actually no pain! I envy not the man whose pity would not stir to see a sparrow bleed or a lamb wantonly put to pain. And as for the cruel man, I shudder at the thought of his depravity. What exquisite pain it must have caused our first parent–how keenly it must have touched the fine sensibilities of their nature–to have had to offer sacrifice! Probably they had never seen death until they brought their first victim to the altar of God. Blood! Ah, how they must have shuddered as they saw the warm life fluid flowing forth from the innocent victim. It must have seemed to them to be a very horrible thing and, very properly so, for God intended them to feel their feelings outraged. He meant them to take to heart the anguish of the victim and learn, with many a shudder, what a destructive and killing thing sin was! He meant them to see before their eyes a commentary upon His threat–"In the day that you eat thereof you shall surely die." He meant Adam and Eve to witness the harrowing appearance as the sentence upon sin was executed, stabbing at the very heart of life, convulsing all the frame, sealing up the senses and leaving behind but a wreck of the beautiful creature and not a relic of happiness for it in the world. How dreadful must have been the spectacle when the first pair gathered around the corpse of their second son, slain by his brother! There were the clots of blood on the murderous club, or the sharp stone, or whatever other instrument Cain may have used in smiting his brother to the grave. How they must have mourned and sighed as they saw the precious crimson of human life wantonly poured out upon the ground and crying to God against the murderer!

Yes, blood is always a ghastly and a terrible thing. It is so, I suppose, because we recognize in it the destruction of life. Is it not so, also—though we may not be able to define the emotion—because we are compelled in our consciences to admit the effect of sin and we are staggered as we see what our sin has done? All through the great school of the Jewish Law, blood was constantly used to instruct the Israelite in the guilt of sin, and in the greatness of the atonement necessary for putting it away. I suppose that the outer court of the Jewish Temple was something worse than ordinary shambles. If you will read the lists of the multitudes of beasts that were sometimes slain there in a single day, you will see that the priests must have stood in gore and have presented a crimson appearance—their snow-white garments all splashed over with blood as they stood there offering sacrifice from morning till night! Every man who went up to the tabernacle or to the Temple must have stood aside for a moment, and have said, "What a place this is for the worship of God! Everywhere I see signs of slaughter." God intended this to be so. It was the great lesson which He meant to be taught to the Jewish people, that sin was a loathsome and a detestable thing—and that it could only be put away by the Sacrifice of a great life, such a life as had not then been lived—the life of the Coming One, the life of the Eternal Son of God who must, Himself, become Man that He might offer His own immaculate life upon the altar of God to expiate the guilt and put

Some of you will feel sickened at these reflections and object to what I have already said as unworthy of my lips and offensive to your ears. I know who these will be—the creatures of taste who have never felt the loathsomeness of sin! Oh, I would that your sins would sicken you! I would to God that you had some sense of what a horrible thing it is to rebel against the Most High, to pervert the laws of right, to overthrow the rules of virtue, and to run into the ways of transgression and iniquity, for if blood is sickening to you, sin is infinitely more detestable to God! And if you find that being washed in blood seems awful to you, the great bath which was filled from Christ's veins in which men are washed and made clean is a thing of greater and deeper solemnity to God than any tongue shall be ever able to express!

I do not think anyone ever knows the preciousness of the blood of Christ till he has had a full sight and sense of his sin, his uncleanness and his ill desert. Is there any such thing as truly coming to the Cross of Christ until you first of all have seen what your sin really deserves? A little light into that dark cellar, Sir—a little light into that hole within the soul, a little light cast into that infernal den of your humanity and you will soon discern what sin is! And, seeing it, you would discover that there was no hope of being washed from it except by a Sacrifice far greater than you could ever render. Then the Atonement of Christ would become fair and lustrous in your eyes and you would rejoice with unspeakable joy in that boundless love which led the Savior to give Himself a ransom for us, "the Just for the unjust, that He might bring us to God." May the Lord teach us—thundering at us, if necessary—what sin means! May He teach it to us so that the lesson shall be burned into our souls and we shall never forget it! I could gladly wish that you were all burden carriers till you grew weary. I could gladly wish that you all labored after Eternal Life until your strength failed, and that you might then rejoice in Him who has finished the work and who promises to be your All-in-All when you believe in Him and trust in Him with your whole heart!

Looking carefully at the text, I would have you notice the name given to the blood of Christ, the ministry in which it was used and the effect that it produced.

First, observe THE NAME GIVEN IN THE TEXT TO THE BLOOD OF CHRIST. It is said to be, "THE BLOOD OF THE TESTAMENT."

You are aware, perhaps, you who read your Bibles thoroughly, that the word here rendered, "testament," is more commonly rendered, "covenant," and although it would be wrong to say that it does not mean, "testament," yet it would be right to say that it signifies both, "covenant" and, "testament," and that its first and general meaning is "covenant."

Let us take it so. The blood of Jesus is the Blood of the Covenant. Long before this round world was made, or stars began to shine, God foresaw that He would make man. He also foresaw that man would fall into sin. Out of that fall of man, His distinguishing Grace and Infinite Sovereignty selected a multitude that no man can number to be His. But, seeing that they had offended against Him, it was necessary, in order that they might be saved, that a great scheme or plan should be devised by which the Justice of God would be fully satisfied, and yet the mercy of God should have full play. A covenant was therefore arranged between the Persons of the blessed Trinity. It was agreed and solemnly pledged by the oath of the Eternal Father that He would give unto the Son a multitude whom no man could number who should be His—His spouse, the members of His Mystical Body, His sheep, His precious jewels. These the Savior accepted as His own, and then on His part, He undertook for them that He would keep the Divine Law, that He would suffer all the penalties due on their behalf for offenses against the Law and that He would keep and preserve every one of them until the day of His appearing. Thus stood the Covenant and on that Covenant the salvation of every saved man and woman hangs. Do not think it rests with you, Soul, for what says the Scripture? "It is not of him that wills, nor of him that runs but of God that shows mercy." He said to Moses, "I will have mercy on whom I will have mercy, and I will have compassion on whom I will have compassion." To show you that salvation is not by human merit, God was pleased to cast it entirely upon covenant arrangements. In that Covenant made between Himself and His Son, there was not a word said about our actions having any merit in them! We were regarded as though we were not, except that we stood in Christ and we were only so far parties to the Covenant as we were in the loins of Christ on that august day. We were considered to be the seed of the Lord Jesus Christ, the children of His care, the members of His own body. "According as He has chosen us in Christ before the foundation of the world." Oh, what Grace it was that put your name and mine in the eternal roll and provided for our salvation, provided for it by a Covenant—

by a sacred pact between the Father and His Eternal Son, that we should belong to Him in the day when He should make up His jewels!

Now, Beloved, in a covenant there are pledges given—and on those pledges we delight to meditate. You know what they were. The Father pledged His honor and His word. He did more—He pledged His oath and, "because He could swear by no greater, He swore by Himself." He pledged His own word and sacred honor of Godhead that He would be true to His Son, that He should see His seed and that by the knowledge of Him, Christ should "justify many." But there was needed a seal to the Covenant—and what was that? Jesus Christ in the fullness of time set the seal to the Covenant, to make it valid and secure, by pouring out His life's blood to make the Covenant effectual once and for all. Beloved, if there is an agreement made between two men, the one to sell such-and-such an estate, and the other to pay for it, the covenant does not hold good until the payment is made. Now, Jesus Christ's blood was the payment of His part of the Covenant! And when He shed it, the Covenant stood as firm as the everlasting hills—and the Throne of God, Himself, is not more sure than is the Covenant of Grace! And, mark you, that Covenant is not sure merely in its great outlines, but also sure in all its details! Every soul whose name was in that Covenant must be saved! Unless God can undeify Himself, every soul that Christ died for, He will have! Every soul for which He stood Substitute and Surety, He demands to have—and each of the souls He must have, for the Covenant stands fast. Moreover, every blessing in that Covenant which was guaranteed to the chosen seed was, by the precious blood, made eternally secure to that seed! Oh, how I delight to speak about the sureness of that Covenant! How the dying David rolled that under his tongue as a sweet morsel! "Although my house," he said, "be not so with God"—there was the bitter in his mouth—"yet," he said—and there came in the honey, "yet He has made with me an Everlasting Covenant, ordered in all things, and sure." And this sureness, mark you, lies in the blood! It is the blood of Christ that makes all things secure, for all the promises of God are yes and amen in Christ Jesus, to the Glory of God by us!

You will ask, it may be, "What is the purpose of this Doctrine?" Its purpose is this—To you who have believed in Jesus, Covenant mercies are sure, not because of your frames and feelings, but because of the precious blood of Jesus! Yesterday you were happy, perhaps, and today you are downcast. Well, but the Covenant has not changed! Tomorrow you may be in the very depths of despair, while today you are singing upon the top of the mountain—but the Covenant will not change. That august transaction was not made by you and cannot be unmade by you! It tarries not for man, and waits not for the sons of men. There it stands fast and settled, signed by the Eternal Signet, and your security is not in yourselves, but in Christ. If Christ bought you—if the Father gave you to Him, if Christ became a Surety for you, then—

"Nor death, nor Hell, shall ever remove
His favorites from His breast;
In the dear bosom of His love
They must forever rest!"

The name of the blood, as we find it in our own translation, is " the blood of the testament." This teaches a similarTruth of God, though it puts it under another figure. Salvation comes to us as a matter of will. Jesus Christ has left Eternal Life to His people as a legacy. Here are the words—"Father, I will that they, also, whom You have given Me, be with Me where I am, that they may behold My Glory." Now, a will, as the Apostle rightly tells us, has no power whatever unless the man who made it is dead. Hence the blood of Jesus Christ, the token of His death, gives validity to all the promises which He has made. That spear-thrust by the Roman soldier was a precious proof to us that our Lord was really dead. And now, Beloved, whenever you read a precious promise in the Bible, you may say, "This is a clause in the Redeemer's will." When you come to a choice word, you may say, "This is another codicil to the will." Recollect that these things are yours—not because you are this or that—but because His blood makes them yours! The next time Satan says to you, "You do not believe as you ought and, therefore, the promise is not sure," tell him that the sureness of the promise lies in the blood, and not in what you are or in what you are not! There is a will proved in Heaven's

Court of Probate, whose validity depends upon its signatures, upon its witnesses and upon its being drawn up in proper style. The person to whom the property is left may be very poor, but that does not overthrow the will. He may be very ragged, but that does not upset the will. He may have disgraced himself in some way or other, but that does not make the will void. He who made the will and put His name to the will, makes the will valid, and not the legatee to whom the legacy was left. And so with you this Covenant stands secure, this will of Christ stands firm! In all your ups and downs, in all your successes and your failures, you, poor needy Sinner, have nothing to do but to come and take Christ to be your All-in-All and put your trust in Him—and the Blood of the Covenant shall make the promises sure to you!

This is a sweet topic. I have not time, however, to enlarge upon it, but I heartily commend it to your private meditations and trust you may find consolation in it.

II. The blood which Moses called "the blood of the covenant" or, "of the testament," was of the utmost importance in the ministry of the tabernacle, for IT WAS SPRINKLED BY HIM EVERYWHERE.

First, we are told that he sprinkled it upon the book. Oh, how delightful this Bible looks to me when I see the bloodof Christ sprinkled upon it! Every leaf would have flashed with Sinai's lightning and every verse would have rolled with the thunders of Horeb if it had not been for Calvary's Cross! But now, as you look, you see on every page your Savior's precious blood! He loved you and gave Himself for you, and now you who are sprinkled with that blood and have by faith rested in Him, can take that precious Book and find it to be green pastures and still waters to your souls!

The blood was then sprinkled upon the Mercy Seat itself. Whenever you cannot pray as you would, remember that Jesus Christ's blood has gone before you and is pleading for you before the Eternal Throne of God. Like the good Methodist who, when a Brother could not pray, cried out, "Plead the blood, Brother!" Yes, and when you feel so unworthy that you dare not look up. When the big tear stands in your eye because you have been such a backslider and have been so cold in heart, plead the blood, my Sister–you may always come where the blood is! There you see that this sin of yours has been already atoned for. Before you committed it, Jesus carried it! Long before it fell from your heart, the weight of it had pressed upon the Redeemer's heart–and He put it away in that tremendous day when He took all the load of His people's guilt and hurled it into the sepulcher–to be buried there forever!

Then the blood was sprinkled upon every vessel of the sanctuary. I like that thought. I like to come up to God'sHouse and say, "Well, I shall worship God today in the power and through the merit of the precious blood! My praises will be poor, feeble things, but then the sweet perfume will go up out of the golden censer and my praises will be accepted through Jesus Christ! My preaching, oh, how full of faults–how covered over with sins! But then the blood is on it and because of that, God will not see sin in my ministry, but will accept it because of the sweetness of His Son's blood."

You will come to the Communion Table tonight, most of you. But oh, do not come without the precious blood, for the best place of all upon which it was sprinkled was upon all the people. The drops fell upon them all! As Moses took thebasin and scattered the blood over the whole crowd, it fell upon all who were assembled at the door of the Tabernacle. Have you had sprinkling with the precious blood, my Hearer? If you have, you shall live forever! But if you have not, the wrath of God abides on you! Do you ask how you can have the blood of Christ sprinkled upon you? It cannot be done literally, but faith does it. Faith is the bunch of hyssop which we dip into the basin and it sprinkles man's conscience frombad works. You say you have been christened, confirmed, baptized–but all these things together would not save one soul, much less all the multitudes who trust in them! They are not sufficient for the taking away of a single sin! But you always say your prayers, you have family prayers and you are very honest and so on! I know all this–but all these things you ought to have done and they will not make amends for what you have not done! All the debt that you have paid willnot discharge those that are still due! Know you not that saying of the Scriptures, "by the deeds of the Law there shall no flesh be justified in His sight: for by the Law is the knowledge of sin"? You may work your fingers to the bone, but you can never weave a righteousness that shall cover your nakedness before God! The only hope for the sinner is to come and cast himself upon what Jesus Christ has done for him—depending upon the groans, and agonies, and death of the martyred Savior who stood for us and suffered in our place, that we might escape the wrath of God!

I hope that there is never a Sunday but what I teach this one Doctrine and, until this tongue is silent in the grave, I shall know no other Gospel than just this—Trust Christ and you shall live! The bloody Sacrifice of Calvary is the only hope of sinners! Look there and you shall find the Star of Peace guiding you to everlasting day! But turn your backs upon Christ and you have turned your back upon Heaven—you have courted destruction, you have sealed your doom! It is by the sprinkling of the blood, then, that we are saved. We must have the blood of Christ upon us in one way or the other. If we do not have it upon us to save us, we shall have it upon us to destroy us. "His blood be on us and on our children," said the Jews to Pilate in their madness—and the siege of Jerusalem was the answer to the cry! Worse than was the siege of Jerusalem to the Jews, shall be the death of those who do despite to the Spirit of Grace and despise the blood of Jesus! But happy shall they be who, giving up every other confidence, come to the Blood of the Covenant and put their trust there, for it shall not deceive them!

III. THE EFFECT OF THE BLOOD OF CHRIST claims our earnest attention—yet the minutes are few in which I can enlarge upon it.

Whenever Jesus Christ's blood comes upon a man, the instantaneous effect is something more than miraculous. Before the application of Christ's blood, the man was distracted. His guilt and its consequent punishment weighed heavily upon him. "Alas!" he said, "I shall soon die, and then Hell will be my lot!" Oh, some of us will never forget when we were in that miserable, burdened state! I declare before you all that when I felt the weight of my sin, I wished that I had never been born!

And I envied frogs, and toads, and the most loathsome creatures, and thought that they were so much better off than I, because they had never broken the Law of God, which I had so wickedly and so willfully done! If I went to my bed, I started with the fear that I should wake up in Hell. And by day the same dread thought distracted me–that I was cast off by God and must perish! But the moment that I looked to Christ–do not mistake me–the very same momentthat I put my trust in Christ, I rose from the depths of despair to the utmost heights of joy! It was not a process of reasoning. It was not a matter which took hours and days–it was all done in an instant! I understood that God had punished Christ instead of me, and I saw that, therefore, I could not be punished anymore–that I never could be if Christ died for me–and I was assured that He did if I did but trust Him! So I did trust Him–with my whole weight I threw myself into His arms and thought, at the time, that He had never had such a load to carry before! But I found that He was able to save, even to the uttermost, them that came unto Him–and what joy and peace I had in that moment it is impossible for me to describe! And I thank God that I have never lost it. There have been time of depression. There have been seasons when the light of God's Countenance has been withdrawn. But one thing I know–Christ Jesus came into the world to save sinners–I am a sinner, and my soul rests alone on Him! And how can He cast me away, since His own promise is, "He that believes and is baptized shall be saved"? I have believed, by His Grace! I have been baptized as an avowal of my faith! And He is not true if He does not save me! But He must be true, He cannot break His word! O dear Friends, there are hundreds here who have passed through the same blessed experience and they can tell you that the blood of Jesus in an instant speaks peace to the soul!

And this precious blood has this property about it that if the peace which it first causes should become a little dim, you have only to go to the precious blood to have that peace once more restored to you!

I would recommend any of my doubting Brothers and Sisters to come to Christ over again as they came to Him at first. Never mind about your experience! Never care about your marks and evidences. Never get piling up your experiences. If you go to the top of some mountains such as Snowdon or the Righi, you will find it all solid and firm enough, but there are some people who want to get a little higher than the mountain, so the people there built a rickety old stage and charge you four pence— or sixpence to go to the top of it! And when you get up there, you find it is all shaky and ready to tumble down and you are frightened! Well, but what need is there to go up there at all? If you would stand on the mountain, that would not shake! So, sometimes, we are not content with resting upon Christ as poor sinners, and depending on Him. We get to building a rickety stage of our own experience, or sanctification, or emotions, and I know not what besides—and then it begins to shake under our feet. Far better if we were like the Negro who said he "fell flat down on de promise, and when he had done that, he couldn't fall no lower." Oh, to keep close to a promise! Job says that the naked embrace the rock for need of a shelter, and there is no shelter like the Rock of Ages—

"None but Jesus
Can do helpless sinners good!"

But I have not told you all the power of this blood, nor could I tell you tonight. That blood gives the pardoned sinner access with boldness to God, Himself. That blood, having taken away the guilt of sin, operates in a sanctifying manner and takes away the power of sin—and the pardoned man does not live as he lived before he was pardoned. He lovesGod, who has forgiven him so much—and that love makes him enquire, "What shall I do for God, who has done so much for me?" Then he begins to purge himself of his old habits. He finds that the pleasures that once were sweet to him are sweet no more. "Away you go," he says to his old companions, "I cannot go with you to Hell." Having a new heart, a new love, a new desire, he begins to mix with God's people. He searches God's Word. He makes haste to keep God's commandments. His desires are holy and heavenly and he pants for the time when he shall get rid of all sin, shall be quite like Christ and shall be taken away to dwell forever where Jesus is! Oh, the blood of Christ is a blessed sin-killer! They say that St. Patrick drove all the snakes out of Ireland. Ah, but Christ drives all the serpents out of the human heart when He once gets in. If He does but sprinkle His blood upon our hearts, we become new men—such new men as all the rules of morality could not have made us! Such new men as they are who, robed in white, day without night sing Jehovah's praise before His Throne!

Sinner, would you be saved tonight? Trust Jesus and you shall be! Sinner, would you be saved upon a dying bed? Trust Jesus now and you shall be! Sinner, would you be saved when the heavens are in a blaze and the stars fall like withered fig leaves from the firmament? Look to Jesus, now, and you shall be saved then! Oh, I would to God that some of you would look to Him! Not for the eyes of your body to do it, but for the eyes of your mind to do it! Think of what Christ is—God, and yet Man. Think of such a Being suffering instead of you! What must be the merit of such suffering, and what an honor to God's Justice that such an One should suffer instead of you! Then depend upon Christ and if you do so, your sins are forgiven you! Believe that they are. Then will you feel springing up within your heart great love to Him who has forgiven you—and that will become the mainspring of your new life! You will start afresh like one that is born tonight. You will, indeed, be born-again, for this is regeneration! Not sprinkling your face with drops of water, but making a new man of you—generating you over again, not by natural generation, but by the Eternal Father begetting you again unto a lively hope by the Resurrection of Jesus Christ from the dead—the true and only spiritual generation! And then, as new creatures in Christ Jesus, you shall go your way through this life up to the eternal life, God's blessing shielding you and crowning you forever.

The Lord grant you His blessing, for Christ's sake! Amen.

THE WATER AND THE BLOOD

"But one of the soldiers with a spear pierced His side, and forthwith came there out blood and water."
John 19:34

IT is with much fear and trembling that I usually stand upon this platform–not that I shrink before the face of the multitude however large, but the weight of the subject which I have continually to bring before your minds fills my own soul with awe. And yet it is with more than usual anxiety I approach my subject this evening, because although it is full of tender interest and touching pathos, I feel that without the unction of the Holy Spirit, it would be insipid and unprofitable. And yet, on the other hand, with that Divine anointing, it is one of the richest topics that can possibly engage our meditation!

Readers of old theology will have remarked how constantly the fathers were accustomed to dwell upon the wounds of Jesus slain. And this fifth wound which penetrated His heart was peculiarly attractive to them. They said a great many things about it. Some, indeed that were fanciful, but other remarks that were truly excellent and well deserve to be treasured up. I would it were more the practice of Believers nowadays than it is to study the very Person of Christ, as well as the Doctrines of the Gospel, and to learn the Divine lessons which are discoverable in the wounds of Jesus as well as the sacred admonitions bequeathed to us by the words of His mouth.

One of these old Divines says that Jesus Christ was typified by our first father, Adam. As Adam fell asleep, and out of his side Eve was taken, so Jesus slept upon the Cross, the sleep of death, and from His side, where the spear was thrust, His Church was taken. He who redeemed us unto God by His blood, formed us as a peculiar people for Himself. The Church is one with Him–she came out of His side, and as He looks upon her, He can say–"You are bone of My bone, and flesh of My flesh. With My blood have I redeemed you." Others have been pleased to compare Christ to the Rock in the wilderness, which was smitten, and this spear-thrust is the great cleft in the Rock. You may remember how Toplady puts it–

"Rock of Ages, cleft for me!
Let me hide myself in Thee."

And he clearly has this in view, for the next lines are–

"Let the water and the blood
From Your riven side which flowed,
Be of sin the double cure,
Cleanse me from its guilt and power."

I do not consider this allusion fanciful, nor can I think it distorts the type. Moses hidden in the cleft of the rock, that he might see God's Glory, had not a standing place one-half so glorious as you and I have when, sheltered in the wounds of the Savior slain, we see the glorious Justice and the Infinite Love of God reconciled in the Person of the dying Lamb.

In the course of reading, I have met with some remarkable expressions in regard to this great wound of Christ. Some have called it, "a gate of Heaven." Why should I object to the title? Do we not enter into Heaven through the wounds of Jesus? It is, of course, a metaphorical expression, yet quite allowable. If the teaching is that there is no other way of access to God except through the torn veil of Christ's body–and that veil was torn in two, indeed, when the soldier with the spear pierced His side–we may, without straining the thought, call that wound one of the gates of Heaven. Another calls it "a celestial window, a window of Paradise," and we have versified that idea in one of our own familiar sonnets–

"Look through Jesus' wounds on me; Another writer, carried away by the consideration of this spear-thrust, calls it "a palace of refuge." A palace! Surely, never kings had such an one! Solomon's palace of ivory was nothing like it! And what a refuge it is! When the poor heart, like the dove hunted by the hawk, needs a shelter, if it can fly to Jesus' wounds, it is sheltered from all its sins. Well does our song put it–

"Come, guilty souls, and flee away
Like doves to Jesus' wounds!
This is the welcome Gospel Day,
Wherein free Grace abounds."

I forget the name of the writer, who, in speaking upon his Master's wounds, seems to get so exalted and carried away by the subject that He calls this wound "the sacred wellhead of the rivers of golden sand which cover all the earth"–two rivers, one of water and the other of blood. Two quickening rivers that carry life through the realms of death. Two purifying rivers cleansing the Augean stable of this filthy world. Two mighty rivers which bear the elect vessels onwards towards the sea of everlasting bliss, not one of them suffering shipwreck on the voyage, for this mighty river is too deep to have quicksands, too broad for the mariner to be cast away upon a rock-bound shore! I like the thought, and so let it be–the sacred wellhead of that river of more than golden sand– the streams whereof make glad the multitudes of God's chosen throughout the earth!

In this wound of Christ, caused by the soldier, I discern four obvious meanings. It has many more, but these four will be enough to occupy our attention this evening.

It was THE MARK OF PROPHECY. In order that it might be fully known that Jesus Christ was the Messiah that was to come, the Prophets had given many marks, all of which must be found in the Person of the Man who should be the Great Deliverer. Among the rest was this one that John quotes, "A bone of Him shall not be broken." This description concerned the paschal lamb, of which it was expressly said by the Lord, through Moses, that they were never to break a single bone of it. Its joints were to be separated after it had been roasted with fire, but not a bone was to be snapped. Now, if Jesus Christ is the Lamb of God's Passover, it is necessary that He should never have a broken bone. And yet it looked as if His bones would be broken. The rough soldier brought up a great iron crowbar and, with an awful blow, smashed the legs of the poor thief who hung on one side of our Lord, but half-dead, in order to hasten his dissolution. It was a strange thing that he passed by Christ, who was in the middle. I know not what it was that made him do so–whether some flash of majesty beamed from that dead face, or whether some singular instinct checked his arm. But he went and administered the dreadful blow to the thief on the other side. And now he came to Christ and perhaps raised the iron rod–when he saw that He was already dead! His head was hanging down upon His bosom and the man saw clearly that there was no need to administer the deathblow to Him. It was a strange thing that his hands should be so restrained. The soldiers of that day were wanton enough. They were just as likely as not to have broken the bones even though the man were dead–but Divine Prophecy must have it so and, therefore, not a bone of Jesus can be broken!

And then the Prophet Zechariah had said concerning the Messiah, "They shall look upon Him whom they have pierced, and they shall mourn for Him as one mourns for his only son." Now up till that moment our Lord had not been pierced, except as to His hands and feet, and this would scarcely have been a carrying out of the word, "pierced." Somebody would have said, "Well, but He never was pierced so as to cause His death–there was no such piercing as the text indicates." But now that the soldier, moved by the mysterious impulse, lifts his lance and thrusts it deep into the side of Christ–now did Prophecy set its mark upon Christ–now did history identify Him–the Man without broken bones yet the Man whose side was pierced! Him for whom Israel should one day mourn! Him whom His enemies should one day confess to be their King!

My dear Brothers and Sisters, has it ever struck you with admiring wonder that Jesus Christ should answer to Prophecies so complicated and types so manifold–should answer even with coincidences the most minute to them all? It would be almost impossible to count the types of Christ which are given in the Old Testament. It would, perhaps, be easy to count the prophecies, but very difficult for anybody to form a character in which all these should be blended and fulfilled! It has been said that if you were to give all these types and all these prophecies to the wisest of men of all ages, and say to them, "You are required to compile a biography of a man who shall answer to all these," they must certainly give up in despair! You can find men who will make a key to fit any lock– by diligence of labor, no matter how complicated key that will fit the exceedingly complex words of all the types of the Old Testament and all its prophecies! How palpable then the evidence is. Our Lord Jesus Christ answers to them all. Just as the stamp in the wax answers to the seal that stamped it, the Providence that transpired corresponds with the predictions that forestalled His course! He went as it was written of Him! There He is and He fulfils types that look the most opposite and prophecies which seem to run counter to one another!

If anybody thinks that the stories told by the four Evangelists are spurious, I would suggest to him to go and write a fifth–to try to write another that would as much correspond with the Old Testament–and with the other four, as those four do with the Old Testament and with each other! And when that task was done, I would then give him another problem to solve before he could have reasonable ground for suspicion that Jesus of Nazareth was not the Messiah. Account for the incredulity of the Jews in the presence of those evidences that have produced conviction among the Gentiles upon any other hypotheses than that which ratifies their own Scripture! If the Old Testament is the Word of God, it seems marvelous to us that men do not receive Jesus as being the Shiloh that was to come, the promised Messiah, the Prince of the kings of the earth! Jewish unbelief amazes us! Yet I suppose if we judged aright, our own lack of faith in Jesus, notwithstanding the rational credit we give to His mission as a popular creed, is still more amazing! If that is gross unbelief which rejects Christ, while acknowledging the Old Testament, what shall I say of you who refuse allegiance to Him and yet profess to believe both the Old and the New? If they that receive the first yet stumble at the second, what shall I say of those who receive both and yet, over the head of this double belief professed, give not their hearts to the Crucified Son of God, and put not their trust in the merit of His precious blood, but still continue afar off from Him by wicked works?

Some time ago, when in Italy, at a town on the Italian side of the Alps, I saw one Sunday afternoon, in a quiet walk alone, a sight which struck me very much and which remains fixed upon my memory. There was outside the town a mountain and the way up the sides of which were different representations of the progress of our Lord, from the Garden where Judas betrayed Him to the place of His Resurrection. The figures were as large as life, carved in either stone or wood, and painted to imitate nature. When I got to the very summit of the hill, there was a church. There was no one in it and I pushed open the door and went in. All was still. It was a large building and all around it were images of the Prophets and the Apostles. There stood Isaiah, Jeremiah, Ezekiel and all the rest–one knew the usual portraits of them. And up in the dome, at the very top of the church, was a large and striking image of the Savior. Now, what struck me about the church was this–that the images of those Prophets and Apostles who stood there had their fingers all pointed upwards, so that, when I went in, I could not help looking up to the top to see what they were pointing at! All round the church there were the words, in Latin, "Moses and the Prophets spoke concerning Him." And there stood Moses and the Prophets, carved in stone, and all pointing to Him! Isaiah had a little scroll in his hand on which was written, "The Lord has made to meet on Him the iniquity of us all." Jeremiah had a scroll in his hand, on which was written, "Behold, and see if there is any sorrow like unto My sorrow, which is done unto Me." I think the church just represented the Truth in that case. It is even so. All the Prophets stand as a complete circle of distinct testifiers and, with uplifted fingers, they all concur with John the Baptist when he said, "Behold the Lamb of God, which takes away the sin of the world." They all point to Christ. If you read the life of Christ and then read what they said of Him, you will be persuaded that this is He which was to come!

II. But to pass on, we may look upon the spear-thrust in the side of Christ as THE ESCUTCHEON OF SHAME.

While our Lord lived, He was the subject of every form of scorn. He was scourged as none but a felon might be according to the Roman Law. He was spat upon and mocked, as even a felon ought not to have been. That crown of thorns, that reed scepter and that old scarlet cloak–who could have invented a more shameful insignia for One who was greater than all the kings on the earth but who was brought exceedingly low? And our Lord's death, itself, was a great portion of His shame. It was a shame for Him to die–and ignominy for Him to die the death of hanging on the Cross. Heraldry has so emblazoned the symbol that we do not ordinarily apprehend the real shame to which Christ was exposed. Were I to preach to you tonight that a certain man who was hanged was very God, people would begin to say, "Why do you preach of one who died on the gallows as a felon?" Literally and truly, that is just how Jesus Christ died, according to the customs of His times. Crucifixion was to the Romans what hanging is to us, only it was worse. It was more shameful, for crucifixion was reserved for the very worst of crimes. Not all murderers were so punished, but only the worst and vilest crimes with murder to aggravate them received this opprobrious doom. People hang crosses round their necks and wear them as ornaments–I wonder whether they would make ornaments of gallows? Yet it means that. It is just the same thing and this is the shame of Christ. This is the very shame in which Paul rejoiced and gloried, that Jesus Christ was not ashamed to be ashamed! That He was willing to be made ashamed and a curse for us! That He was content to be treated with all the scorn that human malignity and inhuman cruelty could heap upon Him!

But, Beloved, when Christ was dead, they might certainly have ceased from their scorn. But no, the brutal Roman soldiers were not very nice as to what they did with living bodies. They would not, therefore, be particular as to what they did with dead bodies! Therefore this soldier, in a mere freak of wanton brutality, thrust his lance into the Savior's heart. It was the last kick of the old enemy. It was, as it were, the last of the spit from the foul mouth of human slander and hatred. It was the last thrust that human malice could give to the Lord of Life and Glory! I see in this the mark, the crowning emblem of the shame which He endured.

Well, and what then? Why, it should teach us, dear Friends, what a shameful thing sin must be! For, though Christ was no sinner, yet when our sins were laid upon Him, look how God treated Him and permitted Him to be treated as an outcast–to be covered with the utmost shame! Ah Sin, what a shameful thing you must be! Blush, Christian, that you should be guilty of it. Blush again, that you do not blush more often! Be ashamed that you are not ashamed of sin, and be offended that your heart should be so stolid over a thing so detestable.

Another thought springs up, namely, that if Christ was put to so much shame for us, how glad we ought to be if we are sometimes allowed to be put to shame for Him! Oh, there are some people who cannot bear shame–they can endure anything else but ridicule and laughter! As John Bunyan says, "of all villains, Shame is the most shameless for he will go and make sport and fun of the Christian's virtues and mock at that which he ought to admire." Well, child of God, supposing today you have your face spat upon for Christ? 'Twere scarcely worthwhile to wipe it off! Ah, if you had to live a dying life, to be thrown in a dungeon, or to live upon the rack–as long as it was done for Him who bore all this for you–the thought might sweeten the wormwood and turn the gall into honey, that you were thus honored to have fellowship with Him in His sufferings! I leave that view of this wound of Christ with you, praying that it may nerve your hearts with a glorious courage as you see Jesus thus shamefully wounded for you.

III. This lance wound was THE SEAL OF DEATH UPON OUR LORD JESUS CHRIST. His enemies were so determined to put Him to death that they dragged His life out of its principal organ and then they pierced it, namely, the heart. It was not possible that Jesus Christ could have lived another moment longer, even had He been alive at that time–but when the heart was touched, death must come. Those who understand anatomy tell us that the pericardium around the heart was pierced and they say that from that there flowed the blood and the water. But I am extremely doubtful whether the pericardium in any state whatever could have yielded a sufficient quantity of lymph, for though there is water there, there is only a small quantity. In the state in which our Savior was, blood and water might have been found naturally in His heart, but only in a very small and infinitesimal quantity. The fountain that flowed from there was miraculous, not natural but supernatural—or if natural, yet so exalted and so increased in quantity as to become in itself supernatural.

Certainly, however, the piercing of His heart was the indication to all mankind that "He was dead already." Now, little as that may seem in the eyes of those of you who do not love Him, it is a most important thing to those who trust Him, for remember, if Jesus Christ had not died, you and I would have perished! It was of no use for our expiation that He sweat great drops of blood unless He had perfected the Sacrifice. The Law required if— if Christ had not laid down His life, the Law would have required ours. In due time, our souls would have been cast into the Second Death on account of sin if Jesus had not died, actually and truly died. But we are quite sure about it now, for His heart was pierced. Indeed, I may say that this is the one keystone of the whole Gospel system, for if Jesus did not die then, we have no Resurrection. If He died not then, He did not rise—and if we have no evidence of Resurrection, the whole of our religion becomes a lie! But, Brothers and Sisters, He did die. His soul left His body. That corpse that was taken by Joseph of Arimathaea was as lifeless as any that was ever committed to the sepulcher! And He did rise again, in proof to us that we who die and those we have parted with on the confines of this mortal life who are, alas, all truly dead, shall certainly rise again and in their flesh shall see God! This is a simple Truth of God for you to hear, perhaps, but never did angel have such weighty news to tell as I have told you tonight—that God was made flesh—the very God that made Heaven and earth took upon Himself our nature and as such He died, literally died for us! The God-Man, the Mediator, Jesus of Nazareth, the Son of God and the Son of Mary, died, was crucified and had His heart pierced for us! And if we depend upon this, we may rest secure. If He died, then we need not die! If He died for us, then we cannot die the Second Death. If Jesus was punished in our place, the sting of death is taken away, the Law is satisfied and every soul that believes in Him shall have eternal life!

IV. But I cannot tarry longer upon that and, therefore, I come to the fourth point. This heart wound of Christ is also to be called THE SOURCE OF PURITY. The text tells us that there issued from it a double flood of blood and water. We are not at a loss to explain this because the Apostle John, in his Epistle, has told us that our Lord "came by water and blood; not by water only, but by water and blood," and he explains it by the connection that Christ came into the world by blood to take away the guilt of sin, and by water to take away the power of sin—by blood to remove the punishment, by water to remove the filth.

Now, dear Friends, let us say that there is no blood and no water that can wash away sin anywhere but in Christ. Allthe blood of bulls could not take away sin, though offered by Aaron, himself, the father of the Levitical priesthood! And all the water in the world, though consecrated by bishops, cardinals and popes, cannot take away a single spot of iniquity! The only blood that can cleanse us from God's wrath is the blood of Jesus Christ, Himself, and the only water that can wash out of us the damning stain of sin is the water which came from Jesus Christ's heart! If you want to be thus doubly washed, go to the Son of God for the washing! Go nowhere else, I pray you, for every other trust is but a delusion and a lie. Jesus Christ can put away the guilt of every sin. Though you have been a drunk, an adulterer, a whoremonger, a thief, a murderer, yet the blood of Jesus Christ can wash you from the accumulated filth of years—and the water from Christ's side can take away your propensities to sin, change your nature and make you holy instead of filthy—can make you pure in heart instead of polluted in spirit! Nothing else can do it. No lie was ever more extraordinary than the lie that baptismal water can regenerate the soul! I marvel more and more that I should find myself living in an age of such idiots and have almost come to think that Carlyle was right when he spoke of our nation as "Consisting of twenty million people, mostly fools." So it seems to be, or else such a dogma as this would have been kicked out of the universe years since—and banished once and forever to the limbo of lunacy as an outrage on common sense! Is God the Holy Spirit confined to water, as that the priest's dropping it on the child's brow can work regeneration in the child's soul? Believe it not, it is a foul lie! But hold you to this—that which alone can work regeneration is the water from the side of Christ— and when faith can get that, and trust that, the matter is done! Faith relies upon the sacred double flood! Then the heart is renewed, the man is changed, the soul is saved by Jesus Christ!

Remember, too, that the water and the blood flowed from the same place and flowed together. And, therefore, if aman would be saved, He must have the two. Tens of thousands would like to escape from Hell, but they have no wish to escape from sin. Are there not multitudes who are very anxious to get rid of the punishment, but are not at all concerned to be delivered from the habit of iniquity? Oh, yes, the drunk would gladly be forgiven, but he would like to keep to his tippling. Yes, the lecherous man would gladly have his constitution restored and his iniquity blotted out, but he must go to his dens of infamy again! Such is not the religion of Christ. The religion of Christ demands of us that if we take Christ,we should take Him for the double purpose—pardon for past sins and to deliver from sins to come. I think it was Celsus, the ancient philosopher, who jeered at the great Christian advocates, saying, "Your Master, Christ, receives all the filth of the universe into His Church! He tells you to go about to find out thieves, drunks, harlots and such like, and to tell them to come to Him! Your religion is nothing better than a hospital into which you thrust lepers." "Yes," said he who argued with him, "you have spoken well. We do receive them as into a hospital, but we heal them, Sir, we heal them! And while into the one door the spiritually and morally blind, cripples, and maimed come in as they are, the Great Physician touches them with His Grace and cleanses them with the water and the blood—and they are not what they were any longer."

Now, am I addressing one man who feels that he is saved by faith, and yet he is sinning as he used to do? Give up that belief, Sir, or it will ruin you! I pray you do not indulge in it, for it is a delusion of Satan! Do I address one man who has a hope that perhaps he can so trust Christ as to be saved, and yet continue to live in his own wicked way? If anyone has told you that, he has told you a lie! Rest assured that you are mistaken! Christ never came to be the minister of sin. He came to save us, not in our sins. He will forgive us all manner of iniquities, but not if we love the iniquity and continue in it! If you hug sin to your bosom, the viper will sting you–and no power, either human or Divine–can extract the poison unless the viper, itself, is taken away. You must have both the water and the blood–and I pray that you may have both.

Now, Christians, I have done when I have put to you one question. Answer it and answer it truthfully. It is this–Beloved Friends, have you got such a hold of Christ as you should have in His double capacity as your Pardoner and your Sanctifier? I know you plead the blood for your remission. I know that is all your hope. I know that the blood of Christ is your comfort and your hope, but have you got the water quite as fully? You have a bad temper, perhaps. Well, it is a pitiable circumstance, but surely, if Christ can forgive a bad temper, He can remove a bad temper, too! Did you ever bring your bad temper to Christ to have it washed away with the water? You should have done so, for He can do it. Perhaps you have got an envious spirit–a murmuring spirit? Naturally so, you are generally depressed and downhearted. Did you ever believe in the power of Christ to kill envy and to lift you up above murmuring? You should do so. You believe that Christ can forgive this sin. Well, that is through the power of the blood–but do you think that the water is less potent than the blood–that Christ can forgive what He cannot subdue? Oh, think not so! Think as well of the Spirit and His sanctifying power as of Christ and His justifying righteousness!

"Well," says one, "I have a besetting sin which I do not think I shall ever quite overcome," My dear Brother, why not? It strikes me that the Christian ought to get his greatest victories from his weakest points–and if you have a besetting sin, I think you ought to be distinguished by its opposite virtue! I do not know that it was so, but I always have a notion that Moses was, by his natural constitution, a thoroughly quick-tempered man. I think so from the fact that when he saw the Egyptian smiting the Israelite, he did not stop a minute, but he slew him at once and hid him in the sand. That looks to me to be the breaking out of the real Moses. But what did he become by the Grace of God? Why, after his spirit was subdued, he became the meekest of men and often was quiet where you and I would have spoken! Now, why should it not be so with us? It strikes me that the worst-tempered man who becomes a Christian ought to make this a strong point and to strive to become the best-tempered. There are some Christians who naturally have a little weakness in their hand and cannot open it well. If they get a little money in it, they are very apt to get their joints tied together very tightly! But, when Divine Grace comes in, I think they should try to defeat the devil by being more than ordinarily generous—so that, whereas other Christians might be content to give less, they say to Satan—"O my enemy, you have held me in bondage in this way, but in wherever else you may get the upper hand of me, you never shall in this, for I will take care that whenever you tell me not to give a shilling, I will give two in order to let you see that you are no master of mine and that I have got rid of the foul sin of stinginess!" Do let us, each one, act upon this great Truth of God, that as Christ has the power to forgive us our sin, so He also has the power to cleanse it away!

And, my dear Brothers and Sisters, let us get closer to Christ! Let us be bedewed more often than we have been before with the water and with the blood! Let us live in the spirit of this double purification and be it ours to find this blessed stream lead us right up to the heart of Christ, from which it flowed, that we may understand the everlasting love which dwells there deep in its eternal fountains—and may rejoice and be glad in it all our days!

THE SAVIOR'S PRECIOUS BLOOD

"The precious blood of Christ."
1 Peter 1:19

We have come in our theological conversation to use that word, "blood," somewhat lightly. I think it should scarcely ever be pronounced without a shudder. "The blood is the life thereof." When shed, it indicates suffering–suffering more intense than that of chastisement or bruising. Wounds are inflicted which make the lifeblood to flow out. In the case of our Lord, Jesus Christ, the term, "blood," brings before us all His griefs and anguish and where the crown of thorns pierced Him. Behold the Man! Think of Gethsemane, where He sweat, as it were, great drops of blood falling to the ground! Think of Gabbatha, the pavement, where they scourged Him with rods, and with the scourge of the Roman lictors where the crown of thorns pierced Him. Behold the Man! Think, lastly, of Golgotha! There they pierced His hands and His feet and, at last, pierced by the spear, out of His side there came blood and water. Pass not lightly, therefore, over such a word as this–blood–the blood of Jesus Christ, God's dear Son! And when you read of its being "precious," remember that the word never had such a wealth of meaning in it, before, in any of its applications. Precious metals–gold and silver. Precious stones–sardonyx, agate and diamond–these are but gaudy toys compared with Christ's precious blood! Precious, for He is God as well as Man. Precious, for He is Jehovah's Darling, the Lamb of God, without spot or blemish! Precious, when you think of God's design. Precious, when you see the effects which it produces. Precious, certainly, to the heart of every pardoned sinner and precious in the song of every glorified spirit before the Throne of God!

It is not, however, my objective, this evening, to pursue the sacred history, so much as to set forth the saving Doctrine, while I remind you of some of the uses of this precious blood. For, after all, the standard of preciousness, when we come to the very essence of it, is not scarcity, but usefulness, for there are things in this world exceedingly scarce and, therefore, precious among the sons of men, which will be left out and treated with contempt when we get into the land where the true standards of value are in use. That is the most precious which is the most serviceable. So in truth, the precious blood of Christ is beyond all estimation! I want to conduct you, step by step, through the application of this blood and its effects upon the heart and conscience. And I shall pause at each step to ask you, dear Hearer, and to ask myself this question–Do you know the blood, the precious blood, in this respect? Have you felt it in this peculiar form of its efficacy? Beginning thus at the first–

THE BLOOD OF JESUS CHRIST IS THE BLOOD OF THE ATONEMENT.

We read of the blood of the Atonement under the old Law. Christ, now under the Gospel, is the Propitiation for our sins. It is through the blood that God, infinitely just, without the violation of His Character, can pass by the transgression of the guilty. It is not possible that any one attribute of God should ever shadow another. He is perfect. He is infinitely merciful, but He will not be merciful at the expense of justice! Justice shall never triumph against mercy! Mercy, on the other hand, shall never cut off the skirts of the flowing robe of justice. It is in the Person of Jesus and especially in the blood of Jesus, that the great riddle of the ages is solved! God can be just and yet the Justifier of him that believes in Jesus. We have sinned. God must punish sin. According to the inexorable laws which God has stamped upon the universe, the sinner cannot go unpunished. His sin is, in fact, its own punishment and becomes the mother of unnumbered griefs. The Mediator steps in–the Son of God and the Son of Man, eternal, and yet as Man, born of Mary and slumbering in Bethlehem's manger–He comes as the Substitute for the guilty. "The chastisement of our peace was upon Him, and by ist." God can be gracious without the violation of the severity of His judgment. His moral government remains untarnished in all the majesty of its purity, and yet He puts out the right hand of reconciliation and love to all who approach Him making mention of the blood of the Atonement of His dear Son!

Are you, then, thus reconciled to God by the death of His Son, or are you still an enemy? Have you ever seen the distance between you and God bridged by the Cross? Have you seen at once how God, the infinitely Just, can commune with you without consuming you, because He poured His wrath upon Christ, instead of you? And then, accepted in Him and for His merits, you live because Jesus lives! Ah, dear Hearer, if you have not seen this, may the Lord open those blind eyes of yours and by His eternal Spirit bring you, with your burden of sin upon your back, to the foot of the Master's Cross, where you may look up and sing—

"Oh, how sweet to view the flowing,
Of His sin-atoning blood!
With Divine assurance knowing,
That it made my peace with God."

The blood of Jesus Christ has another effect upon us, namely—

II. IT CLEANSES FROM SIN.

Surely we can never fail to remember that choicest of all Scriptural texts, "The blood of Jesus Christ, His Son, cleanses us from all sin." There is such music in it that when the spirits before the Throne of God desire to have a song of which they might never grow weary, they select that sentiment, and they sing before the Throne that they have washed their robes and made them white in the blood of the Lamb. Their purity before God is due to the fountain filled with blood wherein their stained garments, all soiled with sin, have been made clean! When the soul comes to Jesus Christ by faith and relies upon Him, then the sentence of the perfect pardon goes forth from God and the soul is purged from all the stains of accumulated years! In a single moment those who were black as Hell become white as Heaven through the application of the blood of sprinkling—for all sin disappears as soon as the blood falls on the conscience! That which the blood of bulls and of goats could not do, the blood of Jesus effectually accomplishes—cleansing from all sin!

Now, dear Hearer, have you ever been thus cleansed? Say not you had never need of cleansing, else you know not your natural condition and your actual transgressions. Man, you can never have seen yourself in the mirror of the Word of God, or you would perceive yourself to be totally defiled and altogether as an unclean thing! You would have bowed yourself before the Lord and joined in the confession, "We have erred and strayed from Your ways like lost sheep. We have done those things which we ought not to have done, and we have left undone those things which we ought to have done. And there is no health in us." Well, if you have ever thus felt your guilt, have you ever realized your pardon? If not, give yourself no sleep till you have! Can you bear to live unpardoned, or in doubt whether or not God has absolved you? Can you ever take any kind of rest, much less indulge your soul with mirth, until the word, "Absolvo," has come from God, Himself, the eternal Spirit bearing witness with your spirit that you are born of God? Happy are they who have been washed! They have need to come each night (even as Peter the Apostle had need) to wash their feet, but they need not except to wash their feet, for they are clean every whit. Jesus has made them clean through His blood! The third step is that–

III. THE BLOOD OF JESUS CHRIST IS THE GREAT PRICE OF OUR REDEMPTION.

Redemption sometimes in Scripture is spoken of as being the same thing as pardon, and I shall not at all dogmatically attempt tonight to draw any nice distinction between the two. "We have redemption through His blood–to wit, the forgiveness of sin–according to the riches of His Grace." But redemption seems rather to be in some sense the effect produced by a pardon than the actual pardon, itself. Man is a slave. As long as guilt is written in God's book against us, we are in bondage. We feel for the present that we are slaves to sin and that for the future, the punishment of sin will inevitably come upon us to our eternal destruction. But the moment we are purged from the guilt of sin, we are set free from the slavery of it! Jesus Christ takes us from being slaves and makes us to be children! He gives us no longer "the spirit of bondage again to fear, but the spirit of adoption whereby we cry, Abba,

Father!" He was slain and He has redeemed us unto God by His blood! And in the liberty wherewith Christ makes us free, we rejoice to see that it was the blood which was the price, thereof, and because He suffered, therefore our chains have dropped off from us. We are free—the Lord's freemen—free henceforth to serve Him with renewed love and renewed hearts because of the abundance of the Grace which He has manifested towards us!

Now, Beloved, have you ever been redeemed by the blood of Jesus? I am not talking to you now about a redemption effected upon the Cross, but have you ever felt redemption in your own spirit from the curse of the Law, from the thralldom of a guilty conscience and from the power of sin? Let me ask you, are you the Lord's freeman tonight? Oh, happy are you, then, for you can say, "Lord, You have loosed my bonds and, therefore, I am Your servant." "We are not our own because we are bought with a price." And inasmuch as we are no more slaves to the Law from henceforth, for the love we bear His name who has redeemed us with such a price, we reckon ourselves to be His servants and we bear in our body the marks of the Lord Jesus! Ah, Friends, if you were never redeemed by the precious blood, then you are still slaves—slaves to sin and Satan—slaves under the vengeance of God and slaves to the Law of God. But may you never be content in slavery! May you pine after freedom, and may Jesus give it to you—give it to you tonight if it is His blessed will! In the fourth place, the blood of Jesus is spoken of in Scripture as—

IV. INTERCEDING.

"The blood of sprinkling speaks better things than that of Abel." It is said to be sprinkled within the veil, so that where the high priest could only go once a year, we may now go at all times, for the blood is there, interceding for us perpetually! Well, in fact, says one of our poets—

"The wounds of Christ for us,
Incessantly do plead."

Even after His death, remember, His heart for us poured out its flood. After death that heart was pierced and blood and water came. So, after His voice was silent and He could no longer say, "Father, forgive them," the wounds were still eloquent–and even when the suffering passed, they still continued to plead with God.

Now, Soul, have you ever come to God through the intercession of the blood? You have said prayers, you have repeated forms of devotion, you have gone to Church or to Meeting Houses. This is all well enough, but have you gone farther? For if not, all outward forms of devotion are but frivolous endeavors that may allure, but will deceive you! Did you ever come to God by the blood and did you ever, by faith, fix your eye upon "the High Priest who ever lives to make intercession for us," who with our names upon His bosom, still offering the blood, stands at this moment before the Father, God, pleading for us who love Him and trust Him? Happy they who look to the interceding Savior and who feel that His blood speaks not revenge, but cries at every vein, "Mercy, mercy for the chief of sinners!" This leads me to remark that the blood of Jesus–

BECOMES THE MODE AND WAY OF ACCESS TO GOD.
We have boldness to enter into the holiest through the blood of Christ. After first cleansing the man and making him fit to come as a priest and a king unto God, then the blood, as it were, takes away the veil and opens up the pathway to God, Himself, for the forgiven and redeemed soul! Never let us attempt to come to God by anything but the blood! All other ways to God, except through the blood of Jesus, are presumptuous. All other fire that we may put upon the altar, except this, is strange fire, and the Lord's anger will go forth against us. May I never plead when on my knees before God anything but the precious merits and the dear wounds of the Man of Sorrows who is now exalted at the right hand of God. How close to God we should come if we did but always bring Christ with us! But what are our prayers when we leave Him behind? What are our devotions when we are met together, or when we are in secret, and we go to the Mercy Seat, but forget the blood that was sprinkled on it, oblivious of the new and living way through the rent body of Immanuel? Come, Brothers and Sisters, let us chide ourselves

for sometimes having forgotten our Lord! And henceforth, be it ours never to think of drawing near to God except by this way of access—the crimson road which the blood has paved for us! To advance farther, the blood of Jesus Christ, according to the Word, is—

VI. SANCTIFYING.

Jesus sanctified His people by His own blood and, therefore, suffered outside the gate. By sanctification is usually meant in Scripture the setting apart of anything for the service of God and so making it holy. Now, the blood separates the saints from all others. It was the blood that was the distinguishing mark of Israel in Egypt. Every Egyptian house was without the blood, but every house of the seed of Abraham had the blood mark upon the lintel and the two side posts, and when God saw the blood He passed over them and spared them in the night of His furious anger. The blood, then, Beloved, if you have ever had it on your soul, is to be the distinguishing mark between you and the ungodly in the Day of Wrath and it should distinguish you now. You should, by your life and your conversation, make yourself to appear to be as the blood has made you—to really be a separated one! We are not of the world, even as Christ is not of the world. We have heard the mandate—"Come you out from among them; be you separate; touch not the unclean thing." We have left the world's sin and we have left the world's religion, too! We have separated ourselves at once from the world's goodness, as well as from the world's vileness, to walk in the path of nonconformity to the world, that we may tread in the footsteps of our crucified Redeemer! And the more the blood is applied, the more the obedience of Jesus is trusted in—and the sprinkling of the blood is relied upon—the more shall we become sanctified in spirit, soul and body by the power of the Holy Spirit. Let us never forget the purifying power of Jesus in the heart. Wherever He is trusted to take away the guilt of sin! And we must ask to see Him sit as a refiner to purify, yes, it must be our prayer that He would take His fan in His hand and purge our hearts as He does His floor! Refining Fire, go through my soul! Oh, sweet love of Jesus, burn up the love of the world! Oh, death of Jesus, be the death of sin! Oh, life of Christ, be the life of everything that is gracious, God-like, heavenly, eternal! So shall it be in proportion as we partake of the power and the efficacy of that blood! The blood, furthermore, is—

VII. CONFIRMATORY.

We must not forget this one effect of it. It is called the Blood of the Covenant—the Blood of the Testament—the Blood of the New Testament. The Covenant was not in force in the olden times until there had been a sacrifice to confirm it. And a will stands not until the death of the testator has been proved to make it valid. The heart's blood of Jesus is, as it were, the establishment of His last will and testament. Jesus, the great Testator, has died, has made an end of sin and His blood is the great seal of His testament and makes it valid to us. If He had never died! Oh, dreadful, "if," only equaled in horror by that other, "if"—if He had never risen again from the dead! But now is Christ risen from the dead! Now has Christ slept and awoke as the first fruits of them that slept! Never doubt the promise of God, for the blood confirms it! Never doubt the love of God, for He spared not His own Son, but freely delivered Him up for us all! How shall He not, with Him, also freely give us all things? If you need evidence as to the eternal goodness of God, His willingness to pardon, His power to save and to bless—look to the Cross of Calvary and see the bleeding Savior—and never doubt again!

Dear Hearer, did the blood so come to you as to confirm your hope, or is your hope a fancy, a delusion? Do you think it needs no confirmation? Have you ever in your moments of questioning and anxiety gone over, again, to the altar where is the Great Victim? Have you said once more—

"

Just as I am, without one plea,

But that Your blood was shed for me!
And that You bid me come to Thee,
Oh, Lamb of God, I come!"

Have you, then, got your consolation back? Have you received the witness of God? Have you heard the voice which bears witness both in Heaven and earth, the voice of the Spirit, and the water and the blood? And have you been satisfied because you needed no better confirmation than the witness of the blood of Jesus applied with power to your soul? The blood of Jesus has another effect of which we ought to think more than we do—that of—

VIII. NOURISHING, CHEERING AND SUSTAINING THE BELIEVER.

To this end the ordinance of communion with Christ in the breaking of bread and partaking of the cup of blessing has been instituted. When we come to the Lord's Table, we have set before us in the broken bread, of which we eat, and in the wine of which we drink, this present fact—that the sufferings of our Master are now at this moment for our nourishment, sustenance, consolation and exhilaration. We have been washed in the blood—we are now to receive, after a spiritual sort, the precious blood of Jesus to nourish our faith, to comfort our hope, to excite in us the liveliest joy and to make us sing and be merry with holy confidence in Him who has redeemed us from all iniquity and made us unto God priests and kings, to reign with Christ forever and ever! There is no cordial for the heart like the blood of Jesus. To think of the atoning Sacrifice is the readiest way to consolation. Our sorrows are not worth a thought when once compared with His! Sit down under the shadow of the Cross and you will find a cooler shade than that of a great rock in a weary land. There is no pasturage for the sheep of Christ like that which grows on Calvary! There is nowhere to be found such wine that makes glad the heart of God and man, as that which comes from the sacred cup of His heart, of which Believers drink by faith when they have fellowship with Him and come into near and dear communion with Him! Although we do sometimes enjoy this without any emblems—without the bread and without the wine—these are still great assistants, blessed exponents, and they graciously help our forgetfulness! We are yet in the body and we need something that shall aid this lagging flesh to see something of the Lord.

Oh, feed then on Christ and do not be content unless day by day He is your daily bread! He who has given you life must sustain that life. He who has taught you how to rejoice must still supply you with power to continue in your daily rejoicing! The blood without cleanses. The blood within cheers, yes, sacredly inebriates the soul till the sinner drinks and forgets his sorrow and remembers his misery no more! And in the fullness of his delight he becomes sweetly oblivious, whether in the body or out of the body, as he rises into almost celestial communion with his unseen, but ever-present Lord! Once again, the blood of Jesus Christ has the effect of—

IX. UNITING CHRISTIANS TOGETHER.

Paul, speaking of Jew and Gentile, says that He "has made both one, through the blood of Christ," and surely there is nothing that unites different denominations of Christians together like the precious blood of Jesus! Brothers and Sisters, we may dispute—I think we do well to dispute over important ordinances and doctrines, for wherein men err we are not to wink at their errors—and neither ask them to wink at ours. I have sometimes heard it said, "Spare such a Brother." Yes, as a Brother—but who am I that I should be spared if I err, or who is he that he should be spared? What are we, or what are our feelings compared with the Truth of God? No, let questions be fought out as kindly, as lovingly, as valorously, as honorably as they possibly can! Truth fears not the shock of arms. Let the controversies go on. I believe that, after all, there is ten times more Truth in this world, now, with all the apparent divisions of Christians, than there would have been if we had been united in a nominal union into some one great church which might, perhaps, have rotted as thoroughly as the old Church of Rome did before the days of Luther! But when we come to the foot of the Cross, what union there is! If the saints in prayer appear as one. If in the praise of the Infinite Jehovah they are one—much more and much more tenderly are they one when they behold Jesus bleeding and dying for them! My heart melts and breaks when I hear Christ preached. He who lifted up Christ would have offended me had he preached some other part of his creed. Had he talked over some Doctrine which I hold to be erroneous, he and I had differed, but when it comes to this, "HE loved me and gave Himself for me–He is the chief among ten thousand, the altogether lovely–His blood is precious"–I feel inclined to cry, "Brother, keep to that! Praise Him louder! Give Him all the honor!–

"Bring forth the royal diadem,
And crown Him Lord of all!"

While we keep to that, we are none of us heretics over that! There shall be no schisms and divisions over the matter. Son of God and Son of Man, Redeemer of our souls from death and misery, all Your mother's children praise You! Every sheaf bows before Your sheaf! Sun and moon, and every star do obeisance unto You, King of Kings, and Lord of Lords, Head over all things unto your Church, which is Your dwelling place, the fullness of Him that fills all in all! Since here we are one, when we get together as Believers, I wish we more often struck that key–the precious blood of Christ–and in our walks and talks with those Christians who differ from us in many points, let us sometimes try to turn those points aside and say, "We do agree to speak well of that dear name which is above every name, that name which charms all our fears and bids all our sorrows cease! That name which is the joy of the Believer on earth and the bliss of the saints in Heaven! I close now when I have noticed that the blood of Jesus Christ may be looked upon by us every day as–

THE GREAT INSTRUCTOR AND THE CARDINAL WITNESS OF DIVINE TRUTH.

God is to be seen in Nature and seen vividly there, but not as He is to be seen in Christ Jesus. Instruction as to the eternal power of the Godhead, some find in the skies above, in the fields around and in the sea beneath. But in the Cross there is more of God than in all the world besides! I have often felt, when I have been rambling in the Alps, that Nature was too small to set forth God. The mirror is not large enough to reflect the face of the Eternal. You stand in the Alps and hear the avalanche, like claps and peals of thunder resounding in the air. You gaze afar off and there it is, and it looks to you like the falling of a few flakes of snow. It is so inconsiderable that the grandeur seems to be destroyed. Though every one of those flakes may be a block of ice weighing a hundred tons, at such a distance the thing grows small. The water leaps down hundreds of feet from the crags, but up in the mountains it appears to be a little trickling creek scarcely worth notice. The very Alpine summits seem to dwindle down to small heaps of stones when one grows used to the scenery. God is too great for this earth to bear Him. The axles of this world's chariot would snap beneath the weight of Deity. We talk of going from Nature up to Nature's God, but the top of the highest Alps is far below His footstool! We do not get any conceptions of God out of Nature worthy of His august Majesty. But in contemplating the Cross, in discerning, there, how God can forgive, how willing He is to save the guilty, how His justice is magnified at the same time as His Grace, I am persuaded that those who have tried both forms of contemplation will tell you that this last is the better by far! You see God through the wounds of Christ as through windows of agate and gates of carbuncle—and you cry, "My Lord, and my God!"

In winding up this poor discourse of mine, let me say to you, Beloved, be more in meditation upon Jesus. I say to myself—Preacher, preach your Master more! Preach Him more after His own sort and endeavor to be yourself more like He! Dear Hearer, live nearer to the Cross. With all your study of Doctrine—and you do well to study it thoroughly—make Jesus Christ the first. Believe in Him. Let Him be your creed. Speak of a body of divinity—there never was in this world but one body of divinity and that is Jesus Christ! And he that understands Jesus Christ has got the only system of theology that is worth knowing! Get right into Him. Some of the early Fathers used to study every wound. They would write a treatise on almost every different spot where He was scourged! They had some tears to let fall and some sweet songs to sing for every step along the Via Dolorosa. Let us not treat lightly what those nearer to the Light of Godtreated so solemnly, but regarding the Master and thinking much of even the littles that concern Him (for the leaves of this Tree of Life are for the healing of the nations), let us study to understand Him and ask to be conformed to Him—even in His sufferings to be like He—

and when we suffer, to see Him in our pangs! Let every grief be a glass through which to look into His life and love, and understand His Grace.

I wish you all knew this, and more than this. Oh, that I could hope that all this assembled company did trust in my Master! Poor Sinner, why not trust Him? You will never be saved unless you do! There is no other door of mercy for you than Jesus! Come, come, come, even though you think He will cast you away. If Christ had a drawn sword in His hand, yet I would bid you come! It were better to fall on the point of His sword than to live without Him! Come and rest upon Him. He never rejected a sinner yet, and He never can! The vilest of the vile can find mercy in Him! And all He asks—and that He gives—is that you rely on Him with all your heart and you shall be saved! God grant that you may! "He that believes and is baptized shall be saved." Obey the second precept as you have attained to the first. When you have believed in Christ crucified, dead and buried for you, then be dead and buried with Him in Baptism! Take the outward symbol of His death, burial and resurrection, and ask to have the inward spiritual Grace that you, being dead to the world, and dead with Christ, and buried with Him, may rise again to newness of life through His quickening Spirit.

The Lord thus bless you, for Jesus' sake!

19205453R00213

Printed in Poland
by Amazon Fulfillment
Poland Sp. z o.o., Wrocław